Praise for *HEAD over HEEL*

'An intriguing book, very well written, well structured, entertaining and sometimes even challenging . . . a delightful and often humorous account of the author's evolving relationship with Italy as he comes to grips with everyday reality there . . . anecdotes provide both humour and vivid images of Italians and Italian life'

Judges of the Grollo Ruzzene Foundation Prize

'A perfect read for a Mediterranean beach, and the author's encounters with southern Italian peasant life are genuinely funny'

Daily Telegraph

'*Head Over Heel* is as good as a holiday. Dramatic, sensual and affectionately amusing'

John Bell, The Bell Shakespeare Company

'Very entertaining, enjoyable and engaging'

Peter Carty, former Travel Editor, *Time Out*

'Cultures collide in this story of how an Australian man meets a beautiful Italian woman in a Dublin bar. What follows is part love story and part life story as the author grapples with everyday life in Southern Italy . . . Harrison evokes excellently the languid atmosphere of small town Italian life'

Italy Magazine

'A funny and touching tale about the cultural divide with a sweet and passionate love story at its heart'

Courier Mail

'A spirited take on life and love in Italy'

Living Abroad

Head Over Heel

Seduced by Southern Italy

CHRIS HARRISON

NICHOLAS BREALEY
PUBLISHING

London • Boston

First published in Great Britain in 2009 by Nicholas Brealey Publishing
An imprint of John Murray Press

An Hachette company

First published in this paperback edition in 2016

3

Copyright © Chris Harrison 2009

The right of Chris Harrison to be identified as
the Author of the Work has been asserted by him in accordance
with the Copyright, Designs and Patents Act 1988.

British Library Cataloguing-in-Publication Data
A catalogue record for this book is available from the British Library.

ISBN 978-1-85788-646-7
eBook ISBN (UK) 978-1-85788-420-3
eBook ISBN (US) 978-1-47364-469-4

Quote from Luigi Barzini is courtesy of Penguin Books

Disclaimer: The author's account of his experiences in this
book are as he remembers them.
The descriptions of his shared experiences are his perceptions
of them at the time; other people in these experiences
might remember them differently.

Printed and bound by Clays Ltd, St Ives plc

John Murray Press policy is to use papers that are natural, renewable and
recyclable products and made from wood grown in sustainable forests. The
logging and manufacturing processes are expected to conform to the
environmental regulations of the country of origin.

Nicholas Brealey Publishing
John Murray Press
Carmelite House
50 Victoria Embankment
London, EC4Y ODZ, UK
Tel: 020 3122 6000

Nicholas Brealey Publishing
Hachette Book Group
Market Place Center, 53 State Street
Boston, MA 02109, USA
Tel: (617) 523 3801

www.nicholasbrealey.com
www.chrisharrisonwriting.com

To my parents – for everything
And to Daniela – for everything else

Contents

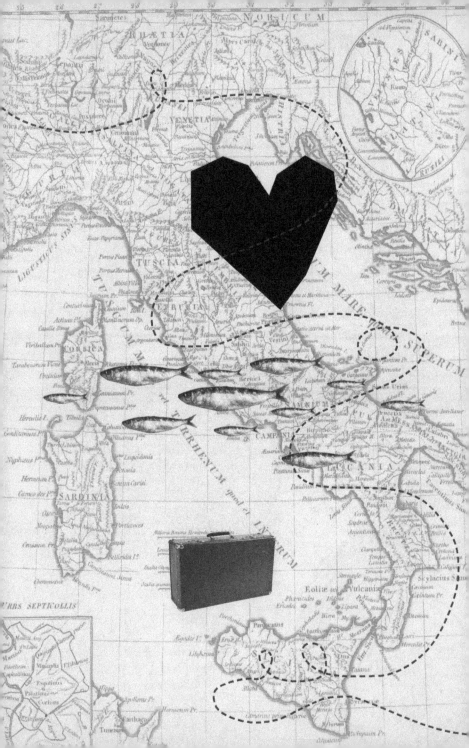

It was the craziest decision I have ever made. I would make it a million times again. She gave me no choice—she intoxicated me. Her liquorice eyes. Her Mediterranean skin. Even the sound of her name was like a summons to all my foolish blood.

Daniela—one L, smile as you say it to pronounce it correctly—was on her second trip to Australia in six months, far too infrequently for both our liking. So I responded with ease in that Sydney hotel, when she stood naked by the window after distractedly interrupting what I had been hoping would last forever, and without turning from the view, she said softly and without intonation: 'Come to live with me in Italy.'

I would do many things for that captivating woman; reason was not one of them.

In the heart of every man,
wherever he is born,
whatever his education and tastes,
there is one small corner which is Italian,
that part which finds regimentation irksome,
the dangers of war frightening,
strict morality stifling,
that part which loves frivolous and entertaining art,
admires larger than life size solitary heroes,
and dreams of an impossible liberation
from the strictures of a tidy existence.

Luigi Barzini

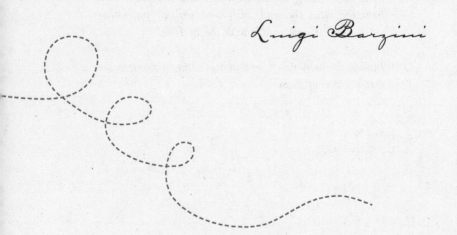

Barzini's challenge

The elderly man from Naples searched clumsily at his feet every time we hit turbulence and yelled 'Where's my stick?' with such nervous alarm that invariably I would find it and hand it to him. A bald head dotted with sun spots and a faulty hearing aid, the passenger beside me had endeared himself from the start of the Rome-bound flight when the roof of our jumbo began leaking. *'La Madonna!'* he had exclaimed, reaching for his cane and shielding himself from the drops of water by stabbing them as they fell.

Mr Bean re-runs and Hollywood fluff—I preferred the antics of my companion to the official in-flight entertainment. He was endowed with the flamboyance of my Italian teacher, Giacomo, with whom I had spent every spare moment of the six months since Daniela's first visit to Australia. Also from Naples, Giacomo was a comical eccentric, whose private lessons—offered gratis when he heard my love story and deemed it his duty as an Italian to help—adhered more to the principles of cabaret than grammar, although singing the verbs on the take-home tape was a great way to make them stick. After our final lesson, dancing on the footpath outside his central Sydney school, shouting *'Buona fortuna!'* as my bus pulled out, he seemed living proof of the Orson Welles assertion that there are over fifty million talented actors in Italy, with the only bad ones to be found on stage and in films.

A week later, using a book as an umbrella, I sipped the glass of wine which my Neapolitan friend had tried to buy me before learning it was free, while he collected a continuous top-up—albeit of water—by catching the drops in his glass. Introducing himself as Aurelio, with the raised voice of the partially deaf he asked why I was heading to Italy. Politeness dictated I shout my reply, meaning passengers in our vicinity involuntarily learnt of Daniela—one L, smile as you say it to pronounce it correctly.

I must confess to stealing the line—'Her name was like a summons to all my foolish blood'—from James Joyce. I didn't think he would mind, given he was partly responsible for my meeting Daniela. Having studied *Ulysses* and other Irish literature at university in Sydney, I left London, where I was later based, to cross the Irish Sea and take a drink at the watering holes of my favourite Dublin characters.

Johnny Fox's is a quaint but lively pub in the hills above Dublin, once a haunt of Irish revolutionary leaders. With its wooden interior and cluttered fascinations, ranging from empty petrol drums to iron bedsteads, Dubliners enjoy a rustic charm with their Guinness which reminds them of home, of history, of Ireland.

Crowded with evening drinkers, the pub's low, uneven ceiling trapped cigarette smoke above our heads, while ground-level cloud swirled and gathered at the window. In typical Irish weather I enjoyed a typical Irish pastime. It only takes a short time in Ireland to spot the link between the weather and the national hobby—indeed some Irish will tell you that the characteristic white head on a Guinness is low cloud.

With an enduring squeak the pub's wooden door swung open, driving an invigorating whisper of cold air through the bar. Roused from stale poses, drinkers surfaced from slouch and stupor, as a bleak Dublin evening was swept aside by a Mediterranean summer.

She moved with the grace of a slow-surging wave whose

impact is great for having travelled far. Three friends in her wake, she approached the bar—elegance, confidence, diminutive, exotic—my first and last infatuation. Gloss-black hair fell straight to her shoulders, reflecting the light in which she glowed, and bronzed skin, while itself dark, seemed to deny the existence of shadow; even at her throat a subtle diamond banished shade. She was an enchanting mix of flesh and fabric, sexual allure through sartorial economy. A simple black singlet revealed sleek shoulder muscles which, under the weight of a jacket draped over her forearm, pulsed slightly like the quivering strings of a harp. And her eyes were the deep rich colour of the liquid I had, on account of her entrance, momentarily stopped sipping.

In addition to James Joyce, I owe my meeting with Daniela to Arthur Guinness, accidental creator of that ambiguous black liquid, actually ruby red, which at first sight appears more an engine lubricant than a social one, until you toss it into your bloodstream and the world changes colour.

Daniela ordered by pointing at what others were drinking, pronunciation of the various beers too difficult even for the spokesperson of four Italian women on holiday, three of whom spoke no English and settled hurriedly on Coke, camouflaging a lack of courage with the right colour at least. Daniela, however, with a little more abandon, pointed at my half-full glass—half-empty until then—sending the barman to the Guinness tap *pronto*, and me, a year later, to her southern Italian home.

The only phrase I knew in Italian at the time would have earned me a slap had I been foolish enough to use it. Fortunately Daniela spoke English rather well. While far from fluent, she could at least understand and make herself understood, though at times we relied on her pocket dictionary to keep our first conversation afloat. But certain expressions need no translation, and several hours later, standing by Dublin's charcoal River Liffey, we exchanged that most delicate of conversations in which so much is said without uttering a word.

Daniela had one day to go before returning to Italy, and

between the sights of Dublin, and my hotel room, we crammed as much into that day as Joyce crammed into June the sixteenth—'Bloomsday' in *Ulysses*, a day in which he too fell in love. But as the hours streaked past we dwelt on the distance between her world and mine. She said she couldn't wait on continental drift to see me again. I loved the remark, and couldn't wait either.

I watched until dark cloud swallowed her plane, then took a ferry across a fierce Irish Sea, lurching like a drunkard on my way back to London.

I returned home to Australia shortly after that, an unlikely reunion now more improbable. Four months would drag by before Daniela came to Sydney for the first time at Christmas, although certain overprotective relatives were made to believe she was headed for Austria rather than Australia. Apart from the following Easter trip (another jaunt to Vienna in the minds of aunts and uncles) it wasn't until June, almost a year since Johnny Fox's, that I would tell this story to a deaf man catching water in a wineglass.

Australia and the impromptu shower behind us, I decided to read since I no longer needed my book as an umbrella. Luigi Barzini was an Italian journalist who wrote what many critics consider the definitive portrait of Italy and the Italian character. Given the nationality of its author, *The Italians* is remarkably self-deprecatory and impartial, a fascinating insight into the Italian way of life. But had I read it before receiving Daniela's invitation, I may not have accepted so quickly.

From the beginning, Barzini cast doubts on my trip to his homeland, disparaging what he saw as futile lust for Italian women by foreign men, 'fascinated by the girls to the point that they often lose all powers of coherent speech and judgement.' In his opinion, I was simply the next hot-blooded fool to become bewitched by a *signorina*'s 'long and shapely legs,

4

lovely and pert face, overbearing breasts and harmonious behind like a double mandolin.' For Barzini, Italian women are provocative creatures with whom the doted foreigner 'can scarcely talk and who would possibly discredit them and make them unhappy if she became their wife.' Er, captain, can we turn this plane around?!

After my initial shock, and several gulps from my wineglass, I decided to take Barzini's words as a challenge rather than a warning. After all, he had really only stated what I already knew—that Daniela's and my relationship would be something of a risk. But I was prepared to take that risk and didn't need Barzini to tell me that infatuation fades.

I was gambling on love and looking for adventure at a time when I should perhaps have been concentrating on a journalism career. I had written for an Australian sports magazine and the editor was offering more work. When I told him I was moving to Italy he was shocked: 'To chase a woman?' But he hadn't seen her eyes. Neither had Barzini.

My parents had, and encouraged me to go. Themselves adventurous, when I was seven they quit excellent jobs and moved their family of five to England for two years so my father could retrain as a Steiner teacher. But that was Sussex. They spoke the language. This was Italy. I didn't. Yet they never said a negative word about my decision. I think they knew from the start that Daniela was special. They even paid for my one-way ticket. Perhaps I should have been offended! Barzini and my editor may not have approved of what I was doing, but my parents sure did.

Having warned me off Daniela, Barzini proceeded to warn me off Italy, criticising his country and suggesting tourists form the wrong impression about real Italian life. Visiting a country rather than living there are two dramatically different things the world over, but in Italy, according to Barzini, the difference is extreme, to the point where 'the Italian way of life cannot be considered a success except by temporary visitors.'

This was not my first trip to Italy. I had visited several times

and, like most enchanted tourists, fallen in love with Italy's effervescent way of life. Touring in summer, I had visited Rome,
Florence and Venice, marvelling at the grandeur of Saint Peter's
Basilica, strolling the patchwork splendour of Il Ponte Vecchio,
and paying far too much for a ride in a gondola on the Grand
Canal. And each time I had left reluctantly, swearing I would
love to live among such artistry, never for a second expecting to
one day be given the chance.

But according to Barzini I had fallen into a trap which snares
most tourists: of judging Italy on its summertime make-up; indeed
the very word 'make-up' in Italian is *trucco*, literally meaning 'trick'.
Real Italian life, claimed Barzini, is more bleak than beautiful;
corrupt, unjust, unenlightened and unhappy, with a dark tragedy
for every colourful tradition. 'It would be a success of sorts if it
at least made Italians happy,' he wrote. 'But it does not.'

I wasn't a tourist this time though, with my residency permit
and a job as a copywriter lined up at a Milan advertising agency—
all organised by Daniela. It didn't mean I had to stay forever, but
it did allow me to stay as long as I wanted. This time I would
see the real Italy and the real Italians, my love for Daniela a
window on her world. And as I'd be sticking around after the
sun set on summer I would discover if Barzini was a poor
ambassador or a gifted observer, though before moving to Milan
in the north I would be spending a two-month summer holiday
with Daniela in the south.

I closed my book and chatted with Aurelio, who confirmed
certain things that Barzini had been saying about the difference
between visiting Italy and living there. Between patchy English
and polished Italian he recounted stories about his island home
of Ischia, including the time he and his uncle, fed up with an
insufficient or, as Aurelio put it, '*costipato*' water supply, called a
plumber to investigate the cause. Knocking through a wall and
following their pipe to the mains, they found a crudely devised
bypass system diverting water first to a villa and then to a hotel,
leaving the remaining dribble for the resident.

I wondered how many international visitors to Ischia had spent a delightful few days in that selfish hotel, overlooking the magical Bay of Naples and making declarations from a sun-lounge that they could happily live in Italy, while the native resident, frustrated and forgotten, dug a hole through his wall like a prisoner attempting escape.

'How do you tolerate that?' I asked Aurelio, knowing he was returning from a visit to family in Melbourne and had an alternative to Ischia should he want it. 'Wouldn't you prefer to live where that sort of thing doesn't happen?'

'*Assolutamente no*,' he replied. 'Ischia is my home. *Il mare mi parla*.'—The sea talks to me.

As the seat-belt sign blinked on and the captain announced rocky weather, I handed Aurelio his walking stick and ordered another drink. Thundering through the night on jet-engines and Jacob's Creek, Barzini's challenge drew closer at twelve bumpy miles a minute. My homesick friend knocked his glass against mine in a toast of goodwill and good luck, then roared with laughter when I told him that Barzini could go to hell. Captain, full steam ahead!

'You know you're back in Italy!' screamed a disembarked passenger attempting impossible conversation over the jet-blast of a Palestinian jumbo. We stood on the tarmac of Rome's Leonardo Da Vinci airport, having lost time in Bangkok drying out our plane and arriving in Italy over four hours late, forfeiting our right to a gangway. Congregating under the wing of our aircraft, we awaited a fleet of buses to ferry us to the terminal while a frantic woman with a walkie-talkie circled us like a sheepdog, screaming: 'No smoking! No smoking! They're refuelling the aircraft to your left!'

From Rome I had to take a one-hour flight to Brindisi, the southernmost airport on the heel of the boot. But because of the delay I had missed my connection and now had just forty minutes to find the domestic terminal and get myself on the second of few flights a day to the Adriatic outpost.

After wrestling directions from a policeman smoking in front of a 'No Smoking' sign (I asked if I could take his photo but, oblivious to irony, he said you weren't allowed to take photos in the airport), I found the check-in counter for transiting passengers, where I negotiated with an uninterested Alitalia rep in a bright green suit for a seat on the plane. Unsightly after thirty hours' travel, I arrived at an unattended passport control booth. With apparent local knowledge and an urgency as great as mine, another passenger disappeared through a side doorway, returning with two reluctant policemen who mocked our obvious haste with their deliberate lack of it.

White plastic belts and pistol pouches on the outside of elegant navy jackets, their uniforms evoked both authority and comedy—a cross between superheroes and lollipop men. Without acknowledging our presence in the slightest, the pair casually opened our passports, half-glanced at mine so sketchily as to not realise it was upside down, then wandered off at the same lazy pace with which they had arrived. After months of working on the necessary documents, my arrival in Italy had gone unquestioned, unchallenged and, without the required stamp in my passport, unrecognised. Weeks later, at an immigration office, their indifference would cause me serious problems.

With twenty minutes remaining before scheduled departure, I found my gate and took a seat among a diverse group of passengers including nuns, priests, children, a sausage dog, a junior football team, holidaymakers and home-comers. An obese man in a chestnut suit read a pink newspaper and smoked a thick cigar, just like the policeman, directly beneath a 'No Smoking' sign threatening a fine of less than the price of a packet of cigarettes.

An announcement told of a gate change and most passengers moved to a new waiting area, swapping with a group bound for

Venice. A little later we swapped again, this time with passengers heading for Palermo, and later still with travellers on their way to Turin. A fourth announcement led our bemused group, feeling it had been made fun of, back to the original gate, where I found the obese man still sucking his cigar with his nose in the newspaper; it's a wonder he hadn't burnt a hole in it.

A further call advised passengers that our flight would be heavily delayed, and that due to a change of aircraft, seat numbers and boarding passes would no longer correspond. We were to choose any seat we liked, as long as it wasn't the captain's.

An hour later another bus arrived to take us to our plane. 'Only in Italy do I buy a plane ticket and catch a bus!' exclaimed one passenger, Italian, making an announcement rather than a statement. Everyone heard but no one blinked, except me, the foreigner and fish out of water, yet to become accustomed to this Italian habit of casting critique across a crowded room, designed less to rectify a problem than enjoy lamenting it.

Our bus travelled taxiways criss-crossing grassed areas baking yellow in the sun, on its way to an antique-looking plane—an MD-80—itself cooking on the airstrip in early summer heat. At the top of a flight of mobile stairs to the aircraft's forward door, the passenger in front of me stopped suddenly and cast a gaze across the hazy aerodrome. '*Signora!*' he yelled down to the Alitalia girl in the shade of the aeroplane's nose. 'Is that a suitcase I can see on the taxiway?' Sure enough, slumped like road kill on the tarmac about 40 metres away was a lonely blue suitcase. Miss Alitalia powered her tiny Fiat Panda and raced towards the fugitive case. 'Just as long as it's not mine,' said the man who had spotted it, as we filed into the cabin, ready now for anything.

I chose a window seat giving me a clear view of the tarmac, onto which a middle-aged woman fainted after climbing from the bus, her young daughter adding to the spectacle by crying over the body as though her mother had passed away. An ambulance crew arrived in the shadow of the wing and declared the woman's ailment to be nothing more than fear of flying, before ushering both of them aboard.

Taxiing to the runway, I noticed a spider in my window whose survival compromised mine; the fact it found nutrition surely meant the window wasn't airtight. But I had neither the language nor the energy to expose the eight-legged stowaway. He'd obviously been there a while and, though visibly ageing, the aeroplane seemed capable of another short sortie.

With a surge from the engines we were light as a feather, sailboats on the Mediterranean slipping under the wing, while the spider waited on a passing insect and totted up its Frequent Flyer points.

Applause as our flight struck the runway in Brindisi, 80 kilometres north of Andrano, a village I had been trying to imagine for almost a year. And Daniela appeared equally anxious to show it to me. As I stepped from the tarmac into the tiny airport, she jumped a railing to the 'Passengers Only' area, dodged a dozing *poliziotto*, and gave me a delicious welcome which, if received by all new arrivals, would soon promote Italy from the world's third most visited country to the undisputed first. Spectators were forgotten after three months' separation. Starved lips were soft. Eyes closed. Breath shared. I held her and her summer dress.

A conveyor belt slid noisily into life and passengers awaited their luggage with nervousness, recalling the runaway suitcase in Rome. 'There aren't even any trolleys!' cried a man in a linen suit and Armani sunglasses. 'A northerner,' Daniela whispered. 'From Padova. I know because of his accent.' As I would later discover, there is a fierce antagonism between Italy's north and south, which Daniela would suffer first hand when we later moved to Milan. But all I knew at that stage was that the man's comment was both arrogant *and* accurate.

Should you wish to smuggle something through Italian customs, arrive at a remote southern airport on a flight that lands at lunchtime, when airport staff, unable to officially enjoy siesta, are on auto-pilot like the plane which flew you there. Then have

Daniela come to meet you. With her arms around my neck and a confidence which shocked me, given by law she shouldn't have been where she was, Daniela stopped the unshaven plain-clothes customs official in his tracks. 'There's nothing in here for you,' she said bluntly, whisking me off to the car where her passionate welcome continued.

'Don't ever do that in my country,' I advised her on the road to Andrano, as she swerved and bullied other motorists with needs less pressing than ours.

'We were only kissing.'

'No, with the customs official.'

'*Va bene,*' she replied obediently, realising it was too early for me to understand that, despite not knowing the contents of my luggage, she had risked nothing, that after my flight the sleepy airport would be as good as closed for the afternoon, and that as he had approached, the customs officer had been far more interested in heading home to a plate of pasta than combing through my underwear. Daniela's presumptuous display had simply done us all a favour. The old rules of life had changed. Barzini said they would.

After an evening swim at the port, Daniela took me to bed, where, despite her distractions, I slept like the dead. Exactly one year separated a day which we had tried to make last as long as 'Bloomsday', from one which, in my haste to arrive, simply wouldn't pass quickly enough. Unplanned, and perhaps ironically, my journey to Andrano—which would never have occurred had Joyce not drawn me to Dublin with *Ulysses*—had taken place on June the sixteenth. My odyssey, however, had only just begun.

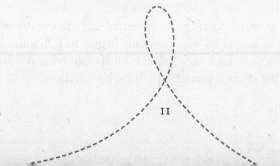

Two days in one—*mattina*

The watermelon seller rises with the sun in a whitewashed fishing village on the heel of the boot. One hand on the wheel, cavalier with experience, he throws his rusty truck around blind and narrow corners of houses edging the street. In his other hand a microphone, connected through his window to an amplifier on the roof, gives his morning cry of *'Meloni, meloni, meloni!'* the decibels to penetrate thick cement walls, turning the waking dreams of Andrano's residents to the theme of his plump, ripe wares.

From a sealed, impenetrable darkness, the light arrives in increments. I see Daniela's feet first, her knees and thighs, then her dancing bottom, echoing the effort of winding a handle to open the roller-shutter from the floor up. Noise and light flood the room as the *serranda* ascends to its stops.

'Have you dreamed about watermelons?' she asks, returning to a bed wet with sweat.

'Has anyone ever fired a gun at that guy?' I ask sleepily.

'You get used to it,' she says, laughing. 'I go to buy one, should I?'

'Aren't you going to put something on?' I yell in her wake. But she's already in the other rooms, opening shutters on a southern village stirring, on the clamorous tones of hasty but unhurried life.

Lying alone in morning heat, in humid air, my ear unveils a village my eyes are yet to see. A *campana* begins to toll, softly but nearby, and I count each lazy strike until the sound is drowned by voices in the street, a squabble perhaps, between men speaking a dialect I cannot decipher. I hear the bell again before a car horn bleats. Another answers. Drivers communicate. The bell again before windows rattle and a tractor labours by. A football scuffs cement. The bell again. How many's that? *'Bravo!'*—children celebrate a goal. Seven perhaps? And then the bestial acceleration of a Vespa—a 50cc motorbike which counters its lack of power with noise. The *campana* is silent. I think it's eight o'clock.

Fifteen minutes later—I am tired after my long flight and have little intention of moving—the bell tolls again, only this time, after eight enduring strikes, a different bell chimes once in a slightly higher tone—a quarter past. At eight-thirty the watermelon seller returns, the dulcet bronze of the bell no match for his screeching amplifier. But at a quarter to nine, in a rare moment of quiet, I hear all eight rings followed by three in the different key. Andrano's *campana*, I calculate, rings 768 times a day. I can throw my watch away.

I am starting to enjoy the commotion, its recurring rhythms, its flaring patterns; listening for how long a quiet moment can last, then laughing when in a few seconds an elderly woman yells an indecipherable instruction or rebuke at a child. The noise seems a ritual of the morning to which I will surely grow accustomed. But the startling squeal which follows, an enduring, agonised howl, tells more of torture than routine, and will take a lot of getting used to. *'Meeeelanzzaaaneeciiicooooorie!!'* Something is drastically wrong.

It's a man's cry, an eye-popping lament, loud and wretched enough to reach every corner of the village. I leap from bed in search of Daniela as the bloodcurdling swansong starts again. *'Meeeelanzzaaaneeciiicooooorie!!'* Racing into the kitchen, I startle her sitting at an elegantly laid table, assaulting a watermelon the size of a beach ball with a knife as long as my arm.

'Che c'è?' she says, blinking.

'I think someone's in trouble. Can't you hear it?'

'Hear what?'

As if on cue the victim republicises his pain.

'*Meeeelanzzaaaneeciiicooooorie!!*'

'That.'

She laughs and moves to hug me, after putting down her knife.

'This is Rocco. A seller of vegetables. The best eggplant and chicory in the village. Do you want some?'

'I thought he was dying.'

'*Stupido*,' she says, giggling, before reaching for her purse and heading into the street.

After several slices of watermelon, Daniela leads me up to her terraced roof and its commanding view of Andrano. Bathed in sunshine and sagging in the centre, the *terrazza* has a knee-high perimeter wall to stop *mamma* falling off while hanging out the washing. Daniela's house is at the centre of the village, on castle grounds officially. To the southern side I can see the medieval *castello*, the piazza and a *campanile* or bell tower, where two dark bells hang side by side. Looking north, at higgledy-piggledy heights are the roofs of simple stucco houses. To the east, olive groves slope to the coast, a fishing boat putters from port, and the Mediterranean sparkles to a far-distant outline of Albanian mountains. Gazing inland, a heat haze has settled over a sun-dried landscape, a desert coastline on which the roots of olive trees strangle stone to survive. Faded colours contrast with the profound blue of the sea. 'This is the Salento,' Daniela tells me.

I am at eye level with the bells as they cast nine-thirty over Andrano; the signal, it seems, for women wearing aprons to take to terraces and hang out washing. Grey rooftops burst into vibrant summer colours as beach towels and bathers pull at their pegs. My first introduction to Daniela's neighbours is from the washing on their roofs. The lady next door likes floral nighties, a man nearby plays a bit of tennis, while a brassière flapping in the breeze tells me that two doors down lives a stout *signora* for whom comfort is essential. There's enough fabric in one pair of her bloomers to make ten of the skimpy knickers hanging on Daniela's line.

'They look like bedsheets,' I gossip. 'Or sails. I'm surprised the house doesn't move.'

'*Criticone,*' says Daniela, slapping my shoulder, before telling me her father used to say that the difference between an old and a young woman's underwear is that you have to move the briefs to see an old woman's bottom, but you have to move the bottom to see a young woman's briefs. I'm intrigued by her anecdote, not for its humour, but for the fact she uses the past tense to refer to a man still alive.

'*Meloni-melanzane-banane-patate!*' Another fruit and vegie seller winds his way through the streets below, prompting an old woman to drop her pegs and disappear from her terrace, only to reappear at street level where the truck is flagged down and a sale is made.

You could survive without leaving the house in Andrano. Simply wait for the bell to toll nine-forty-five and head into the street, where antique trucks thread their way through town. The drivers' raucous spiels, delivered with much-rehearsed musical cadence, are amplified by home-made sound systems and dusty narrow lanes. Many chant in dialect; a direct address to a local audience. Food is the main merchandise; what else would you expect in southern Italy?

'*ZucchineZucchineZucchine!*'

'*Patate Calimera, patate zuccarine!*'

'*Funghi-melanzane-peperoni-meloni!*'

'*Pesche fresche. Cinque euro 'na cascia de pesche!*'

Thanks to Andrano's street vendors, my vocabulary looks set to become stocked with vegetables, as does Daniela's fridge.

Other entrepreneurs peddle household items. '*Articoli da bagno, articoli da bagno!*' cries one, offering bathroom accessories—scales, mirrors, mats and mops. '*Mula forbici!*' shouts another, hoping to sharpen our scissors. '*Voglio la murga! Cambio la murga!*' This old guy, Daniela tells me, swaps kitchen utensils for *murga*—used cooking fat which he turns into soap. No thanks.

'HousewivesHousewivesHousewives! Step into the street for this golden occasion. Four brooms for only ten euros!'

'Isn't that considered offensive?' I ask Daniela.

'*Perchè offensivo?*'

'Well, if he drove around yelling "housewives" in Australia, he wouldn't sell many brooms.'

'*Perchè?*'

We were worlds apart.

'*Materassi! Materassi!* We have all the quality you seek in a single or double mattress!' But no one is seeking such quality this morning. With no takers, the truck soon arrives at the end of the street, where the driver is forced to reverse and his towering merchandise threatens to wipe out a balcony on which an irate woman thrashes at the truck with a broom, itself a housewife special perhaps. It's like something out of a Fellini film, yet Daniela finds my amusement the only surprise in a routine morning.

Like floats in a parade the vendors continue to pass. Trousers, shoes, water and wine. Just about the only thing you can't buy from home is a newspaper. But it's summer and there's not much in the news, for while Italy is hard at work, it's only in the pursuit of pleasure.

With the bells tolling ten and two, Andrano begins to quieten. A heartless sun climbs higher and residents flee to the sea. Daniela suggests we do the same, though I'd be happy to keep watching the village. I don't know it yet, but the most wonderful present Daniela will ever give me is this first day in her town. My guide, my lover, and my interpreter, her patient explanations inspire an affair beyond our own, an unlikely affection between myself and Andrano, the ceremonies of its locals and the rituals of a day organised around the musical instruction of the *campana*, its incessant ring an ironic reminder of the passing of time where it appears to have stopped. Gazing across the rooftops, I have the impression it could be any day; ten, twenty, fifty years ago. And if you remove the television aerials and the motorised life passing below, perhaps even hundreds of years.

Daniela flicks her car into neutral and rolls us down the hill to the port. Curled like a fleeing serpent, the road winds through olive groves, centuries old, caught in gnarled and ghostly poses. 'When I am a child,' says Daniela, 'I think olive trees change shape when I turn my back.' Olive trees are the Salento's signature, with over ten million of them in Puglia—the heel of the boot—accounting for 60 per cent of Italy's olive oil.

'They are beautiful,' I say.

'They are survivors,' says Daniela.

Towards the bottom of the hill we pass rows of beach houses before arriving at the Porto d'Andrano—a swimming-spot for the brown-skinned only. The beachfront is jagged rock, hostile to bare feet. No sand, just craggy hollows and dramatic grottos. Wading is not an option. You dive into cavernous blue, transparent, crystalline, its sparkling surface dancing on the hulls of fishing boats among which we swim. Creaking under ropes, each wooden craft displays a limp Italian flag, faded and tattered by sun and season.

Having grown up on Sydney's northern beaches, I am at home in deep water and adapt quickly to the dangers of my new surroundings, which amount mainly to getting in and out without cutting your feet or diving onto submerged rock. But my confidence is shattered when I stand on the sharp three-inch spikes of a *riccio*—a sea anemone, my scream silencing the buzzing port.

Locals stare at the embarrassed outsider.

'So that's why everyone is swimming in plastic sandals,' I gasp at Daniela.

'*Si, amore.*'

She is yet to say she loves me, but she is calling me 'her love'. It feels nice . . . much better than the pain in my foot.

Daniela's car finds the hill-climb home more trying than the descent, and once at the top we gather speed and drive straight past the house, accelerating.

'Where are we going?' I ask, my foot on her glove box.

'Zia Maria's,' she replies. 'Nobody can take out *ricci* spikes better than Aunt Maria.'

Zia Maria, who thinks I'm Austrian rather than Australian, does a wonderful job on my foot and we're soon heading home with figs, spinach and an apronful of lemons from the tree in her yard rolling around our back seat.

Up ahead on the shoulder of the road, a middle-aged man in a navy-blue suit blows a whistle and brandishes what appears to be a large red-and-white lollipop. It's a *vigile*, Daniela tells me, smothering the brake with her sandal and muttering '*La miseria*'. But when we get close, the municipal policeman recognises my driver and waves us through.

'Very thorough,' I say.

'This is Giovanni,' begins Daniela, acknowledging him as we pass before going on to recount his life story.

Originally from Poggiardo, a town to the north, he was transferred to the area ten years ago and quickly established a reputation as the meanest *vigile* around by handing out fines for even minor offences, something to which motorists—and colleagues—were unaccustomed. But then he fell in love with a woman from nearby Castro and has hardly issued a fine since, ever ready to negotiate even on severe offences. 'A changed man, all because of a woman from Castro,' concludes Daniela in Italian.

'So does he know as much about you as you do about him?' I inquire in English.

'*Probabilmente*. He waved you through as well, didn't he?'

'But I've only been here a day.'

'That's all it takes.'

Daniela's English has improved dramatically since we met. She's having a few problems with the past tense but I'm only interested in her future. Having studied English at school, she's had a head start with her second language but I'm working on closing the gap. Daniela is helping me do that, while I'm helping her refine her English. We are both teachers and students, speaking a patch-work of English and Italian. It's fast becoming a hybrid tongue, as fun as it is unique. Everything is a springboard to a new word or phrase, Daniela's knackered car on the road home no exception.

'*Knackered. Knackered,*' repeats Daniela. 'My car is *knackered.*' She stresses the new addition to her vocabulary.

'That's it. *Knackered.* And in Italian?'

'*Sfinita. La macchina è sfinita.*'

'*Sfinita,*' I imitate. '*La macchina è sfinita.*'

The bell is ringing twelve when we arrive at Daniela's gate. Her neighbour, Pippo, has parked his car across her garage, as he often does, she says, resigned rather than angry. Daniela punches her horn three times—'This is usually the solution.' Sure enough, out waddles Pippo with the short hurried paces of the elderly at speed, one finger thrust in our direction indicating this won't take a second.

'What sort of car is that?' I ask Daniela, waiting in ours.

'That,' she replies, as though pausing for presentation, 'is a Fiat from 1964. It's called *La Giardiniera.*'—The gardener's model. 'Popular with the farmers because he can put tools flat down in the back.'

It looks to be an early attempt at a station-wagon and has three doors, two of which open backwards. It is no longer than a modern-day motorcycle, and no taller either.

Pippo climbs into the cabin and slams the door, causing the boot to spring open.

'Do you know about Newton?' asks Daniela. '*Per ogni azione . . .*'

'. . . there is an equal and opposite reaction,' I interrupt.

'Pippo's Fiat is perfect example of this theory.'

Unaware of his contribution to physics, a stooped Pippo clambers out, sidles round the back and puts his hand up once again—this won't take another second. After closing the boot he climbs back in and pulls his door more gently this time. But the back door shifts again and the silent comedy is repeated.

'I am sure I watch this a thousand times,' says Daniela. 'It drived my father crazy. He tell Pippo to go in the window but he says he is too old.'

Pippo settles for leaving his door ajar and twists the ignition key, causing the entire machine to vibrate like a dog shaking water from its back. The noise is a rasping wheeze, summoning ancient pistons to perform. Hobbling like its owner, *La Giardiniera* moves away, but no sooner are we inside the gate than it is back across the drive.

'What if we want to go out again?'

'I'll beep.'

After a shower to rinse off the salt, Daniela says she needs to go and buy a couple of things before the shops close for lunch, that she prefers to go by bicycle, and that she has prepared a bicycle for me because you can't get by in Andrano without one, if only because you can't get the car out of the garage. It's a woman's bicycle; like the neighbour's underwear built for comfort rather than speed.

The best Italian mosaics are the roads in Andrano. Bumping across town, my headlamp pops from its plastic casing as I crash from one pothole to the next. As tough on testicles as on tyres, the furrows and ruts make riding a straight line difficult; cyclists who try to avoid them appear drunk at the handlebars. It's like riding a bull at a rodeo.

With a squeak of brakes we pull up at the Co-op general store, where Daniela introduces me to Antonio, the town butcher. Standing in front of the shop with a little girl and a mangy kitten, he is trying to convince the former to take the latter home with her. The cat is mewing pleadingly, twitching its nose at airborne aromas filtering through a fly-curtain.

Inside the store, dusty stock lines the walls and a woman clicks a pricing gun at packets of pasta. Behind the butcher's counter, above a clump of waxen rabbits with their limbs outstretched, as though skinned while on the run, hangs a little blue heart bearing the words: '*E' nato un bambino*.'— A son has been born.

'*Auguri!*' congratulates Daniela. 'What's his name?'

'*Paolo*,' replies the proud father.

'*Che bello*,' says Daniela, clasping her hands in front of her chest before ordering some slices of prosciutto and mortadella.

I had foolishly told Daniela that a sandwich would do for lunch, but riding home past open windows in a cobblestoned lane behind the church, the smells of home cooking cause my nostrils to flare like those of the cat. Enticed by the aromas of grilling fish and roasting meats, of garlic, eggplant and *Zucchine Zucchine Zucchine*, my sandwich days are long gone.

When the bell sounds one-thirty, it echoes along streets deserted for the first time since sunrise, together with a clink of cutlery, the theme music of television soaps and the hum of table chat. Even if you weren't nosy, which Daniela assures me everyone is, it would be difficult not to know at least your near neighbours intimately. As we tuck into spaghetti with white wine and clams, which Daniela has prepared at short notice, we hear a young boy on the street trying to teach stray dogs to sit. His father calls him to come inside because he's wasting his time, it's a miracle most are even standing.

When the bell tolls two-thirty, shutters are closed to re-create night. Andrano becomes a ghost town during siesta. A ride around the village on my bicycle reveals even traffic lights are spent, the blinking semaphore of an orange light lending an eerie feel to deserted streets. If I didn't know Andrano was sleeping I would think it abandoned. Heat has baked the town into silence, slumber and stillness, and it's impossible to look at the whitewashed houses for the reflection of the sun.

Back at Daniela's we lie on the bed with the *serranda* half-drawn and enjoy a moment's silence. At three o'clock the *campana* tolls at a funereal pace for several minutes, a sombre reminder of the death of Jesus at that hour. Shortly after the bell stops I hear the sweet singing voice of a child. Enticed outside, I find a girl of perhaps five dancing naked on the balcony of a house across the street. Squeezing spongefuls of water over her head, she is singing: '*Voglio l'amore, voglio fare l'amore.*' Convinced my rudimentary Italian is playing tricks on me, I head back to the bedroom to find Daniela approaching sleep. Touching her shoulder, I whisper: 'Is that girl saying what I think she's saying?'

'*Che cosa?*'

'I want love, I want to make love.'

Daniela listens for a moment.

'*Sì*,' she replies, groggy with heat and sleep.

'Dancing naked on her balcony?'

'So?' says Daniela absently, before falling asleep.

I finally nod off after fully closing the *serranda* on the precocious serenade and a bell tolling three-forty-five. The room is black once more. If not for Daniela's breathing, I'd be lost.

Two days in one—*sera*

Daniela's bronzed bottom dances again as she opens the *serranda* from the floor up. Noise and light flood the room, and if not for the bell tolling four-forty-five I would swear it to be the start of a new day. Instead, it is merely the second half of the old one. With the worst of the afternoon heat past, Andrano is restored to life.

Fifteen minutes later a sweet organ melody reverberates around town, hypnotising the street dogs who howl a haunting accompaniment. It's the angelus, Daniela tells me, an age-old Catholic devotion which has also become the present-day signal for Andrano's shops to reopen for the evening. This is the time when the *Andranesi* do their chores, the pleasures of the Mediterranean a memory of the morning. But I had more idle plans—to watch them doing so.

Daniela's house is one of few set back from the road. With an elevated porch behind a geranium wall, it is the perfect place, and the safest, to watch the afternoon pass along Via Dodici Apostoli, a bustling street leading from the *centro storico* to the edge of town. Littered with potholes and patchwork repairs, the cramped two-way road is not a place for the fainthearted. Driving appears to be just one of many uses for the roads in Andrano; others include knitting, tapestry, ironing, football, cards, chatting, sitting, farming, and—if you're a stray dog—dozing.

Supervising the interaction of human, animal and mechanised traffic is religious protection at either end of the street. At our end a ceramic Madonna surrounded by candles and imitation ivy, while at the other a life-sized statue of Padre Pio, a twentieth-century Italian saint, watches over the intersection and all who sail through its illegibly faded STOP sign. Pin-up boy for the pious, this kind-faced figure in a brown tunic is on eternal duty outside the mansion of a Vatican cardinal, an illustrious resident for so small a village. A plaque at the padre's feet reads '*Ti aspet-tiamo*'—'we await you', although the broken glass atop the mansion's towering perimeter wall might make the weary pilgrim think otherwise.

With our feet on Daniela's wall and a pink *aperitivo* in our hands, we watch an afternoon unfold. Passing portraits of the *Andranesi*, typical in Daniela's eyes, peculiar in mine.

Two doors down, an elderly woman washes her wall from a ladder with its base in traffic, her bucket swinging from the second-top rung. Three boys on bicycles pedal by, one of whom points his head to pass between wall and ladder like a barnstormer in search of thrills. At the last second he wakes to over-ambition and swerves wildly, avoiding—somehow—both a loss of control and the base of the ladder. The woman, whose name, Daniela says, is Maria Pia, moves to throw her sponge at the daredevil but he's already disappeared round the corner. So she descends, moves her ladder closer to the wall and scrubs from a rung lower down.

A bow-legged man rolls a tractor over a plastic sheet laden with grain, his wife following behind picking out imperfections with him as much as his harvest. The sheet covers half the street. If the farmer put his tractor away, passing cars could press the grain for him.

A droning engine precedes the arrival of what looks a cross between a moped and a wheelbarrow. 'This is an *ape*,' informs Daniela. *Ape* (pronounced Arpeh) means 'bee', and like the Vespa, meaning 'wasp', is so named because of its buzz. A three-wheeled motorbike with a tray on the back and a cabin with handlebars inside, it is essentially a motorcycle utility. The monotonous moped hums past the house, a sunburnt wife perched in the tray on a mound of freshly plucked vegies whose roots shed a little brown earth every time they ride a bump. In the tiny cabin behind the driver's head is a picture of the Madonna; if he ducked it would appear she was driving.

Shaped like a tortoise, and almost as slow, a Fiat 500 chugs past our vantage point steered by a boy standing on his father's lap. A cyclist with a kitchen sink in his basket and an S-bend around his neck is overtaken by a shirtless man breezing by on a Vespa, side-saddle, legs crossed and cigarette between his lips. Another *ape* arrives from a side street, stopping at the intersection where it is ambushed by a group of children who snatch tomatoes from the tray. Spotting the theft in his mirror, the farmer leaps from the cabin yelling *'Disgraziati!'* at scampering feet.

A boy cycles by with a harmonica in his mouth, pedalling furiously and blowing a discordant burst of notes with every breath. A grey-haired man rolls past, a bucket hanging from either end of a broomstick across his bike's handlebars. Protruding from his mouth is a ragged clump of mint on which he munches, his jaw working harder than his legs.

Skipping along the street, a boy in tight swimming trunks cracks a coconut on the wall of the house opposite. With only a towel around his waist, the owner of the house eventually emerges to see who knocked. Finding no one, he surveys the street once or twice, scratches his head and disappears back inside.

Trudging the street in worn-out sandals, an African man pushes a rickety cart laden with sundry items ranging from car mats to calculators. He lives on the edge of town, says Daniela, and manages to feed a family of five with what can only be meagre profits.

A bent old woman turns the corner and heads our way, trembling slightly and limping significantly. Disturbed, according to Daniela, she wanders Andrano without compass or purpose, gaze on the ground, face hidden by a shawl. Indeed I only see her face when she looks up to spit.

In an attempt to find fresh air and escape the heat of the

house, two women put plastic chairs on what would be their veranda if the road didn't meet their door; doormats are dirtied by tyre-tracks rather than footprints. Dressed in widows' black, they knit as best you can while sitting on a busy intersection. The younger must be sixty-five, the elder approaching ninety, and her feet—stockinged despite the heat—dangle inches short of the ground. Dodged by teenagers on two-wheel terrors, they continue their needlework, seemingly oblivious to danger and din.

Another black widow pedals past our lookout, *tulipani* in her basket suggesting a visit to the cemetery.

'Where do they buy their black dresses?' I ask Daniela. 'They're all the same.'

'How can I know?' she replies. 'You think we have shops just for widows?'

'Nothing would surprise me,' I say, looking further along the street at a woman ironing between parked cars. Could it be *that* hot in her house?

'*Buona sera*,' call a group of nuns in chorus on their short walk from the nunnery to six o'clock mass in the church.

'*Buona sera*,' we reply.

'How's *papà*?' one asks Daniela.

'The same,' she replies, plaintively.

The sister would know that, but no doubt thinks it polite to ask.

Fully dressed now, the man opposite adds himself to the scene, sweeping the street outside his front door. Between his broom, Maria Pia's ladder, the grain and tractor, some poorly parked cars, the lady ironing and the women knitting, Via Dodici Apostoli has become an obstacle course. Safe transit involves weaving from one side to the other, a manoeuvre which cars slow down to perform but which Vespas find more exhilarating at speed. I appear to be the only one who finds each near-miss unnerving, and I'm in the safest spot.

Sporting a navy suit with crimson lapels and polished silver buttons, a young *vigile* approaches on his bicycle. I'm convinced he'll try to untie the knots in the road, blow his whistle at the farmer, wave his lollipop stick at Maria Pia. Instead he challenges himself to steer the bottleneck 'no hands', affording him all the authority of the ten-year-old boy behind him doing the same.

Death and destruction somehow avoided, the real *vigili* of Andrano's streets must surely be the fine-bone Madonna and the terracotta padre, who have seen an otherwise perilous afternoon conclude without incident, the only snarls those of two stray dogs competing for territory belonging to neither.

Vapour trails turn pink high above the sea. The bell strikes eight and the sky begins to darken. I had forgotten the *campana*. Hadn't heard it since the angelus. Was it because of the commotion in the street or was a mysterious town becoming familiar?

A full moon soars from behind the sea at a speed which makes the world seem flat. Fishing boats dot the Mediterranean, their lamps like candles on a shimmering birthday cake. Having stewed in the sun all day, Andrano begins to cool. A faint breeze roams the streets. The dark brings energy.

The bell tolls nine before we start dinner, an Italian habit to eat late, if only because of that mountainous lunch. Daniela has prepared a Sicilian recipe: *melanzane alla parmigiana*—fried eggplant and prosciutto topped with parmesan and basil. Her mother is Sicilian, so most of the recipes Daniela has inherited come from that Mediterranean island where *mamma* is currently on 'holiday' with *papà* and from where she telephones as we are finishing dinner.

From the kitchen I listen to Daniela's conversation, enjoying her calm responses to her mother's affectionate persecution.

'*Si mamma.*'

Yes, she lightly grilled the eggplant before adding the ham.

'*Si mamma.*'

Yes, she bought the parmesan from the store in Tricase.

'*Si mamma.*'

Yes, she used breadcrumbs.

Daniela convinces *mamma* that her recipe hasn't been adulterated, and that apart from my arrival, all is routine at home. Then she asks about *papà*. Roaming a fenced garden, eating plants and swearing at the mirror—it appears, sadly, that all is routine there as well.

They talk for nearly an hour, although it seems they're about to finish every five minutes. Italian goodbyes are like operatic deaths: just when you think they are spent they flare up again. Each time Daniela says goodbye the conversation takes a fresh turn. I think that's why *ciao* means hello *and* goodbye.

We are setting mosquito coils to repel the nightly plague of *zanzare* when we hear the playful melody of a concertina which Daniela suggests is coming from the piazza. I propose we go and watch, so Daniela puts on a summer dress and we step into the street, following the music like hunters on a scent. But to our surprise the lively tune fades as we reach the piazza, deserted but for an old man on a bicycle with a watermelon in his basket. His tyres squeak on shiny stone as he disappears down a dark alleyway. We look about, intrigued, disoriented by the music and our failed search for its source.

The subtle illumination of butterscotch stone lends Piazza Castello an enchanting sense of history. Guarding the town square are three ancient buildings: La Chiesa di Sant'Andrea—a squat twelfth-century church named after Andrano's patron saint; the *municipio*—a genial town hall with arched olive-wood doors, and the showpiece Baroque castle, Il Castello Spinola-Caracciolo, with cobblestone courtyard and ornate limestone balcony. Between the bygone buildings, where Daniela and I stand bemused, is the smooth stone public square: market place, meeting point, heart of the village.

Daniela leads me down a dimly lit side street, guessing the music to be coming from the bar. But again the sound softens as we approach, and turning a corner we find only shadows, a stray dog scratching, an old man smoking on a step. The music appears to be roaming the streets as we are; slowly, randomly in the still, humid night. Hand in hand we pass Andrano's staple shops: *barbiere*, *tabaccheria*, *fruttivendolo*. And at every turn the serenade falls away, another laneway leads nowhere, and but for a scattering of elderly residents cooling themselves, the town seems deserted.

'*Buona sera*,' says Daniela to a hunched man in a white singlet, sitting in a doorway with a cane across his knees.

'*Buona sera*,' he replies, routinely.

'Do you know where the music is coming from?'

'*Dalla piazza*,' he replies in an obvious tone, making our same assumption.

'*Grazie*,' says Daniela, preferring not to contradict.

Several twists and turns later we come across a derelict house, its door boarded up and weeds growing in its front wall. Tattooed above the door is a faded street number beside a little white plaque displaying a new address. Daniela tells me that the house belonged to her grandfather who used to repair bicycles on the premises. 'My father want to restore it,' she adds, 'before he get sick.'

Another neglected address has a poster on its wall advertising a circus which came to town years ago. The crumbling façade has become something of a billboard, with an ad for a football competition and a faded announcement of nuptials between Luigi and Serena, who'd have children by now. A few doors down, a *manifesto di morte* leans against a house announcing the death of one of its occupants. The poster will be displayed for several days, says Daniela, until the deceased has been laid to rest in the cemetery on the edge of town.

Having wandered most of the *centro storico*, we abandon our search for the music and return to the bar near the piazza. Andrano's acoustics had been playing with us it seems, enticing us on a tour of the village. The bell is less shy about being discovered, however, and crashes eleven and one above our heads.

We buy some peach gelato and watch a group of boys trying to seduce a group of girls. Draped over impotent motorbikes, the Casanovas wear wraparound sunglasses despite the fact it's approaching midnight. Gelled hair, pointed collars and jeans fraying fashionably. With equal attention paid to appearance, the maidens mill around, giggling and licking ice-creams. In a motor-ised mating routine, the boys check their reflections in wing-mirrors before stinging the night into low-octane life, hoping the tongues of their admirers won't be content with gelato alone.

We walk home via bocce lanes behind the castle, where every so often two lead balls collide and a group of old men in singlets exclaim 'oooohhhhh' in enthused unison. Two teenagers are having a rock fight in the castle park opposite Daniela's house, in a friendly enough manner until a wayward stone strikes the headlight of one combatant's Vespa. 'You're dead,' screams its owner, running his hands through the dirt in search of larger, sharper missiles.

The bell tolls twelve as we prepare for bed; early in Andrano, but I'm exhausted. Accustomed to the heat, Daniela quickly falls asleep, while I toss and turn for over an hour—jet-lagged. Giving up, I pull on a pair of shorts and take a beer onto the porch. Despite the hour, children's voices float through the streets and the traffic builds again along Via Dodici Apostoli. The street is busier at 2 am than at 2 pm.

Stray cats run for cover—it's drag race time! For the Madonna and Padre Pio, the night shift is even more demanding than the day. Raucous Vespas dash past the house, two, sometimes three abreast, ridden by soft-centred hooligans, high on the sugar in their ice-cream. I should be alarmed but I'm quite enjoying the show, although the audacious noise leaves me wondering how I'll ever get to sleep.

The bell strikes three before the street is quiet and I'm back on the mattress next to my slow-breathing mystery. I kiss her shoulder and she stirs slightly. It's been an unusual day, in a town beyond my imagination, with a woman beyond my dreams.

Andrano hushes, cools, rejuvenates, in preparation for a new day, which, apart from the sea anemone in my foot, I hope will be the same as the old one.

As if disturbed by the novel silence, the watermelon seller will soon jolt awake, feel for the keys to his rusty truck and crank up his screeching amplifier. And in their darkened houses, the waking dreams of Andrano's residents will turn to the theme of his plump, ripe wares.

Crristoper Arrison with H in front

In Luigi Pirandello's novel, *The Late Mattia Pascal*, the protagonist feigns his own death in order to escape what he calls 'the tragedy of Italian civil status'—the impossibility of evading bureaucracy to live a free and peaceful existence. During the tedious process of becoming a resident of Daniela's country, at no time was I desperate enough to emulate Pascal. I would never have killed myself, though I could have killed others on occasion. Being in Andrano was a great deal more enjoyable than obtaining official permission to remain there, and I had it easier than most.

Soon after arriving in Italy, my work visa and residency permit required completion at a string of public offices. Before visiting each office Daniela would brainstorm a contact, someone who either worked there or knew someone who did. Any acquaintance would do, no matter how tenuous the claim to friendship; a third-removed cousin or a friend of a friend, just as long as they could open the side door or meet us out the front. When I asked Daniela why we couldn't fix the documents ourselves, she looked at me as though I had arrived from a foreign planet rather than a foreign country. 'Why do you worry?' she asked. 'There is not a choice. This is Italy.'

Each contact needed to be thanked, which was where I came in; my only real role in the entire process. When arriving at Italian customs feeling like a smuggler of Aboriginal artefacts, I had assumed the dozen boomerangs Daniela insisted I bring from Australia to be gifts for family and friends. I didn't realise they were actually sweeteners for well-connected friends, scissors with which to cut red tape. Designed to leave and return, the boomerangs were Daniela's way of thanking those who ensured I wouldn't have to do the same. But even with tricks up our sleeves we still had to roll them up.

Sixty kilometres north of Andrano is the Baroque city of Lecce, capital of the Salento. In July alone we made over fifteen visits to its smoke-filled public offices, an unwelcome interruption to the sedate routines of summer. In tongue-out temperatures with no air-conditioning, the 120-kilometre round trip was a trial for both Daniela and me, but it was Napoleon who suffered most.

I lost no time in christening Daniela's car, an Elba, after the emperor exiled to the island of the same name. A scarlet hatchback made by Innocenti Motors, he'd clocked over 200,000 kilometres and, by the look of his bodywork, been to war more often than his namesake. In torrid July heat he rattled to and from Lecce as reluctantly as we did.

Our expeditions to Lecce invariably started with a stop, at one of the last houses on the road out of town—the *api* petrol station. The owner of the simple stucco dwelling that is identical, in most respects, to other houses in Andrano, has converted the next-door block into a two-pump driveway and painted walls, pumps, pylons and awning a garish canary yellow, the colour of the multinational company to which his poky franchise belongs. Along the rear wall of the station is a flower garden, where yellow azaleas provide a loyal finishing touch to a thriving business affectionately named 'California' by the old guy on the pumps.

'*Benvenuti in California!*' he yelled each time we pulled in. '*Pieno Signori?*'

'No, just twenty, *grazie*,' Daniela would reply, declining his automatic offer to fill 'er up. He only asks as a joke. A '*si*' would startle him. *Benzina* costs €1.30 (over AU$2.00) a litre in these parts and we'd have doubled Napoleon's value had we filled his tank. Part of that exorbitant price is comprised of taxes, some of which are even warranted, while others—like the tax levied on petrol to help fund Mussolini's Abyssinian war campaign, and which is said to have never been removed—are more difficult to justify. *Benzina* is a huge financial burden on Italians. I even heard a story of an armed hold-up at a petrol station where the traumatised assistant moved instinctively to the till, only to be redirected towards the pumps by the barrel of a gun.

With no guarantee Napoleon would outlast a full tank, Daniela only ever bought enough *benzina* for our immediate journey, the reason every trip to Lecce took us via 'California'. The eccentric owner quickly became my first friend in Andrano. I called him 'Signor Api', explaining that in the real California such a title might translate as 'Mr Happy'. He was delighted with the nickname and started using it himself. It seemed a fitting moniker for such a cheery old soul, for if anyone could leave you feeling happy after paying through the nose for petrol, it was a larrikin like Signor Api.

A short man of seventy with a wise and wrinkled face, Signor Api wore a lopsided pair of reading glasses while pumping petrol; aligning all those zeros—when Italy used the lira—would have damaged anyone's eyes. It's a tradition of the Italians not to pump their own petrol. Even at a station where a discount is offered for self-service they prefer to wait and have it pumped for them; strange considering they drive as if they'll wait for no one. Boisterous and bright, while pumping our petrol Signor Api shouted wisecracks from his position at the tank, meaning we listened from the cabin whether we wanted to or not.

That particular morning, Napoleon was covered with bougainvillea from the tree in Daniela's drive, an adequate trigger for the tongue of a small-town sage, who raised head and hands to deliver his lines.

'Outside the car, petals of flowers soon to fade. Inside, an everlasting rose.'

Daniela was less enamoured with Signor Api than I was, particularly now she had to translate as well as tolerate his remarks. He was still keen on her though.

'You're the most beautiful woman in Andrano,' he declared. 'And perhaps even the province.'

'Perhaps?' repeated Daniela, feigning insult.

'Well, there are lots of women in the province, and they can't sneak through Andrano without me spotting them.'

While Daniela's beauty was not in question, neither was the fact that few women who stopped at 'California' were spared this dubious accolade.

As he continued his banter, a van with Bari numberplates pulled up, its driver asking directions for Diso, a town less than 2 kilometres away.

'Head for Rome!' yelled Signor Api. 'Head for the world's most picturesque capital and you'll not miss Diso, dear fellow.'

'Which way to Rome then?' asked the courier, whose tight schedule didn't allow for jest.

Signor Api stamped his foot like a soldier standing to attention and pointed to the road tapering out of town. The courier gave him a wave, made a mental note that the *Andranesi* were to be avoided, then headed for the capital. *'Tante belle cose!'* shouted Signor Api, his customary farewell meaning 'all the best', the same farewell he then gave us as we pointed Napoleon towards Lecce for our first assault on the immigration office.

The first stretch of the road to Lecce, though designated *una strada provincale*—a secondary road, is little more than a country lane. Erosion on both flanks means most people drive down the middle, yielding only to oncoming cars or when being overtaken. The speed limit is 70 kilometres per hour, but we sat on 100 and were often overtaken—by a man shaving on one occasion. Uneven stone walls separate the road from olive groves, wheat fields and abandoned stone huts with wild grass on their roofs.

The speed limit drops to 50 and cars to about 80 where the *provinciale* passes through the towns of Marittima, Diso, Ortelle and Poggiardo. Whitewashed houses line its edge and motorists entering from side streets must poke their bonnets into the narrow main street to sight oncoming traffic, something they too often feel before they see. Rather than touch their brakes, to which most Italians appear allergic, drivers already on the *provinciale* warn of their approach by beeping horns and flashing lights. Life in a house on the corner can't be peaceful.

Stop signs referee most intersections. Some are so faded it is only their octagonal shape which reminds of their disciplinary role. They are like mistletoe, an optional obligation to be observed or ignored depending on advantage. 'Who goes first here?' I asked Daniela, as she pulled out of Marittima and I strangled my door handle. 'The most courageous,' she replied, her foot on the accelerator.

At a crossroads in Poggiardo, an Albanian family has taken advantage of a traffic light to set up a drive-thru market. While waiting for a green, motorists can peruse fake Persian carpets, lampshades, fans, drills and other sundry items, while sunburnt children in dirty clothes wander between cars selling tissues and cigarette lighters. We gave a coin but refused the merchandise, hoping they'd sell it to somebody else.

Once past Poggiardo it's *superstrada* to Lecce. The official speed limit is 90 but most cruise at 130. We did the same, only because it's less dangerous to accompany missiles than obstruct them. The shoulders of the road were strewn with litter and defunct electrical appliances. The carcass of an Alsatian lay under a buckled guard rail. A stray, said Daniela, better off dead.

Despite the heat we closed the windows to pass the Pedone pasta factory and an olive oil plant, their stench thick and foul like the smoke belching from industrial chimneys. Soon afterwards, on a hazy horizon, the city of Lecce appeared, sweltering on flat land kilometres from the coast. Polluted and uninviting, each time it materialised I hoped it was a mirage.

The *superstrada* joined the Lecce ring-road, on which a scrum of cars ignored any concept of precedence and jostled for position. Lanes, where painted, were totally disregarded. Drivers punched their horns at the first hint of inconvenience, despite passing a sign just a few seconds prior declaring it illegal to do so. After blazing across country bitumen we were idling in city traffic, surrounded by eyesore apartments and immigrant beggars on intersections. *Benvenuti a Lecce.*

Stunning in the centre, unsightly at its edge, a beautiful Baroque skeleton with unattractive flesh. Like most Italian cities, the elegant architecture of Lecce's lavish *centro storico* contradicts its unkempt residential surrounds. Such antique cities seem ill at ease with modern expansion. But Lecce's history is its highlight, not its take on modern life. In a similar evolution to Andrano but on a larger scale, Lecce's pre-Christian founders were roaming Greek communities. The city was then fought over and ruled by a succession of warlords including the Roman emperor Marco Aurelio, the Normans, and then for three and a half centuries by the Spanish Bourbons. Around the middle of the nineteenth century, patriotic uprisings unified Lecce with the rest of emergent Italy, and today the flag of a proud republic stands outside the public offices of what has become the administrative capital of the Salento.

We parked Napoleon between two communal bins as a dishevelled young man approached. 'Car service, *signora*,' he informed Daniela. 'I'll look after it.' Daniela thrust him a coin which he slipped in his jeans before sitting on our bonnet, a menace to all who approached our car, if only until we were out of sight. It was a minor Mafia-style transaction, a demand dressed as an offer, with failure to pay implying he might really 'look after it'. Although Daniela resented these paltry extortions she rarely refused to pay, figuring a coin a small price to pay to protect herself from the protectors.

They were queuing into the street outside the *Ufficio Immigrazione*, Africans, Kurds, Slavs, and now an Aussie, patiently waiting in the hope of being told they could stay. A division of the *Questura*—the police headquarters, its one service window was manned by a plump policeman, plainly uninterested in the rigours of work. Cap on the counter, he squinted in smoke from the cigarette between his lips. Those queuing seemed tense. They had been waiting for hours, many just to see if their permits had been completed. An African man in a caftan, when told his wasn't ready and that he should return in a month, protested: 'This is the third time I've waited three hours just to be told to come back.'

'So?' shouted the policeman behind perspex protection. 'When I want to go to the bank I need to apply for a day off work.'

I wasn't sure who was complaining to whom.

'Are you in the queue?' a Slavic man asked Daniela in fluent Italian.

'No, go ahead,' she replied. 'We're waiting for someone.'

'Ah, you've got some help,' he said, noticing my documents. 'Lucky you. Last time I came with my lawyer who wore a miniskirt and we waited two minutes. But she couldn't come today. Where are you from?' he asked me.

'Australia.'

'Australia? What the devil are you doing here?'

I looked at Daniela.

'Ahh,' he said. 'Love, war and money are the three reasons people change country. You've changed for the best reason.'

I smiled. He continued, needing to talk.

'It's the documents that are the problem. These offices are awful. Italy's not that bad, though. It's a nightmare to get the permit, but once you've got it you can move around the country and look for a job. In Germany they gave me the documents quickly but I couldn't move more than twenty-five kilometres from the office. I said to the officer: "Twenty-five kilometres? I'm not your dog."'

We all laughed.

'Have you lived here long?' Daniela asked.

'Nearly four years,' he replied. 'Forgive me, *signora*, but I don't like Italy much. But it's my only home. Yugoslavia doesn't exist anymore.'

The queue moved. He took a step forward, we took a step back, our trump card on the way.

Ten minutes later that trump card arrived when two black Lancias with tinted windows pulled up, double-parking the street to a standstill. '*Ecco Riccardo*,' declared Daniela, straightening her blouse. From the second car emerged a local police chief, heavily overweight, with a bald head and goatee. Only his smile softened daunting features. Handsome and imposing, he had the appearance of an underworld figure, indeed my first impression was that he looked like the *Mafiosi* he was paid to collar. His escorts lit cigarettes and leant against Lancias as Riccardo, arms outstretched, moved towards us.

'*Carissima Daniela*,' he cried, kissing her cheeks. 'He's arrived then finally?'

'*Si, si*,' said Daniela, touching my arm. 'Chris, *ti presento Riccardo*.'

Shocked at the style of Riccardo's arrival, I stuttered: 'It's a pleasure to meet you.'

'I've already met you on paper,' he replied, crushing my hand and kissing my cheeks. '*Dai*, let's get this done so we can go and have a drink.'

We followed Riccardo to the front of the queue, where the policeman at the window recognised him and touched a switch under his counter to throw an adjacent door ajar. A series of offices branched off a grey marble corridor. Riccardo led us to the furthest and entered without knocking. The man on the phone cut his conversation short.

'*Buongiorno ispettore*,' said Riccardo. Without waiting for a reply, he introduced Daniela and me before explaining the purpose of his visit, finishing with the words *permesso di soggiorno*—permit of stay. The inspector took a drag of his cigarette before opening a grey filing cabinet next to his grey desk. Everything in the office was grey: the telephone, the manila folders stacked from floor to ceiling, even the coughing occupant. There were no computers and everything was either sprinkled with ash, dust or age: the sagging shelves, the stationery, the crucifix on the wall. The only thing fresh and crisp was the form the inspector pulled from his drawer and on which he began to write.

Despite copying my name from my passport, the inspector misspelled it on the form—Crristoper Arrison, the way he and indeed most Italians, other than Daniela, pronounce it, rolling the R of my Christian name and leaving the H off my surname.

'No, it's *Harrison* with H in front,' corrected Daniela, spotting the inspector's clumsy calligraphy. 'And *Christopher* has one R and two H's.'

'*Accidenti*,' muttered the inspector, before taking another form and offering cigarettes we refused.

Italians have difficulty with the English alphabet. There are only twenty-one letters in their *alfabeto*. Missing are J, K, W, X and Y, and while the letter H does exist, it is always mute and begins only a handful of imported words like 'hotel', pronounced *otel* in Italy.

Arriving at the 'date of entry' section on the form, the inspector thumb-searched my passport until his sunburnt brow furrowed.

'There should be a stamp in your passport saying when you arrived in Italy.'

'When did you arrive?' Riccardo asked me.

'June the sixteenth.'

'He arrived on June the sixteenth,' said Riccardo, expecting the blank to be filled.

'But why isn't there a stamp?'

In improving Italian I recounted the tale of the lazy immigration police at Rome airport.

'But they should have stamped this visa the Italian Consulate gave you in Sydney,' insisted the inspector, holding up my passport.

'But they didn't,' interrupted Daniela.

'They didn't stamp his passport, inspector,' said Riccardo, clearly accustomed to his word being the last. But on this occasion, unfortunately, it wasn't.

Italy has enormous problems with illegal immigration. In 2001 alone, some 20,000 *clandestini* came ashore along the peninsula's coastline, risking their lives in rudimentary vessels in the hope of swapping poverty for prosperity. For most, Italy was not the destination but the entrance, the Continent's umbilical cord, a 1000-kilometre stepladder into the belly of greater Europe. As the Italians say: 'If you can't get in the front door, climb in through the window.'

While not quite accusing me of having arrived by dinghy, proving my legal entry into Italy was not something the inspector was prepared to overlook. Fortunately I was a Frequent Flyer and had retained my boarding pass out of habit; proof, surely, of my conventional arrival. I put this to the inspector and Riccardo looked at me admiringly, his broad smile suggesting I was going to fit right in. You need to be good at contingency plans to live in Italy.

The inspector was happy to compromise, ordering me to bring the boarding pass when I returned to complete the permit with documents I would spend the next few weeks collecting. He then licked the back of a €20 tax stamp, which Daniela had bought from a nearby tobacconist, and placed it next to my passport photo on the application.

'*Finito*,' he said, stamping both the stamp and the photo.

'What's next?' asked Riccardo

'*Impronte digitali*,' replied the inspector.

We walked to the front of another queue and into another office without knocking. Sheets of white paper with black hand-prints were scattered about the room, which looked like a kindergarten for criminals. Riccardo told the officer in charge of fingerprints to do mine next.

'Where are you from?' asked the plain-clothes officer, as he painted my hands with a sticky black substance.

'Australia.'

'Australia? What the cabbage are you doing here?'—I loved this Italian nicety, replacing *cazzo* (fuck) with *cavolo* (cabbage).

'I'm starting work in Milan in September.'

Daniela nodded; I had told the policeman all he needed to know.

'I'd love to live in Australia. I'd go there in a flash if I could. Tell me, are the police more severe in Australia than in Italy?'

I didn't have an answer. Fortunately it was a rhetorical question.

'How long is the flight?'

'Twenty-four hours.'

I was tempted to tell him to retain his boarding pass.

I washed my hands and we left the *Questura*, stepping into the oven outside. Feeling guilty for having jumped the queue, I gave the former Yugoslavian a timid wave. In forty minutes he had progressed a few metres but wasn't yet inside the building. Riccardo insisted he buy us a drink, signalling to his minders by patting his stomach and pointing to the bar opposite.

'Sharing a coffee is an Italian tradition after achieving something together,' he said, before putting his short black away in two sips. 'A way of celebrating our success against the State.'

He shared a sly smile with Daniela.

'I can't thank you enough for this morning,' she said.

'Thank you doesn't exist,' he replied, eyeing his watch. 'Hi to mum and dad,' he added, before kissing our cheeks and breezing back to his dangerous life.

When we returned to the car its minder was missing but sadly Napoleon was still there. Parked between two bins, he looked a little like a third. But he mustered the strength for the journey home and soon we were diving into the emerald depths of Andrano's port, where the morning's trial dissolved in the sea amid fishing boats, ice-cream and Daniela's scarlet bikini.

What began with our first trip to the *Ufficio Provinciale del Lavoro*, where I had to register my job and set up a taxation arrangement, became two solid weeks of office-jumping. Backwards and forward between labour offices, the INAIL office for workers' compensation and the INPS office for taxes and pensions, where

I received a tax file number which, with its sixteen characters, was only half as long as the queue to request it. Staffed by procrastinating public servants sucking on cigarettes, each office was equipped with grey telephones like those of the *Questura*, a range of rubber stamps on revolving racks, paper to the ceiling, crucifixes on peeling walls, faded EU and Italian flags, and only in cases of absolute necessity, an old Olivetti computer. Not only had time stopped in these offices, it had done so a long time ago.

Frustrating days were delightfully punctuated by Daniela and the Mediterranean. After a morning's queuing we would spend the afternoon drifting on a boat around coastal caves, the anchor working harder than the motor. I took my Italian textbooks and Daniela tested me as I splashed round the boat. A mistake cost a kiss. I made some on purpose. An afternoon with her adventurous tongue was worth a morning's misadventure biting my own. Floating between heaven and hell. Italian life is like that.

The next hurdle was the *Ufficio del Lavoro*, where my work visa would be issued—eventually. Daniela had somehow managed to befriend a contact at the office, a young woman with her own experience of foreign 'affairs'. Her *storia d'amore* had been with an American man who had failed Barzini's challenge and returned to the States. Curiosity as to whether Daniela and I would fare any better was my only explanation for her interest in our case. Whatever the reason, Daniela had smartly nurtured a friendship with the woman, who told us to come to her office in the afternoon when she could give us her undivided attention.

At three o'clock on a summer's afternoon Andrano is fast asleep. But someone is up and about. With only a fly-curtain separating bowser from bedroom, Signor Api is ever ready to dart out and sell some gas. We tooted quietly to avoid waking the village and he appeared in his standard summer uniform: green singlet splashed with oil stains, grey shorts with a belt made from rope, and tattered sandals on feet with toenails in need of a clean. If he was talkative in the morning, he was garrulous in the afternoon. Daniela blamed the home-made wine he drank with lunch, so potent that most of the village suggested drinking his petrol would damage him less. Taking our key to the fuel cap he went to work, fast enough for a Formula 1 team. Until the muse arrived and the race was lost.

'I don't like the nude anymore,' he proclaimed. 'There's nothing left to desire. All the women on TV are naked. They disappoint my imagination. Where's the winter woman gone? It's always summer on channel 5.'

While Signor Api spoke to the breeze, a teenage girl waited outside the house directly opposite. Driven by an older man, an Alfa arrived into which she climbed before the pair raced off. 'Ahh . . . the modern appointment,' began Signor Api, entitling what was to come. 'The woman strolls from the house and the vagabond whisks her away. *Facile!*' He slapped one hand across the other. 'Time forgets what I went through. The only reason I'm not with my beautiful girlfriend of fifty years ago is because I got too close in front of her parents. The only way they would let me hold her hand was by putting a wedding ring on it first. But I anticipated the times I lived in. I taught women love. To kiss even. Ah, what's our Lord up to? When you're a young man you fancy older women and when you're old you want the young ones.'

Perhaps objecting to her husband's prattle, Signor Api's wife stuck her head through the fly-curtain and barked a comment in a dialect even Daniela couldn't decipher. But his reply was abundantly clear: he was working, she'd have to wait.

'Gossip was the problem,' he continued. 'Making love was not a sin. Making love and telling someone was the sin . . .' And on he went. Each trip to 'California' was a philosophic mix of petrol and prose, and each erudition was 'God's natural law'. Even the overabundance of breasts on channel 5. I couldn't help liking him.

He closed the fuel cap and swapped its key for a €20 note.

'Where are we headed today?' he inquired.

'Lecce again,' I replied. 'We're still working on my documents.'

'Still? *Mamma mia!* And they say things are perfect in this country. I tell you, the only thing perfect about the Italians is our appetites.'

He slapped our bonnet and burst out laughing as his wife stuck her head out again.

'Who says things are perfect in Italy?' I asked Daniela, as we set out for Lecce.

'Signor Api,' she replied, switching the fan on high.

With a graffitied façade, a broken window and an Italian flag on the roof, what looked the ideal place for patriotic squatters was in fact the office we were after. Daniela asked me to stay in the car. I had lost my temper the previous day after waiting over two hours for documents which on the phone were reported to be ready but weren't. I hadn't said anything I shouldn't, but had raised my voice in English, something Daniela suggested was counter-productive.

It was a scorcher—38 degrees, and the trip to Lecce had been tense, with Napoleon running a temperature. Hence my frustration when Daniela emerged from the building with the news we would have to repeat the journey the following day because her contact hadn't turned up for work. I suggested we try our luck with a colleague but Daniela disagreed. I still couldn't swallow the concept of having to know someone to get something done, but my foreign thinking clashed with her local knowledge. The heat was intense and things boiled over. We shouted. We fought. I protested. She convinced me. And when she spoke English to deprive bystanders the details of our dispute, with that cute clumsy accent and mistimed intonation, suddenly I couldn't wait to get her home, even if it meant agreeing to tomorrow's return trip.

It took two more trips to find the woman at work, but just as Daniela had maintained, when she did finally turn up our documents were processed with ease. Daniela gave her a boomerang, although I thought she didn't deserve one.

Almost a month had passed since Napoleon's first advance on Lecce. We had amassed a wad of paper on which the T's were finally crossed, the I's dotted and the H's inserted. We could now return to the *Questura* to finalise my application for the *permesso di soggiorno* and then start the rest of summer.

We were late for our appointment at the *Questura* on account of a religious procession which blocked the road through Diso for fifteen minutes. It was the first time I had seen a stagnant line of Italian cars whose horns weren't being thumped like game show buzzers; Italians respect their saints more than they do fellow motorists. We found Riccardo waiting by the service window, observing an altercation between the *poliziotto* on duty and an African man wearing a gold necklace outside his caftan.

'Your application has been delayed because of what happened in Otranto.'

'I was only selling CDs.'

'*Illegal* CDs.'

When we entered the inspector's office he muttered '*Buongiorno*', pointed at me, narrowed his eyes and guessed: '*Arrison?*'

'*Perfetto,*' I replied.

He reached for his phone and put a fat finger into hole number 9, which he cast through a three-quarter circle. Then he lit a cigarette and waited for a reply.

'It's Poggi,' he said, spraying the mouthpiece with smoke. 'Bring up the folder for Crristoper Arrison.'

He listened a moment.

'Crristoper Arrison with H in front,' he elaborated.

Poggi's cigarette was approaching his knuckles when his phone rang. He picked up and listened intently, his brow creasing slightly.

'Listen to me,' he said abruptly. 'Arrison with H in front of Arrison.'

They don't pronounce it, they don't hear it, and now some poor policeman in the bowels of the building couldn't see it either.

'Look under A,' suggested Poggi as an afterthought.

Riccardo opened the inspector's window to let air in and smoke out.

'*Bravo*,' said Poggi, relieved, adding '*fai presto*' before hanging up.

When my folder arrived, Poggi inserted our documents as well as a photocopy of my boarding pass which he stamped as authentic. He then returned to the 'date of entry' section on the application and filled the final blank. As relieved as we were that the process was over, the inspector extinguished his cigarette, stood up, shook our hands and informed us that we could return to collect the permit in a month.

'A month?' questioned Riccardo, encouraging a revised estimate.

'Well,' hesitated Poggi, 'I'll see what I can do.'

Driving home, the Lecce ring-road was clogged to a standstill. An elderly farmer trudged between cars selling freshly plucked carrots with their tops attached. Some of the dirt from his produce had lodged in his beard, an undisciplined growth that covered his mouth and would have sparked like kindling were he smoking. Head bowed, he said nothing; if anyone wanted him they'd let him know. I watched as he laboured past my window, his tattered shirt, his shabby sandals.

'I hadn't imagined this place to be so . . .'

'*Strano?*' suggested Daniela.

'Ancient.'

'It's backward and frustrating,' she said, surprising me. 'But somehow it gets inside you. Every Italian complains about Italy. But if we leave, we miss something and we don't know what it is. It's impossible to describe.'

'Do you want some carrots?' I asked.

'No, I'm going to cook *linguine ai frutti di mare*.'

Linguine ai frutti di mare . . . I thought she said Italy's allure was impossible to describe.

We joined the *superstrada*, accelerating. My documents were complete and we were on cloud nine. But two *carabinieri* standing by their squad car on the shoulder of the road soon brought us back to earth. One waved a lollipop stick while his colleague held a submachine gun. Might and impotence side by side, they looked a comical pair, the Laurel and Hardy of law enforcement. One was fat, the other skinny, and between lollipop sticks, knee-high boots, striped trousers and hats too small for their heads, they aroused ridicule rather than respect. As we pulled over, the larger officer slipped his baton in his boot, bullet-proof vest lodging under his chin as he leaned in our window. '*Documenti per favore.*'

A random document check takes a bit of getting used to for an Australian. Daniela reached for her handbag and I grabbed my interim permit on which the ink was barely dry. But the *carabiniere* had lost interest in our documents, distracted by an unusual sight in the car. Yellow Post-it notes were stuck about the cabin, bearing the name of items to which they were attached. The steering wheel, horn, glove box, dashboard, gearstick and handbrake were all labelled. Daniela's idea—a novel way of learning vocabulary. There were patches of paper everywhere. It looked as if Napoleon had cut himself shaving.

The *carabiniere* summoned his heavily armed colleague and the two men shared a laugh.

'Can I ask why, *signora*?'

'My boyfriend's learning Italian.'

'Where are you from?'

'Australia.'

'Australia? What the cabbage are you doing here?'

'I'm starting work in Milan in September,' I said fluently. Practice makes perfect.

'Your Italian seems to be coming along well.'

I touched Daniela's arm.

'I've got a good teacher.'

'What language do you speak in Australia?' asked the one with the gun.

I assumed he was joking and looked at Daniela, whose expression indicated he wasn't.

'*Inglese*,' I replied, stifling shock.

'I'd love to learn English. My brother speaks a bit of French.' He looked at Daniela. 'Do you speak English, *signora*?'

'*Si*.'

'You lucky thing. And where did you two meet . . . ?'

As cars raced by, most of them speeding, the highway patrol gleaned our love story. When it was finished they wished us good luck. The officer with the machine gun even waved as we pulled out. Whether they realised it or not, they had forgotten to check our documents.

The medical check is the final hurdle for those seeking residency in Italy, deliberately last in case the process leading up to it has driven the applicant mad. The reward for passing is a *libretto sanitario*—a ticket to free government health care.

When Daniela called her family medico, friend first and doctor second, he insisted we come round immediately, saying he was very much looking forward to receiving his first Australian patient, although he suggested Daniela register her *canguro* with a vet as well. Driving to the after-hours appointment at Dr Nino's home, Daniela said he was a good medico because he remembered what was wrong with you from one visit to the next. I hoped there was more to his CV than that.

In the nearby town of Soldignano, Dr Nino's freshly painted villa reflected the afternoon sun. We walked through a garden of lemon trees up to grandiose front doors, which a moustachioed man opened onto a palace of antiques and leather lounges, artworks and statuettes. The opulence of the house was at odds with the neglected township outside its gate, litter on the street and a starving stray dog. If you could take an x-ray photograph of these southern villages, to view the plush insides of houses lining ramshackle streets, you would glimpse the Italian attitude to common property. 'The street belongs to no one,' they say. But what about the dog?

Tall for an Italian, Dr Nino retold the kangaroo joke in case Daniela hadn't passed it on. Then he gave me a stringent medical, which involved drinking the best part of a bottle of his home-made *limoncello*—pure alcohol with a hint of lemon. I can only assume his motive for such a medical was that, were I sick, his eccentric elixir would either kill or cure me. 'Nino made it with lemons from our garden,' boasted his wife, whose contribution had surely been nail polish remover. They insisted I drink, to the point of putting the glass in my hand; if they could have drunk it for me they would have. By the end of the 'medical' I was chatting with their parrot, who, to my disgust and their amuse-ment, spoke Italian better than I did.

Dr Nino received a boomerang. I got a headache that came and went.

After a month's racing around on roads belonging to no one, Andrano had its first Australian resident—Crristoper Arrison with H in front. And while I could prove my new civil status with any of a dozen *documenti*, the real indicator of my belonging to Andrano was the fact I could hum its five o'clock angelus by heart. Should the *Carabinieri* ever wave me over and I've forgotten my documents, perhaps such a feat might amount to something. If not, I'll tell them another love story.

Festivals and funerals

When the bell tolls midnight on New Year's Eve, the *Andranesi* pack into La Chiesa di Sant'Andrea to receive spiritual nourishment, a divine start to another year, and to hear their town's octogenarian priest read the annual village statistics for births, deaths and marriages. But in recent years, Don Francesco has been confirming what a dwindling number of gatherers already knew, that Andrano's clerics have been burying rather than baptising.

We would soon be leaving too, if not quite so permanently. There are few jobs in a southern Italian fishing village for an Italian let alone an Australian, so come September, Daniela and I would start work in Milan. I had a job as a copywriter at her brother's advertising agency, while she had organised a transfer to an inner-city primary school. At the end of the school year in June, Daniela had left the *scuola elementare* where she began her teaching career nine years earlier. Justifying tears at their favourite teacher's bad news, an eight-year-old boy spoke for the class when he told her: 'We are not robots. We have hearts, you know.'

Apart from a side trip to Sicily en route to Milan to meet Daniela's family, we still had the first weeks of August, a month-long national holiday, to enjoy the eccentricities of a town I was sad to be leaving so soon after making its acquaintance. And I couldn't have chosen a better time to discover Andrano and surrounding towns, when despite enervating temperatures the Salento is vibrantly alive.

August on the heel of the boot is a marathon of festivals, when towns like Andrano pay homage to history. Every evening there was a different village to visit, where residents were showering thanks and adoration on either religious protectors or favoured foodstuffs—all they needed to survive. When offered the choice of a *sagra*—food festival, or *festa patronale*—religious festival, much to Daniela's relief I invariably voted with my stomach.

In the seaside town of Porto Badisco at the *Sagra del Riccio di Mare*, I wrought my revenge on the sea anemone that punctured my foot. Armed with special cutters to protect against spikes, fishermen prised out the reclusive molluscs and served them with local bread and wine. Revenge was sweet, much sweeter than the taste of a crustacean better left at the bottom of the sea.

In the town of Depressa, named after its low-lying position rather than the mental health of its inhabitants, we went to the *Sagra della Pasta Fatta in Casa*—the Home-Made Pasta Festival. It was doughy and tasteless, and I shocked Daniela and several purists within earshot by confessing my preference for Barilla in a packet. Daniela had found herself a philistine.

In a gastronomic tour, Daniela ferried me from one smorgasbord to the next: the Olive Festival in Torre Dell'Orso, the Fish Festival at La Marina di Torre Vado, the Eggplant Festival at Collemeto, the Horsemeat Festival in Secli', the Snail Festival in Cannole and the Pizza Festival in a village whose name I can't remember but where a group of chefs made a pizza almost as big as the piazza. My favourite was the *Sagra delle Cozze* in Castro, where I polished off two plates of spaghetti and mussels cooked in white wine followed by several scoops of peach and lemon gelato. Spartan by comparison, Daniela's favourite was the *Sagra della Frisella* in Specchia Gallone, where an entire evening was organised around a hard wet bread topped with tomato, olive oil, salt, rocket and oregano. Daniela adores the infinite variations in staple foods like bread. An inherited trait no doubt, the traditions of tougher times when such staples were all people had.

Even in the finest restaurant she fills her stomach with bread before the entrée arrives. I don't know why I take her.

Weight gained at the food festivals was quickly lost at the bizarre *Festa del Ballo,* a fifteen-day dance spectacular culminating in the town of Melpignano on *La Notte della Tarantola*—The Night of the Tarantella. Performing a frantic carnal wriggle known as the *tarantola*, dancers imitate victims of what is now considered a psychosomatic condition dating back over a thousand years. Documented cases existed throughout the south of Italy, but the condition was particularly rife in Puglia, home to the city of Taranto from where the tarantula spider gets its name.

It was widely believed that the tarantula's bite made the victim, or *tarantato*, a slave to the giant spider by whom they became possessed. The *tarantato* began to tremble when the tarantula moved or mated, prompting musicians to arrive with violins and tambourines to play what became known as the *pizzica*—the 'pinch' or 'bite' of the tarantula—as a form of musical therapy to help the voodoo-like torture pass. Victims begged musicians to play faster and closer because the vibration of air from the instruments relieved the pain of the bite on the skin, helping to disperse the coagulation of the blood.

The movement of the *tarantato* was convulsive, rhythmic and repetitious, beginning slowly and climaxing in a trance-like erotic ecstasy. People danced for days on end and were said to have assumed spider-like capabilities. One *tarantato,* an otherwise exhausted eighty-year-old, was reported to have danced for three days and to have crawled to the roof of his town's church, while a woman danced into the frame between the legs of a wooden chair, where she remained trembling and contorted for a number of awkward hours.

Scientific investigation supported some genuine cases of *tarantismo*, however more weight was given to an alternative theory when it was discovered that most victims were women. Socially and sexually repressed, they were believed to be justifying the liberating musical and erotic expression, which under any other circumstances would have been unacceptable, by claiming to have been bitten by the spider. This permitted a luxurious lapse in etiquette, from stripping in public to blasphemy in church.

Despite its psychosomatic stigma, the disorder still exists. Every year on 29 June in the town of Galatina, 30 kilometres north of Andrano, the few remaining *tarantati*, who insist their bodies to be possessed by a spider, gather in the church of San Paolo to ask the patron saint of *tarantati* for deliverance. There, I am told, they are made to drink pungent water from a well containing snakes, frogs and spiders. An immediate urge to urinate is deemed evidence of dispossession. How vomiting is interpreted I'm not sure.

We drank something far more palatable on *La Notte della Tarantola*, a crisp white wine which cost the equivalent of three dollars a bottle from a local vineyard. The frenzy of the *pizzica* filled Melpignano's piazza and even I gave the 'Tarantula' my best effort, but erotic trances in public don't come easy to me. Daniela suggested I'd been caught in a spider's web rather than bitten by its owner. Her English friend from Lecce was even more critical of my unorthodox style, saying I looked like a randy ostrich with a nervous tic. I was far better suited to watching a throng of scantily dressed young women with an annual excuse to show off their writhing, well-tanned bodies.

In the early evening of August the second, I was sitting on the porch watching the street scene as usual when a *vigile* strolled by and attached a 'Special Event—No Parking' sign to our front wall. Every 10 metres or so he attached another poster to a light pole, rubbish bin or someone else's wall, informing residents that tomorrow's religious procession would pass among their homes.

At seven o'clock the next morning I was woken by a chorus of destruction so violent it seemed the Saracens were invading again. Walls shook, mudguards on our bicycles rattled, window panes wobbled, Daniela's print of Gustav Klimt's *The Kiss* fell from its hook, and two Chihuahuas in the neighbour's garden vomited in fear. And by the time the cannon had been fired from Andrano's castle a dozen times, almost the entire Salento was aware that tonight was Andrano's *Festa Patronale della Madonna.*

Culinary fetes are minor events compared with a town's annual homage to its personal spiritual protector. Most of the townships scattered about the Salento host such a thanksgiving in summer. Almost every evening I would hear a rumble in the distance which seemed to foretell the miraculous arrival of a storm, a faint chance of rain for the sun-dried south. But dashing to the roof I would discover the thunder to be merely another cannon firing from a far-off turret, or a fireworks display on an upwind horizon. No *Festa Patronale* was without fireworks; more important than the party itself is boasting to surrounding towns of its magnitude.

On Daniela's agnostic advice I had avoided the religious festivals of other towns, but as a resident of Andrano I could hardly neglect my own. For the past 300 years the *Andranesi* have honoured their divine patron, *La Madonna delle Grazie*—The Madonna of Mercy, with an extravagant town party in early August. The Madonna is co-patron of Andrano, sharing the responsibility with Saint Andrea—patron saint of fishermen—from whom Andrano gets its name; that way the town enjoys two public holidays instead of one. Even in towns where she is not the official protector there are shrines to the Madonna on roadsides and in piazzas. But in Andrano she's extra special, the frontispiece of many a private dwelling, whose occupants often place a window box in their front wall in which the sacred virgin stands, benevolent and dusty, forever on guard over all inside.

Shortly after our neighbour, Umberto, had cleaned and calmed his Chihuahuas, they began barking once again at the arrival of the procession. First came Don Francesco and a group of clerics with gold staffs, at their holy heels four thickset men balancing a life-sized statue of the Madonna on their shoulders, then a lively brass band playing with greater enthusiasm than expertise, while at the tail of the human serpent, which slithered through the streets for most of the morning, were several hundred faithful in disordered rows, chatting among themselves and doing their best to restrain fleeing children with the correct vocabulary for a religious procession.

At eleven o'clock the church bell rang frantically for half an hour. Then, after a few seconds of remarkable quiet—perhaps the Madonna's only miracle all day—stray animals scrammed as the daytime fireworks display commenced. Intrigued, I ran to the roof, where the powder of hundreds of explosions burst against a blue backdrop like flak in war-torn skies. Having followed me to the *terrazza,* Daniela anticipated my question, screaming that the significance was in the timing of the explosions, which only a panel of judges could discern. Unaware the menace was choreographed, Umberto's Chihuahuas ruined their owner's carpet once again. The din was total, thrilling, absurd.

At two o'clock the town paused as revellers regained their strength, and perhaps their hearing, for the long night ahead. A gypsy family had set up camp in the castle park opposite our house. Two naked children looked on as their mother washed their brother, pouring water over his head and rubbing his skinny body with her hands. The father slept on a dirty mattress thrown on the road behind a beaten-up car, whose boot was crammed with toys to be sold at the party later. Washed as sketchily as their occupants, the children's ragged clothes had been flung out to dry on a waist-high hedge. Andrano was asleep, the only objection to the gypsies coming from a stray dog that had made the hedge his home and whose flea-ridden tail the children pulled as they waited their turn for a shower.

A short time later I heard Umberto shouting at a *vigile* who had been passing on his motorbike. With my translator asleep, I struggled to understand their disagreement but assumed it concerned the itinerant family within metres of Umberto's front gate. Their altercation continued at length. When it was finished,

I went outside to find the gypsy family asleep and two stray dogs copulating in the middle of the street—the southern Italian version of a speed hump. To Umberto's clear disgust, the *vigile* was obviously powerless to move the nomads on, and it wasn't until the party got under way around eight that they plucked their clothes from the trees and moved to the buzzing piazza.

At around the same time, Daniela said her yearly prayer to the Madonna. Nothing extravagant, just her usual request for a hailstorm to smash the tacky decorations in the piazza. Thousands of tiny lights in colourful patterns had been mounted on three-storey wooden scaffolds framing the village square. The flick of a switch turned the subtle stone piazza into Las Vegas, a neon prison of palm trees and waterfalls, a garish amusement arcade. The castle, the church, every permanent feature of the piazza was eclipsed by the lights, as if turning on the party meant turning off the village.

The stilts supporting the kitsch bulb arrangements were held in place by fishing wire tied to everything immobile: balconies, bell towers, street lamps and statues. Though gigantic in structure, the whole lot could have been brought down with a pair of scissors and a basic understanding of the domino effect. But Daniela preferred the religious implications of her hailstorm, which the superstitious community would interpret as a sign their offering to the Madonna had gone unappreciated, saving the village a fortune in future years. Someone had to tell them the party was a waste of money. Daniela figured it might as well be the guest of honour.

The heat from the lights was intense—like standing in a microwave oven, suggested Daniela, who clearly wasn't enjoying the party. She would have gone home had I agreed, but I was determined to understand her objection to the event, which, judging by the thickening crowd, was a minority opinion.

At the top of the square was a stage on which the brass band huffed and puffed. The roads feeding off the piazza were closed to traffic and lined with toy stalls, shooting arcades, merry-go-rounds and a miniature Ferris wheel which, if any taller, would have electrocuted its passengers in the lights. A pig's head marked the beginning of the food stalls. A makeshift bar sold beer, wine and bottled water. Parents bought their children helium balloons—dolphins and Dalmatians—which hovered above the crowd on red ribbon leads. Villagers sat around on plastic chairs, chatting over the band which executed Verdi and Rossini for six hours straight.

Immigrant families, mainly Asian and African, who spent August between one festival and the next, sold miscellaneous gadgets and fashion accessories including microscopes, blood pressure machines, water pistols, binoculars, socks, fake handbags, imitation watches, pens that doubled as cigarette lighters (perfect for the frustrated writer) and—just in case the lights got too bright—sunglasses. The only religious tone to the entire evening was the blind eye turned to these immigrants by *vigili* too busy dealing with traffic snarls in surrounding streets to ask to see their documents.

Semi-live merchandise was also on sale, its popularity indicated by the fact its vendor was asleep. Behind him was a filthy tank occupied by around fifty fish competing for the last traces of oxygen in water that could cure a *tarantato*. Hanging above the tank were tiny bird cages, undignified gaols so cramped their trapped occupants couldn't even turn around. The saintly spirit of the *festa* didn't stretch to all God's creatures.

Partygoers were smartly dressed. Daniela suggested most of the women would have bought a new dress for the occasion. The men were also well turned out. Several wore black wigs, failing to realise that the lights of Las Vegas betrayed the difference between natural remnants and bogus locks.

To remind themselves it was a religious occasion, most people stopped in at the church before joining friends under the lights. To do so they had to step over the gypsy woman sitting with her legs across the doorway, a plastic begging bowl in the folds of her skirt. Her husband was in the crowd selling toys, while their three children, pocket height all, were nowhere to be seen.

We bumped into Umberto and asked about his altercation regarding the gypsies. 'Gypsies?' he replied over the brass band's take on *The Barber of Seville*. 'What do I fucking care about gypsies? I was complaining about the fine for not wearing a helmet on my motorbike, given to me by a man who rode past my house today doing the same thing!' He was incensed, disappearing into the crowd yelling *'ipocrisia!'*

Southern Italian villages don't need a newspaper because word travels faster in the piazza. Strolling the stones, passing the *Andranesi* in their loose summer clothes, I realised how much they must have known about us by how much Daniela knew about them. Not a person wandered by for whom Daniela didn't have an anecdote, amusing or tragic, which she recounted when its subject was out of earshot. At a southern Italian village festival, there's as much colour in the partygoers as in the party lights.

Smoking a pipe on the steps to the church was a shoemaker, famous for eating a contract in front of a salesman he no longer wished to pay. Licking an ice-cream outside the *tabaccheria* was a doctor with a penchant for pyromania, deregistered after setting several garbage trucks aflame. Supervising his son on the Ferris wheel was a man searching town for the person who stole his *motorino*. Apparently his chronic back problem disappeared along with the motorbike, and he wishes to thank the thief and give him the keys rather than bring him to justice. Wary of a ruse, the thief is staying quiet.

Many of the anecdotes were tinged with tragedy, like that of the middle-aged man and woman sitting by the bar—the Romeo and Juliet of Andrano. Shortly after they married, he came home to find a suicide note confessing adultery and his wife slumped next to a half-drunk bottle of bleach. After drinking what remained, the husband ended up in the same hospital as his wife, where, in slippers and dressing-gowns, it all came out in the wash.

Not so happy an ending had befallen an old woman now eating a handful of hazelnuts in the castle courtyard. Returning home from the post office one pension day, she found her husband being held at gunpoint by two bandits in balaclavas. Ordered to hand over the pension money, the woman turned out empty pockets, saying the computers were down at the post office and that the thieves should return tomorrow. Incredibly, they did, along with the *Carabinieri*, who disarmed and unmasked the woman's son and his best friend. The only thing close-knit about some Italian families are the balaclavas.

We bumped into Daniela's bank manager, Errico, whom I'd met the week before when opening an account at his branch. After exchanging pleasantries with his wife and daughter, Daniela informed him there was no ink in his ATM machine: 'We have to shade over the receipt with a pencil to see what's written on the paper.'

'So? In Sicily that's how people vote,' replied Errico, laughing at his own joke. 'We do things differently here, Crris,' he continued. 'Yesterday I phoned a man to tell him I couldn't honour the cheque he'd given his mechanic because he had no money in his account, so he suggested solving the problem by writing a cheque to the bank for the same amount.' He laughed again and slapped me on the arm.

To the rear of the stage we met Concetta and another of Daniela's travelling companions in Ireland. Dressed in bright orange paramedic uniforms, they were leaning against the door of the *Misericordia* or First Aid Station, on standby should anyone suffer heatstroke in the lights. '*Buonasera paramedici*,' I said, before inviting the pair to the bar for refreshments. In between rolling her tongue around three scoops of pineapple ice-cream, Concetta explained how she and her volunteer colleagues had been trying for years to raise enough money for Andrano to buy its own ambulance, saving any future bleach drinkers ten valuable minutes on the trip to hospital. 'The money for the ambulance is up there,' shouted Concetta, pointing her cone at fireworks flashing overhead. What a shame Errico's client couldn't just write her a cheque.

I was beginning to appreciate Daniela's derogatory opinion of Andrano's *Festa Patronale*. Originally a religious procession followed by a gathering to share the modest spoils of bread, vegetables and the rare indulgence of meat, today it has become an excessive and crass attempt to prove that better times have arrived. But with so many public utilities still primitive or non-existent, Daniela believes the party to be a harebrained waste of a staggering €40,000—around $80,000. And the 5000 *Andranesi* are tight-fisted compared with the 1500 residents of Diso, who donate over $200,000 annually for a neon knees-up in honour of Saint Filippo and Saint Giacomo, making Andrano's bash look as though a couple of absent-minded oldies have left their lights on for the night.

There are few forward thinkers like Daniela in Andrano, however. Most people give generously when party organisers door-knock a town with the streets of a war zone and whose sewer system consists of a *pozzo nero* or 'black well' under the house. But Andrano's mayor could never oppose the town party, which gives thanks to the Madonna for protection on roads that will always be dangerous, if only because the cost of the party prohibits their improvement. The religious rituals must be observed. God will provide. Daniela and Concetta simply feel that, as times change, He should provide different things, like an ambulance for those motorists relying on the Madonna for road safety.

Walking home after the *festa,* I saw a boy of perhaps fourteen perched on a stone wall. A snare drum across his knees and drumsticks protruding from his pockets, he was waiting for a lift after keeping the beat at the back of the band. His parents would be along at some stage to pick him up. There was no rush—it was only 2 am and crowds were still thick. I had visited few places in which a child could wait alone at such an hour armed only with drumsticks. I put my arm around Daniela. For all its faults, it was thrilling to be living in such a place, if only for a short while.

Andrano woke with a headache for which the party wasn't responsible. We knew something was wrong when we pulled into 'California' and had to beep twice before Signor Api, undeserving of his nickname for once, trudged through his fly-curtain, shoulders slumped and head bowed.

'Andrano is black today,' he said. 'Have you heard?'

'*Che cosa?*'

'We lost one of our sons last night. Francesco's boy, the surveyor. A car accident.'

'*Madonna!*' exclaimed Daniela, disbelieving.

'He was with two friends who died as well. They were going on holiday to Rimini. Apparently he fell asleep at the wheel.'

Signor Api pumped our petrol in silence as rare as it was sad. When finished, he pointed at a promotional poster for his petrol company featuring a *Tyrannosaurus rex*.

'He's the luckiest of all,' he reflected. 'King of the world and he didn't even know it.'

We had no idea what he meant.

When we arrived back at the house, the same *vigile* who had stuck the Special Event sign to our wall was replacing it with a less festive poster: '*Lutto Cittadino*'—'Citizens in Mourning'. Andrano's celebrations were over.

Such a tragic death brings the town to a stop. All festivals, private and public, are cancelled out of respect. Shops close, a special mass is held and residents observe a minute's silence. But only tragedy or celebrity provokes communal mourning. More natural passings, like that of Tonio, a ninety-year-old friend of Daniela's family, later that month, are part of everyday life in a town with such an elderly population.

Between the Signor Api grapevine, the *manifesto di morte* and cobblestone gossip, Andrano's residents quickly learn they are one fewer. Daniela's mother even found out about Tonio's death from Sicily and phoned to ensure we would represent her at the funeral. Along with friends, relatives and the town pharmacist who used to deliver his medicine, we gathered at Tonio's home on the evening before his funeral to comfort immediate family and pay second-last respects.

The following afternoon mourners gathered once again at the home of the deceased. At five o'clock the town bell tolled a funereal call, the signal for us to convey Tonio, through streets closed once again by an overworked *vigile*, to Andrano's modern and inelegant church—La Chiesa di Santa Maria delle Grazie. The bell rang from the moment our mournful march started until the moment it stopped; having dictated the movements of Tonio's life, it was now orchestrating those of his death. An empty hearse rolling slow at our heels, our procession curled among tightly packed houses. Stoic faces watched from doorways, stony and expressionless, like the lethargic bell which echoed around town, informing residents that one of their own was on his way to the grave.

At the head of our hundred-strong column, the coffin was carried by the brothers of Andrano's *Confraternita*—a religious society to which Tonio had belonged. Dressed in white tunics and blue shawls tied at the neck by a pink ribbon, the dozen old men held up banners, staffs and crucifixes bearing emblems of their fellowship. The *Confraternita* is over 1000 years old and was founded to unite Christians in religious discussion and preach throughout the town. As we snailed through Andrano, Daniela told me how her grandmother had tried to convince her father to join the society, which, for an annual fee, offered the benefits of a guaranteed grave at the cemetery and an honorary funeral escort by the brothers. But her non-conformist father had loathed the idea. Nowadays the *municipio* provides residents with a final resting place, graves which the dwindling brothers of an effete fellowship are rapidly filling.

After a ten-minute march we arrived at the flat-roofed church, used for funerals because of its larger size. Tonio was put on display at the altar and mourners filed past to pay last respects.

The air was hot and heavy. Suffocated by a tie on a 38-degree day, at one point I had to resist the temptation of fanning myself with a Bible. Realising I was in a foreign environment—the church not the country—Daniela kept one eye on her hymn sheet and the other on me. Dressed in heavy robes, Don Francesco was himself suffering. He conducted a swift service that culminated in 'amen', one of the few words in his blessing I understood. Our procession was soon back on the pavement, accompanied once again by the bell which would toll monotonously until we reached the cemetery.

Andrano's graveyard is on the southern edge of town, meaning our procession had to traverse Piazza Castello on the ten-minute walk from the church. It seemed an appropriate route, a chance for Tonio to say farewell to his village: La Chiesa di Sant'Andrea in which he'd married, the *municipio* where he'd paid his taxes (including €10 a year for the light on his wife's grave), and the bar where he'd gambled, smoked and shouted coffee and opinion. Crossing the square with the bell tolling loud, Daniela told me that Tonio had spent every day of his ninety years in Andrano. It was something he boasted about. He had never seen Italy, let alone the world. Andrano was his world. Small and simple. A full stomach and a healthy family. What more was there?

Bystanders dipped heads and hats as we paraded Tonio past them. Our slow march continued in stifling heat until we reached the cemetery's main gate, where a road sign displayed the word 'Andrano' with a red line through it—the end of the road for both the town and for Tonio. Beyond stood olive trees, assorted crops and primitive tool huts made from the same stones as the unmortared walls separating one ancient livelihood from the next. Beyond that . . . the heel of the boot, a long swim, then Africa. Towering above the cemetery was a 10-metre mobile phone mast. Life goes on.

Prestigious family tombs, almost miniature chapels, lined the rectangular confines of the cemetery, while at the centre stood a six-tomb-high edifice for the dead; graves in Andrano are above rather than below ground. Coffins slid into the cement structure like drawers in a cabinet, sealed with a marble plaque inscribed with a brief biography and a photo, usually black and white, of the occupant. Levels one to three could be reached from the ground, while a raised metal platform gave access to levels four through six. From their vantage point, Andrano's deceased have a view of surrounding fields, which, like Tonio, many had worked all their lives. Considering their trade, they seemed wrongly denied the earth's eternal embrace. Life's comrade should at least be death's companion.

Near the cemetery's main chapel, whose walls also contained stacked remains, were the private tombs of the royal families who had lived and died in Andrano's castle. The tomb closest to the chapel was that of the Caracciolo family, containing, among others, the last of the princesses, Ippolita, after whose death in 1963 the castle was bought by the *municipio*. Daniela's grandmother had been a confidante of Ippolita and, until recently when she joined the princess for good, would regularly clean a royal tomb that is now dusty and in disrepair.

As Tonio's coffin was taken to the chapel for a final blessing, Daniela whispered that she had done her bit as *mamma*'s representative and suggested we have a swim while the sun would still dry us more quickly than a towel. We said hushed goodbyes and walked home to the sound of the chapel bell and cicadas in olive branches.

Much later, on Daniela's terrace, watching the sun sink behind the town, I surprised her by saying I was sad to be leaving Andrano. I would have liked to stay longer: to see autumn soften arid colours, to hear Signor Api's winter wisecracks, and to attend midnight mass on New Year's Eve. But Daniela was less sentimental about our next move. She assured me that come the end of August, when the sun lost its sting and the watermelon its taste, those who had raced home to Andrano would return to the cities with equal haste. Ironically, despite 40-degree summer temperatures, it was winter the *Andranesi* considered harsh.

Summer brought life to the Salento. Winter was spent waiting for its return.

So Milan and work awaited. But what about Andrano? Another resident in the tomb today and another two departing soon. Don Francesco's New Year's mass looked like bad news once again.

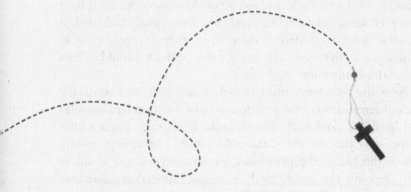

The statement

Two kilometres from Andrano along an unsignposted track roamed by foxes, rabbits and very plump mice, is a restaurant known as Pietralata, whose outdoor tables stand among olive trees over three centuries old. After a lazy day by the Mediterranean, there are few evening pleasures as simple and affordable as a glass of wine, a game of table soccer and pizza under the stars. Pietralata is informal Italy at its best: conversation, a pack of cards, artichoke hearts and moonlight.

Having spent many summer evenings at Pietralata's uneven tables, when the time came to farewell Andrano as well as Daniela's friends and colleagues, the relaxed pizza restaurant seemed the perfect choice of venue. And as usual we had a fabulous evening, until the bill arrived and Daniela discovered her handbag was missing. I would have paid had I not acquired the habit of leaving my wallet at home. Such trivial items belonged to the organised life I had abandoned a couple of months back. I had become a kept man, with neither a key to my name nor a use for my pockets other than as a place to rest well-tanned hands. Fortunately, Daniela knew the owners and could pay next time.

The following morning Daniela's handbag was on our doorstep with just the cash from her purse gone astray—the fee for home delivery perhaps. Everything else had been left intact: mobile phone, credit cards, even a ring that at least looked expensive; I had given it to her and was slightly offended the thieves hadn't taken it.

Grateful for the return of her possessions and prepared to write off the cash, Daniela's problem was that she had cancelled her credit cards. When she rang her bank to inform of the thieves' change of heart, she was advised to report the temporary theft to the *Carabinieri* within forty-eight hours, ensuring that if any money had been spent on the cards she would be reimbursed by the bank's insurance. Sound simple enough? Enter the *Carabinieri* . . .

The butt of Italian jokes, Italy's paramilitary police force is famous for needing a squadron to change a light bulb, or for manning the exit of a bank while thieves slip out the entrance. Ridiculed by those it is their duty to police, members of this clumsy constabulary are considered dimwits and well-dressed fools, incompetent, lazy and intellectually as thin as the peninsula they patrol. When the *Carabinieri* arrive on a crime scene, many victims consider their problems to have worsened.

We arrived at the *Carabinieri* station in Loritano as the town bell struck seven. It lacked the gaiety of Andrano's *campana*, the result of a more modern metal, suggested Daniela. To avoid queuing we had planned on visiting the station during siesta; Daniela was finally coming round to my way of thinking. But the officer who answered our call to check if they were open (a necessary measure even at the police station) said the chief would need to sign such a declaration and he wasn't due back before seven. To save a return trip, why not wait until then, suggested the underling. The Italians were too hard on these *Carabinieri*. This officer's approach seemed most efficient.

Unlike the whitewashed houses between which it stood, the station was set back from the road, with entry to its courtyard blocked by a barred gate. Daniela rang the buzzer twice before an officer unbolted the station door and leant into the first cool of twilight.

'*Si?*'

'We need to make a statement.'

The lock on the gate buzzed open and we moved towards the weather-beaten building. The *carabiniere* was on his own and stretched as though we had woken him.

Four metal chairs comprised the furniture in a spartan waiting room. Drab and dreary, the only colour was the red stripes down the legs of the officer's black trousers (so they don't confuse them with their jackets, goes the saying) and pictures of brave officers performing stunts in the fight against crime: scaling mountains, abseiling from helicopters and holding onto sleds pulled by huskies. But the bald, pot-bellied policeman who ushered us into his office was a world away from the athletic young men posing for cameras while pulling ripcords.

Daniela declared herself to be the caller whose handbag had been temporarily stolen. She also reminded the officer that he had told her to come at seven because the chief would be there, at which point she was told that the chief wasn't there and she would need to return the next day. Sensing frustration, the man offered at least to compile the statement so it would bear today's date, then the chief could simply sign the declaration tomorrow, or whenever he showed up for duty.

A crucifix was the only decoration in an office whose furniture seemed borrowed from a primary school classroom. Scratched into the desk were the words *Forza Juventus!* The local team from Lecce didn't get the sort of results that warranted the defacing of furniture. A fan scattered paper from a table in the corner, there were no computers, and the standard-issue grey telephone was distinguished from those of other public offices by a red light above the dialling circle. Metal bookshelves bulged with jaundiced paper and fraying folders tied closed with ribbons. Dated and dusty, it was the sort of room that made putting today's date on the declaration feel like telling a lie.

The *carabiniere* lit a cigarette and took a form from his top drawer. Between it and a blank sheet he placed a ragged piece of carbon paper, before winding all three through the spool of an antique typewriter. An Olivetti, naturally, the shabby machine had no button head on the number 5 key and the exposed piece of metal looked uninviting to touch. The letter T was written in pen on a grey key, the odd one out, while others, the originals, had once been black.

The officer used a single forefinger to type Daniela's details which he copied from her licence. After several minutes of painstaking tapping, including a search for a small object with which to strike the sharp number 5—Daniela lived at number 15—he returned her licence and reclined in his chair.

'*Allora*,' he said, shortening his cigarette. 'What time did this occur, *signora*?'

'Around half-past ten,' replied Daniela.

Attempting to type 22:30, the officer hit the 3 key but the metal arm didn't move. Annoyed, he struck it again, but the key appeared to be blocked. He seemed embarrassed, and hesitated.

'Er, I'm sorry but the three isn't working. Could we make that ten-forty?'

Eyebrows raised, Daniela and I exchanged a glance.

'I suppose so,' replied Daniela.

'No later though,' I joked in English. 'The restaurant closes at eleven.'

'Where is your boyfriend from, *signora*?'

'Australia.'

He looked at me.

'Australia? What the hell are you doing here?'

You know the rest.

Before altering history, the *carabiniere* gave the 3 one last chance, jamming a fat finger down hard this time. The key pounced like a snapping mousetrap, only to then stick to the paper against which it slapped. He leant forward to retrieve the key, sending it back to its place among the others with the flick of a finger. Glad to be finished with the numbers, he tapped the ash off his cigarette and reclined in his chair once again.

'So, where were you, *signora*?'

'Pietralata in Andrano. You know the pizza place in the countryside?'

'*Si, si*. And you lost the handbag there?'

'No, the handbag was stolen there.'

'Stolen?' He looked surprised. 'But you told me you'd lost it.'

'No, I told you it was stolen,' insisted Daniela. 'That was the first thing I said on the phone.'

'But stolen is a completely different story.' He looked at his typewriter. 'And a completely different form.'

'*Allora?*' challenged Daniela. She addressed him as she would a child at her primary school, and as far as his typing was concerned, that was where he belonged.

He spun a knob on the side of the typewriter to shoot the form into his hovering hand. Then he opened another drawer, found a different form, separated it with the same piece of carbon paper and off we went again. In uncomfortable silence, interrupted by the erratic tapping of keys, he compiled the document until reaching the previous impasse, leaning forward once again to retrieve the 3 of ten-thirty, before adding to the statement without consulting us this time. At the end of each line he stopped to read his composition aloud, punctuation included, while running one hand through the other, a picture of creative contemplation. His tale was an elaborate one, and Daniela tried her best to stifle a laugh when he described the thieves as '*ignoti malfattori*', a literary turn of phrase promoting petty criminals to 'unknown evil-doers'.

Satisfied with the introduction he looked up at Daniela, needing to research his novel further.

'And what colour was the handbag?'

'Er, black,' hesitated Daniela, holding up the subject of the story. 'It's this one.'

His eyes scampered left and right. He muttered inaudibly. He looked at the old Olivetti, then at Daniela. Despite answering her call, he had clearly forgotten the details of the handbag's nocturnal adventure. He pointed at the bag which, according to the statement he was preparing, was still in the hands of '*ignoti malfattori*'. He appeared nervous, and was reluctant to say what he said next: 'But that's not stolen, *signora*.'

Daniela raised a hand to silence the man and spare him further embarrassment. She paused, drew breath and cast me the trace of a smile. Then she went from the top, recounting her story as slowly and deliberately as the officer had been typing. 'As I said on the phone, this handbag'—she held it up once again—'was stolen last night but was returned to me this morning. On the advice of my bank, I need to declare it out of my possession from ten-thirty last night until eight o'clock this morning. That way, if the thieves used my credit cards before dumping the bag, any money spent will be reimbursed.'

Calmed by her clarity, the *carabiniere* played his first correct card of the match.

'Why can't you just ask the bank if any money was taken?'

'The bank won't know if any money was spent until tomorrow afternoon, so they advised me to declare it just in case.'

The officer understood but saw no way forward for a novel with a flawed plot.

'But this form is for stolen property, and you have the handbag now so I can't say it's stolen, can I?' For a bald man he sure knew how to split hairs.

I surprised everyone, including myself, by making a suggestion in perfect Italian.

'Can't you say the bag was stolen and then returned?'

'But the form is for items stolen and missing. If I fill it out, as far as we're concerned the bag is *still* missing.'

'Isn't there a form for things stolen and returned?' asked Daniela.

'*No, signora.*'

Daniela thought for a moment. If thirty-two years in the south of Italy had taught her anything it was how to improvise.

'What if we pretend that the bag hasn't been returned? That it's still missing. Then could the form be filled out?'

The *carabiniere* gazed out the window and stroked his alfalfa moustache.

'I don't see why not,' he replied, cautiously, certain there should have been reasons why not, only he couldn't think of any.

'Ah,' sighed Daniela. '*Alleluia.*'

Devoid of his former enthusiasm, the officer leant over the Olivetti. When he then asked Daniela to list all the items that had been in her handbag, she cleverly replied that only her purse had been in there, avoiding the potential for further confusion. After a few minutes the statement was almost complete, the *carabiniere* reading its conclusion aloud: ' . . . and I am declaring this theft within forty-eight hours so as to be reimbursed by the bank should any money have been taken under insurance policy number . . . '

He looked up at Daniela, who had closed her eyes.

'What is the insurance policy number of the bank?' he asked.

Frustration filled the room once again, mine because I thought I couldn't possibly have understood and Daniela's because she knew she had.

'What is the insurance policy number of the bank?' he asked again.

'How should I know?' snapped Daniela, angry now. It was the first time I had seen her face redden anywhere but at the beach. 'That's the bank's affair. It's not an insurance policy between me and the bank. It's just a benefit of having their credit cards.'

'But I need the number or I can't complete this.'

'Why did you write it in the first place?'

'*Mi scusi?*'

'That type of policy doesn't have a number.'

'It must have.'

'It doesn't.'

Stalemate. Daniela and the *carabiniere* exchanged desperate glances. I put my hand on her shoulder, hoping to calm her down, while pondering the sort of response this sleepy station could muster should that red light on the telephone start flashing.

The *carabiniere* lit another cigarette, cracked a knuckle and eyed the document. Watching him think reminded me of the number 3 key which stuck when engaged. Daniela was about to speak when a thought finally entered his head. 'Why don't you call the bank tomorrow and ask for the number of the insurance policy? That way we can complete the form when you come back to see the chief.'

It was an absurd proposal, but by then Daniela would have confessed to murder if it meant ending the ordeal. In fact she was tempted to drop the whole thing, considering it better to lose money to thieves than sanity to those paid to catch them.

Relieved it was over, we were escorted to the waiting room where the photos of daring crime-fighters still hung from their rusty nails. Abseiling from a helicopter would remain a dream to this pen-pusher, or key-pusher rather, who seemed more suited to the ejection seat. Now I realised why the *Carabinieri* provided material for every comic in the land. If nothing else, the trying evening had been an incentive to stay out of trouble.

The officer put on his hat, nicknamed *la lucerna* because it resembles a miner's lantern. In order of importance he grabbed cigarettes and keys before locking the station door and following us into the street. As we drove off in one direction in Napoleon, he went the other way in a matchbox Fiat Panda.

'Where do you think he's off to?' I asked Daniela.

'Probably to look for my handbag,' she replied. 'According to his form it's still missing.'

The following morning we called Errico at the bank, hoping he might save us a return to the station. No money had been taken according to his computer, but he repeated that certainty required forty-eight hours and suggested we persist with the declaration. When told that the *Carabinieri* wanted the insurance policy number, he sniggered and asked rhetorically, 'You went to Loritano, didn't you?' He described how officers from the same station had once stormed his bank to foil a robbery taking place at the post office. He confirmed that the bank's insurance policy didn't have a number, then asked us to tell the officer in question to do Italy a favour and join the mounted *Carabinieri* as the horse.

We were left with no alternative. Back we went to Loritano.

This time the gate was buzzed open by a trim officer with shiny shoes. Inside the office a smart new laptop sat alongside its ancient ancestor. The two machines looked as different as yesterday's policeman and today's. We breathed a sigh of relief. We had finally found the chief.

Once again we were alone. There was either no crime in these parts or the *Carabinieri* were so inept at solving it that no one bothered to declare any. Daniela explained our visit, gave a summary of yesterday's antics and said that, as she had expected, there was no number for the insurance policy. After a lengthy search for our form, which was eventually found still in the typewriter, *Il Comandante* glanced at his subordinate's handiwork and crossed out the final paragraph. Daniela then signed the declaration before the chief added his initials and thumped it with a rubber stamp.

'This is yours,' he said, handing Daniela her copy.

Daniela thanked him for his efficiency.

'It's nothing,' said the chief. 'And if the stolen property turns up,' he added, 'be sure to let us know.'

Had Daniela politely agreed to do as the chief asked, folded the form and slid it neatly into the handbag it declared stolen, the trial would have been over. Instead she made her first mistake. It was one of the few times I would accuse her of being too honest.

'But the bag has turned up.'

'*Mi scusi?*' said the confused chief. 'It's been returned?'

'*Si.*'

'It doesn't say here that it's been returned.' He scanned the document again. 'Why didn't you say so last night?'

'I did,' replied Daniela. 'I told your colleague that the bag had been returned the following morning, but he said that meant he couldn't complete the form so we pretended it was still missing.'

The chief blinked repeatedly.

'What time did you say you came in yesterday?'

'At seven.'

'*Porca la miseria,*' he swore softly, a sympathetic smile appearing as he recalled the duty roster. 'I must apologise, *signori.* Would you mind telling me the whole story?'

The chief listened intently as Daniela did so. Then he read the declaration from the top, slowly this time and aloud: 'While dining with friends at a restaurant by the name of Pietralata in the Andrano countryside . . . ' He looked up at us. '*Cristo,*' he said, laughing. 'Did my colleague ask what you had for dinner?'

With immense satisfaction, both on our part and his, the chief reduced the statement to rubbish and tossed it in the bin. On a new form, identical to the old one, he typed a brief statement declaring the bag, purse and credit cards stolen and out of our possession for twelve hours. He used the Olivetti adroitly, but, like his colleague, found a small object with which to type Daniela's prickly address. The buzzer sounded in the waiting room as he was finishing the revised version, and he tapped a few more characters before excusing himself and rising.

The unkempt man on whom he opened the door had a messy crop of greying hair and eyes alive with anger. He wore shorts, sandals and a summer shirt which stretched so tightly over a distended belly that its buttons seemed set to burst.

'*Mi dica,*' said the chief—'Tell me'—but he was going to hear this man's story whether he asked for it or not.

'I must denounce someone,' said the man with menace, narrowing his eyes as he spoke.

'Who? What's happened? *Stai calmo, signore.*'

'My neighbour. I must denounce my neighbour.' The cadence was robotic. 'Next door to my house there is a garden. For the last two months my neighbour has chained a dog there which barks day and night. I haven't slept in two months. My family hasn't slept in two months. You must come now and do something about my neighbour.'

The chief held up two open palms.

'Calm down right now and listen. You must go and speak to your *vigile*. I cannot intervene in such a situation.'

'I have,' said the man, desperate. 'My neighbour *is* the *vigile*.' The chief raised his eyebrows, the irate man his voice. 'You must come and do something. I don't blame the dog. My neighbour is the problem. And if you don't come and do something right now'—he shook his hands to deliver his threat—'I'll kill him this very day! I will! I'm absolutely serious. I'll murder him!'

His warning echoed around the empty waiting room. The huskies looked on from cooler climes.

'*Calmo!*' insisted the chief.

'No. Let's be clear on this. I'll murder him today!'

No doubt these were threats he had shouted at home for the past two months, only now he believed himself capable of actually carrying them out and had frightened himself into going to the police. As melodramatic as it was, in a way he had done the right thing, turning himself in *before* committing the crime. *Il Comandante* realised he had no choice but to intervene in some way. He shut the station door with his foot. 'Take a seat,' he said to the desperate intruder. 'I'll be with you when I've finished with the *signora.*'

While yesterday's circus had justified Italy's mockery of the *Carabinieri*, or at least certain officers, I couldn't help thinking that they were little helped by the complexity of the average Italian crime and the inherent comedy in the average Italian. Home-delivered handbags complicate the most straightforward of thefts, and now the actions of a law-enforcer were pushing someone towards becoming a law-breaker. It was difficult to excuse the fiasco of the previous day, but for every citizen with a story about an oddball *carabiniere*, there is surely a *carabiniere* with a story about an oddball citizen.

The chief completed our form in distracted silence, his mind on the volcano in the next room. When finished, once again he and Daniela signed the statement, the third and final version of a document we would never need given the thieves had spent no money on the cards. After what we had suffered to get the form, I rather wished they had.

We thanked the chief and passed his furious visitor in the waiting room. He was pacing like a tiger in a cage and, judging by the burst blood vessels in his eyes, the chief faced some difficult diplomacy. But at least he was up to the task. I shuddered to think what might have happened if the man's anger had won out around seven the previous evening. After first advising him to go and kill his neighbour, making the choice of form simpler, the underling would have at least been sharp enough to insist the murderer stay in town, if only because he was obliged to return and have that form signed by the chief.

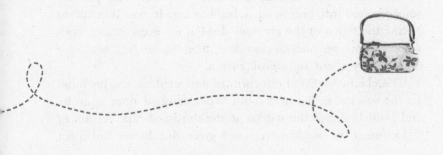

The broom tree

Signor Api knew something was up when we said yes to a full tank of petrol. Noticing Napoleon bursting with suitcases, he inquired with more than the usual nonchalance, 'So where are we off to today?'

'Sicily,' replied Daniela. 'And then Milan.'

'*Lampo!*' he exclaimed—'Lightning! It looks like you're going for good.'

'I guess we are.'

I climbed from the car to shake Signor Api's hand and he pulled me close to touch the leather cheeks of his face against mine—left and right.

'You'll be back,' he said, keeping my hand. 'Both of you. And there'll be a *bambino* in the back seat, not suitcases.'

'If you say so,' said Daniela.

'Nothing to do with me. It's God's natural law.'

Signor Api filled our tank and emptied Daniela's wallet.

'All the best,' he shouted, as we departed 'California' and Andrano. And with over 2000 kilometres of Italian asphalt ahead, his final cry of '*Buona fortuna*' was addressed to Napoleon as much as to us.

My first indication that Daniela was different from the average *Andranese* was the fact her holiday house was in Sicily. Much of middle-class Italy owns a second home, more often than not by

79

the sea, so for most of the *Andranesi* it's less than a kilometre from the first. Every summer they load up their cars and roll down the hill to beachfront retreats, where they spend the mosquito months on the same stretch of sea as last year and next; on the same stones in fact, swimming where they have always swum, among faces they have always known. Their unadventurous routine is portrayed by the popular summer song, '*Stessa Spiaggia, Stesso Mare*'—'Same Beach, Same Sea'. It's an anthem almost, describing a population which, when it comes to summer holidays, changes only its bathing costume.

Daniela's family had a different routine. They still went to the same beach every year but it was a long way from Andrano. Daniela's mother, Valeria, is Sicilian. Her father, Franco, was born in Andrano but was uncharacteristically against the idea of having a holiday home so close to his rest-of-year residence; he wasn't going to spend the summer racing between the two houses fetching some forgotten item or other. So every year, while the rest of the *Andranesi* were completing their summer exodus without troubling second gear, Daniela's family were making the 900-kilometre journey to a Sicilian hillside near Valeria's home city of Alcamo, where they were eagerly awaited by a legion of aunts, uncles, cousins, friends and the picturesque Gulf of Castellammare.

Their private hillside is divided into plots shared among Valeria and her two sisters. These sisters and their families spend the rest of the year in apartments just a few kilometres up the road in Alcamo. Much to Franco's satisfaction, when he was well enough to appreciate it, they spend most of their summer holiday racing between the two properties fetching some forgotten item or other.

A dear friend of Valeria's lives in a seaside hamlet on the Gulf of Taranto, handily positioned around a third of the way between Andrano and Alcamo. Driving by without dropping in would have been insulting and un-Italian. Pulling off the through-road and sounding our horn brought a dozen people—the youngest five and the eldest eighty-five—to the pavement outside a three-storey house. Daniela had only intended to stop for refreshments, but with twenty-four cheeks to kiss hello, and at the insistence of every mouth between them, we ended up staying the night.

Three generations lived in the house, one for each floor. Children on top, parents in the middle and grandparents on the ground. The whitewashed building was something of a flow chart: with the passing of time its occupants gradually worked their way down, until one generation went underground and the next moved in on top. The garden was as fertile as the family who kept it, apricots plopping to earth near the house and pears ripening down the back. Between trunks of trees were children's toys and a dozen free-range chickens. Things were happy, noisy and busy—the southern Italian stereotype.

The following morning, nearing the toe of the boot in Calabria, we joined the *Autostrada del Sole*—the Highway of the Sun, famous for summer traffic and infamous for summer fatalities. A succession of long tunnels and tall bridges straddle alpine relief more suited to Austria than southern Italy, demanding concentration from motorists with their minds already on holiday.

Passage across the 3.6-kilometre Strait of Messina, separating Sicily from mainland Italy, is by car ferry. Politicians debated suspending a road across the water but the price in lira was longer than the bridge. We queued for an hour to board a towering ship which even carries trains across a body of water whose currents can be wild in bad weather. Legend has it that two sea monsters, Cariddi on the Sicilian side and Scilla on the Calabrian, are responsible for the many lives lost in these turbulent waters, including some of Ulysses' shipmates who drowned here during the *Odyssey*.

Despite being surrounded by water, Sicily's first and last impression is one of despairing thirst. Closer to Africa than to Rome, it is positioned at the toe of a boot which appears set to kick it back to the desert continent from which it freed itself millions of years ago. Water is scarce on this sun-baked island, in fact the only natural liquid Sicily manages to produce in any great quantity—apart from wine and red orange juice—is the burning lava of Mount Etna. From the docks of Messina we drove past the 3000-metre volcano en route to Catania, before heading for the heart of the island.

Alcamo is situated towards Sicily's western shore. To traverse the island, Daniela had decided to take the inland route which she described as 'scorching but safe' compared with the coast road. Without a sea breeze to cool the engine, Napoleon overheated as rapidly as we did. Forty-five degrees and no air-conditioning. The asphalt was melting and so were our tyres. It was lunchtime and the road was abandoned. All around were starving fields of yellow grass, baking earth, prickly pear and olive trees. Passing towns were as rare as clouds and the screech of cicadas filled suffocating air. The earth was ablaze, yet it was enchanting—an endless mirage. Until Daniela imitated Etna, vomiting from the heat, and we raced for Palermo and the cool of the sea.

The first time you drive a car in Italy, do it somewhere other than Palermo. With Daniela out of action it was down to me to steer Napoleon through the heartland of Garibaldi. You swerve rather than drive through Palermo. We were five abreast on what would have been a three-lane road had anyone bothered to paint lines on it. Stop signs were suggestions and red lights as optional as milk in coffee. Faded and forgotten, zebra crossings were less an aid for pedestrians than for emergency crews in search of their bodies. I managed to avoid accident if not incident. Daniela soon felt sick again.

To the left of the highway stood the bleak tenements of Palermo's residential outskirts, imposing eyesores of discoloured concrete and clothes hung to dry. To the right, the *centro storico*, elegant but decaying Arab-Norman architecture defaced by pockets of World War II ruin. Palermo's urban blight is the work of *Cosa Nostra*, the grisly Sicilian Mafia which, through collusion with government administrators, developed the city to its profit and whim.

Cosa Nostra is the real deal when it comes to organised crime. Responsible for 10,000 deaths in the decade before 1993, its blood brothers are notorious for dissolving rivals in acid or tying them up in such a way that, by resisting, they strangle themselves. *Incaprettamento* or 'goat strangling' it's called, a preferred method of murder because, when rigor mortis sets in, the body is in a position which allows it to be easily transported in the boot of a car. Untouchably well connected, *Cosa Nostra*'s 'men of honour' are in complete control of Palermo, a city whose leaders are elected by voters either long dead or born on 31 February.

The man who had the most success in combating *Cosa Nostra* was magistrate Giovanni Falcone, and leaving Palermo we took the *autostrada* on which the Mafia paid him back. Just when I was starting to relax behind the wheel, Daniela leant over and casually informed me that the road beneath us was once blasted into a 7-metre-deep crater by explosives hidden in an underground drain. Falcone, his wife Francesca and their three bodyguards, whose car was launched into an olive orchard, were all killed. With many of the attractions stained with blood, enjoying Palermo requires a strong stomach and a weak sense of justice.

After passing the exit for Punta Raisi, the airport from where Falcone's ill-fated motorcade had departed, Daniela dialled her mother's mobile: '*Stiamo arrivando mamma.*' It was dusk, the sky was crimson and the temperature had dropped to a refreshing 35 degrees. Giving orders from the passenger seat had done wonders for Daniela's nausea. She had spent the last few kilometres of our journey preparing me for her father, who, at fifty-nine, had succumbed to a precocious and debilitating onslaught of Alzheimer's disease.

Having spent the past six weeks in a house adorned with his artwork, to a certain extent I knew Franco already. His inspirations at least: the personality of landscape, the privacy of a man's mind, female beauty and the pleasures of family. Franco was obviously a complex character before the disease had rendered him simple. 'Please smile if you can do it,' said Daniela. 'He gets confused if he sees that a person is unhappy.' I assured her I would try and had fully expected to manage.

'Right here,' she said, indicating an unpaved laneway disappearing up a hill. With Daniela reaching across to sound the horn, we bumped along the track until arriving at a clearing, where about twenty people were shouting and waving, and a woman held a silent man's arm.

The exuberant bunch had been waiting for me as much as for Daniela. From the moment Napoleon's door squeaked open I was adopted as one of the family. We kissed our way through the crowd, Daniela throwing me the names of relatives whose cheeks arrived seconds later: 'Zia Tina, Zio Tonio, Nonna Lina, Nonno Totò, Antonio, Fabio, Marisa, Sergio, Luisa, Salvatore, Lucia . . .' Faces arrived so fast that I forgot my left from my right, which was fine until I met Daniela's 100-kilogram cousin Antonio in the middle. Lurking at the back of the pack was Daniela's bearded brother Francesco; sometimes there's a lot to be said for a firm handshake. I hadn't come to Italy to kiss Francesco, I had come to kiss his sister.

With her arm through Franco's, Valeria gave me a smile I found difficult to return. Her husband's mental absence was more striking than his physical presence, and despite Daniela's prep talk I struggled to camouflage dismay. Daniela kissed the grey stubble on her father's cheeks. 'Ciao papino,' she said with forced enthusiasm, as though trying to coax a smile from a baby. Franco's forehead creased, he mumbled an indecipherable word, and although looking through her, a tear glazed his eye as he caught the memory of his daughter.

Valeria was Franco's anchor. His livewire legs marched on the spot and if she'd let go he'd have walked to the horizon. On Daniela's suggestion, I offered him my hand, which he rubbed with two fingers. 'He's painting,' said Valeria. 'He does that.' After a few brushstrokes he opened his eyes, turned his head sharply and said 'sì' to an imaginary voice. It broke everyone's heart but Franco's. But still his family smiled.

Before illness took hold, Franco had been a teacher, an artist and a musician. As an artist he held exhibitions throughout Italy, and as a musician he taught violin and piano, composed music for the table harp, and played jazz concerts with Mussolini's nephew in Milan. His family first realised he was suffering from something sinister when, one summer, among other puzzling lapses, he forgot the way to the holiday house which he knew like the back of his hand. In the five years since that wrong turn, Valeria has become the nurse of a husband who no longer knows her name.

A stocky woman with russet hair and rosy cheeks, Valeria's fair skin made the summer a trial, but trial she was used to. Her two children had obviously inherited their olive complexions from Franco.

'Velkom,' said Valeria in pre-prepared English. 'Voodayou lika-derink?'

The hillside laughed, then applauded, *'Bravissima! Bravissima!'*

Valeria's freckled face reddened. '*Andiamo dentro*,' she said more naturally, beckoning me inside while swatting her hand at the group which was still clapping. She took my arm now that Daniela had hold of her father's. 'Keep this shut or Franco will wander off,' she said, leading me through the gate of a concrete fence surrounding her house and garden. Relatives returned to their respective houses as the five of us went inside, Valeria leading me, Daniela leading Franco, and Francesco following behind after hearing the gate click.

Valeria spoke quickly. Without Daniela's pleas to slow down I often failed to understand her. Never mind, certain questions I had wanted to ask—such as do Italian housewives really buy four brooms at a time—she answered without saying a word. They most certainly do. One was leaning against the kitchen door while the other three were hanging upside down in a lone olive tree at the centre of the garden. When she did speak slowly, Valeria often revealed more about Sicily's personality than her own. After taking our order for a beer and a glass of water, she banged about the kitchen cupboards for such a long time that Daniela eventually called out: 'Don't worry about the beer if you can't find one, *mamma*.'

'It's not the beer I can't find,' replied *mamma*. 'It's the water.'

Francesco spent the evening grooming himself. Three years Daniela's junior, he was expensively undressed, Armani swimming trunks stretching tight around his stomach. His bonsai goatee had been cultivated with precision and a tattoo on his shoulder spelt something in Japanese. Driving to the bar to buy bottled water, he spent more time fixing his hair in the rear-view mirror than watching the road, doing little to dispel the Casanova cliché I attached to self-admiring Italian males. Inclined to shout rather than speak, he was boisterous when leading a conversation and uninterested when others had the stage. Impatient with my Italian, he made few attempts to converse with me. On the rare occasions that he did ask me something, he usually interrupted my reply. It made me nervous. I rushed words that were slow in coming and in doing so chose the wrong ones. I knew better than to take it personally—he was hyperactive and waited for no one. But it did inhibit me slightly, a shame considering that, with those who gave me time, my Italian was coming along well. I was to have a complex relationship with Francesco. As my boss, my landlord and the self-appointed guardian of his sister, he would find my early days in Milan more trying even than I would.

And then there was Franco, sweet Franco, who spent the evening pacing the room only to find himself lost in its corners. Daniela would turn her father around until he spied open space and marched on. Now and then he blasphemed or told a piece of furniture to fuck off. He fossicked for small items which he either moved or stowed in his pockets; the TV remote control was in the sink and Daniela's keys in the fridge, thrust into the butter like Excalibur in stone. I soon got used to his pacing; he was back and forwards like a pendulum and every bit as regular. Alzheimer's had wasted his body and humiliated his mind. Yet every so often he would strike a smile which lifted the room, revealing, albeit briefly, that he remembered what it was to be happy.

A reunited Italian family chats long into the night. It was gone two before we went to bed, or staggered I should say; Zio Tonio had brought round a couple of bottles of his home-made wine as a 'velkom' present.

Our room was a downstairs granny-flat, its private entrance accessed by a flight of stone steps at the side of the house. Between terracotta pots at the window I could see down the valley and across the gulf, where the lights of a cargo ship blinked on the dark Tyrrhenian Sea. Even with the door closed I could hear a swarm of Vespas on the beachfront, their surging engines, their screaming pilots. But after two days on Italian roads nothing could have kept me awake. I was asleep before hitting the mattress, which, like the brooms, had perhaps been bought from a passing truck.

We spent seven days on the hillside working hard at being lazy. Seven sweltering days separated by night but not sleep. Seven holidays which had the rhythm of clockwork, despite Alcamo's *campana* being out of earshot.

I opened the door each morning on the same calming sounds. Gravel crackled under Franco's shoes as he paced the pebbled garden, muttering to himself and the voices in his head. Across a sloping olive grove separating our house from his, Nonno Totò sang on his balcony. Having spent several years as a prisoner of war, just the fact it was morning merited a tune. '*C'è Scirocco!*' yelled Nonna Lina, broadcasting her daily weather forecast. It wasn't blowing yet, but come siesta, the desert wind she predicted would have baked life to a standstill, and the evening *aperitivo* would have Saharan sand floating in it. A chorus of cicadas brought the land-scape to life, their hypnotic concert enticing me to grab a book and flop under a tree. But there was much to be done on this idle day. Morning meant a trip to the beach before it was too hot even to swim.

Cousins gathered in the clearing between their houses before departing in a convoy of cars. The sun was strengthening and there was no time to waste on trivialities like seat-belts. We travelled in Antonio's Fiat Uno, me clutching Daniela's arm in the back while Francesco and his cousin shared a cigarette up front. Had I wanted to wear a seat-belt, the ragged back seat had none. A picture of the Madonna obscured the fuel gauge, justifying blasphemy if we ran out of petrol. The roads were patchwork and uneven. Each time we hit a bump the air-freshener hanging from his rear-view mirror emitted a scent. After a few kilometres the cabin smelt like the perfume section of a department store. Antonio drove fast, his size fourteen sandal suffocating the accelerator and snubbing the brake. I relaxed slightly after we passed a Vespa with an entire family on board, including a dog balanced precariously on the handlebars. There's always someone worse off than yourself.

Antonio dropped us off at a beach called Guidaloca before setting off in search of a car park. He was gone most of the morning. Our convoy had split, we had lost the others and a crowded beach meant calling mobiles to find them. Italian beaches are packed tight during summer. In an attempt to counter overcrowding, at the end of June each summer's beach laws are broadcast, laws that make fools of *carabinieri*. In the region of Lazio, for example, beach umbrellas must be 4 metres apart, while in Emilia Romagna it's 2.5 metres. But the umbrellas on Guidaloca lacked such order. Sicilians either find beach laws bothersome or figure that, having broken so many laws on their way to the beach, it would be hypocritical to start obeying them on arrival.

Guidaloca was shaped like a slice of melon and its water looked just as refreshing. After dumping towels on the beach, Daniela and Francesco ran for the blue while I scaled the headland on my way to a World War II watchtower. Built from the stone of the headland, it was perfectly camouflaged, the attraction, no doubt, for the teenage lovers I surprised inside. Despite their vantage point they had failed to see me coming. It's little wonder the Allied invasion of Sicily was a cakewalk.

Sexually strict parents oblige their children to satisfy private curiosities in public. For many Italian teenagers, erogenous zones are located in Fiats. On our way to a restaurant one evening, we passed a car park which Daniela claimed would later be full of people sitting closer than handbrakes normally allow. I thought she meant one or two. But on our way home around midnight, both cars *and* occupants were bumper to bumper. Randy young couples in Naples don't even bother with lovers' lanes, they simply park on any street and paste the windows with newspaper. A daughter with an encyclopaedic knowledge of current affairs is not something a Neapolitan father brags about. To ensure the undivided attentions of their partner, some men prefer to paste the windows with the sports newspaper. Maybe that's why *La Gazzetta dello Sport* is pink—to enhance the mood.

Back at the tower, I excused myself and returned to the beach, where things were just as steamy on the stones. A mismatched pair were in an amorous pose on a plastic recliner. The man's hair had receded, his stomach had advanced and he was greying as fast as he was tanning. Thirty years younger, his companion was naked but for a black G-string, a ring on each finger and scarlet nail polish on her toes. Besotted and blasé, she played with the crucifix in her lover's chest hair and kissed him about the face. All fat self-importance, like a *Mafioso* on holiday, he feigned indifference to her attentions, but the bulge in his swimmers revealed otherwise.

Many Italian men take a mistress, especially in Sicily, where they say eternal love lasts two years. Daniela's class were studying ancestry one morning when an eight-year-old child drawing a family tree raised her hand and asked: '*Maestra*, where does daddy's special friend go?' To hell, if you ask mummy. The summer sun must nourish infidelity because a third of all divorces are filed in September, the first month of autumn. One newspaper even publishes cheating hotspots. According to *Il Messaggero*, polygamous people holiday in Versilia, while the monogamous sun themselves on the island of Elba or in Rome. That's probably because on Roman beaches the law stipulates 4 metres between beach umbrellas. The closer to the Vatican, the further apart the towels.

Francesco decided we should rent a pedal-boat to visit coastal caves. I felt sure we would surprise another teenage couple but was happy to tag along. Daniela suggested I do the talking to improve my Italian. Queuing at the boat stand I rehearsed the simple sentence in my head. When my turn arrived I delivered it fluently and with no trace of an accent: '*Possiamo noleggiare un pedofilo per favore?*' Perfect Italian. Grammatically flawless. So why had Francesco burst out laughing and Daniela covered her mouth with her hand? Because I had asked to hire a 'paedophile' rather than a 'pedal-boat'. '*Pedalò*,' corrected Daniela. 'Not *pedofilo*.' My confidence was shattered and I was back under Daniela's wing. I hadn't even known the word for 'paedophile' until uttering it by accident. As we laboured out to sea, the man on the stand checked his hand-written sign to be sure it was my mistake.

Daniela and I swam in the caves while Francesco trapped crabs, ripped them apart and ate them raw. Both in Sicily and Puglia I enjoyed paddling in the placid sea, but have to admit I found unruffled water rather dull after a time. Having grown up surfing the Bondi breakers, I associate going to the beach with wipe-outs rather than relaxation. In Australia I took a surfboard. In Italy I took a book.

After an hour's lease we returned to the beach to find Antonio and the group reunited. We sunned ourselves until tummies began rumbling and Daniela declared it time to go. Arriving at Antonio's Fiat we found its wing-mirror smashed and hanging by a thread. '*Va bene*,' said its indifferent owner. 'I never use it anyway.' Antonio drove even faster when hungry and we were soon back at the hill, where Franco was still pacing the garden and Valeria was hollering about what my underwear had done to her washing.

Daniela translated her mother's lament as best she could. Uninvited, Valeria had collected our clothes from the granny-flat and added them to her wash. Hanging on a clothes-horse in the garden were a pair of my burgundy Rios which she was convinced had put streaks on her sheets. The underpants in question, I am embarrassed to say, were so old and faded that there was very little burgundy left in them. It seemed unlikely they would start losing colour when they hadn't done so for years. But Valeria was adamant they had ruined her cycle. Daniela tried to defuse the trivial tragedy, one of many in the average day of an Italian family, by suggesting it was the different washing powder that had made my underwear run. It was the beginning of her role as mediator. 'That's got nothing to do with it,' dismissed Valeria. 'Don't buy red underwear, Crris. Buy white ones.' Being adopted as one of the family was going to have a downside.

A thermometer nailed to the broom tree read 40 degrees in the shade, and as forecast by Nonna Lina, the *Scirocco* was blowing strong. Activity on the hillside came to a stop. There was nothing to do but stay inside, eat for an hour, then rest for another three. I was glad we had private quarters, the cool room under the house. Thanks to Valeria's open mind, her daughter was far more comfortable in the granny-flat than she would have been surrounded by newspaper in the car.

As in Andrano, the second half of the day began around five, when Daniela assumed the role of tour guide and whisked me off to places of interest near Alcamo. First up was the ancient city of Erice. Perched on a mountaintop overlooking the sea, according to legend it was founded over 3000 years ago by the son of Venus and Neptune. I should have photographed the town's eighth-century walls, the twelfth-century castle and the cobblestone lanes so narrow they must be walked single-file. But I didn't. I had intended to. I had even bought a guidebook. But next to the bookstore I found a *pasticceria* which sold fruit made from marzipan, a sugary Sicilian specialty. So I sat on a bench scoffing miniature bananas, an orange, a mandarin and a peach, while watching the sun set on the seaport of Trapani over 700 metres below.

Next stop was the ancient treasures of Segesta. Erected in 420 BC, the 36-column Doric temple was billed in my guidebook as 'the best preserved Greek architectural site to be found anywhere'. Quite a claim, but one archaeologists dispute less than whether or not the Greeks intended to put a roof on the building. Another topless attraction was Segesta's amphitheatre, a primitive arena carved from rock atop Mount Barbarian, venue for summer performances of Greek tragedies other than the Olympic Games.

Other excursions took in the monument to Garibaldi at Calatafimi, which commemorates a famous victory of his Red Shirts over the Bourbons, and as much of Palermo as the heat and our resultant late starts would allow. We would return to the hill after sundown, to be greeted on the driveway by the scents of dinner, which, I must confess, enticed me more than the treats in my guidebook.

Every evening Valeria laid a table in her garden for twenty, to which neighbours would bring food for forty. A typical feast began with Zia Tina's *antipasti,* which included prosciutto with sugarmelon, pizza slices, bruschette, fried eggplant, zucchini and peppers in olive oil. That alone would have done me. But Luisa's *primo piatto* was next, a daring but delicious mix of baked potato and mussels. Then Nonna Lina's horsemeat pieces in tomato sauce. 'Eat quickly,' said Antonio. 'It was a racehorse.' The meat was stringy, yet surprisingly tasty—although I couldn't help thinking that I may have been eating something more intelligent than me. Valeria usually prepared the *terzo piatto:* kebabs of liver and other animal sundries the origin of which I preferred not to ask. Fruit followed for those whose arms could still reach further than their stomachs: watermelon, apricots, peaches and figs. And then came the *coup de grâce,* an onslaught of calories called *cannoli siciliani*—a sweet comprised of flour, sugar, chocolate and white wine, fried into a wafer in the shape of a hollow bow tie filled with ricotta cheese and chocolate. Stuffed, both diner and dessert.

As swift and well choreographed as a set change at the theatre, at the end of each course Sergio circled the table with a rubbish bag into which we tossed everything except our glasses. His cousin Luisa followed him round handing out plastic utensils for the next course. Everyone contributed to the meal in some way. Zio Tonio provided his home-made *prosecco*—a white wine as dry as the countryside in which the marathon meal took place. And all the while Valeria fed Franco at the end of the table, holding him still and wiping his chin with a serviette now and then.

Dinner table conversation concerned what was on the dinner table, in fact talking about food seemed more vital to my hosts than actually eating it.

'How do they cook spaghetti in Australia?' Nonna Lina asked Daniela.

'They massacre it,' replied Daniela. 'They don't know how to cook it *al dente.* They don't realise that it cooks while you taste it and while you drain it, so if you turn it off soft it becomes much too soft. A spaghetti needs a vertebra.'

'Quite right,' said Nonna Lina, proud of her granddaughter.

After dinner, Sergio circled the table with another rubbish bag into which we threw everything: plates, cups, serviettes, cutlery, even the paper tablecloth was discarded. The only evidence of the feast were some saucepans and Nonno Totò's belching, for which his wife apologised. Totò was unashamed of his vulgar emissions. On one occasion, the grey-haired man held onto the table as a thunderclap of recalcitrant air escaped a more southerly orifice. '*Scusate*,' he said, 'I heard of a man who held it in and died.'

Despite protests from my hosts, I insisted on carrying the rubbish to the bin on the street. It was the least I could do, and besides, a stroll down the hill helped digest the mountain I had eaten. Valeria and her sisters were trying hard to please their guest, so I pleased them by eating everything they put in front of me, including a possible descendant of Seabiscuit. In Sicily, gaining friends means gaining weight.

I upset Zio Tonio one evening, however, by refusing to eat his afternoon catch. He was proud of the molluscs he had cut from a submarine cave and on which most people splashed a few drops of lemon juice before slurping them from their shells. But they were much bigger than the oysters I was used to, and looked weepy, sickly, like a slug with a skin condition. Zio Tonio offered the tray hopefully.

'*No, grazie.*'

'*Perchè?*'

I showed him the palm of my hand in a gesture of polite refusal.

'I just don't want one, thank you.'

He pushed the tray closer.

'*Perchè no?*'

'I just don't want one, thank you. I'm not hungry.'

'*Ma perchè?*' he insisted, looking at Daniela for an explanation. She said something that discouraged him but he was clearly as offended as I was uncomfortable. I hoped this didn't mean the end of his home-made wine. The Sicilians were the most generous people I had ever met. They were also the most insistent.

The younger men packed away tables, the women washed pots and pans, the older men lit pipes and loosened belts. Everyone then returned to Valeria's garden, to sip liqueurs on recliner chairs while discussing the day's events. It was my favourite part of the day, listening to their lives with no risk of being offered anything other than alcohol.

Antonio became agitated when recounting his afternoon trip to hospital. He had taken his mother, Zia Tina, who had cracked her head open after slipping on an olive in her kitchen. The doctors had asked Antonio to sign a document which, on close inspection, stated they had done a CAT scan when they hadn't. '*Mi sono sciroccato,*' said Antonio, describing how it had made him hot and bothered like the African wind.

'You almost cracked the doctor's head as good as mine,' said his mother, adding accuracy.

Zio Tonio burst a spray of whisky into the air when Daniela recounted my paedophile gaffe. The hillside erupted. *'Bellissimo!'* they all agreed. *'Straordinario,'* winced Antonio. They clutched their sides and slapped their legs. Without trying, I had won their hearts.

The only person who hadn't returned to Valeria's garden after dinner was her brother-in-law's precocious daughter, Marisa. The long-legged fifteen-year-old was avoiding her possessive father, Fabio, who was angry with her for refusing to return the mobile phone which her boyfriend had bought her. Convinced the boyfriend was trying to keep tabs on his daughter, Fabio had insisted she stop seeing him and imposed a curfew on the girl, sparking a Sicilian squabble that could be heard in Tunisia.

Fabio's concerns, and curfew, seem justified when you realise that more Italians are killed by friend than by foe. The previous weekend, three women had been murdered by jilted lovers who then disposed of themselves, one with a screwdriver apparently— the Italian version of DIY. In the last eight years more than 900 people have met their maker this way. Italian beaux obsess over their belles. When the government proposed an electronic locator bracelet for prisoners under house arrest, less interest was shown by prison authorities than by jealous boyfriends, who saw it as a superior measure to the mobile phone which could be switched off or ignored when 'otherwise engaged'.

Valeria's garden was the obvious choice for our meeting circle. It caught the evening breeze, had the best view of the gulf and, more importantly, was fenced off so Valeria could relax while Franco wandered. With his shorts bulging over a nappy and the elastic shot in his socks, he shuffled among chairs, stopping every so often to put pebbles in his pockets, laugh randomly or launch blasphemy at the broom tree. Around midnight, Valeria gave him some medicine that would shut him down until morning. *'Buona notte Franco,'* said the group as Valeria led him towards the house.

He padded behind her like an old dog on a frayed lead, a sad end to a happy evening.

Aunts, uncles and grandparents drifted home shortly after, leaving 'children' to play cards before heading out later. We played a game called *Scopa*, not with a standard deck but with Sicilian cards. There are four suits comprising swords, coins, goblets and clubs—not the three-leafed variety but the wooden sort a caveman would carry. The idea of the game is to collect cards from the table with the equivalent number of another suit. *Scopa* is Italy's most popular card game and doesn't take long to learn. According to a famous handbook there is only one rule: 'Always try to see your opponents' cards'.

At an hour when in Sydney I was used to an evening winding down, in Sicily it was just beginning. Around 1 am, in convoy once again, the promise of fresh air and gelato lured us back to the beach, where crowds of summer insomniacs paraded the promenade. Hundreds were there, watching others and being watched, an obstacle course of narcissists dodged by Vespas and speeding cars. Approaching sunrise we returned to the hill, where Daniela and I collapsed on sheets my underwear had allegedly stained.

After my fourth consecutive sunrise the morning trip to Guidaloca was beyond me. I woke around midday and did what I had been wanting to do since arriving on the hillside: take a recliner chair, a book and a glass of beer to the olive grove. To call it a day before the day had started and, above all, to be alone. In Sicily, time on your own is as rare as rain. I think that's why it's impossible to play Solitaire with Sicilian cards.

Sipping slow and reading fast, I was engrossed in Peter Robb's history of *Cosa Nostra* entitled *Midnight in Sicily*. The diabolical tale revealed more about Sicily than my guidebook to stone structures built by people long dead. This was the unfinished story of unsettled scores. The words on the page were more deafening than the cicadas in the trees. *La Mafia* was invisible, yet tangibly close. Too close perhaps. In 1985 the biggest heroin refinery in Europe was discovered under *Cosa Nostra*'s control just a kilometre from the broom tree. And 70 kilometres to the east, the unassuming town of Corleone was home to the most infamous *Mafioso,* Salvatore Riina, prompting Hollywood to give the name to its jowly boss of bosses, Don Corleone. I was holidaying in Mafia heartland—the ingenuous countryside. Above suspicion, it bred men of secrets who controlled the towns, the cities, the island.

Enthralled by the bloodshed, I had failed to notice the arrival in the olive grove of two men. Dressed in dark suits and sunglasses, it seemed the elegant thugs in my book had materialised. The sun at their backs, their shadows loomed across me. Shielding my eyes, I identified Antonio and Fabio. I was relieved but confused, by their clothes mainly; surely in such heat you would only wear a suit to either a wedding or a funeral, neither of which had been discussed at last night's meeting circle.

Fabio took off his sunglasses before explaining their visit. 'Would you like to come to confession with us, Crris?' I was slumped in the sun-chair as though part of the fabric, a menace to no one but the insect which had drowned in my beer. What the hell did I have to confess other than my wish to be left alone by these invasive Sicilians? Was the paedophile lapse back to haunt me?

'Daniela heard we were going and suggested we ask you to join us.'

'Oh did she?'

I looked up the slope towards the house to find Daniela perched on a concrete wall, waving and smiling, clearly enjoying the scene she'd created. For once my poor Italian came in handy as I invented an excuse which none of us understood. But my stutterings were unnecessary. Fabio and Antonio could keep straight faces no longer. Bloody Sicilians. Practical jokers.

Daniela arrived with a beer and climbed into the chair with me.

'Why you didn't go with them?' she asked. 'You should confess what we do this morning in the grandma-flat.'

'*Granny*-flat.'

'*Ah, scusa.*'

Sicily is an island of contradictions. Where eternal love lasts two years, but I fell in love with the same woman every two hours.

'*C'è Scirocco!*' yelled Nonna Lina, and the hill had the day's weather. But by the time the dusty blanket arrived that afternoon, Daniela and I would be on the road to winter. Summer's flame was fading. It was the last day of August. Come September we'd be in Milan.

We weren't the only ones leaving. As the temperature dropped, beachfront bars would close and snow would grace Mount Etna, the two sisters would return to their apartments in Alcamo, Valeria would drag Franco back to Andrano, and Francesco, Antonio, Sergio and Luisa would join us in Milan. There they would spend the winter eagerly anticipating their next summer break, with the same people in the same place—*Stessa Spiagga, Stesso Mare*. I wasn't sure if such an unvaried life would leave me bored or reassured. All I knew was that I missed the hillside before we'd even left.

In the same carnival fashion with which they had welcomed us, the group gathered in the clearing to see us off. Only Nonna Lina was glad we were leaving. 'Guests are like fish,' went one of her many maxims, 'after a while they stink.' We were given gifts of food and several bottles of Zio Tonio's *prosecco*. Accepting them meant repacking the car and offloading some clothes. I tossed Valeria my burgundy underwear. 'Give them a wash, will you?' It felt good to make them laugh, intentionally.

Taking leave of *mamma* was more difficult for Daniela, whom she was leaving alone with *papà* for the first time. As the reason for her departure, I felt a little responsible and appreciated Valeria's lack of resentment towards me, which, according to Daniela, was not to be underestimated. Given that I was robbing Valeria of her only daughter, Daniela believed many Italian mothers might have been less welcoming.

After kissing our way back through the crowd, I told Valeria as best I could that I admired her courage with Franco, that I considered her incredibly stoic, and that above all I revered her ability to laugh in the face of a situation that would make others cry. 'Well,' said Valeria, 'I'm Sicilian, not Italian.' Her tone was matter of fact. 'We're a different breed.'

Having been ruled by many but cared for by few, like her thirsty island Valeria has no one to rely on but herself. Obstinate, and without complaint, she will nurse her dying husband to the end.

A stray dog sniffed at Napoleon, loaded with lasagne and marzipan as he rolled down a gravel driveway leading to a main road and Milan. A cheerful group of twenty waved from a clearing on a hilltop. A Sicilian woman continued her hold on a silent man's arm.

A kilometre of sausages

The seasons changed overnight. We closed our eyes on summer skies and awoke in autumn fog. The city at our window had vanished, and drawing the curtain merely revealed another veil, thin and weightless, yet thick and heavy, under which Milan would sulk the entire winter. Southern summer was a memory. Northern winter a reality. No watermelon seller, no morning swim, only screaming sirens and blaring horns: a medley of mechanical rumours betraying the frenetic nature of life under the fog. The honeymoon was over.

Rolling in from the Po valley and nestling against the Alps, Milan's winter cloak is as miserable as the city it obscures. Having been to Milan several times, Daniela suggested the veil actually did the charmless city a favour and was only objectionable for what it unmasked when it lifted. 'Many poets have tried to make the fog to appear romantic,' she said while dressing for work. 'But they all have failed.' Then she too vanished, off to the children she was having difficulty convincing that days didn't last for six hours and nights for eighteen.

My first impressions of the city beneath the fog were pieced together from the newspaper and an Italian–English dictionary. The national daily, *Il Corriere della Sera*, devotes its final page to Milanese chronicle. More a summary of pertinent information, invariably it read something like: Agenda—work. Weather—fog. Sunrise and Sunset—irrelevant. Air Pollution—extreme. Traffic—blocked. Yesterday's Crime Figures—robberies 60, car thefts 102, snatched handbags 68 . . . How I longed for

Andrano, where the sun shone bright and stolen handbags were returned.

By Italian standards, a weather summary on the back page of a newspaper is cursory. Italians place great importance on the weather, holding it accountable for everything from toothache to libido. They trust only the most qualified meteorologists. An air force colonel in military uniform reads the weather on TV. In keeping with the Italians' love of praise, his weather map is signed by its designer. Fishermen needn't fear what appears to be a nasty low pressure trough between Sicily and Sardinia; it is merely the flamboyant autograph of a computer technician. No one is average in Italy.

During autumn and winter, however, the *Milanesi* don't need a detailed forecast, partly because they know it already—fog—and partly because, even if by some miracle it were favourable, the only place they're going is the office. Whether they can see their designer city or not is irrelevant. They are here for one reason only—to work.

Milan is Italy's wealthiest city. On previous trips to Italy, as many tourists do I had skipped this commercial and industrial capital, preferring to spend limited time and money on Rome, Florence and Venice. Guidebooks to the city devoted more pages to shopping than sights, leading me to assume she lacked the charisma of sister cities.

Like Francesco, Antonio, Sergio and Luisa, as well as thousands of other southern Italians, we too had come to Milan for the work and soon settled into the city's singular pastime. Daniela enjoyed the challenge of an inner-city primary school. Compared with Andrano, where the school day finished at lunchtime, she was working longer hours and teaching students from various countries, many of whom spoke less Italian than I did.

Her day was lengthened further by the fact her new school, named after the general responsible for Italy's biggest bloodbath on the Austrian front during World War I, Luigi Cadorna, was a forty-five-minute drive from Francesco's apartment. Having lived all her life in a town where the only traffic jams were caused by stray dogs or religious processions, Daniela was unaccustomed to the rat race. Whenever she became stressed, I had to remind myself that her life had changed almost as much as mine.

Francesco's apartment was in a suburb of Milan, a tatty outskirt to say the least, but he preferred to live less centrally because the reduced rent allowed him the luxury of a spare room, a room he now rented to his sister and me. In the evenings, when Francesco returned from his downtown agency, we worked together on ad campaigns required in English for overseas clients. Writing copy was easy. Communicating with Francesco was difficult. My boss spoke slowly for no one, and my Italian needed to improve *pronto*.

A contestant on an Italian quiz show is stuck on a multiple choice question regarding marble. He has narrowed down the answer to either *marmo bianco*—white marble, or *marmo nero*—black marble, but is undecided between the two. Giving him a clue, the host asks which one sounds better and encourages the contestant to articulate both. He complies, slowly, unearthing the music in mundane words. '*Marmo bianco, marmo nero. Marmo bianco, marmo nero.*' The man's eyes light up. '*Marmo bianco* sounds better,' he replies confidently.

'Is that your final answer?' asks the host.

'*Sì.*'

'*Perfetto!*'

The Italian rule of thumb is: if it sounds good, stick to it. Bear that in mind if you're ever learning the language.

Italian grammar adheres to complex principles, until those principles make a phrase discordant and can be swept aside in the name of beauty. At my Italian course in Sydney, Giacomo had dismissed questions regarding grammar rules with an answer I found unsatisfactory at the time—'Because it sounds better, *basta*.' Several years on, I realise there is no better explanation.

Italian is widely considered the most melodic of the Romance languages. King Charles V of Spain said:

When I'm talking to my horse I speak German,
When I'm talking to diplomats I speak French,
When I'm talking to God I speak Spanish,
But when I'm talking to women I speak Italian.

If you want to upset an Italian ear, subject it to the angular tongue of the Germans or the cold, efficient, sterile talk of the Swiss. To an Italian, rhythm and melody are far more important than efficiency, precision and perhaps even meaning. Italians enjoy speaking their language and view it as a pastime rather than a means to an end. In their eyes, or mouths rather, it's a dynamic organism, an instrument with which to make music, a brush with which to paint.

Energised and harmonised by vowels and double consonants, Italian words massage the mouth of the speaker and tickle the ear of the listener. Saying the word *stuzzicadenti* (toothpick), for example, will do more for your mouth than actually using one. Likewise, 'taste buds' in English sounds somewhat bland, while *pupille gustative* goes close to satisfying them.

Italian sentences are like symphonies, composed with the onomatopoeia in words like *zanzara* (mosquito). There is harmony in humdrum words like *pipistrello* (bat), *schizzinoso* (fussy), *malavventurato* (unlucky), or *inoperosamente* (idly). Even place names are fun to say, like Squinzano, Poggibonsi, Domodossola, or people's names, like Baldo Bologna and Marco Magnifico. Bob Matthews in English equates to Roberto di Matteo in Italian. And Joe Green is Giuseppe Verdi. Who would you rather be?

There is, unfortunately, an ugly side to this beautiful banter. Speaking Italian is addictive and most Italians would prefer to talk to themselves rather than stop. But verbosity inhibits clarity, with frustrating results. Ask a German where the bank is and they'll either tell you or say they don't know. Ask an Italian and they'll tell you regardless of whether they know or not. Their tongues are far too hyperactive for terse replies like 'I don't know'.

The other downside is that Italians dislike listening almost as much as they love speaking. Community service announcements on Italian TV don't aim to stop people smoking, littering or drink-driving, instead they try to stop them babbling. '*Chi ascolta cresce*' is their catchphrase—'Whoever listens, learns'. Errico the bank manager told me that if you don't shout in Italy you won't be heard, something conversations with Francesco duly confirmed. Raising one's voice to speak Italian is a form of social Darwinism, a fight for survival in a conversation. As a result, learning Italian also means learning how to interrupt, to bellow, to dismiss and to shout down.

For the newcomer, there is a danger that the enthusiasm required to converse in Italian can influence the composure with which they speak their native tongue. After a short time in Italy, the undesirable habits that came with Italian had crept into my English, alienating friends and family who mistook passion for aggression. Cut off the Italians mid-sentence, swat your hand at them, call them fools; they'll still be your friends and will have done worse to you. Do it in Australia and you'll be drinking on your own.

Unaware of the pitfalls, I fell in love with Italian and began talking so much I almost got stretch marks on my tongue. Giacomo knew his language was addictive when he planned his course. By first teaching us colourful expressions, he ensured I became so excited by what Italian did to my mouth that I was prepared to tolerate what its intricate grammar did to my head. My first French lesson at university was grammar based, meaning I could take or leave my second. But after Giacomo's first lesson I had the audacious ability to ask a woman to my bed, ensuring my attendance at lesson two on the off-chance she accepted.

But learning a language in a vacuum results in a superficial knowledge. The way to really tame a foreign tongue is to live among those for whom it is not foreign, to imitate their pronunciation and impersonate their tone of voice. Through no fault of Giacomo's, I learnt more in one week in Italy than in one month in Sydney. When you are immersed in a language, like a fish hook in the sea, it's impossible not to fluke a fish or two. Slowly and surely the words begin to build, one after another, like snowflakes on pine branches.

Keeping your ears peeled is the key. There is never a moment's rest. Indeed some of the best lessons are learnt during relaxation time. You don't need a professor of linguistics to teach you the first person plural. A one-eyed football commentator is just as handy. 'Corner kick for us!' cried the commentator/Inter Milan fan. 'My goodness we're playing well today.'

A trip to the beach in Andrano taught me the difference between the formal and the informal address. In Italian, *tu* means 'you' informally, while *Lei* means 'you' formally. I struggled with this mark of respect for superiors and strangers, not only because there is no equivalent in English, but because I found its use illogical and a trifle insincere. A friend of Daniela's had objected to a Doberman who moved its bowels in the water, muddying the Mediterranean and leaving a floating mine at the swimming spot. Stefano complained to the owner quite tactfully but she attacked him more forcibly than her dog could have done. 'My dog's cleaner than *you* are,' she snapped. As she didn't know Stefano, she used the formal *Lei* to address him. Italians abuse each other with respect.

Televisions make great textbooks. Over the summer I watched the Italian soap opera, *Incantesimo*—Enchantment, and stocked my vocabulary with vital words like lover, affair, pregnant, elope, miscarriage and murder. And that was just for one character; a fairly average week.

The biggest obstacle to learning a foreign language is pride. My tip is to learn the word for 'window' and throw pride out of it. If you can't laugh at yourself and are not prepared to hire 'paedophiles' rather than 'pedal-boats', you might never be humiliated but you'll never excel. Inaccuracy is a moss-covered stepping-stone towards accuracy, and I slipped on it often. I even asked the butcher in Andrano for a 'kilometre' of sausages rather than a 'kilogram'. 'You must be hungry,' he replied, friend first and smart-arse second. The only reason locals appreciate foreigners who attempt to speak their language is because it gives them something to laugh at.

Recounting an episode of *Incantesimo* to Daniela, another beneficial practice, if excruciating for the listener, I said that a nurse had put a prematurely born baby in a 'dehumidifier' rather than an 'incubator'. It didn't survive, unfortunately. Dehydrated most likely.

In Italian, the past tense of the verb 'to discover' (*scoperto*) is unnervingly close to that of the verb 'to fuck' (*scopato*). In my early days in Milan, I rushed home to tell Daniela that I had 'fucked' a shop on the corner which sold international phone cards, a Japanese restaurant behind the bank, and, perhaps the hardest for her to accept, a woman who translated official documents for less than the woman at the Australian consulate.

Given her blunders with my language, Daniela rarely criticised my slip-ups with hers. Walking home from the shops one evening she said she was so tired she could stop and have a 'snap' under a tree. When I criticised the clothes that a male character wore to his wedding in *Incantesimo*, Daniela defended his fashion sense, saying she'd seen other 'brooms' dressed the same way. But perhaps her most laughable lapse came when we were completing my residency documents in Lecce. With only one office left to visit, Daniela happily declared that we had made it to 'the final turtle'. Her English, however, had a few more 'hurdles' to jump.

It's not just beginners who make mistakes. Even experts make Freudian slips. Several months after our move north, while I played mixed-doubles tennis in Milan, a fire broke out nearby with smoke wafting over the court. When sirens finally sounded, an Italian friend declared, 'Here come the blow-jobs' (*pompini*) rather than, 'Here come the firemen' (*pompieri*). His partner served several double-faults before regaining her composure.

The more I erred, the more I learnt. The more I learnt, the

more I realised that the beauty of the language masked a litany of complexities, knots I needed to untie if I was going to read and write Italian. I wanted to avoid the trap of simply learning conversation, easy to do when learning a foreign language in a foreign country. So while Daniela and Francesco were hard at work at school and office, I was hard at work in the apartment teaching myself Italian.

The textbooks Daniela bought me covered contemporary cultural topics with the most commonly used vocabulary. Like the newspaper, they depicted what was happening outside under the fog. Chapter titles read like a list of modern evils: pollution, traffic, Mafia, crime, and examples of the conditional tense were explained by Italy's most common cause of inconvenience—the strike. 'Maria and Peter would have gone to Paris for the weekend but the airlines were on strike. They would have driven but there was a petrol strike as well.' It appeared walking was their only option.

When Daniela returned from work we would take a walk around the streets, where much of the morning's lesson was dramatically brought to life. The similarity between what I studied in the textbook and what I witnessed outside was stark, too stark in regard to chapter 9: 'It's a difficult life for pedestrians'.

Wading through a minefield of tall grass and dog turds—the Milanese version of a park—we were startled by an abrupt screech of brakes and a dull metal thud. Running to the scene, we found two men shouting and waving arms, employing the same gestures I had studied in chapter 6: 'Gesti'. One of few cheerful chapters in the textbook, it was devoted to commonly used hand gestures, as vital to Italian conversation as vocabulary and grammar. The famous joke—'How do you stop Italians from talking? By chopping off their hands'—is old because it's apt. Italians' hands are as active as their mouths and work in swashbuckling accompaniment. Daniela can only talk while driving if she steers with her knees.

'Gesti' was a series of illustrations with arrows indicating which way the hands must be moved to communicate without speech. Below each picture was a phrase or expression, usually emphatic, for which the semaphore stood. Pushing one finger into your cheek and twisting it means 'this food is delicious'. Scraping your fingers under your chin and away from you signifies 'what do I care?' And touching all five fingertips together like the petals of a closed flower, while shaking your hand back and forth as though mixing a cocktail, means 'what the hell do you think you're doing?'

There are other gestures, unfit for print in the textbook, which you will often see exchanged between angry motorists or rival football fans. Obscene sign language such as extending your pinkie and index finger to do 'the horns', suggesting that someone is a cuckold, the husband of an adulteress. I saw this mainly on Sicilian roads, far more frequently than I saw blinkers or brake lights.

The two men on the Milan street were exchanging gestures from chapter 6 in their disagreement over an accident from chapter 9, while a young man was lying face down on the road in front of a blue BMW, twisted and limp as though he'd fallen from a height, and with his head in a pool of blood. Insisting she would faint if she saw the blood close up, Daniela helped by phoning an ambulance from behind a tree. I ran to the felled pedestrian and tried to communicate as best I could over the shouting match on the street. It was the unluckiest of days for the victim: collected by a car whose driver was more interested in convincing a passer-by of his innocence, only to then have first aid administered by a tongue-tied foreigner who knew little more than how to ask a woman to his bed and several obscene Sicilian gestures.

The victim blinked occasionally, so he was alive in any language. In broken Italian I asked if he could feel his arms and legs, but his lack of response indicated he was either critically injured, couldn't understand me, or both. Chapter 9 had a happy ending, with the victim scrambling to his feet and brushing off the dust before calling his lawyer, another essential Italian lesson. But a happy ending appeared unlikely here.

A crowd gathered and Daniela's ambulance arrived, followed by a team of doctors who erected portable curtains and administered 'second aid'; I had been 'first', if not much of an 'aid'. I've no idea if the pedestrian survived. All I saw after that was a *vigile* manning the curtain, parrying the overcurious trying to peek inside by touching all five fingertips together like the petals of a closed flower, while shaking his hand back and forth as though mixing a cocktail—'what the hell did they think they were doing?' The driver continued his debate with the witness, seemingly oblivious to the blood he had spilt. The accuracy of my textbook had been proven in tragic fashion.

'Ciao, Daniela. I was just watching the midday news. Gorbachev died this morning.'

After a month in the apartment with only my textbook for company, I was slipping less and less on that mossy stepping-stone. So when I called Daniela at work to tell her the ex-President of Russia was now the late ex-President of Russia, I did so with such confidence that she passed the news among her colleagues. But the evening bulletin, which Daniela and I watched together, contradicted my version of events. The following day at school was an embarrassing one for Daniela, with colleagues informing her it was actually Gorbachev's wife who had passed away.

Whether to continue locking myself away with the textbook or attend an intensive language course was a question I had been debating for some time. I hadn't for a second expected Gorbachev's wife to help me decide.

From an abundance of language schools I chose the aptly titled *Il Centro*, so named because of its central position in the cobblestoned Brera district, which despite heavy traffic and elegant buildings coated with exhaust is otherwise Milan's most attractive quarter.

The five-morning-a-week two-month course was tough. The fiery red-headed *maestra*, nicknamed *Il Generale* by my classmates, was slightly shy of five foot, but that was all she was shy of. Stunting her height further were elaborate metal earrings, wind-chimes almost, which stretched her freckled ears and touched her rigid shoulders. Short-haired and bullish with a ring on every finger, she spoke quickly and only in Italian. English was outlawed. Indeed any language other than Italian was ignored. Even if you raised your hand to say you had no idea what she was talking about, her response was a burst of gibberish otherwise known as Italian.

Invariably dressed in leather, the pint-sized polyglot showed no mercy when dressing down adults who had failed to do their homework. Her nine o'clock interrogations of the tongue-tied were as demoralising as they were beneficial. Few would deny being frightened of her. A whip would have been at home in her hands. She had cast us into the proverbial deep end, the bottom of which none of us could touch, but *Il Generale* soon had us swimming with the fluency of fish.

A bustling foreign city can be as cryptic as the tongue of its inhabitants. *Il Centro* helped familiarise both, the course tempering the language and my morning trip to school revealing the personality of misty Milan. Charmless perhaps, but I discovered there were some things worth seeing under that blanket of fog.

The bright orange bus ride to the city was the morning's first adventure, a twenty-minute journey which the driver seemed desperate to pull off in ten. 'Where did you get your licence?' he screamed one morning while swerving around a car that had run a red light. Detecting the driver's Neapolitan accent, a female passenger three rows from the front baited, 'Maybe he got it in Naples.'

'Has someone back there got something to say?' asked the driver ominously, his eyes scanning the rear-view mirror rather than the road.

'No,' replied the woman. 'Just an observation. I think that driver probably came from Naples because he passed on the red.'

'Shut up, *signora*,' suggested a man behind her. 'In Milan we pass on the red too.'

We took a tight corner and standing passengers squeezed the overhead railing.

'I drove a bus in Naples for fourteen years and never had an accident until I came to Milan,' claimed the driver.

'Having to obey the rules must have confused you,' retorted the woman.

Heated but harmless repartee is a pastime in Italy, and I soon learnt to enjoy situations which I had first thought bound for violence.

There were of course mornings when nothing out of the ordinary happened on the bus. Passengers read the paper or spoke on the phone, while any pedestrian who delayed the driver's quest for a personal best received a blast of the horn he used more often than the brakes.

The bus terminated near Piazza Duomo, Milan's central piazza, which at eight-thirty in the morning was buzzing with those who needed to be elsewhere by nine. I may have been clinging to notions of Andrano but to me the words 'central piazza' had a village ring to them, conjuring scenes of markets and street talk, an idle atmosphere. In a commercial metropolis of 2 million people I had expected the social role of the piazza to become lost. But while the atmosphere in Piazza Duomo is hardly intimate, the heart of the city has remained in the hearts of its residents, who do what they can to have their hectic schedules include a trip to the square, and perhaps take a walk between its foaming fountain and pooping pigeons.

I could have taken a tram from home that would have dropped me outside the school, but preferred to take a bus which left me a ten-minute stroll across the *centro storico*, past the marble magnificence of the world's third largest cathedral. The Gothic Duomo, which dates from 1386, is a craggy masterpiece of turrets, belfries, gargoyles and statues, from whose tallest spire a gold Madonna blesses the cityscape at her feet—when she can see it, that is. When the fog finally clears, she glistens in the sun atop her marble perch, which, in unison with the cathedral, absorbs the pale pink sunset.

Early winter. The *Milanesi* hunched their shoulders under heavy jackets and cocooned their necks in woollen scarves. Striding purposefully, they pointed their heads like dogs in a downpour, observing little other than pavement and wristwatch. Women were dressed ostentatiously: gold-armed sunglasses, fake tans, high-heel boots and fur coats. One heavily made-up woman had a mink on her back and a Malamute on a lead. Dead or alive, both furs were fashion accessories.

Japanese tourists milled about, buying anything with 'Italia' written on it and taking photos of each other. Only a contortionist could cross Piazza Duomo and avoid appearing on a Tokyo mantelpiece. To avoid one photo I starred in several others. And don't open your umbrella when it rains unless you want to become the leader of a giddy touring party from Osaka.

A bicycle bell scattered tourists and pigeons as the Rinaldi Express postman weaved among the throng. Pedalling antique mounts (new bicycles don't seem to exist in Italy), Milan's bicycle couriers, a fleet of middle-aged men in navy-blue suits, deliver the post with style rather than speed, whistling while they work.

A group of students on a school excursion leant against a wall of the Duomo. Most were wearing Nike, in fact it looked as though their teacher had checked the roll on their clothes. One played with a remote-control car before it was mown down by a cyclist who failed to spot it in the fog. The man dismounted, kicked the plastic toy and made the gesture for 'what the hell do you think you're doing?' at its remote controller. He was quite right, the piazza is supposed to be closed to cars.

Two policemen were trying to repair a sagging bumper bar on their squad car. One tried to reattach the appendage gently before his colleague pulled him away and kicked it hard, causing it to sag even further and setting off the caged Alsatian in the back. Two *carabinieri* on foot patrol stopped to lend a hand, a rare moment of collaboration.

The same beggar sat on the steps to a seminary behind the Duomo each day. Every two weeks he would disappear for a day, before returning to the cold concrete step in fresh pants and shirt, his beard shaved and his hair cut. It was a well-thought-out spot—aspiring priests can hardly ignore an outstretched hand. But I was inclined to suggest he venture round the corner to the Grand Hotel Duomo, where another savvy scrounger collected bothersome shrapnel from guests departing the luxury hotel. Her collection cup was the only thing tatty about her. She even wore lipstick. Not bad for a beggar.

Leaving Piazza Duomo, I strolled the polished patterned tiles of the Galleria Vittorio Emmanuele II. The grandiose building in the shape of a cross is named after the first king of Italy and links Piazza Duomo with Piazza La Scala, the site of what many claim to be the world's most beautiful opera house. At that early hour, the elegant shopping mall was being spruced for another day's trading. Waiters tied cushions to chairs outside exclusive cafés, while Prada's front window was meticulously cleaned to give a sharp view of even sharper prices.

On the first day of my Italian course, I stopped at a bar where Daniela and I had drunk coffee the previous weekend after viewing Da Vinci's *Last Supper*. The *barista* had charged Daniela 70 cents for an espresso which, two days later, cost me and my awkward Italian the tourist price of close to double. Despite being fleeced, I often breakfasted there on my way to a course whose results I could assess by the price of my coffee.

Almost as often as I was overcharged, I was called back by a waiter determined to hand me my receipt. Time and again I forgot the irksome law requiring me to keep proof of purchase for 100 metres from point of sale. This ineffective tax avoidance measure is policed by Italy's fourth ineffective police force, *La Guardia di Finanzia* or 'The Receipt Police' as Daniela calls them.

In grey and yellow uniforms, they patrol shop and street inspecting register and receipt, ensuring shopkeepers have an honest record of takings in their till.

Absurd laws are open to absurd interpretation. A barman in La Spezia was fined €250 for offering a glass of water to a beggar who was caught without a receipt, while a barman in Milan was fined the same amount for sipping one of his own drinks for which he hadn't paid. I rather hoped it was the waiter who had overcharged me.

Collusion between shopkeeper and customer makes evasion of the law simple. Daniela went to a hairdresser who offered her a discount if she accepted a receipt for less than the amount she paid. If Daniela was stopped on leaving the salon, she would say her hair had not been cut, merely styled for a wedding, a version of events that would be confirmed when the Receipt Police cross-examined the hairdresser.

Receipt in my jeans and caffeine in my veins, I left the bar for the final leg of my morning trip to school. In the heart of the Brera district, live mannequins stood motionless in a Calvin Klein shop-window, intriguing shoppers who sensed something was up and stared until winked at by the models. It was a marvellous gimmick. Even I walked in and bought an overpriced turtleneck.

On the same bustling street, a waiter balancing a tray on the points of his fingers threaded among frantic traffic to deliver coffee, cigarettes—and receipts—to nearby shops. As passing vehicles ruffled his apron, the fearless matador didn't spill a drop. He obviously hadn't read chapter 9 of my textbook.

A one-armed man attempted a three-point turn in a car that was blocking traffic. Cigarette between his lips, he swung the wheel as best he could, pulling it down then blocking it with his elbow. The impatient driver of a tour bus put his fist on his horn but failed to provoke a reaction from the driver, if only because he had no spare hand with which to make a rude gesture.

Enjoyment of the casual scenes on my morning walk to school, tinged as always with humour and mayhem, ended abruptly on arrival when *Il Generale* would be waiting for me, an eye on her watch and a question on her lips. Despite the noise, the pollution, and the chaos I had witnessed on the streets, by far the most stressful place was her classroom. We hated her the way army recruits hate their drill sergeant, who then turns them into the finest of soldiers.

Thanks to Gorbachev's late wife, *Il Centro*'s early starts, virtual reality textbooks, public humiliations, biased football commentators, bastard waiters, indiscreet Dobermans, and a great deal of trial and error, Daniela and I began to converse purely in Italian as my knowledge of her language surpassed her knowledge of mine. As Italian became my plaything and Milan my playground, my relationship with Daniela grew more meaningful. Each new word was a key that unlocked a door to her personality. Stunted English had been enough to reveal her as whimsical and kind-hearted. Effortless Italian now showed her to be quirky, illogical, intellectual and brave. If I had loved her in English, I adored her in Italian. She was as beautiful as her language, and I couldn't get enough of either.

No foreigners . . . or southerners

Il postino placed his forearm over the intercom buttons to every unit in the apartment block and pressed. The building's nervous system pulsed, a seven-storey egg-timer that startled residents, including Francesco's sausage dog, Liuto (lute), named after the long-necked musical instrument he vaguely resembled. He sprang from the bed on which he'd been dozing, slipped on parquet in his rush to the door, and with midget paws scratching for traction, careered snout-first into the wall in the hall. Panic stations in the apartment, like a cockpit with a red light blinking, an alarming yet appropriate fanfare given it heralded a miracle—the arrival of the post.

I was concentrating on a frosted shaving mirror the first time I heard this commotion and was so startled I considered myself lucky my razor was blunt. Six weeks earlier to the day, my parents had sent me a parcel from Australia, so I raced for the intercom as excited as Liuto, convinced it had finally arrived.

'*Si?*'

'*Postino.*'

'*Arrivo.*'

I thumbed a switch on the intercom to release the downstairs door, wiped the remaining shaving cream from my face and darted to the lift. '*Fuori Servizio*'—'Out of Order'. Dressed in pyjamas, I took three stairs at a time.

Criticism, complaint, rebuke or reprisal are forgotten in the excitement of the post's late arrival. 'Better late than never' would be an appropriate slogan for *Poste Italiane*. Since moving to Italy

I have received Christmas tidings at Easter, been congratulated on my thirtieth birthday shortly before my thirty-first, and invited to a wedding months after the honeymoon.

A trip to the local post office helped explain such delays. A slouching woman used a paintbrush to daub my postcard with glue and affixed a stamp which failed to cover her clumsy artwork before tossing my missive into the international bag, where it no doubt attached itself to a card for an Albanian lady celebrating a baby who might be a teenager by the time congratulations arrived. Change was then administered from a Quality Street chocolate tin. And this was Italy's snappiest city?

At Andrano's post office they don't affix stamps in front of the customer, they write the value of stamps they will 'later' attach to the envelope. One August I sent a postcard to friends in Ireland whom I then visited in September. The postcard arrived after I did, and from the date on the stamps I realised that the card had spent eight days in the post office before being dispatched. What's the difference between a strike day and a normal day at an Italian post office? On a strike day they put a sign out front to explain why no one's working.

After twelve flights of stairs I arrived in the foyer to find the postman sorting mail from his brown leather satchel.

'*Postino?*'

'*Si.*'

'You buzzed me.'

'I may have. I buzzed everybody. I needed the door opened.'

'Oh, I thought you needed me to sign something. I'm waiting for an important parcel.'

'I'll buzz you when it arrives,' he said, turning back to the pigeonholes.

Not wishing to waste the trip, and even less inclined to retackle the stairs, I waited for Francesco's post while observing the routine of the man who delivered it. Individual apartments were not numbered so he took each letter addressed to the building, read the name of the recipient, scanned thirty pigeonholes labelled by surname and when he couldn't find a match tossed the letter on top of the mailboxes. Is it any wonder the service is slow?

Named apartments make life difficult for the postman, particularly when, for tax purposes, owners opt not to declare tenants because contracts attract the attention of the Receipt Police. As a result they leave their own surnames on intercoms, pigeonholes and front doors. Visiting friends must know your landlord's surname if they wish to be buzzed into your building. When inviting someone round for the first time it's not uncommon for the Milanese to say: 'See you at nine and the doorbell's in the name of Di Costanzo.'

The postman's job might be more pleasurable if the Italians derived as much humour from the literal meanings of their names as I do. Most Italian letterboxes make amusing reading, especially when couples display both their surnames. One pigeonhole in Francesco's building reads: Panico e Pace—Panic and Peace. Two doors down live an incompatible couple by the name of Guerra e Pace—War and Peace. Fortunately their neighbour is a certain Salvatore Capace—Capable Saviour, just in case Mr War gets the upper hand next door.

Italian surnames are most comical when their meanings reflect an aspect of their bearers' personality, as though the literal meaning has rubbed off on them. It's difficult to get more than a few reluctant pleasantries out of Daniela's old school friend Davide Timido, and Valeria's friend Stefania Frigida remained a spinster all her life. Coincidence often makes a surname's literal meaning funny. On the evening news, I once saw Giovanni Lava reporting from Mount Etna after the volcano's eruption. But I also had a skin cancer check with a Doctor Tan in Sydney, so perhaps I should give the Italians a break.

My favourite Italian book is the phonebook. I scan the columns in search of titillating titles, wondering what each name reveals about its bearer. Does Elvio Mezzogufo—Elvis Half-an-owl, suffer from insomnia? Is Crucifisso San Filippo—Crucifix Saint Phillip, religious? Is Signor Massimo Peloso—Mr Max Hairy, balding gracefully? And does Pietro Calvo—Peter Bald, have a full head of hair?

Some Italians have names with positive connotations like Marco Magnifico—Mark Magnificent, and Maria Bella—Maria Beautiful. But spare a thought for Carla Vacca—Carla Cow, and Anna La Rana—Anna the Frog. Does she have a son called Kermito? Fortunately for Anna, Italians tend to ignore the connotations of names, apart from Italy's most famous tycoon and playboy, Gianni Agnelli, for many years head of the Fiat empire. Before the Italian release of *The Silence of the Lambs,* Agnelli, whose surname literally means 'Lambs', refused to have his name linked with the film and got the title changed to *The Silence of the Innocents.* If all lambs were that powerful we'd probably all be vegetarians.

By the time the postman had finished sorting there were more letters above than inside the pigeonholes. In Francesco's box I found an envelope addressed only to 'The Southerner', containing a poem entitled *Preghiera per i Terroni*—A Prayer for the Peasants. *Terroni* is a derogatory term meaning 'person of the earth', levelled at southerners whom northerners find uncivilised. The postman hadn't delivered the unstamped hate-mail, so I assumed it had been placed there by someone in the building who considered Francesco, Daniela, and perhaps even me, undesirable by origin.

My small parcel still at large, I returned to the apartment, catching a ridiculous glimpse of my half-shaven stubble before awaiting Daniela's return so she could help me translate the poem. She laughed when I told her the title, but her smile disappeared as she scanned the lines.

Preghiera per i Terroni

Oh mio caro buon Gesù
Fa che non ce ne siano più.
Fagli capire che non sono voluti
E pulisci l'Italia da questi cornuti.

Da Roma in giù un grande ciclone
Che cancelli per sempre i dannati terroni.
Pioggia, vento e temporali
Solo e soltanto sui meridionali.

Translating poetry is more difficult than writing it, but here goes:

Good Lord Jesus
Rid us of them please.
Make them realise they're not wanted
And cleanse Italy of these cuckolds.
From Rome down bring a great cyclone
That eradicates the damned *terroni*.
Rain, wind and thunder
On the southerners alone.

A Milanese friend of mine once commented: 'Foreigners don't usually consider Italians racist, but it's only because we are so prejudiced against fellow Italians that we have no hatred left over for foreigners. We would be the best racists in the world if foreign people settled here to the extent that we have settled in their countries, because we get so much practice among ourselves.'

It's a question of geography. Italians dislike each other according to city or region and believe negative traits to be indicative of place. If you're tight-fisted you must be from Genova, if you're arrogant you're from Florence, if you lack humour you call Milan home, if you're a snob then Padova's your pad, if you're conceited you belong to Bologna, if you're obstinate you're sure to be Sardinian, and if you hail from anywhere south of Rome you might as well be African.

Northern Italians believe the First World stops around Rome, beyond which the uncultivated *terroni* inhabit the underdeveloped south. Some northerners even suggest they should have to take their passports when venturing south of the capital. The *terroni* are regarded as a primitive underclass which many northerners believe Italy would be better off without. Umberto Bossi, leader of *La Lega Nord*—The Northern League, is a high-profile subscriber to this view. The rough-spoken xenophobe champions tearing the country to shreds, with the north governing the north, the centre the centre and the south the south.

But the problems of a divided nation cannot be solved by estranging it further. The history of Italy is one of north–south disparity stretching as far back as the 1500s, when the Spanish conquered the south of the country and established the 'Kingdom of Naples' which lasted for over three and a half centuries. While the north was a series of prosperous sovereign states, the south was comprised of a largely illiterate peasantry to whom education was denied in order to facilitate rule. The benefits of the Industrial Revolution were reaped in the north but denied to the south, where the Spanish, content with the advancement of their home-land alone, were indifferent to progress.

Even after Garibaldi liberated southern Italy from Bourbon rule in 1861, uniting 'The Kingdom of Italy' ruled by Vittorio Emmanuele II, development in the south lagged far behind that of the north, where roads, schools and factories were the order of the day. The south, almost disregarded, became known as the Mezzogiorno, literally meaning 'midday'. Not sure why. Maybe because that's when they stop work.

Throughout the 1900s the southern problem was largely ignored, and under Fascism it was illegal to even refer to the Mezzogiorno—the nation's weakest link. Some financial help arrived in the 1950s with the 'Mezzogiorno Fund', but between corrupt local government and Mafia self-interest the money was dealt to the already rich, justifying northern accusations that the south was crooked and should fend for itself.

In the decade which followed, over a million southerners migrated north in search of the wealth which had stuck there like sand in a blocked hourglass. An even greater number tried their luck overseas, mainly in America and Australia.

Historical differences help explain the rift, but the modern problem is due to present failures as much as past events. The south has since enjoyed heartier times, with a limited industrial revolution of its own, a more educated and skilled blue-collar class, a growing white-collar class, second occupations which escape the eye of the Receipt Police, a boom period in the 1980s when the government traded jobs for votes, and generational wealth in the form of property, which is soaring in value as the Mezzogiorno becomes a tourist attraction.

But prosperity has been a lopsided affair which has turned southerners in on themselves. Their lack of community conscience and inherent mistrust of authority, which whether foreign or Italian has rarely been anything but self-advancing, gives southern Italy a medieval persona, alienating it further from the modernised north.

How could I have fallen for an uncivilised *terrona*? And how did the simpleton masquerade as the most refined woman I had ever met? Daniela admits certain attributes like melodramatic outbursts and raised voices make southerners appear unrefined, but prefers a southerner's hot temper to a northerner's cold hypocrisy. She says the northerners are *inconsistente* when they spend ten months of the year decrying the south as an African outpost, yet come July and August, as if sun cream were an antidote for chauvinism, they have little difficulty lowering themselves—quite literally—to enjoy enchanting southern beaches and Mediterranean cuisine. 'It's no wonder they come here for our food,' asserts Daniela. 'Polenta is the only thing they know how to cook up there. Do you know polenta, Chris? It's a subspecies of couscous. And they call *us* Africans.'

With few unified moments in the course of its history, Italy has arrived in the twenty-first century with 600-year-old problems and hate-mail in its letterboxes. After her initial shock, Daniela took the blow on the chin. As light-hearted as ever, she merely considered the *Preghiera* evidence that the northern philistines were capable of poetry after all, given that, as she points out, the bulk of Italy's literature has been created by southerners. Touché.

The phone rang at length before an old man picked up.

'*Pronto.*'

'*Buongiorno.* I'm calling about the flat to rent.'

'Where are you from?'

'Lecce.'

'I don't rent to southerners.'

Daniela pulled the phone from her ear as the old man slammed his down.

We had never intended to live with Francesco for long. Sharing a flat with your boss and your girlfriend's brother, especially when they're one and the same, is far from ideal. We wanted to live alone, and certain habits of Francesco's suggested he was disposed—and perhaps destined—to do likewise. For starters, the six-foot tank of piranhas implied peculiar taste, and Liuto's scattered puddles and sticky surprises suggested the dog either didn't get enough walks or was frightened of the fish. Harder to bear was Francesco's recent split from his childhood sweetheart. Lucinda once came by the apartment while Francesco was at work to seek my opinion over who was entitled to the sundries of their relationship—CD racks and lampshades—to which I replied that she was, if she took Liuto and the piranhas as well.

But our search for privacy was fast turning up nothing, firstly because Milan's rental market is as vicious as taking a bath in Francesco's fish tank, and secondly, for the reason that had cut short Daniela's phone call, her being southern along with my being foreign made us unattractive to many landlords.

Francesco had experienced similar prejudice when he moved to Milan five years earlier. One woman pointed to the washing machine in a flat he was inspecting and asked if he'd ever seen such an appliance. When Francesco objected, the woman apologised, saying she meant no offence and was genuinely interested in knowing if whitegoods had yet arrived 'down there'. Now it was Daniela's turn to suffer the injustice of moving north. She took heart from the fact that Francesco had eventually settled well and, in her optimistic way, was convinced we would do the same.

Daniela had one thing in her favour. A card up southern sleeves. She was a *statale*—a government employee, who probably couldn't be sacked were she to overthrow the republic single-handed. It was as good a guarantee of reliable rent as you'll find in Italy, north or south, and a reliable return on their investment properties helps the northerners shed prejudice even faster than clothes in the southern sun.

But after several frustrating weeks, during which Daniela would rush home from school at lunchtime to call about apartments already let before breakfast, we realised that either I began calling first thing or we'd be sharing with Francesco indefinitely. At that point I was speaking Italian as fluently as a tightrope walker steps a tightrope: slowly, surely, but one false step and I fell. Due to the fact that many landlords direct agents to exclude foreigners as suitable tenants, I was hardly the man for the job. Most of the property files I saw on estate agents' desks were marked in bold at the top: *NIENTE STRANIERI*—NO FOREIGNERS. Such words even appeared on the file for the property I ended up renting, an apartment which took weeks to find.

Italian cities are like rotten fruit—the best part is the pip. On Milan's *periferia*, eyesore apartments abound like weeds in a neglected garden, depressingly dreary and unkempt. The city's classical beauty was scarred by the explosion of southern migration, which saw cheap housing erected without planning permission and with haste defying taste. I wanted to live my Italian experience among Old World architecture, if not in it, then close to it. With Daniela's school as my reference point I searched as centrally as possible, for we agreed that small and stylish was preferable to large and sterile. The hunt was on.

Sparrows were stirring when I went out to brave the winter

wind and buy the morning paper, but the private placements I called were either already let, diverted to answer phones or led slyly to *bancadarias*—search agencies which demand the equivalent of $200 before letting potential addresses slip. Before learning how to spot them, I once ended up in the waiting room of a *bancadaria* where an agent was doing her best to calm a landlord with whom she had fallen out. Over what? Those pestilent foreigners. 'Of course you're right,' said the agent, squinting through her own smoke. 'I wouldn't want them in my house either but I thought their situation was different.' This was going to be tough.

I gave up on private ads and began calling listings under estate agency banners. This would also incur a fee but, unlike the *bancadarias*, *after* they found us a place to live. I called on the dot of opening time and recited Daniela's checklist of questions in Italian: Where is the apartment? What floor? Is there a lift? Does it work? I made only one mistake, asking if a unit had a roof (*tetto*) rather than a bed (*letto*).

If I survived the first round it was their turn to ask questions, which usually meant explaining why I was reading from a check-list. I replied that I was Australian, with a permit of stay, a steady job and a *statale* due home for lunch a little later. The next round of questions was more personal but easy enough to answer thanks to practice with Daniela. How old were Daniela and I? Were we married? Did we have children? Any pets? What work did we do? One agent hesitated before saying: 'I'm embarrassed to ask but the landlord only wants tenants with a degree. Do you or your girlfriend have one?'

'Between us we have three.'

'That's probably too many.'

According to the checklist, I was to then ask for an inspection time, insisting as best I could on being first to view the flat. Apartments are in such demand that interested parties block them with a deposit after the briefest inspection. On several occasions, after tiresome journeys on tram, tube and foot, I arrived for appointments to find the agent locking up and his pockets plump with cash. No time can be taken to consider a property or compare it with another, for both will disappear in the time it takes to decide. Two apartments slipped through our fingers while we discussed the practicality of a bathroom without a window or a kitchen so small the fridge was in the pantry.

Having arranged inspections at potential properties, I set out mid-morning with a mobile phone, a map of Milan and a handful of tickets for the *metropolitana*. Gypsies wandered the stuffy trains twisting Bohemian tunes from antique accordions. A child followed, shaking loose change in a paper cup. They swapped carriages at every stop, maximising their audience and stretching their one melody as far as possible.

Both above and below ground I was in Milan's bloodstream, racing between appointments until the city became familiar. Only once did I lose my way, missing an appointment in the elusive Via Copernicus. I turned the map in my hands for several minutes but still couldn't work out whether I was going around Via Copernicus or whether Via Copernicus was going around me.

Demand for apartments is so hot that owners needn't clean or tidy when preparing them for inspection. One unit I saw had waste in the toilet, another food and rags in the sink. Those in our price range were cramped to say the least, with aeroplane toilets and bidet-sized baths. The Milanese live in dwarf digs, with the pokier pads close to the centre. Many can be heated by turning on the toaster or vacuumed from the one power point. Michele, a friend of Francesco's from Palermo, lived in a studio flat with 18 square metres of floor space including the balcony, less than the size of his garage in Sicily. But for a young civil engineer, Milan is where the work is, even if that work only affords a cage-like existence in a miserable metropolis.

After a while I discovered that 'foreign' actually meant Albanian, African, Asian, Eastern European or black, but such precise prejudice wouldn't fit on the property files. Being Australian wasn't a handicap after all; in fact most landlords warmed to the prospect of having a tenant from a country they admired. It obviously hadn't occurred to them that Australia is about as far south as you can get, unless you rent your apartment to a penguin. How absurd that I should have been more attractive to Milanese landlords than Daniela—a fellow Italian.

After six weeks' searching we faced the prospect of Christmas at Francesco's. What do you give a lover of killer fish for Christmas? A bathing suit? Then, one frozen morning, fog free no less, I was first to inspect a smart and affordable *monolocale*—studio apartment—in a reasonably central location. Close to Milan's main cemetery, the best-kept part of town, the apartment was only slightly bigger than many of its tombs. Twenty-eight square metres, €600 a month, and an Irish pub just a stumble away in the direction of the cemetery; my mother always said drink would lead to the grave. It wasn't perfect, but it would do. The search was over. Christmas on our own.

I paid the agent a blocking deposit before accompanying him to the office. When I called Daniela to tell her to drop everything and join us, I hoped her relief would lead to forgiveness for the apartment's algae-green walls. In fact they quite resembled those of the fish tank we were desperate to escape, as did the landlady its savage occupants. The young woman from Padova, who promptly arrived at the agency to question us further and complete the contract, made it abundantly clear that she was making an exception by renting Daniela her flat. I suppose we should have been flattered. When the deal was closed I saw the agent strike a line through *NIENTE STRANIERI*.

Before putting us on his books, the agent proposed a deal with the unabashed ease of someone who makes a habit of ignoring the law. If we didn't care to pay tax on the agency fee, an arrangement in his favour as much as in ours, he would reduce the price significantly and enter our transaction in a book which could be made to disappear in the time it took the Receipt Police to climb the stairs. If we wished to pay the tax, however, the price would increase and he would enter our exchange in the official register. I wondered who was the more corrupt: the northerner proposing fraud or the southerner seriously considering the offer.

We declined the offer of coffee by saying we were double-parked, to which the agent replied 'So am I' before reaching for cigarettes. Driving back to Francesco's, home for a day or two yet, we passed an abandoned park whose waist-high grass was scaling a sign declaring the park to be in need of a sponsor. Perhaps if they paid those taxes . . .

A quick drink to celebrate, before preparing invitations for the housewarming party, including directions to the flat and the name on the doorbell.

It would have been nice to conclude this account with news of my parcel's eventual arrival, but *Poste Italiane* deliver happy endings as often as they do the mail.

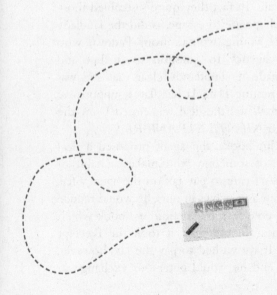

Love songs, cleavage and conversation

January's cold conclusion is a seven-day shiver from the twenty-fourth to the thirtieth, known as *i giorni della merla*—the days of the blackbird. Legend has it that a large white bird, in an attempt to escape Italy's coldest week of the year, sought refuge in a chimney from which it emerged black. While the legend may be questionable, the cold is all too real. Siberian winds invade the city and the evening sky turns a shade of orange. But the teasing colour is as warm as a mirage is thirst-quenching.

For Milan's homeless it's a week of tougher than usual improvisation, with many a tramp driven to trespass by sub-zero temperatures. Such was the plight of one iced itinerant found snoring on the back seat of Daniela's car one morning. She woke the vagrant and rewarded him for not stealing the coins in the console by donating them towards his breakfast. Saying nothing, the man trudged off with all he owned under one arm, eyeing the vague promise of spring at the corner of the sky.

The harsh winter was worsened by circular emails in my inbox each morning regarding the annual Boys' Weekend back in Oz. While I froze in Milan, old schoolmates in Sydney were zipping across the harbour on my best mate's catamaran, beer in hand for extra ballast. For the first time I was homesick.

Fortunately our new apartment offered warmth and well-being. Francesco's friend Michele had insisted we cook fish on our first night as tenants in order to ward off evil spirits, a Sicilian tradition, although I suggested changing the locks would be a sounder guarantee. Between my cynicism and his superstition we had little in common. When he arrived for dinner and saw our tiny flat, Michele—who lived in 18 square metres, remember—declared: '*La Madonna!* It's enormous. And you've got a full-size fridge!' Five years in Milan had warped his concept of size and space.

A 30 per cent surcharge was levied on our utility bills because we were residents of another province. However, the damage from this unwelcoming law was minimal as we discovered one of the few benefits of living in a matchbox—it could be heated by lighting a match. Our deaf neighbour helped us economise further as we could hear the nightly news without troubling our own television, and, being a first-floor flat, it was more than adequately lit by a street lamp about a metre from our window. It was a pleasure to finally have our own place, the strenuous result of overdue privacy warming it even more.

Although I had the sneaking suspicion Milan wouldn't be home for long, we were settling in better than expected. I was happier in my new job teaching English than I had been copy-writing with Francesco. Whether hurt or happy to see the back of me, Daniela's brother had been most agreeable regarding my bid for independence, even helping me look for work and, on one occasion, before I changed field completely, teeing me up an interview at the publishing house of one of his clients.

During the interview I scanned the pages of the publisher's portfolio—the monthly magazines of the *Polizia* and *Carabinieri*, in which I found glossy heroics similar to those on the station walls in Loritano. The large office was minimally furnished with a marble floor and an echo, so what I didn't understand first time round I picked up on its return. Reading between the lines of the job description, I realised my skills as an English speaker were sought purely to call America in search of two scoundrels who had taken their money for an internet contract and run. I was quick to refuse what sounded more a yarn for the publisher's glorified newsletters than an offer of gainful employment.

The idea of teaching came to me in the Irish pub near home,

where I struck up a conversation with the only Englishman in the bar. Danny had been living in Milan for fifteen years and had nothing positive to say other than that the locals were 'so crap at golf' that he won every tournament he entered. He loathed the place, describing it as 'the Third World disguised as the First'. Everything bothered this twitchy expat: the people, the pollution, the football played by 'girls who cried when tackled and kissed when they scored', the lifestyle, the rubbish, the fog, the furs, the fake tans and above all the fashion, which he described as 'superficial nonsense for superficial people'. But Danny loved one thing—his wife, who just happened to be from Milan. What they had in common was anybody's guess.

Seeing me as a potential ally, or at least an objective ear, Danny shouted several rounds of overpriced Guinness, 'merry mud' as he called it, and we vandalised our livers while he vented his spleen. The way the Italians drove was Danny's biggest gripe, particularly because his eldest daughter was approaching driving age. 'The only chance she's got of driving on these streets is inside a fucking armoured tank,' said Danny into his pint, a view he knew well. Then a Vespa roared past the bar, maximising its noise and irritating the Englishman who shot to his feet yelling: 'I hope you die, fella, alone and in pain!' I think it's fair to say that Danny wasn't sold on *la dolce vita*.

Like a prisoner with no escape plan, chain-smoking Danny was tense. His love of his wife was obviously greater than his hatred of her country, yet she was costing him sanity, self-respect and a fortune down the pub. A fast-talking, slow-ticking time-bomb, the Englishman was something of a warning: having failed Barzini's challenge he was proof that I might too. I made myself a promise to abandon my adventure should I ever resemble him. Which is why it made no sense that I then accepted his job offer. Having identified the enemy, I went and joined its ranks. Perhaps I was more Italian than I thought.

Despite never having taught English before—not necessary according to Danny—the challenge was less the job than getting to and from it alive. I worked from three until nine at a private college about a forty-minute drive from home, and in my six-month career made only slightly more money than the cost of damages incurred while commuting.

Daniela had herself been involved in a three-car quarrel on her way home from work one afternoon, and had replaced Napoleon with a second-hand Lancia bought from a friend of Francesco's. It was no armoured tank, but it offered more protection than its predecessor on roads that had driven Danny to drink and soon did the same to me.

Even the most cautious Italian drives as though a pregnant passenger's waters have broken; the rest engage in a dangerous cross between dodgems and a demolition derby. The most hazardous part of my daily commute was Milan's *circonvallazione* or ring-road. Despite being as wide as a runway, something most people seemed convinced it was, it had no lanes marked in either direction and more black spots than a Dalmatian. Motorists drove as if theirs were the only vehicles on the road, flashing lights to scatter slower cars and beeping horns if disobeyed; like the film *Speed,* it was as if they had bombs on board that would detonate if they stopped. I usually cruised around 20 kilometres an hour over the speed limit (whatever that was) and was menaced, flashed and forced to yield by those who found my going sluggish.

Allergic to the briefest delay, when traffic became blocked some motorists even mounted the footpath to avoid the impasse. Those who did queue hedged their bets on which line would move away first by positioning themselves between both, a time-saving tactic which achieved little other than lengthening both queue and chaos. Zebra crossings were faded and ignored, as were the pedestrians who braved them. I stopped at one to let a woman cross and she curtsied and blew me a kiss.

Accidents were par for the course. On one trip I witnessed a motorcyclist collect a double-parked car while attempting an inside pass of a bus. He was one of over 7000 people who died on Italy's roads that year. *Vigili* arrived and drew a chalk outline round the corpse. Driving over it for the next few days felt like treading on the man's grave. Then it rained and he disappeared.

The biggest menace were the Vespas because heavy traffic failed to slow them down; in fact most daredevils, like in Andrano, welcomed the thrill of obstructions. Vespas are motorcycles when it suits their riders and bicycles when it doesn't. It's a split-second transformation, the time it takes to mount the gutter and blaze away on the footpath. They terrorise motorists and pedestrians, causing half of city accidents. Examples of perpetual motion, they weave to the front of queues like fleas up a dog's back, before dodging delay and buzzing away without a foot ever touching the ground.

One afternoon I saw two boys on a Vespa run a red light and scatter pedestrians on a zebra crossing like seagulls on a beach. An elderly man launched his shoe at the pair who by then were nothing but the smell of four-stroke. A *vigile* witnessed the lunacy and blew his whistle until red in the face, but realised pursuit was futile on a bicycle. Italy's municipal police must be the most impotent on the planet, serving little purpose at intersections other than decoration. In fact their elegant uniforms are so elaborate they once caused a strike over how much paid time should be allocated to putting them on.

If Vespas welcomed traffic for the thrill it provided, beggars did the same for the food it provided. Haggard homeless manned almost every intersection, men, women and children, window cleaner at the ready or a feeble hand outstretched. Many were maimed or deformed. An Albanian I passed each day had lost a leg and three fingers. By the time he struggled to the windows of most vehicles, they had already moved on. But I waited and flipped him a coin no matter how long it took his leg to collect my alms, often earning me a beep from the bastards behind.

City beggars relied on traffic congestion for donations because if they relied on red lights to stop traffic they'd have been waiting forever. The students for whom I risked my neck each afternoon complained that English was difficult because of its many double meanings, to which I replied that they had underestimated their own language, for only in Italian does *semaforo rosso*—red light— mean 'stop' or 'go if you can'. 'That's different,' one objected. 'A red light is advice, not an obligation.'

Most of the accidents I was involved in resulted from similar contempt for red lights, the most serious caused by a driver who disregarded a red at a roundabout, collecting my tail and prompting me to perform an elegant if frightening pirouette. Apportioning blame is difficult with a man capable of disregarding a red light while cradling a baby in his arms, speaking on the phone and allowing his nine-year-old to roam the cabin as he would a jumping castle.

If you think red-light cameras could solve the problem, think again. In my time at the Italian wheel I've only seen two, in the tiny southern settlements of Diso and Marittima. And the one in Marittima only makes the intersection more dangerous, as drivers dodge the sensor pad by veering onto the wrong side of the road.

Another accident was actually caused by my refusal to ignore a red; bloody law-abiders, always causing problems. Stationary at an intersection, I was being beeped because I wouldn't budge, when a Vespa scurried past, relieving me of my wing-mirror and furrowing a scratch in my door. Amazingly the rider blamed me for the sideswipe, swatting his hand and shaking his head. I was still cursing by the time I arrived at school, where 'I told you so' greeted me as I stormed through the door. Danny was openly sympathetic but quietly delighted. He had found himself a drinking partner.

My rewards for arriving at school were the fear of driving home—the shambles just described, only in darkness and thick fog—and a bunch of idle students interested in gaining a foreign friend more than a foreign tongue. At their companies' expense, lawyers, accountants and architects showed up for class without pen or paper. Those paying their own way were a little more studious but just as inclined to chat. I was happy to let them talk, reminding them every so often to do so in English rather than Italian.

Invariably my drive to work became the topic of conversation. The students helped me understand the bedlam on the bitumen, at times lamenting with me, at times admitting to being part of the problem, but more often doing both with unblinking hypocrisy. A young bank clerk called Angelo, beginner in English but expert on Italy, tried to calm me one evening after my late arrival due to heavy traffic—a slight role reversal but never mind. The standstill had been caused by a police car parked in the middle of the road. I could see its flashing lights from the back of the queue and was ready to forgive the delay if it meant some justice on the roads. But when I finally passed the car fifteen minutes later, the *poliziotti* I had expected to find writing tickets were laughing together in a kerb-side café, hats on the bar while they devoured a pizza. Angelo listened to my story before saying: 'Yes, but they were not police because Italy does not have a police force. Well, actually we have four, but none are any good. They should get rid of all of them and give us one we can trust.'

Mistakenly believing Angelo's ear sympathetic, I shared my gripes about Italians behind the wheel. He agreed that the road toll was an avoidable disaster, but claimed it to be the result of too many cars in too little space rather than a reflection of the talents of Italian drivers whom he insisted were 'the best *natural* drivers in the world.'

'So it's got nothing to do with the speed you drive at, Angelo?'

'*Assolutamente no.* If we had to obey your stupid speed limits our road toll would be worse from people falling asleep at the wheel.'

I waited for a smile that never came.

'And nothing to do with people ignoring red lights and not wearing seat-belts?'

'Seat-belts are dangerous because they are uncomfortable and restrict movement. I've only worn a seat-belt twice and both times I had accidents.'

It was the only ride Angelo would ever take me for.

If, by some miracle, my trip to school had been uneventful, the conversation would find fuel in some other debacle I was digesting. This was because most students wanted to know what I thought of their country, and while I tried hard to flatter, which usually meant banging on about food or cathedrals, an honest response was often a negative one. But I soon realised that they were as frustrated with certain facets of Italian life as I was, and that criticism, provided it was voiced more tactfully than Danny's rants, was not a novelty.

An attractive travel agent named Katia asked me how I found life in Milan on the very day Telecom Italia broke their umpteenth promise to connect my phone. Fuck food and cathedrals, she deserved to know the truth, even if the buxom brunette with a fur handbag should have been conjugating the verb 'to be'.

Our new apartment had a phone connection, we just needed to have it activated and be given a phone and phone number. The first day we called Telecom they said they would call us back (on the mobile I assumed) to advise a time when a technician would come by the house. We heard nothing for the next two days so on the fourth we rang and were advised to fax certain documents which would speed up the process: *carta d'identità, codice fiscale* and so on. On the fifth day they failed to call so Daniela called on the sixth and was told they'd be coming at midday on the seventh day—it sounds like the Creation, but that was a breeze compared to this.

When the technician didn't show, Daniela called and discovered that Telecom Italia was on strike. On the eighth day we called and asked if our appointment for yesterday was valid today. Yes it was, they assured us, but then didn't turn up anyway. On the ninth day they said they were coming tomorrow, reminding an exasperated Daniela that by law they had ten days to respond to our initial request, and that tomorrow was really only the seventh day because the weekend didn't count and neither did the strike day. Time was going backwards.

On the tenth day a technician stuck a screwdriver in our socket, twisted it to the left slightly, gave us a hefty bill and made for the door.

'*Il telefono?*' inquired Daniela.

'The telephone will be delivered in the next ten days,' he replied.

If we needed a phone urgently, said the woman at Telecom Italia, we could go to one of the following addresses and pick one up. We followed her directions to a butcher shop, where a man with a skinned rabbit in his hands said he was tired of people asking for telephones rather than sausages. The second address checked out but they had no phones in stock, so we bought one at an electronics store and the saga was over, as was Katia's English lesson.

I had expected the comely travel consultant to raise one of her plucked eyebrows at my tale of woe, but instead she nodded her head and recounted a similar fiasco. While fiddling with the top three buttons on her blouse, which no doubt her boyfriend would have preferred done up, Katia went on to explain that public-sector workers in Italy can neither be sacked for incompetence nor promoted for diligence, and that the private sector is only marginally better due to arcane laws that favour employees over employers. Apparently it goes back to the aftermath of World War II, when the government thought the best way to counter unemployment was to make sackings illegal. The teacher was learning more than the students.

Other than Katia's plunging neckline, my favourite part of the job was walking into a classroom and finding vocabulary left on the whiteboard by the teacher of a previous class. Like an investigator sifting through clues, I would guess at the topics of ghost conversations by analysing their remaining parts. With a keen eye on current affairs this was often an easy process. One Monday afternoon, following a weekend when football giants Juventus had controversially been handed the championship, much to the dismay of Milan supporters, I inherited a whiteboard featuring the words: rigged, referee, bribe, disgrace, corner-kick and Rolex watch. And the day after Silvio Berlusconi was elected *primo ministro*, despite his hailing from Milan the whiteboard once again sang of scandal: fixed, corrupt, dishonest, monkey, circus, narcissistic, dwarf.

Sometimes the puzzle was more cryptic and took longer to solve. Once I was so mystified by the combination of: snorkel, tongue, spa bath, prawn cocktail, ear infection and moonlight, that I was forced to admit defeat and ask the teacher of the class before mine what her conversation had been about. Apparently her student had been on holiday to a Red Sea resort in Egypt.

I doubt there are simpler jobs than holding conversation classes with Italians. It was a different story with foreign students, however, like tight-lipped Viktoria from Moscow, the twenty-something mail-order bride of a wealthy Milanese businessman. Perfectly beautiful with golden hair and the soft-rose cheeks of a Russian doll, Viktoria conducted herself with high-heeled confidence despite the fact she had about as much liberty as a deer trapped in headlights. Her buyer was over sixty and kept her among other display items in his Milanese mansion. There she lived with the children from previous marriages who were older than their shapely step-mum. Herself reticent, Viktoria became something of a talking point at the school. When she arrived for class in a black Mercedes, the secretary would stick her head around the staff room door and announce: 'The princess will have her lesson now.' But this princess was far from happy. Her sapphire eyes were as empty as they were alluring, and during our clumsy conversations she drew verbal sketches of the 'perfect' life that left the speaker as sad as the listener.

But the majority of students were talkative Italians with whom conversation flowed into friendship. Friendship forged with oddball characters like Claudio, who invited me to his father's winery to help bottle a delicious home-made vintage. Short and shifty with a smart-alec smile, Claudio was seventeen and still at school, where he may have laid the foundations towards his dream of becoming a vet if he studied as much as he talked. For most of our lesson Claudio's Shakespeare reader remained closed, while he tried to sell me an array of discount merchandise including Armani at half-price, mobile phones at cost, and free entry to Milan's most popular nightclubs. One afternoon I made the mistake of telling him that I had missed out on tickets to the famous Milan–Inter Milan derby at the San Siro stadium. My mobile rang later that night.

'You have two options,' said Claudio. 'I've got one friend with two tickets which he'll sell you for one hundred and fifty euros each, or I've got a mate who prints them himself who'll give you two for twenty-five.'

Claudio urged me to take the cheaper option.

'Where would I be sitting?'

'Er, you wouldn't be sitting,' he replied reluctantly. 'You stand in one of the stairwells and if the police come you just walk to another part of the stadium.'

'Sounds like a ticket to prison, Claudio.'

'No no. Don't worry. We use them all the time.'

'So why does your other friend have tickets worth a hundred and fifty?'

Only Shakespeare could stump Claudio quicker.

I fashioned another unlikely friendship with a man named Raffaele whom I taught English on Thursdays and played tennis with on Sundays—when he wasn't at the football, that is. Raffaele was a member of the *ultras*, hardcore supporters who made a nuisance of themselves by lighting flares and hurling fruit, coins, insults, bottles and anything else not tied down. The *ultras* of San Siro even smuggled a motorbike into the stadium, set it on fire and threw it off the top tier onto the crowd below. Red-faced security officials' only defence must have been that the *criminali* had perhaps brought the bike into the stadium in pieces and assembled it inside.

Mild-mannered outside the stadium, Raffaele made it clear

that he was being sent to class by his boss and would sooner talk football in Italian. On one occasion he was excited to hear that we were both going to the same match, a Champions League fixture between Chelsea and his beloved Milan. The evening after the game, Raffaele showed up for class with a question on his lips, pertaining to English no less—there's a first time for everything. 'What were the English supporters calling out all night?' When I eventually found an adequate translation of 'fucking Eyetie cunts', even ribald Raffaele was shocked. '*La Madonna!*' he exclaimed. 'Even we're not that bad.'

Friendships were made more easily in one-to-one classes. Aware of the intimacy of such encounters, the school had glass doors to each classroom. At their first lesson most students broke the ice by bringing up food, not literally of course, with some asking what my favourite Italian dish was and one even offering to cook it for me. Tiziana was a flirtatious brunette with a pert, proud and protuberant bust kept on display despite the winter. Taller than most of my male students, she carried hourglass measurements with daunting confidence; even had I been interested in conjugating anything other than verbs with her I would have been too inhibited to make the first move. Stylish and seductive, she was far too occupied socially to ever find time to study, and I can't remember a lesson when she didn't receive a call, either from a fashion boutique advising that her order had arrived, or about hair and beauty appointments being confirmed or rescheduled.

Two days before her exam, Tiziana pressed me for the answers, making it clear that were I interested in finding where her fake tan finished it would certainly be worth my while. When I politely declined she realised she would fail and skipped the exam altogether. She had done the course to prepare for an Alitalia entrance test which I presumed she would skip now as well. But a month later she dropped by the school to let me know she'd passed and was working at the check-in desk. To celebrate I shared an innocent glass of champagne with her at the bar over the road, careful not to spoil the moment by asking where she had found the answers.

Claudia from Sicily was more subtle than Tiziana but likewise put sex before study. Although teachers weren't supposed to do translations, I had difficulty refusing her strawberry-blonde requests to translate love songs of her own composition. It was when she insisted on singing them to ensure correct pronunciation that I was forced to object, not only because she expected me to join in, but because there were ten other classrooms in close proximity and I was a worse singer than I was a translator.

Lessons were not all love songs, cleavage and conversation. In group classes mainly, I strove to improve the students' English as much as they had my Italian. Most found English frustratingly complicated and one even brought in scientific evidence to explain why. Francesca from Bologna, five o'clock Wednesdays and Fridays, had found an article in *Il Corriere della Sera* which suggested English to be harder to learn than Italian, German, or even Japanese, because of the way words are pronounced differently from the way they are spelt: I am *shore/sure* you *know/no* what I mean. The scientists claimed that English employs two parts of the brain as opposed to just one for Italian, where words are pronounced as they are spelt. 'Could you take that into account when marking my next exam?' asked Francesca, so sweetly that I thought I might.

Francesca was my favourite student because she brought her sausage dog to class. Bruno the bilingual Dachshund sat patiently at the desk beside his mistress and growled at anyone who disputed it as his rightful place. After putting a question to the class I would go round the room for answers, only to arrive at Bruno looking up brightly with the pink of his tongue poking out. He seemed to enjoy his studies and attended more regularly than some of my two-legged students. Francesca's exam results were always superior to her performance in class, to such an extent that I accidentally offended her by asking if she wrote the answers on the flip-side of Bruno's ears.

Francesca's biggest problem with English was that of the majority of her classmates—pronunciation. English demanded she do things with her tongue that it was reluctant to do, like say the word 'the' for example. The definite article moved her tongue in the vicinity of her front teeth, somewhere Italian didn't force it to go and which felt unusually sharp as a result. Italians have great difficulty with the 'th' sound; one child even burst into tears during class for fear she would bite off her tongue. Francesca would only attempt the word after hearing me say it a dozen times and then showing her my tongue was still intact. She eventually got the hang of it, after cleaning up the spit from several failed attempts. Only Tiziana nailed it first go, but her tongue was used to a challenge.

I often learnt more about my students when teaching them English than when conversing in Italian, like the time I was explaining *should* and *shouldn't*. The textbook provided some hypothetical examples which I read to the class like a quiz.

'You're stopped at a red light but there's nothing coming. *Should* you go or *shouldn't* you?'

'*Shouldn't*,' replied the class in chorus.

It was heartening to think they at least knew the laws they ignored.

'You're in an airport and you want to smoke. There's no sign saying that you can't but an airport is a public place. *Should* you smoke or *shouldn't* you?'

This time their correct response was ruined by one man who said: '*Should*. Even if there is a sign—*should*.'

The same stubborn student had difficulty with the difference between *supposed to* and *obliged to*. After examples from the textbook, his face was still blank, so I thought up some more and the penny finally dropped.

'Ah, like taxes,' he said, smiling.

'Sorry?'

'We are *supposed to* pay them.'

Once again I reluctantly marked a wrong answer right.

The staff room was as much fun as the classroom. My colleagues were a peculiar bunch of expats, Brits mainly, who had fallen in love with either Italy or Italians and stumbled upon teaching as mistakenly as I had. Regardless of how long they had lived in Italy or how fluently they spoke Italian, there remained that displaced part of them that Italy could never satisfy as a night down the pub with fellow castaways could. Apart from Danny, we were the happiest of shipwrecks.

If, by Wednesday, none of the staff had mentioned our Friday night drink, Danny would pipe up and remind us. He would arrive at the pub first and reserve a table which he was invariably under by the time company showed up. But Danny didn't need company, indeed his most interesting conversations were the ones he conducted with himself after several pints of his murky pleasure. I found it entertaining to sit back and listen while he ruminated on topics such as how the hotel across the street had lost one of only two stars. Band-Aids covered the second star on a sign outside the grimy building, a downgrade Danny described as: 'Crummy, hygienic, and the most honest thing I've seen in Italy in over a decade.'

Concerned that his frank hatred of Italy would cloud my own experience, I had tried to distance Danny. But our fear of the roads united us and he saw me as something of a confidant. So when the phone rang after eleven one evening, who else could it have been? I picked up to hear his booming voice unusually meek and trembling.

'What's wrong, mate?' I asked. 'The Guinness worn off again?'

'Worse. I've run over a nun. Meet me at the pub, will you?'

Danny had skittled the sister in his Citroen. Fortunately she was only bruised. He on the other hand was a wreck and took three pints to pacify. When he did finally relax, he sat back in his chair and declared: 'Thank God she was a nun. Anyone else would have sued me rather than blessed me.' My work was done. He was his irreverent self again.

If Danny demanded I drink, David demanded I gamble. A

middle-aged Irishman who had first come to Italy as a teenager to mow lawns at a Roman convent, he had since married and moved to Milan where he'd been teaching, and gambling, ever since. What disturbed me about David's dependency was not the money he wasted but the obscure things he found on which to bet. If I arrived at work and there was a plum cake in my in-tray, David's team had come up trumps in the Siberian third division.

He lived above a betting shop run by a Croatian who could offer him good odds on Hungarian wrestling, Belgian water polo, even the Eurovision Song Contest. I refused to flutter on foreign fixtures but joined him every week playing *Totocalcio*—where we had to pick the results of Italian football matches, *Totogol*—where we had to guess how many goals would be kicked by certain clubs, and *Totosei*—another football tipping competition which I bet on to satisfy David but still don't understand enough to describe. Given the fact we never won, I'm not sure he did either.

The owner of the school, Rachael, had lived in Italy for twenty years and spoke fluent Italian with a Yorkshire accent. An eccentric expat, she too had inter-married but was happy with her decision to do so. Unlike Danny, who was always threatening to move back to England, Rachael was convinced she would never return to Blighty for more than a summer holiday; whether this was out of affection for Italy or the barrels of money her English school reeled in I wasn't sure. Like many foreigners who adopt Italy, she referred to it as 'home' when complimenting and 'abroad' when criticising. She disagreed with Danny over the lifestyle and said Italy's charm was only visible to the charming, an insult Danny took on the double chin. But on the subject of law enforcement, Rachael was scathing. In twenty years she'd had seven cars stolen, one of them twice and which, the second time round, she found abandoned under a bridge on a main road. 'The police couldn't find it when they were supposed to be out looking for it,' she said, 'but I stumbled across it while shopping.'

The only rule in the staff room was that the door remain shut during exam time so that no student could spot their contribution to the comical errors we wrote on the whiteboard. Certain mistakes were too delightful not to be shared:

I'm sorry I couldn't come to your party last weekend but I was taking a grope in the mountains. David knew the ski instructor well and said he had marked it correct because it probably wasn't a mistake.

My sister has tin legs and a blonde hair. 'She sounds tremendous,' Danny had scribbled alongside. 'Is she free on Friday night?'

I got a beautiful bug for my birthday.

Every Easter we catch a fast dog to Corsica.

Last week my dog bought my wife.

Roberto Benigni wanks in the cinema. 'I'm not his biggest fan either.' Danny again.

They all laughed. But I couldn't help picturing a fat Sicilian telling his friends about the fool of a foreigner who asked to hire a paedophile for an hour, and sympathised as much as I laughed.

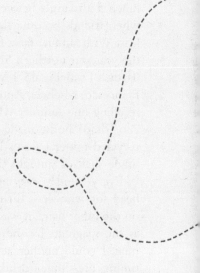

Sunday Night *Spaghettata*

Having flown the family coop, a group of southern friends relocated to Italy's north, where they formed another family whose intimacy was based on distance. It was not your average Italian family, today among the smallest in Europe, it was the Italian family of old, of stereotype and Fellini: half a dozen people with napkins at their collars crammed around a table sipping wine and slurping spaghetti.

Sunday is a sacred day. After religious obligations early, Italians lunch with family before spending the evening with friends. But when friends become family, Sunday evening becomes a family feast. With familiar faces from Sicily who worked in Milan during the year, our northern Sunday evenings had a distinctly southern flavour. Daniela and I would dine, drink and play *Scopa* with Francesco, Michele, Antonio, his wife Adele, Sergio and Luisa, recalling one summer while planning the next. Accompanied by Zio Tonio's home-made white, which he shipped us regularly in recycled mineral water bottles, Sunday Night *Spaghettata* was a single shaft of sunlight through Milan's cement sky.

Every Sunday evening like clockwork, Daniela and I would head for whoever's turn it was to host the spaghetti soiree. If, on the other hand, it was our turn to cook, I would be as twisted as the spaghetti by the time guests arrived at around half-past nine; I could neither accustom myself to eating so late nor to timing pre-dinner drinks accordingly. My Italian friends were shocked by how much I drank, particularly as I told them I was drinking far less since moving to Italy. And when I said that in

Australia we fill the bath with beer when hosting a party, I confirmed their suspicions that I was descended from a long line of alcoholics.

Unless you've fallen off your moped, stumbling or slurring your words is considered bad form in Italy. Drinking is perfectly acceptable. Getting drunk is not. It's a question of culture. Having been given wine at the dinner table since they were old enough to ask what it was, my Italian friends hadn't arrived at eighteen salivating for the illicit drop. The legal drinking age is not an issue in Italy, indeed many Italians don't even know what it is. Not because they're so drunk they've forgotten, but because they're so sober they couldn't care less. The age of consent, however, is a completely different story.

Italians don't need alcohol to anaesthetise inhibitions. On the beach in Andrano over the summer, I had joined in sober sing-alongs with Daniela's friends that would have taken my Australian mates several bottles of bourbon to attempt. It didn't take spirits to raise spirits, and I found it refreshing to retire to bed on a Saturday night without the ceiling spinning.

Sunday Night *Spaghettata* wasn't for teetotallers, they simply wouldn't let a drop of alcohol past their lips were it not in the slipstream of food. This ensured they never got drunk, even if they tricked themselves into thinking they were drinking less by only half-filling their glasses. Daniela's cousin Antonio stifled a grin when denying that half-filling a glass twice was the same as filling it once, and who was I to ruin canny traditions with boring truths? When the night was over they grabbed car keys without questioning alcohol intake. None of them knew the legal limit, and none of them had ever been stopped by police, who probably didn't know either.

The idea of a shared Sunday meal arose after the eight of us had been to a park to throw a boomerang I had given Michele. I had expected him to do as other friends who'd received a boomerang had done, either display it on his mantelpiece or lose it in a bottom drawer. Instead, the excitable Sicilian demanded a lesson in how to throw it, and given my nationality, he assumed I knew.

Where can you throw a boomerang in Milan? Open spaces are not a salient feature of the city and throwing it in most parks would mean losing it in unsponsored grass. Now there was an idea: lose it on the first throw and be home in time for the football. Finding a launch site proved difficult, and just when I thought we had given up on the idea, Adele, who lived outside Milan in a suburb called Rho, suggested the park near her and Antonio's apartment. 'It's enormous,' she said. 'And well maintained.' Michele clapped his hands and I reluctantly agreed, thankful I hadn't bought him a didgeridoo or I'd have been giving a recital.

The following Sunday we gathered at Adele and Antonio's before heading to the park in convoy, just as we had done in Sicily on our trips to the beach. Hundreds of parents, children and pets were soaking up some novel sunshine, far too many to hurl a deadly weapon whose only chance of returning was in a bag marked 'Exhibit A'. Like an overzealous astronaut, Michele refused to abandon the launch and insisted we wait until the crowd cleared. Towards dusk, with the temperature dropping faster than the number of picnickers, my students eyed their teacher eagerly, the long delay having raised their expectations.

'Did the Aborigines use it for anything besides sport ?' asked Michele, taking the boomerang from its original wrapping paper and handing it to me.

'They used it for hunting, didn't they, Chris?' said Daniela.

'*Si*,' I answered vaguely, trying to recall the list of instructions on how to throw the damn thing; in their eyes, to have read from it would have been like needing the words to sing my national anthem.

'For hunting?' repeated Adele. 'What's for dinner then, Crris?'

I took a hopeful backswing and launched the bent stick dead straight, before it plummeted to earth and was set upon by a cocker spaniel.

'Looks like spaghetti,' said Antonio. 'Shall we go back to our place?'

Every Sunday evening from then on, the group gathered to share what's called a *spaghettata*—a simple bowl of spaghetti. The staple ingredient didn't mean our meals lacked variety. In fact I doubt whether I twice ate spaghetti done the same way unless specifically requested, usually by yours truly. Food is one aspect of life that improves when you live rather than travel in Italy. Like the language, though more fattening, it was something I simply couldn't get enough of. In Australia I ate to live. In Italy I lived to eat.

My favourite was Daniela's *spaghetti alle vongole*—spaghetti with clams and white wine. Also delicious was Luisa's *spaghetti alla Mediterranea*—a simple dish she described as 'the real Italian flag', with green *basilico*, white spaghetti and red *pomodoro*; if eating it was treason then I was willing to hang. Adele's specialities were either *spaghetti alle melanzane*—tomato and eggplant, or *al gusto vivo* with tuna, mushrooms and tomato. Her husband's *spaghetti ai funghi* was delightful, as was his *mare e monti* with seafood and mushrooms. Francesco liked to experiment in the kitchen and often attempted sauces of his own invention. I rarely asked what was in them, but always counted the fish in his tank just in case he'd tried *spaghetti alla piranha*. Sergio could whip up a *carbonara* in minutes, and Michele's *aglio, olio e peperoncino* was so spicy it almost heated his tiny flat. My contribution involved buying dessert from the *pasticceria* down the street and making sure everyone's glass was half-full.

Describing the role of the Italian family, Luigi Barzini wrote:

Where legal authority is weak and the law is resented and resisted, the safety and welfare of the individual are mainly assured by the family. The Italian family is a stronghold in a hostile land: within its walls and among its members the individual finds consolation, help, advice, provisions, loans, weapons, allies and accomplices to aid him in his pursuits. No Italian who has a family is ever alone.

A southern legion on a northern battlefield, our Sunday night family served the purposes Barzini describes in every department except loans and weapons, unless you count the boomerang. A source of counsel and support, it was often used to round-table problems that were depriving someone of sleep: relationships, car accidents or some cryptic Italian law. Italians are wary of State and statute and will consult family when dealing with either. But with the lowest birth rate in Europe, Italian families are no longer the reserve of wisdom they were when Barzini was writing, so Antonio was forced to consult his second family on an obscure law causing him headaches over a new addition to his first.

I was climbing a mountain of Barilla when Antonio asked: 'Crris, how does the name A-S-J-A sound in English?'

'Depending on how you pronounce it, like a detergent or a continent. Why?'

Adele was expecting a baby girl whom Antonio wished to name Asia. But he had heard of a case in Torino where, due to a 1930s law stipulating no child could be named after a geographical place, one child had been forced to change her name. Other than tampering with the spelling of the name, Antonio was researching the issue as best he could. He had even found the website of a famous Italian actress, Asia Argento, and sent her an email asking if she'd encountered any problems sharing her name with a continent. He was yet to receive a reply, so Sunday Night *Spaghettata* that particular evening was spent searching for a solution to his dilemma.

Antonio had received conflicting reports as to whether the dubious decree still existed. Apparently one office said it did while another said it didn't. This worried the already proud father of one, who was less concerned by the actual law than the potential for misinterpretation by those policing it. Taking the wrong advice now could result in the arrival of a letter, anytime between his daughter's birth and death, demanding she change her name and throwing her life into disarray. Francesco had recently received a similar letter claiming he had underpaid his tax five years ago and could he please prove otherwise or pay a fine. Together with his *avvocato*, he devised a confusing response and that was the last he heard of the matter—well, for another five years at least.

I was less surprised by the bizarre law than by the fact no one else at the table found it bizarre. Au fait with the absurd, they merely listened intently before advising Antonio on his best course of action. Every member of the panel made a suggestion. Francesco first proposed they turn the child's nickname into her real name by calling her Anna on the forms and Asia to her face. After a few more half-glasses of wine, he said they could even call her Beatrice on the forms as long as Asia was the name to which she grew accustomed. Antonio was sceptical, saying those who didn't know his daughter personally would call her by her official name, causing trouble at school and in later life. Daniela suggested it was Francesco who'd have trouble in later life and told her brother to shut up.

Michele suggested Antonio declare he was naming the baby Asia after the nut or the bird rather than the continent. He said he didn't know if such a nut or bird existed but neither would the people at births, deaths and marriages. This preposterous suggestion proved Michele the real nut, and he too received a serving from Daniela, despite it not being her turn to cook. For all its flaws, the Italian government sure spices up dinner conversation.

'What about spelling her name A-S-I-E?' suggested Luisa, who went on to question the existence of the law by saying friends of hers in Sicily had recently named their daughter Ginevra— Geneva in Italian.

'Perhaps they spelt it with a J,' said Sergio.

'No,' replied Antonio, 'every region is different and they probably don't have this law down there, that's all.'

'There's an idea,' said Luisa. 'Go home to have the baby and register her in Sicily.'

'But we've changed our residency to Milan,' replied Antonio. And I thought naming the child was the easy part of parenting.

When you breeze through Italy as a tourist and see a policeman smoking in front of a 'No Smoking' sign, illegal immigrants peddling stolen goods as freely as ice-cream, and Vespas swarming the streets with all the order of flies on a carcass, not for a second do you imagine the existence of men like Antonio: disciplined, obedient and going to great lengths to avoid contravening the law. Like those tourists, before meeting Antonio I had wrongly assumed Italy to be a lawless land of glory without hope, in which statute, like stop sign, went unobserved without scruple.

Contrary to popular belief, however, Italians lead highly regimented lives under one of the most cluttered constitutions on the planet. Italy is saturated by senseless statutes: the distance from a shop for which a receipt must be kept, the space between beach umbrellas, and now the naming of children. They are whimsical regulations which Barzini believes

> could paralyse every activity in the land if they were suddenly applied. Nobody knows how many of them are still valid, nobody knows for certain what some of them really mean. Often not even recourse to the records of what lawmakers said years before when debating them in parliament reveals their significance and precise purpose.

I was next in line to give my opinion and suggested naming the baby H-A-S-I-A with H in front. When brows furrowed I wrote the word 'hotel' on a piece of paper and asked Antonio to pronounce it. 'Otel,' he said, obviously, as though I was wasting his time. Then I wrote 'Hasia' and held up the paper again. Antonio's expression changed from sneer to smile. '*Incredibile*,' he declared. 'How did you think of that?' I kept my account of the immigration office in Lecce to a minimum. The silent letter had silenced the debate. Time to raise half-glasses and celebrate.

'Have you started cooking yet?' Michele asked Daniela over the phone one Sunday evening.

'*No. Perchè?*'

'Change of plan. Can we have the *spaghettata* at my place tonight?'

'If you want, but what's up?'

'I need Crris to call New York to find me a hotel and I don't want to use your phone.'

'I thought your travel agent had booked for you.'

'So did I.'

I found the change of venue irritating, not because Michele needed my help to call New York, but because dinner at Michele's was something of a trial. The problem was not his cooking, nor that his apartment lacked the elbow room for eight people to taste it at the same time, but that he lived in the very centre of Milan, where finding a pot of gold at the end of a rainbow would be easier than finding a car park.

Italians own more cars per head of population than any other country in Europe. Their love of the automobile is famous, less so their squabbles over parking them all in a country with more cathedrals than car parks. A man in Naples murdered his neighbour over a parking dispute, and in Sicily two seventy-year-old men bit each other's ears off over who was entitled to 3 metres of asphalt. It's a far cry from the French who, in certain parts of Paris, leave their handbrakes off so other motorists can nudge their cars forwards and backwards to create more space. The Italians demonstrate no such camaraderie.

Like Hollywood police cars arriving at a crime scene, Italians park with creativity and flair. Precision, order and the rights of others are ignored. If a motorist spots two parking spaces separated by a line, which in Milan would be akin to striking oil in your garden, they will park over the line and snare both spaces. Legal options are soon exhausted and motorists have no choice but to mount the footpath or double-park. Any spare concrete is considered fair game, be it across tram lines, bus zones or pedestrian crossings. This keeps Milan's *vigili* in employment, handing out parking tickets as deftly as a dealer in a game of poker.

Even when you're lucky enough to land a legal car park you're still not safe from the bicycle brigade, as I discovered one morning watching the stuff of silent comedy. Before heading into town to do some shopping, I stopped at the bar below our apartment for coffee. From my table by the window I observed a council worker boring a hole in the pavement, while a colleague rang doorbells up and down the street. He was looking for the owner of a car that was causing problems, not because it was illegally parked—or at least, not yet. When I returned home round lunchtime, the workers were gone, there was a 'Disabled Parking Only' sign cemented into the pavement, and a bright yellow rectangle painted around the car. The car was still there when I left for work that afternoon, as it was when I returned home that night. Only now, flapping against the windscreen in the bracing winter breeze, was a ticket for parking in a disabled car park without the required permit. I'll never watch *Candid Camera* again after living in Italy.

Although I was yet to taste someone's ears, the parking situation in Milan was fast whetting my appetite, so when Michele summoned us to his apartment unexpectedly, I jokingly demanded that he come and pick us up. To my surprise he agreed, saying it was on his way home from the airport where he would collect his girlfriend, Carla, who was flying in from Palermo to accompany him to New York. It was to be their first overseas holiday together—subject to my finding them a hotel, of course. But between Michele's search for a car park in Milan, and mine for a hotel room in Manhattan, I considered myself to have the easy job.

When they arrived to pick us up, Carla and Michele were bickering over the booking, which Michele claimed was the travel agent's mistake. Apparently, when he had gone to pick up the tickets and hotel vouchers, the consultant said she had no record of his requesting accommodation with the airfares. In his anger, Michele foolishly paid for the tickets and declared he would find the hotel himself. But when his internet search turned up nothing only twenty-four hours before departure, Michele became stressed and invited an English-speaker to dinner. He hadn't realised it was a holiday weekend in New York, and that The Big Apple, like his small apartment, was bursting at the seams.

The cloud over the trip was straining a delicate situation further. Carla had only told her parents that she was going to Milan for the week. That she was actually destined for New York was to be confessed either later that evening or after arriving in the States, when her parents couldn't stop her from going, if only because she was already there; perhaps she figured she'd have more chance asking forgiveness than permission. But with my initial calls for a hotel room drawing blanks, Carla's lies were coming true. She did indeed look like spending the week in Milan, an observation made by Francesco which caused Carla and Michele to start squabbling again, Daniela to berate her insensitive brother, and the spaghetti to overcook.

For the first time since its inception, Sunday Night *Spaghettata* was a stressful affair; Michele had chosen the wrong night to invite his Japanese friend, Hiroshi. In a glorified cupboard that served as kitchen, bedroom, dining room and lounge, there were ten of us, counting Hiroshi, in Michele's poky pad. Nervous tension filled the room, and with the heater on high it felt as if we were in the saucepan rather than the spaghetti.

Everyone was occupied and pre-occupied. I phoned hotels and called out questions I couldn't answer myself, like would

two singles do? '*Assolutamente no,*' interjected Carla, whose father
would have disagreed. Antonio and Sergio sat with Adele debating
the quickest route from her office to the hospital; she insisted
on working despite a stomach so stretched it looked as though
Asia might arrive while I was chatting with America. Michele
prepared a perfunctory *carbonara* while cursing travel agents,
protective parents and the woman he was supposed to be taking
on a romantic holiday come morning. Francesco listened intently
to my telephone conversation, every so often informing Michele
that he hadn't a clue what I was saying but that my tone sounded
positive. Hiroshi sat in the corner thinking he was in a madhouse.
And Daniela, Luisa and Carla sat on the bed comparing experiences with overprotective fathers.

Herself no stranger to bending the truth, or at the very least
omitting letters from countries she planned to visit, Daniela
sympathised with Carla over her nervous parents. But Daniela
had visited Austria rather than Australia for the benefit of aunts
and uncles rather than her father, who was already ill by the time
we met. Had he not been, she mightn't have even made it as far
as Austria.

When his teenage daughter went out for the night with tanned
legs and a miniskirt, Franco would remind Daniela of her curfew
by asking what day it was. If Daniela replied 'the fifteenth', Franco
would say that she was either home before the sixteenth or she'd
never see the seventeenth. Daniela resented the curfew but was
thankful her father wasn't as severe as Luisa's, who spat on the
doorstep when his daughter went out and said if she wasn't back
by the time it dried he would come looking for her.

A father's obsession with his daughter's safety often demands
she lie in order to grow up socially and sexually; in fact fibbing
is considered foreplay by some Italian teenagers. Sons suffer similar
persecution. For every protective Italian father worried about his
daughter, there is a protective Italian mother devoted to pampering
her prized boy; pampering which is often excessive and which
gave rise to the saying 'Jesus Christ must have been Italian because

he lived at home until he was thirty and his mother told him he was God'.

Psychologists in women's magazines warn Italian mothers that *mammismo distruttivo* hinders rather than helps. A letter in a personal help column written by a distraught mother asked for help in controlling her jealousy when she saw her thirty-five-year-old '*bambino*' cuddling his girlfriend. She begged for advice on how to avoid inventing excuses to interrupt the embrace, like a jealous Poodle on hind legs scratching at trouser bottoms for attention.

Some mothers are not in the least ashamed of their intrusiveness. On *Stranamore*, a TV show where couples in crisis air differences with a view to reconciliation, one woman gave her lover—who was sitting in the studio audience to remain anonymous—an ultimatum: 'It's either me or *mamma*,' she said. 'Stand up if you choose me.'

'I choose you,' said the man, standing up.

'No he doesn't,' said his mother, standing up beside him.

But *mamma* only intrudes because *figlio* loves to let her. The mollycoddled *mammoni,* as they are known, are as devoted to their mothers as their mothers are to them. Roberto Benigni summed it up perfectly in the film *Johnny Stecchino*. Playing a Sicilian *Mafioso*, he looks deep into the eyes of a wife pleading for attention and says: '*Amore mio*, there is only one woman in my life, and that woman is you and my mother.'

Mothers deny sons nothing and are denied nothing by sons, whose marriages often fail because wives tire of competing with mothers-in-law. A friend of Valeria's in Andrano often stopped by to complain about her husband, who gave his mother a key to their house, let her rummage through drawers to see if jocks or socks needed mending, and complimented his mother's cooking but never hers. Valeria always managed to solve her friends' problems, if only because they saw Franco when they visited and realised their complaints were insignificant by comparison.

Overprotective parents will do anything to avoid separation from their children, even invent illness or disability in extreme cases. Daniela has a friend whose mother became mysteriously ill every time her daughter mentioned moving to Milan to study psychology. Why move away to study strange behaviour when you can do so at home? Other parents were less manipulative but equally reluctant to loosen the leash. When I told a student at the English school that I was required to pay board to remain at home after high school, he said that when he finished school his parents would have paid him to stay at home.

Other than Carla, who still lived at home, the rest of the group had flown southern nests to further careers in northern Italy, something their parents had accepted in time but which had turned their love to anxiety; the family fortress had been breached and they could no longer protect their children from a corrupt and dangerous world. Deserters were monitored daily when Telecom Italia went off-peak. Throughout Italy at 10 pm millions of pockets play a tune, prompting sons and daughters to check their watches and respond 'Ciao mamma' with utmost certainty. At Sunday Night *Spaghettata*, the group actually prepared for *mamma*'s call by fishing phones from bags and pockets as ten o'clock approached.

Calls from Michele's mother made for amusing listening, and in such a small apartment it was impossible not to eavesdrop. In her soft-soled shoes and apron, she worried herself sick. Her country boy was in the city, that perilous place she once visited to have a hip operation. She watched the evening news through white-knuckled fingers, convinced that any tragedy she saw in Milan had befallen her Michele. When seven large pieces of ice fell freakishly from Italian skies, with the largest piece coming to rest in Milan, Michele's mother called to make sure it had missed her son. Stubborn and set in her ways, she still waited for the discount rate before ringing to ensure he was alive.

On another occasion, after snow had fallen in Milan, again the evening bulletin caused Michele's mum to panic. '*Non ti preoccupare mamma,'* comforted Michele, answering his ten o'clock check-up. 'I'm on the sixth floor. You need more than a few centimetres to get up here.'

Despite her nervous disposition, only once was Michele's mother so overwrought she spurned the discount rate and called during the day: when Michele's father fell from an olive tree and broke his shoulder—and the ladder. With her hands full nursing her husband, she was hoping her son would fly home for a few days, because, unlike his father, the olives weren't plump enough to fall on their own and needed to be picked.

But now it was Carla who grew nervous as ten o'clock approached. Manhattan wasn't full after all and I had found her and Michele a room. Very shortly she would confess to her father, who would either impose his will, or change it. I suggested she make sure he wasn't up an olive tree when she delivered the knockout blow. But Carla was in no mood for jest and had only prodded at her *carbonara*, not because it wasn't Michele's best, but because she was about to hear her father at his worst.

When her phone rang, Carla fled to the bathroom, from where she emerged shortly after with a forced smile on her face and a bottle of beer in her hand; to make me feel at home Michele had put six of them in his bath. Keeping her audience waiting, Carla sat down at the table and lit one of Sergio's cigarettes.

'*Allora?*' asked Michele. 'How did it go?'

Carla coughed a cloud of smoke and grimaced at the cigarette.

'I can't understand my father,' she said. 'First he tells me not to go, then he tells me not to come back.'

Two weeks later, I was driving to work when my own mobile rang. Little A-S-I-A had been born. No H in front. Antonio was going to take the risk. All being well we would see her next weekend, at Sunday Night *Spaghettata*.

Campanilismo

We had been living in our apartment for six months when we heard the church bell at the end of our street for the first time, a rare midday silence allowing us the sound of twelve indolent rings. For a few blessed moments the traffic noise ceased, stubborn horns and howling sirens usurped by mellow bronze. '*Che schifo di campana!*' declared Daniela, who was off work with the flu for the second time in a month. 'That's a tired bell. It sounds like a dry tongue slapping against the parched walls of a mouth that doesn't want to sing anymore.' I am yet to hear a better example of *campanilismo*—love and loyalty to one's hometown bell and the unique way of life that its ring orchestrates.

The *campana* in an Italian piazza is like a heart pumping blood to the body's organs. So vital is its role in the workings of a town that, despite starvation, the first thing the residents of Adano ask of the liberating Allied forces in John Hersey's *A Bell for Adano* is the replacement of their bell, which Mussolini had seized to melt down into bullets. 'The spirit is more important than the stomach,' says a villager to an American major. The Milanese have different priorities, however, and the role of the bell becomes lost somewhat when its ring is only heard by mice in the bell tower.

Daniela had an inherent affection for Andrano's bell and its calm choreography of sedate routines. Her disparaging remark about the bell in Milan was just one in a series of outbursts that made me realise it was Daniela, rather than the bell, who was worn out. Without saying so, she had come to question our staying in Italy's commercial capital. So when her mother phoned to say that her terminally ill father had had an epileptic fit, fallen down the stairs, cracked his skull and was hospitalised, the idea of moving home to help was entertained more seriously than it might have been were we happy in Milan.

Daniela disliked the city's bleak concrete character. Without the sun to warm her skin she felt like a foreigner in her own country. She was alienated by the robotic existence of the Milanese, their joyless addiction to work, and was tired of teaching stressed children who thought the babysitter was their mother. She could forgive the Milanese their contempt for the south but not their lack of respect for the health of their own city, which was coughing and sneezing even more than she was. Unlike Daniela, however, Milan couldn't take a day off work when it fell ill.

Milan records more cases of ailments linked to air pollution than any other Italian city including Naples, where fresh air is sold in a can. The European Union warned Milan that its pollution levels were exceeding EU limits to a dangerous extent, yet on 'European Day Against Air Pollution', when all major European cities including London, Paris, Rome, Madrid, Athens and Munich were closed to traffic other than public transport, Milan declined the invitation to freshen its air, saying it needed to work and could the EU please save the environment outside office hours.

I was also disappointed by Milan. As Daniela had suggested during our first week there, it wasn't the fog that bothered me as much as what it unmasked when it lifted. How could such a wealthy city appear so neglected? The centre was elegant but the suburbs were eyesores. Even high-priced residential areas looked squalid. And common property was as well groomed as a beggar's beard. On my way to work I saw people walking dogs in grass so wild that the only trace of the hidden hound was the lead in its owner's hand.

I found the people more charming than the city, despite their addiction to money and their talent for hypocrisy. Quick to brand southerners uncivilised, at times they are themselves ill-mannered. After paying rent punctually for six months without fail, we were woken by our landlady at 9 am one Sunday asking why our rent wasn't in the letterbox. 'It's the first of the month,' she told a semi-conscious Daniela. 'With your rent I pay my bills. If you can't pay you must give me eight days' warning so I can make other arrangements.'

'And can you pay your bills on Sunday morning?' asked Daniela, who had the envelope ready for the following morning, the first *business* day of the month.

Still in her pyjamas, Daniela went down and put the envelope in the mailbox, ignoring my request to cross out the *'gentilissima'* before the name, a common Italian flattery declaring the recipient to be 'extremely courteous'. I thought it more appropriate to write *'fortunatissimo'* on an Italian letter, given that 'extremely lucky' would better describe anyone receiving mail delivered by *Poste Italiane.*

Milan was wearing down both our spirits and our savings. Italy's most expensive city doesn't justify the cost of living there. While the Milanese were energetic—pushing, rushing and losing sight of simple pleasures—their city felt exhausted, stale and sterile, bored by its own bleakness. I was tired too; tired of cheating death on the road to work, of hunting out car parks that didn't exist, of spending my entire day off queuing to pay bills, of the sinking sky, the forgotten sun and the beggars on almost every corner: cold, hungry, desperate and, far too often, deformed.

At first Milan broke my heart; in time it destroyed it completely. A young boy in the rags of a tracksuit stood at my car window holding cigarette lighters with his good arm while the other, a mangled stump, hung at his side. He tapped on my window but I stared straight ahead at a near-naked woman on a billboard advertisement taking photos with her mobile phone. A few months earlier I had donated loose change, in the early days I had even budgeted for each beggar before leaving home. I had bought countless lighters even though I rarely smoked, but now

I simply ignored the pathetic presence in the rain. Driving away I glanced at my mirror and saw the child return to the rubbish-strewn kerb. Looking back I saw no way forward. I was immune to his suffering. It was time to leave Milan.

But was Andrano a realistic alternative? With no English-speaking friends I would be far more isolated than in Milan. But isolation would be great for my Italian. Here was an opportunity to swap north for south and city for sea, to live in a part of Italy as intriguing as it was remote. Daniela could apply for a transfer back to her former school, and now that I no longer worked for Francesco, I could teach English wherever I pleased. But surely not in Andrano? Some of the locals didn't even speak Italian.

As daunted as I was excited, somewhat foolishly I asked my students what they thought of the idea. None of them had actually visited the south but that didn't stop them from tearing it to shreds—climbing aboard the bandwagon is far simpler than stopping it. 'You're mad,' said an outraged Claudio. 'Don't do it. You'll die down there. And don't call it Italy. It is the *south* of Italy. They are two very different places.'

Angelo appeared offended that someone he had befriended was capable of such a proposal. He screwed up his face like a child eating greens and said: 'I don't think you realise what it's like down there. They are backward and illiterate. You'll go crazy. No woman is worth following to the south.'

Surprisingly it was Raffaele, the hardcore football hooligan, who was the most diplomatic. Leaning towards me as though what he had to say was classified, he whispered: 'Be very careful if you go down there, Crris. Eight out of ten southerners get angry quickly. I saw it on the news.' Only Raffaele could render racism endearing.

Their bigotry only bolstered a mood of defiance in me. I was deaf to hearsay and saw through blind gossip. The two months I had spent in the south had been delightful and unique. But that had been a holiday: sun, sea, sex and spaghetti—anywhere's paradise if that's your itinerary. Residing in Andrano permanently would no doubt ruin the novelty and perhaps, more crucially, my relationship with Daniela.

If I hadn't reflected on our relationship before now it was because I hadn't felt the need. I was still as besotted with Daniela as I had been in Ireland, when I thought our affair would last as long as my pint. The passion we felt for each other had survived the unusual arrangement of living together from the start. There had been no alternative, the distance between our homes demanded all or nothing. Dating would have been next to impossible, though good for my Frequent Flyer points. But now Barzini's alarm bell began to sound. Summer distractions had turned to winter decisions and the future was as foggy as Milan. How easy to fall in love. How difficult to make it last.

But we had already come further than Barzini predicted. Initially, I admit, I had lusted after a stylish girl with whom I could hardly communicate. But then I fell in love with a sensitive woman who realised our bond was complicated and so nurtured it like the *basilico* growing steadily in *mamma*'s garden; stray cats pissed on it from time to time but that merely added flavour.

Daniela's character made our relationship possible. She remained patient when a two-hour film took us double that time to watch, and knew immediately what I hadn't understood and stopped the film on cue, while in the cinema she leant across and whispered a translation. I was far too busy trying to understand the film to even contemplate popcorn or kissing her.

She never pressured me to learn her language, nor did she discourage me when I made mistakes, something I confess I did to her and which, for some reason, she forgave me. She reprimanded friends who spoke fast, as she did those who used dialect. 'Just the official language, thanks,' she would say. 'How would you feel if he started ranting in English?'

Having watched her father's tragic decline from professor to patient, she was courageous, hardy and headstrong, all of which are desirable traits when another grown man who needs looking after enters your life. From the moment I arrived in Italy, Daniela was my lover, teacher and friend. That we were still together almost a year later was testament to her mastering this mixture of roles.

There were of course testing times born of conflicting cultures and contrasting minds. Daniela disliked my precision and I her imprecision. I was punctual. She was late. I was organised. She was scatterbrained. My language was direct. Hers was decorative. She accused me of impatience and being set in my ways. I accused her of failing to understand the loneliness of linguistic isolation, the pressure I was under, and just how much I had compromised to start a new life in her country. 'There's nobody who is forcing you,' was her clumsy comeback, said with such a cute accent that I rather thought that she was.

Our principal cause of tension was Daniela's loose respect for the truth. Her lips were alive with polite little lies—transparent and effectively harmless, yet lies all the same, causing confusion if nothing else. One afternoon, during that first summer in Andrano, she proposed a walk from Acquaviva to Castro—two seaside locations a few kilometres apart. Believing such a walk to only be possible along the thin and twisted coast road, dangerous to drive let alone walk, I declined the offer and suggested a swim instead. '*E dai,*' pleaded Daniela. 'There's a footpath.' So off we went. But I soon discovered that she had invented the footpath to convince me to come on the walk. She had done so for my benefit, you understand; apparently I needed some exercise.

What was illogical to me was logical to Daniela, who can say she is coming when she is in fact going. She once called me at home saying '*arrivo*' only to turn up over an hour later. 'I was heading home,' she protested when she finally showed up. 'I just had to do some shopping and feed Anna's cat on the way.' But once I realised liberties were never taken with vital truths, I found it fascinating rather than frustrating to live with a woman capable of the delicate logic behind 'I didn't forget, I just didn't remember'. It wasn't my birthday she was referring to, so what the hell. When it did come around, she came home with a parcel in which I showed interest. 'Go away,' she discouraged. 'There's nothing in here for you except something.'

More annoying was her inflexibility. Coming from a country with few traditions, I never quite grew accustomed to Daniela checking her watch every time I suggested doing something or calling someone. Shortly after arriving in Italy, when I couldn't have done so myself, I suggested she call Riccardo the police chief who'd offered to help with my documents.

'Now?' she replied, scandalised. 'He'll be eating. I'll call later.'

I reminded her after an hour and again she consulted her watch.

'Now? He'll be sleeping. I'll call later.'

The afternoon ticked by.

'What about now?'

'Are you serious? It's after five. He'll have gone out. I'll call this evening.'

Sometimes I capitalised on the fact the Italians are creatures of habit. During summer I had the entire Adriatic to myself between 2 and 4 pm. Few Italians will risk a swim until at least two hours after a meal. It's suicide, apparently—you'll get cramp and sink like a stone. They used to queue up to watch me drown. Daniela could have sold tickets. But the fact I never went under wasn't enough for them to question their routine. And Daniela accused *me* of being set in my ways?

The culture clash added spice but caused little more than squabble, recurring, frustrating, but par for a complex course. Overall the relationship was as delightful as it was difficult, and any reluctance to move south was in no way due to doubts about my feelings for Daniela. What I was less certain about was whether those feelings would be compromised were I to become dependent on her. In Milan I was at least remotely self-sufficient. In Andrano I would simply be remote.

My plans for the future had never involved living in a tiny Italian outpost. Before meeting Daniela I had made a modest start in journalism and hoped to rise up the ranks at either a magazine or newspaper. But as Woody Allen said: 'If you want to make God laugh, tell him about your plans.'

He was certainly laughing at Franco's. Daniela's father was deteriorating and her mother phoned more and more, not to ask her daughter to come home, but to hear a voice other than her own. Franco's voice was gone; his measured one at least. All he uttered now were random phrases, fitful and ungoverned, like the detached tail of a lizard. It was heartbreaking for the family to watch their father reduced to rubble, and I fully understood Daniela's need to nurse the man who had held her at birth, touched the dimple on her chin and said: 'Must be the angels' seal of approval.' She adored him. I'd only met him through the memories of others and I adored him too. Daniela's mother needed her. Did I let her go, or go with her?

I was still to answer that question when a tearful Daniela, who hadn't slept well for weeks, whispered at 2 am that she was applying for a transfer home. Sixteen months had passed since that night in Sydney when she asked me to move to Italy and I said yes before she finished the question. Tonight, however, I hesitated when she asked me to join her in Andrano. I didn't say yes, but I didn't say no either. Instead I told her of my need to return to England for a while, to reflect on the happiest but hardest year of my life, to spoil myself with my language, visit old friends, recharge my batteries and renew my spirit of adventure. And most of all, to look over my shoulder and see if I could find any future in the past.

I held Daniela in the darkness, stroked her hair and dried her tears. Thin in my arms, my summer girl felt cold. I thought how happy her students would be—their favourite teacher returned, how happy her mother would be—her daughter back safe in the nest, and how sad we would be—too different to have similar paths. Daniela once told me that had her father been well we might never have met. Now that he was ill he might divide us just the same.

Then tyres screeched outside and a voice yelled *'Vaffanculo!'*—'Go fuck yourself!' Life in Milan would continue without us.

Daniela's transfer was approved by the Education Department, but Danny disapproved of my resignation from the English school. We broke our lease without penalty, although the landlady insisted we paint the kitchen if we expected the return of our bond. 'Tomato sauce must remind her of the friends she doesn't have,' said Daniela, as I concealed the remnants of Sunday Night *Spaghettata*. Our stay in the apartment had done little to reconcile north and south. As far as we were concerned, our landlady typified the money-minded Milanese. And as far as our landlady was concerned, we were southern slobs.

Like bookends of time, our final days in Milan were spent in the same place as the early days—Francesco's. I would leave my things there while in England. I didn't have much, the spoils of a year in Italy were in my head, my heart and at the panel beaters. As new nine months ago, our Lancia now had more dings than a Chinese phonebook. Only vital repairs would be performed in expensive Milan. The rest could wait until Daniela's return to Andrano, where such things cost half the price or are done by a cousin.

Danny and other colleagues had organised a farewell evening, and being early drinkers, had arranged to meet on the steps of the Duomo at six. Daniela and I took a tram that should have dropped us in Piazza Duomo, but approaching the *centro storico* the traffic became blocked. Before long, the driver shut down the stationary tram and opened the doors to let in some air; it was mid-June and the short-sleeve evenings were warm and pleasant. A hundred metres ahead was a complex intersection where, despite traffic lights, a tangle of trams, buses, cars, bicycles,

Vespas and pedestrians rarely managed to agree on who should cross the cobblestones first.

Horns blared as the traffic built; Italian drivers blame the car in front for even kilometre-long queues. Trams were banked up nose to tail, a bright orange serpent along which it was impossible to tell where the number 16 finished and the number 4 began. Vespas dodged and weaved before themselves coming to a reluctant standstill, except for one impatient rider who scattered pedestrians on the pavement. Faces appeared at apartment windows, shopkeepers took to crowded footpaths, and a nun emerged from the Church of San Tommaso, craning her neck in the direction of the intersection which now had even God's attention.

But not everyone was looking on. A couple in the seat in front of us continued their oblivious kiss. He was the cocksure Italian heart-throb: Versace slacks, sun-lamp tan, shoulder-length hair and upturned collar. She was English, pale and plump, as new to Italy as she was to her lover. Frisky thirty-somethings, they had met only recently—'Maybe even on the tram,' whispered Daniela—and the only language they had in common was the wet one being shared regardless of the fact they had an audience.

When she finally realised they were on stage she pushed Romeo away, adjusted her shirt and sat straight. Taking in the world around him, he wrestled out a pleasantry.

'Verry much . . . *traffico*,' he said, rolling his R in both tongues.

'Accident?' she asked.

'*Penso proprio di si.*'

'What?'

'*Si, si.*'

She looked about her and appeared to grow nervous, as foreigners often do in Italy when horns are blaring, sirens are sounding, voices are raised and arms are waved. Such a scene is commonplace to Italians but to the visitor it can seem like the end of the world. After peering out the window in the direction of the din, he took the woman's hand and said: '*Andiamo*. We walk.'

When they had gone I took Daniela's hand and copied his patchwork command: '*Andiamo*. We walk too.'

I ridiculed because I remembered. We had been them. In an Irish pub rather than on an Italian tram but we had been them. In fact, the more I thought about it, I had been both of them. Less than a year ago an Italian accident scene had made me nervous as well. A year later, calm and indifferent, I took Daniela by the hand as though she were the startled newcomer. With local knowledge I led her through a pack of cars itching and inching to go nowhere, crossed another bloodstained intersection on which a woman lay motionless, brushed aside bystanders like branches across a forest path, then took a short-cut leading directly to the Duomo, whose magnificent white marble had turned pink in the setting sun. The subtle glow of the Duomo remains my most pleasant memory of *Milano*. It wasn't enough to bring on second thoughts about leaving, but it was a most handsome farewell.

Pollen filled the air on the morning of departure, swirling through the streets like springtime snow. Daniela and I had spent every day of the past year together. Now came our first goodbye, tender and tense. Her delicate hand seemed fashioned for mine, filling contour and crease as though sculpted into place. Letting it go felt like defacing a work of art. Daniela was distressed and I feigned strength, but watching her car take the corner threw shadow across my world, like lying on a beach when storm clouds plunder the sun.

I took a bus to the airport and tried not to think about her. She'd be approaching Modena by now, stereo up and window down. I checked in for the flight to London. I'll bet she's listening to the Crowded House album I gave her, humming along and tapping the wheel. I had a coffee while my departure gate changed. Bologna was her next way-point, then the Adriatic coast, then

600 kilometres with the sea by her side. My flight was called. Valeria would be cooking something special. Some Sicilian home-coming dish most likely; there were culinary traditions for every occasion. I boarded the plane and found my seat. Probably some sort of meat or fish which is supposed to bring luck to those who've been away. The captain announced a delay. Town tongues would wag; Daniela was returning home on her own and the piazza would buzz with speculation as to why. The wheels rolled finally as I turned the pages of a book I wasn't reading. I wonder if her father will recognise her . . .

My plane entered the runway, raindrops stretching as it rolled like thunder before climbing through cloud and pointing its nose towards England.

Daniela rode a bump in the road to Andrano, where the town bell was ringing madly, singing the praises of midday in spring and the welcome return of one of its own.

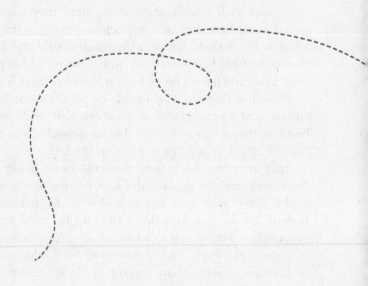

The bitter*sweet life*

One of many contradictions which characterise the Italians is the fact they have migrated throughout the world while remaining hopeless travellers. It seems strange that gifted improvisers find adventure bothersome and spend foreign holidays searching for the comforts of home, their beloved *Belpaese*—the beautiful country. Luisa took her coffee percolator with her the one time she ventured abroad, the morning odour enticing a queue of compatriots outside her hotel room. And Carla found siesta impossible in Manhattan, until a pharmacy selling eye masks and ear plugs rescued rural habits from the mayhem of a metropolis.

I found such travelogues amusing until they resembled my own. I could have slept in a tree before moving to Italy, yet here I was at my friends' house in England, tossing and turning in the comfortable bed where two years earlier I had slept like the dead. James and Jenny's house had no *serrande*—those heavy Italian shutters that function like eyelids on windows, and despite a curtain, and several glasses of Guinness that made my eyes as heavy as the clouds at the window, it seemed closer to midday than midnight in my lonely room in the loft.

After counting sheep until the cows came home, I opened the curtain and sat up in bed. From my window a meticulous garden, lawn mown in stripes and a neatly trimmed hedge. Beyond, a road with lines down the middle, sealed, smooth and rubbish-free. Heavy rain splashed on its surface before draining away most efficiently. Such a downpour would destroy the roads in Andrano, eroding them beyond an already miserable state. I lay back and lost myself in thoughts of Daniela, dodging puddle and pothole on her beaten-up bike. Perhaps she was better off without me, given such depressions had only depressed her since I'd arrived to point them out.

For the Italian in me it was too early to sleep. Back in Italy we'd have been heading out around now, or moving on to *secondo piatto*. But for the Australian in me it had been a late night and all was silent in Sussex bar the rain on the roof. Half of me was tired, the other half raring to go; I wasn't sure if I was suffering from insomnia or schizophrenia. I turned on the light and tried reading my book, but a history of the Sicilian Mafia entitled *Excellent Cadavers* made a bloodstained lullaby.

Though struggling to sleep, I was thankful my hosts had gone to bed early as it had been a somewhat tense evening. From the moment we met at the airport, I realised that the nature of our friendship had changed. I had expected a festive welcome, like the one I'd received in Sicily. Instead I got handshakes and smiles, pleasant, but not enough. Handshakes no longer expressed the joy of recovered friendship, so I'd hugged James who reluctantly obliged but probably would have punched me had I puckered up. I was used to being greeted like a returned war hero rather than a traveller in need of a bed.

I had expected to have so much to talk about that, as in Sicily, I would unload my suitcase from the car the next morning. But the first thing James and Jenny did was show me to my room and explain their system for saving hot water. And dinner conversation had been forced. They spoke about work and mortgages, while I recounted tales of an itinerant year to which they paid only polite attention. They were expecting a baby but needed no help choosing a name; such was the dull efficiency of their government they were free to name it what they liked.

A year in Italy had also broadened the minds of my taste buds, and I found that English fare had become bland. I didn't say anything impolite, though I almost turned my nose up at their Parmesan in a packet, managing to stop myself just in time.

My mother's cooking had also suffered by comparison. I had previously been an undiscriminating eater, devouring anything she dished up provided it was dead and hot. But when Daniela and I had visited for a week in January, suddenly I was asking what was on the evening's menu. It made her nervous. She was used to empty plates and compliments rather than half-eaten meals and criticism. It was Daniela's fault: by spoiling me she had also spoilt my mother's cooking.

Apart from the fact I'd become a culinary snob, my parents had been delighted to see me. So too had my ageing dog, who, delirious with excitement, forgot the front door was made of glass. An Italian glazier would have taken twice the time to arrive. It was good to be home.

Or was it? My Aussie mates made more of a fuss than James and Jenny but still seemed distant, suspicious—perhaps—of the changes in me: Prada shoes and Armani strides. Fashion-wise, blending in in Italy means standing out in Australia. Most of my friends were settling down, having kids and moving into middle management. I could still squeeze all I owned into a backpack. They talked about how expensive Sydney had become since the Olympics. I talked about Signor Api. It's a tumultuous moment when an Australian realises he might have more in common with a southern Italian petrol station attendant than with his compatriots.

Back in Blighty it was the same. James suggested we watch a film after dinner, so I left my photos in my bag, my stories in my head, and settled into IKEA furniture for an equally pre-fabricated instalment from Hollywood. What had happened to me? A year ago I enjoyed banal blockbusters as much as I did shepherd's pie. I would never have found fault with the hospitality of my hosts. Half-watching the happy ending, I realised, somewhat sadly, that I no longer related to old friends and interests, and that while increasing my experience and broadening my horizons, living overseas had alienated me from former pastimes which, ironically, I now found foreign.

The downside of knowing two worlds intimately was feeling totally at home in neither. I had grown up between England and Australia, my mother was Ukrainian, my girlfriend Italian, and now 'home' was a word I could say in three languages without knowing what it truly meant. The Italian in me was incomplete in England. The Australian in me would always be homesick in Italy. At Italian beaches I longed for the breakers of Bondi. At Bondi I missed the calm Mediterranean. It was a privilege to know both, but privilege can be perilous.

I was a fool to search the English for the merits of the Italians, just as the Italians could never possess the attributes of the Aussies. The fact James and Jenny could no longer entertain me was my fault not theirs, and why had I hoped to entertain them with stories to which they couldn't possibly relate? James could never grasp the joy in a game of *bocce* behind Andrano's castle. It was like asking Francesco to appreciate an Ashes test match at Lords. They were different worlds, separated by a tightrope on which I currently swayed, desperate to find the right way to go.

On the whole I was thrilled to be back in England. My tongue returned to its default setting and my eye to its love of order. I never thought it would relax me to see motorists parking with precision or stopping at zebra crossings. And I felt like hugging shoppers queuing patiently in the supermarket, or pedestrians putting their rubbish in the bin. Civility removed stress from everyday life and I found myself breathing easier. I enjoyed my afternoon stroll through the village. Shops were open during the day! And buses arrived at bus stops rather than an out-of-breath *vigile* with news of a flash transport strike. But the joy of returning to my former world was overshadowed by what I had left behind in my new one; not just Daniela, but an elusive Italian beauty which I couldn't see until it was out of sight.

A year ago in a Lecce traffic jam, while a farmer sold freshly plucked carrots between cars, Daniela had praised the invisible charisma of her country, saying that even Italians lament Italy's obvious imperfections yet, when they leave, grieve for the loss of something they cannot describe. At the time I was new to Italy, the real Italy of queue and corruption, and simply couldn't relate to such concepts. From where I stood things looked unenlightened and unappealing: paradise for a holiday, hell for a way of life. But a year later I sat up in bed, watched the rain fall on an English garden, and was forced to admit that Daniela was right—there was something in those carrots after all. Some spell that endeared me to a country I had criticised, to the subtle qualities in blatant people whose bad points were their good points and whose weaknesses were their strengths. They were abstract qualities impossible to define—the riddle of the *Belpaese*. But with no *serranda* on my window, it was a riddle I had all night to solve.

Tourists adore Italy because they breeze through in summer and glimpse a transitory personality, the sparkling disguise of a bleak reality. They follow their guidebooks to the historic highlights of a modern mess, queue to see frescoes rather than to pay phone bills, and believe life in Italy to be wonderful because the Italians tell them it is so. As Gore Vidal says in *Vidal in Venice:* 'most people come here to find something that they have never known before. For the visitor it is sort of a waking dream. Naturally, no Venetian ever dreams this Venice, but every Venetian works to evoke it for others'. Real Italian life is far removed from the tourist experience. Venetians don't ride in gondolas. Many couldn't afford to even if they so desired.

Hollywood cinematographers have played a role in this deception. Sticklers for stereotype, it is invariably summer in films set in Italy, with the lives of well-tanned characters revolving around sex and other diversions. The Italian Riviera was the ideal place to set *The Talented Mr Ripley*, for example. Where else do you sun yourself while sipping Cinzano, seducing beautiful women and squandering your allowance? Even when Italian cinema tackles serious topics, films such as *Life is Beautiful* can distort grim realities to a frivolous extent. But who's looking for reality? Escaping it is much more fun.

Travel writers are also to blame. Many fail to see that life in Italy can be frustrating rather than fun, and foolishly declare that a relaxing of the rules would be a wonderful way to live. In *Neither Here Nor There*, Bill Bryson spends the first night of a whirlwind trip through Italy dining with an expatriate American friend, whose twenty years in the country have left him with nothing positive to say. Bryson, on the other hand, has been in Rome just a few hours and can't understand his friend's objections. He heaps praise on the Italians, saying he finds it 'very attractive' that they won't queue, pay their taxes, turn up for appointments on time, undertake any sort of labour without a small bribe or believe in rules of any nature.

A few days later, Bryson has changed both city and opinion. Fed up with the mutinous life, he complains: 'Why can't the Florentines see that it would be in their own interest to sweep up the litter and put out some benches and force the gypsies to stop being so persistent in their panhandling and spend more on brightening the place up?' At first the 'who cares' attitude, *menefreghismo* it's called in Italian, seems a tempting escape from ordered society. But after spending some time defending his place in a queue, Bryson's fondness for discipline triumphs. Pretty soon the American, who came to Italy in search of *la dolce vita*, is 'desperate to get out of there' and runs to catch a bus into sane Switzerland. When Barzini said 'the Italian way of life cannot be considered a success except by temporary visitors', he failed to realise that sometimes even they are not impressed.

But most tourists leave swearing allegiance to illusion, convinced the mirage they have witnessed is real. Seduced by fashion, food, art and architecture, they make a reluctant return to former lives, mind and mantelpiece stacked with stereotypes of the colourful country they cannot wait to revisit. They are besotted with *Italia*, having even fallen in love with the Vespas, those impotent Italian icons buzzing round the piazza. It looks like such fun, wind in the hair and lovers' arms holding on. What a wonderful way to live . . .

What tourists don't see from their room with a view is a man in Andrano driven mad by the motorbikes. He has called the *Carabinieri* countless times to denounce the drag races outside his front door. Now the irate vigilante takes to the street swinging a lasso above his head. 'I'll kill you before the summer is out!' he yells, launching the noose at his teenage tormentors. Blasphemy announces the fact he has missed, then his wife rushes out to calm him down. Life goes on and so do the bikes, gathering speed for another pass. Hands clasped like talons, he goes inside and lights a cigarette, imagining it's a fuse connected to the fuel tank of every Vespa in the land. Meanwhile tourists all over the world continue to dream of his Italian nightmare.

Summer is an annual honeymoon in an otherwise unhappy marriage. Until you've lived with the Italians beyond summer you've seen only their silhouettes. Casting light upon them reveals scandal and surprise. Suddenly that famous effervescence goes flat. Even the gelato loses its flavour.

Only those who stick around discover that 'the sweet life' can turn sour. I was happiest in Italy while I too was a tourist, and enjoyed watching the news until I understood what was being said. The sexy newsreader seemed far too busy striking a pose and arranging her hair to be the bearer of bad news. But as my Italian improved I realised that she was telling me what the guidebooks had overlooked: that seventy-five people had died on the roads over the weekend, that Italy's fifty-fourth government since World War II had been dissolved during the ad break, that yet another young boy in Naples had been killed defending his Vespa from thieves, that the Mafia had murdered again—be it the Sicilian, the Calabrian or the Neapolitan, that football matches had been fixed, judges had been bribed, degrees had been sold and the Prime Minister had been charged with corruption—again. Et cetera, et cetera, et cetera. It made your head spin.

In Italy the word 'government' is synonymous with 'corruption'; it's like ice-cream and summer—expected bedfellows. As a result, the population has as much respect for its politicians as its politicians have for the population; mutual contempt, a blind eye for a blind eye. Daniela's only interest in politics was the day off she enjoyed each time a government collapsed and her school was used as a polling station to elect another.

Her indifference to politics might appear irresponsible, but when you are called to the polling booths as frequently as your bladder calls you to the bathroom, to vote for MPs and PMs who have been tried for murder, colluding with the Mafia and ignoring every law it is their duty to uphold, cynicism seems justified, a form of self-protection if nothing else.

This is where a paradox creeps in. Only by ignoring Italy's imperfections have the Italians perfected their lives. By snubbing their nation's shame they have found its main strength—escapism. Escapism so colourful that it slaps misery across the face. *Life is Beautiful* turned a holocaust into a fairytale. Benigni waltzes to his death playing the fool in an attempt to save loved ones from a life more brutal than beautiful. His forced smile masking a tragic fate, he personifies Barzini's claim that 'there has never been a race of people so fundamentally desolate and desperate as these gay Italians'.

One of Italy's foremost social commentators, Beppe Severgnini, says the Italian ability to shrug off scandal is due to a concept known as the *Terrazza Law*. 'We may have had a lousy day,' says Severgnini, 'we may have been told that we are going to have to pay more taxes because someone in government has made off with another few billion lire. But in the evening we can have a meal *al fresco* with our friends, maybe on a *terrazza* under a clear sky, and our bitterness evaporates. This is *The Terrazza Law*. If we had British weather in Italy our politicians would have come to a sticky end long ago.'

A TV show depicted this blind eye turned to serious issues more radically than Severgnini. A regional broadcast, it featured a naked woman standing next to a journalist who read from a music stand. It was utterly sexist, although I'm fairly sure I was the only person in Italy to pick that up:

> The unemployment rate in Puglia has risen dramatically in the last year. Do you care? Government funding for hospitals has been cut drastically in the last six months. Concerned? The European Union has passed new laws disfavouring the export of foods typical to Puglia which could cause massive job losses. Is anybody listening? No, of course you're not! *(He had started shouting.)* You're all too busy staring at her tits to listen to the problems in your region. And even the people in power, who could do something about it, are staring as well. That's why I need to shoot you all tonight. Because you haven't heard a word I've said!

The only difference between this regional broadcast and most national shows was the man with the conscience, because breasts are pretty much broadband. Italian television is designed, quite literally, to titillate rather than educate. Endless variety shows feature near-naked nymphs who dance, wrestle each other in hot tubs and bend over backwards—and forwards—to entertain. Even when the women are decently dressed, cameras on the floor shoot up their skirts while those on the roof peer down their shirts. Anything goes as long as the mundane lives of viewers are diverted by sensation, as long as the pomp has no circumstance, and as long as base instincts suppress higher faculties.

Politics is far less important than poly-tits, as Italy's porn-star-parliamentarian proved. Cicciolina rode the tart ticket all the way to the lower house, where she offered to run the country 'with her tits out'. But the fake blonde with real boobs wasn't around for long, as she could reveal the bulk of her policies by unbuttoning her blouse. Nevertheless, she got there. It's difficult to imagine she would have done so in most other countries.

But most other countries take themselves too seriously for

Italian tastes. The founders of Humanism are suspicious of those who strive for perfection rather than pleasure, and believe the worth of a nation to be measured by the quality of its food and wine rather than its postal service or hospital waiting lists. Daniela's world had different priorities from mine. I had criticised hers for its lazy approach to law and championed mine for its efficiency. But after a year in Italy, returning to England felt like entering a nanny state. There were too many rules: keep off the grass, don't feed the birds, switch off your mobile, no ball games. Everywhere I looked I was told what to do. From anarchy to tyranny in a two-hour flight.

There were no bare breasts on English TV, instead menacing ads threatened the consequences of failure to pay one's TV licence or car tax. Give me the breasts any day. In an English WC a sign forbade me to flush paper towels down the toilet. In an Italian public toilet there is no sign, but no paper towels either. In England when a streaker runs across the field at a sporting fixture, the cameras turn away while the commentators discuss the weather. In Italy the uncensored footage makes the highlights package. Stuck in a traffic jam, the driver of an Italian tram opens the doors to let in some air. The English bus driver is required by law to keep his doors shut in case passengers wander off and get themselves killed. These were the differences between Daniela's country and mine: leave people to their own devices or control their every move.

While I searched for a country with a conscience, I was unsatisfied with Italy. But once I began respecting the *Terrazza Law*, I was less bothered by people disrespecting all the others. For better or worse, Italy's virtue is its vice. It offers a break from society's search for excellence and, in doing so, achieves excellence of another sort: private pleasure over public progress, for some a sign of failure but for the Italians a sign of success. Having previously condemned this egocentric existence, to suddenly support it would be a huge contradiction, and a tiny indication I had become more Italian than I thought.

Italy appealed to my love of the absurd. Nothing ever changes, yet life is full of surprises. The peninsula doesn't do what it says on the packet. It looks like a boot but it's actually a stage, trod by actors who refuse to follow a script. Their improvised show is something of a circus: hilarious, dangerous, chaotic, erotic. Life is a performance in which nothing is as it seems or should be. Italy is not the place to live if you want what's written in the TV guide to correspond with what's on TV, nor will it ever be home if you want road signs to lead where they say they do. But if, on the other hand, you are willing to get lost, you might just find yourself in this peculiar place.

Compared with other advanced nations, the Italians have non-conformist agendas, preferring food to finance, sex to the stock market, and juggling relationships to balancing the budget. These priorities have earned Italy a kind of affectionate pity from the rest of the world, as though it were the runt of an otherwise flawless litter. Internationally it's a figure of fun, ridiculed for its inability to wage war rather than complimented on its passion for peace. It was heavily criticised for its indifference to the threat of the Y2K bug—the turn-of-the-century computer syndrome that was predicted to paralyse the world. Those clever countries that wasted fortunes preparing for a phantom crisis never acknowledged that Italy's lack of interest might have been intuitive rather than ignorant. But a country that can relax the rules and still become the fifth largest industrialised nation must be doing something right.

Italians find perfection less interesting than imperfection and rank effervescence above efficiency. Daniela's idea of hell is paradise. Like most Italians, she believes there is order in disorder and tranquillity in chaos. What she saw in a perfectionist like me was anybody's guess. I often complained about the noise outside the apartment, the surge of engines and the screech of brakes. But Daniela heard nothing except life. Silence, she assured me, was the sound of death.

Life in Italy comes down to a choice: either tolerate the 'sour' to enjoy the 'sweet' or return to a world fond of order and efficiency, with less tragedy but less comedy. I found that choice difficult because I felt such conflicting emotions; Italy both enticed and repelled me in the same breath. Its allure was masked by its defects, yet its defects were its allure. Those who love Italy are among its most vocal denigrators, those who hate it among its staunchest defenders. Bill Bryson declared himself smitten with the place and was gone in the blink of an eye, while his expat friend was critical of a country he would probably never leave. And I was somewhere in between, my love–hate relationship with Italy making me anxious to leave while eager to return.

After wasting an entire night wondering whether to live with a woman I couldn't possibly live without, I finally fell asleep around dawn with a pair of black underpants over my head—the best substitute for a *serranda* I could find in my suitcase. Now all I needed was some real Italian coffee and I'd soon feel much more . . . at home.

Desperate to hear her voice, I rang Daniela early the next day.

'*Pronto.*'

It was her mother.

'*Ciao Valeria. Sono Chris. C'è Daniela?*'

'No, she went to the beach with Concetta. It's a beautiful day. No *Scirocco.*'

'That's fine. I'll call later.'

But Valeria liked a chat.

'How's your holiday going, Crris?'

'Terrible. Everything's changed. Everyone's changed.'

Valeria laughed.

'It's you who's changed. Come on back to the *Belpaese.* You're more Italian than my daughter. Oh, and bring some of that stuff called . . . er . . . Blu-Tack? Is that what it's called? Daniela's told me all about it. Sounds amazing.'

'They've got white Blu-Tack now, Valeria. It won't stain your white-washed walls.'

'Even better. Bring some.'

Valeria had a habit of making difficult decisions seem easy.

After just twenty-four hours in England, I flew back to Italy that afternoon. James and Jenny thought I was mad, but who wants to watch a film in rainy Sussex when they could be diving into the Mediterranean and soaking up the Andrano sun? Summer was returning to Italy. So were the tourists in search of *la dolce vita*. And so was I, convinced it didn't exist but ready to search for it again.

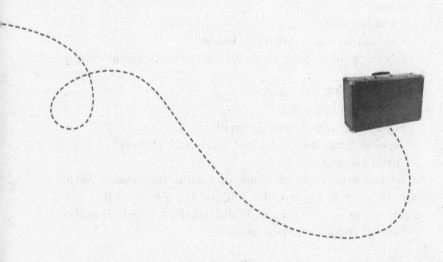

The Adriatic Express

When travelling from Milan to Lecce on the morning train, don't waste time searching the departures board for your platform number. Simply scan the trains in Mussolini's massive *Stazione Centrale*, the sleek Eurostars with their snouts speckled by the blood of continental insects, and among these slender speed machines you'll find a rusty old rattler that looks unlikely to roll beyond the station let alone make the thousand-kilometre journey south. Behold the Adriatic Express: too slow to murder a mozzie and on which the graffiti could have been sprayed while it was moving.

Daniela's brother had booked me a seat on the slug after I rang him from London asking to collect my belongings, stay overnight and leave for Lecce the following day. Francesco had been most generous, even picking me up from the airport on my arrival from Heathrow. Any ill feeling from our failed business venture was forgotten. It was lovely to see me again, he said, before apologising for the state of his apartment given he hadn't yet cleaned up after our farewell party.

I had arrived at Francesco's in the early evening, shortly after which there came a knock at the door. His nosy neighbour had somehow heard of my itinerary, most probably through walls as thin as their wallpaper, and asked if I would mind taking a parcel of food for her son—a soldier stationed near Lecce. I told her I'd be happy to, not realising that when she said 'parcel' she meant a suitcase the size of my own. She cooked all night and was waiting for me at her front door when I left Francesco's the following morning. '*Attenzione*,' she said, holding the suitcase horizontally. 'Could you carry it this way please? I wouldn't want the sauces to run.'

Across town traffic was heavy and I was running late despite the time-saving efforts of my taxi-driver, who threw his Fiat through back streets, half steering, half holding on.

'What time's your train?' he asked over his shoulder.

'Nine,' I replied, choking the door handle.

'That's the thing with Italian trains. You know when you depart but not when you arrive.'

Better *when* than *if*, I thought, declining to respond so the madman might watch the road.

Less than a minute before departure, lugging my own gear and an unknown soldier's dinner, I ran for my carriage towards the front of a train which was so long it stretched off the platform. I clambered aboard as a whistle was blown and the carriage doors slid shut—a frantic but fitting farewell to a city I will always remember as breathless. As if to take a run up, the train rolled backwards for a few seconds before jolting in the right direction and hobbling from the building into bright July sunlight. For the second time in three days I said goodbye to Milan, hoping this time I wouldn't return quite so quickly.

Milano–Bologna

The intercity lurched across a tangle of tracks until clearing the station's exit. As we set course for the south, apartments gradually thinned to factory then field. The carriage had a corridor along its left-hand side and closed compartments of six chairs— three forwards and three backwards—along its right. The walls of my compartment were decorated with pictures of the four seasons, but we stopped so often for no apparent reason that I began to think I'd see at least two out the window. Between the prints was a cracked mirror, a sign on the window warned in four languages that it was dangerous to lean out, and there was a 'No Smoking' sign on the door. It stopped no one from lighting up, but few objected because the smell of smoke masked the stench of urine coming from the toilet at the front of the carriage. And I had rushed back to all this? It was going to be a long trip.

The lazy locomotive dragged its burden of carriages, uncomfortable and overfull. Passengers without a reserved seat sat in the corridor and were trampled over by those who did on their way to claustrophobic compartments. *Trenitalia* oversold the service on which passengers didn't have to book a seat if they didn't mind standing, and being early July, the start of school holidays, there were plenty of people willing to do so if it meant a quicker escape to the sea. Both man and beast were excited at the prospect of fleeing Milan. One passenger nursed a turtle who registered its desire for water by passing some of its own. Turtle piss has a foul stench, and I soon forgot the other odours that filled our circus train.

It was easy to see why the south was scorned. I had ridden trains all over northern Italy that were fast, clean and reasonably reliable, even if fifteen minutes late was as punctual as they could manage. But this antique collection of carriages was surely being banished to the bottom of the boot in the hope it wouldn't return. The author Guido Cerenotti must have been riding something similar when he wrote: 'These Italian trains of sufferance. This filthy travelling shed without any timetable, palely close to something from the Andes or Calcutta.' The only thing missing was livestock, although passengers were packed in like sardines. And of course there was the turtle, incontinent little blighter. The strength of its shell was no compensation for the weakness of its bladder.

If a boot is Italy's shape, it is also its perfect metaphor. The Adriatic Express was a faulty zipper which often snagged on its way across the polished leather at the top of the boot—the north, down to the scuffed, broken and worn-out sole—the south. As that zipper slowly descended, tooth by tooth, station by station, it opened the boot a little more and allowed me to feel its fit for the first time, to experience the discomfort of a crude heel that would call for stoicism and a sense of adaptation were I to survive the blisters.

Our slow march forward was like a journey back in time, the warnings of my students ringing loud in my ears. While living in Milan it had been a courtesy to Daniela to pretend the difference between north and south wasn't as drastic as they suggested. Now I began to think I had underestimated that difference, and what I'd dismissed as blind racism was in fact clear-sighted critique. When deciding whether to accompany Daniela down south, perhaps I should have listened to the man on the national news, who held up a water bottle for the cameras and announced: 'This is my urine. I had no alternative. Six hours on a train with no toilet. Why does this only happen from Rome down?' It was a good question, as indeed was why I was heading there. But I gritted my teeth and blocked my nose. 'Rome down' was where I was going, albeit at a crawl.

An announcement welcomed passengers to *Trenitalia*'s service to Lecce, and informed us that 'Chef Express—The Travelling Restaurant' was now open in carriage five. It listed an array of snacks and reminded passengers to keep their receipts until they had left the train. The tentacles of *La Guardia di Finanza* reached everywhere.

I spent most of the two-hour trip to Bologna chatting with a woman by the window, whom I discovered to be English when asking if she would mind shifting her bag in the overhead rack so I could position another travelling restaurant—the soldier's suitcase—horizontally. Detecting an English accent in the unrolled R of her obliging reply—'*certo*'—I inquired where she was from.

'London. You?'

'Sydney.'

'Well, well, well.'

Mary was, or had been, beautiful, and was determined to hold the years at bay with clothes from her daughter's wardrobe, a kilo of make-up and a litre of perfume—somewhat wasted in a train that stank of urine. Fifty-five going on thirty, Mary was confident and engaging, the sort of woman you might wish to be your girlfriend's mother. She touched my arm when she spoke and leaned towards me when asking questions, like what was I doing on what she called 'the train from hell'.

When I told her I was relocating to a fishing village on the heel of the boot, she gave me the phone number of an English friend who worked for a chain of language schools in Italy, with, if she remembered correctly, a branch in Lecce. 'Call her,' she said. 'She'd be keen to have a native English speaker working in such a remote region.' I was delighted. Daniela's main concern regarding my move to the south was poor job prospects, a problem I might now have solved before arriving. I have a talent for counting chickens before they hatch.

As though providing punctuation, the train stopped as I finished my story and restarted when Mary commenced hers. Fifteen years ago she had married an Italian millionaire whom she had since left, 'making a lot of money on the divorce', and was now living in Como with her 'new man' who was 'half my age but double the fun'. Her beloved 'Robbie', playful English for Roberto I presumed, was an art dealer who attended exhibitions all over the world while Mary 'caught up with him at weekends'. Perhaps she felt young in the presence of old paintings. This weekend her Robbie was in Bologna for an auction. Or was he?

As the train approached the capital of Italy's Emilia Romagna region, Mary repeatedly dialled Robbie's number on her mobile and grew more and more frustrated each time he failed to respond. I left her to her calls and watched fallow fields slide by, feigning, like the rest of the passengers in our vicinity, a lack of interest in her manhunt. Eventually she gave up on Robbie and rang his hotel instead. 'But he must be staying there,' she protested, 'I booked the room for him myself.' Her fluency suffered when she became flustered, making her second language, and her second husband, even harder to pin down.

Over the next twenty minutes Mary tried his number a dozen times. When he finally answered, she turned towards the window in a vain attempt at privacy; the only alternative was the toilet and that was out of the question for a woman in Armani. 'What do you mean you've just woken up?' she asked in English, reducing the number of eavesdroppers in the compartment to one. 'You're supposed to be at the auction in ten minutes. And why aren't you staying at the hotel I booked for you?' Mary put her finger in her ear as a passing train rattled our windows, the most inelegant pose she had struck in years. 'Listen, we'll discuss it later,' she shouted. 'I'll meet you at the gallery in an hour.' Then she snapped the phone shut and fixed her hair in case shouting had messed it up. Regaining her composure, she leant towards my ear. 'He changed hotel on me,' she whispered. 'Oh well, they're all the same.' Whether she was referring to hotels or Italian art dealers I wasn't sure, but smiled agreement in either case.

Mary stopped chatting after that, her confident air succumbing to the rancid air of the carriage. For the remainder of her journey she tried to distract a suspicious mind with a crossword puzzle, but succeeded only in reinforcing in angry pencil the clues she had solved earlier when Robbie was where she thought he was.

Like a lame dog with its tongue out the train limped into Bologna, already exhausted with its journey just begun. I carried Mary's bag over the human obstacle course in the corridor, handing it to her once she was safely on the platform. 'Goodbye and good luck,' she said softly, a farewell I echoed, only to regret the implication. She double-kissed me like an Italian and turned towards the exit, stepping cautiously in high heels as though walking on thin ice, something I imagined Robbie would be doing for a day or two.

Bologna–Rimini

In 1980, the railway station in Bologna was rocked by an act of terrorism when a bomb exploded in the waiting room, killing eighty-five people. The mid-summer massacre, until then the worst terrorist incident in Europe, was eventually attributed to the *Nuclei Armati Rivoluzionari*, a group of Neo-Fascists with a gripe against the government.

Other than its darkest hour, I knew little about Bologna, but had been keen to visit since reading Charles Richard's book *The New Italians*, in which he described the city as 'the Italy that works'. Such praise didn't extend to trains passing through, unfortunately—or at least not to mine. Without explanation we waited for half an hour in the station. Had I known of the stopover I might have ventured out for a look at 'the Italy that works'. Instead I stuck my head out of 'the Italy that didn't work', escaping the stench and watching every train except ours put the station behind it. Time dragged and I was beginning to regret not having paid the extra to fly down south.

'*Mio Dio!*' exclaimed a large woman entering our small compartment. 'This train stinks.'

'*E' disgustoso,*' agreed the lady sitting opposite.

'*Offensivo,*' added the girl next to her, who I assumed to be her daughter.

'It will improve when we start moving,' I assured the newcomer, who placed her broad Bolognese bottom in the seat Mary had vacated.

'If we ever start moving,' quipped the girl.

'I swore I was never going to catch this train again the last time I caught it,' said the large woman, who later introduced herself as Patrizia.

'It's the smoke I can't stand,' said the man on my left, slamming the compartment's door and tossing his paper on the floor. 'I can't tolerate people who smoke in the non-smoking carriage.'

Littering is okay though.

'The problem is that half the carriage is smoking and half is non-smoking,' explained the woman opposite. 'What good is that? Of course the smell is going to travel to the non-smoking area.'

'That's not it,' contested her daughter. 'It's the people who smoke in the corridor whether it's a non-smoking section or not.'

'But if every passenger had to have a seat,' interjected Patrizia, 'the corridor would be clear and we wouldn't have this problem.'

And on they went, Italians lamenting Italy, a broken record playing over and over as the train staggered out of the station.

Introduced by inconvenience, Italians everywhere talk about one thing—Italy. About problems for starters: the delay, the smell, the smoke. But soon afterwards, their fury forgotten, about food, cities, holidays, a new law and an old way around it. After sharing anger we swapped addresses. I would even end up playing tennis twice a week with the man next to me, Renato, who turned out to be from Tricase, a small city to the south of Andrano. Had Italy's smokers lit up where they should, Renato would never have spoken up and I might never have met the man who became my closest friend in the south, even if he proved to be as unreliable as the train on which we met.

As we traversed the top of the boot heading east and to the coast, I realised why I had returned to Italy. United by hardship, my new friends were telling stories of the grace in disgrace and the service in disservice, of couples they knew who had met when 'he' arrived to find 'her' sitting in their double-booked seat. When daylight saving stops and clocks are wound back, Italian trains stop for an hour so they will eventually be on time. 'That's how my brother met his wife,' said Patrizia, 'waiting on a train that was waiting on the clock.' Inefficiency can be a better ice-breaker than most chat-up lines. I'm not sure how *Trenitalia* copes when clocks go forward an hour. And as for Alitalia . . . ?

Only a forgiving type can enjoy the enigmas of Italy. Anyone with an eye for detail will find the country derailed. But when it comes to train travel, who is better off: punctual strangers or mates running late? Do you want a clean train or the friends you'll meet on a dirty one? I had never ridden such primitive public transport. Our sorry string of carriages inched across the landscape like a crippled caterpillar, already an hour late only three hours into its journey. But on board I found a job, a friend and, a little later, a dozen pasta recipes. Such positives fail to excuse the negatives, they are merely Band-Aids that make those blisters from the boot just that little bit more comfortable.

Complete strangers an hour ago, we were joking and laughing together when the train neared the coast, salt in the air and sky azure blue. Cirrus clouds reminded me of Australian skies, an emotion I shared with my new-found friends. 'Why would you live in Italy when you can live in Australia?' asked Patrizia. Would she ever have believed it was because of experiences on dodgy trains like this one?

Rimini–Pescara

Low-budget babes in bikinis—and out of them—were the cast of the raunchy Italian film *Rimini Rimini*, a bonanza of bosoms shot in Italy's answer to Surfers Paradise, minus the skyscrapers but with plenty of other erections. For Italy's young singles, Rimini's discos and deckchairs provide the essential ingredients for a summer break: sun, sea, flesh and fornication. Even those who fail to find a mate get close enough to claim intimate, if not carnal knowledge. And that's just on the beach! Cramped alongside thousands of other holidaymakers, they rent a 2-metre plot of sand, a sun-lounge and a beach umbrella; the sort of holiday I imagine to be as relaxing as a stampede. But many passengers thought otherwise and the train, or at least its corridor, emptied somewhat. The turtle remained, however. Like the other tourists who stayed on board, it preferred the more picturesque bays and beaches further south.

A whistle sounded, a horn honked and the word Rimini slid

by the window, slowly at first then almost too fast to read before disappearing abruptly. Sea air filled the carriage as we began our descent of the peninsula, the sparkling Adriatic a soothing sight on the left. On the right was the *autostrada* Daniela had driven two days earlier to reach the same destination. Beyond that, in stark comparison to the beachgoers on the other side of the train, were farmers working fields surrounding hilltop villas that were guarded and shaded by cypress trees. To the left a holiday, to the right hard work, and in the middle a museum from where I watched both.

The corridor now clear, ticket inspectors in goblin-green jackets came through the carriage. As lethargic as the train, they punched holes in tickets and advised passengers alighting in Ancona to move four carriages down if they wished to step onto a platform; the twelve-carriage train was too long for most stations. When I went to the window on the other side of the carriage to stretch my legs and wave at children building sand-castles on the beach, as we rounded each bay I saw the rear of the train bent back on itself like a dog worrying fleas.

During my walk I noticed a fire extinguisher in a glass case. '*Rompere in caso d'incendio*' advised a sign, above an English trans-lation telling me to 'crash glass in fire event'. I have never understood why Italians go to the trouble of translating something without first going to the trouble of finding someone who speaks both languages. During my first summer in Andrano I had thought about buying a kayak. Nothing too flash, just a small canoe I could paddle to Albania and back on a sunny afternoon. The bilingual brochure I picked up boasted the boats to be 'optimum for use in funny sport'. *It's a Knockout* perhaps? And I bought a pair of earplugs in Milan which, according to the packet, were 'good for students to concentrating on noisy books'. Legs stretched, I returned to my cell, hoping we made Lecce without a 'fire event'.

When I entered the compartment they were discussing Australia and what the concept of open space must be like. I fielded all sorts of questions, some of which were easier to answer than others: What's the population? How long does it take to fly there from Italy? Are your politicians honest? How much does meat cost? What's the most popular dish? Is it true that Australians are cannibals or is that the New Zealanders? Do you ride the kangaroos?

This last question was posed by Silvia, the attractive young woman travelling with her mother. I deduced that Silvia hadn't seen much of the world, not only from the naivety of her question but because, as Renato suggested when she later left the train, she had perhaps spent all her pocket money on a boob job. Renato's theory wasn't a stab in the dark but based on certain 'hard evidence' which, since leaving Rimini, had snuck out of Silvia's shirt. Her top buttons must have slipped during bumpy track changes, either that or because of the train's constant vibration. Had we been travelling on a smooth Eurostar the sensuous stowaways might never have surfaced.

Sitting directly opposite, Renato and I immediately noticed what looked to be the most comfortable spot on the train. But Renato's unabashed staring soon alerted the girl's mother, who, with a subtle signal, made her daughter aware of the slippage. I had seen a Ruth Orkin photograph of an American girl on an Italian street being ogled by men who made no effort to disguise desire. Hands in pockets they smile and stare as the girl fastens her collar and flees. At first I disliked the photo because the woman looks distressed. But now, after living in Italy, I have realised its vulgarity is accurate.

Like several other passengers who walked into the wall when spotting Silvia, Renato found it impossible not to stare at a beautiful woman, or in this case, parts of a beautiful woman that were staring at him. Renowned bottom-pinchers, Italian men are candid about their cravings and refuse to accept that a natural urge can be considered a vice. But many foreigners find their blatancy disrespectful, as I found the Orkin photo at first. They desire respect while the Italians respect desire. But who is the more honest? I pretended not to look at Silvia's chest in case she spotted me and objected, while Renato fixed his gaze like a missile locking onto a target. We both desired the same thing, only Renato didn't deny it.

Italian men and women are comfortable with sex. To them *sesso* is not a dirty word but a human necessity, perhaps even more essential than food. When Roberto Benigni appeared on stage at the San Remo Song Festival and begged the ravishing female host for 'just a few seconds under your skirt', he was applauded by both male and female spectators. It took me a while to get used to a society which considered such behaviour decent. I had been somewhat uneasy when I went to the cinema in Tricase to see the film *Malèna*, in which the beautiful and buxom Monica Bellucci plays a sexually deprived war widow who squeezes lemons across her breasts on balmy Sicilian evenings. I wasn't uncomfortable because of what I was watching but because of who I was watching it with. The ten-year-old boy next to me licked his ice-cream indifferently as Bellucci all but masturbated. Such a film would have carried either an R or M rating in Australia. In Tricase it was for general exhibition. Why should the boy's parents have hired a babysitter just because Bellucci took her daily dose of vitamin C differently from most people?

Italian women are worshipped rather than respected. On 8 March, International Women's Day, admirers shower them with mimosa to celebrate *La Festa della Donna*. Bunches of the yellow flower are sold at traffic lights. It's the one day of the year that beggars stock something motorists actually want and washing windscreens can wait.

Such festivals are healthy but an abundance of films like *Rimini Rimini* and Italian TV in general have done little for the feminist cause. So why don't Italian women mind? When Daniela and I watch TV, I'm the one who finds the nudity excessive. We'll be having lunch with her mother while two women mud-wrestle, and Valeria—retired schoolteacher and regular church-goer—will actually barrack for one of them. It's a question of culture. Daniela has grown up thinking women come out of cakes. My Australian ex-girlfriend didn't think women should even bake them.

Renato would have had little in common with my ex-girlfriend, for whom Italy would probably have been far too sexist. But for many women, and even for a famous feminist, its stance on sex is liberating rather than lewd. 'What do we find in Italy that can be found nowhere else?' asked Erica Jong in *My Italy*. 'I believe it is a certain permission to be human that other countries lost long ago.' Renato would have agreed with her, although he'd much prefer to examine her thighs than her theories. He fell asleep after Silvia buttoned her blouse. The only scenery he was interested in had been locked away.

Pescara–Bari

The sealed silence of an air-conditioned Eurostar ruins the romance of train travel. Like soldiers farewelling loved ones on their way to the front, passengers leant from windows when the Adriatic Express stopped at a station. Platforms were crowded. For every person departing, five came to see them off. Boyfriends relinquished girlfriends with passionate kisses. Husbands dismissed wives with the briefest of pecks. '*Ciao Giovanni!*' someone shouted. '*Buon viaggio!*' screamed someone else. '*Salutami la nonna!*' yelled a mother to her daughter. '*Stammi bene,*' said a father to his teenage son. A baby was passed up to the window for a kiss, a woman was serenaded by a group of young men, and an old man tripped and fell on a step. Every stop was a big event, and when you looked at the train, every start a little miracle.

The ceremony wasn't reserved for those departing. Six *carabinieri* waited by the carriage next to mine from which stepped a man in a pinstripe suit. He handed a briefcase to one officer and a birdcage to another. The armed men accompanied the new arrivals towards the exit, two in front, two behind and one at each side. Whether the escort was for the man or the bird I couldn't tell. Perhaps the budgie had witnessed a crime and they were waiting for it to talk.

On tiptoe above the crowd, a guard waved a ragged red rag. Cigarette between his lips and cap under his arm, he craned his neck towards the front of the train in the hope that the driver would see him. Ten minutes later, still smoking, the same guard thrust a green rag at the sky; I could only assume that with all that smoke the man's lungs lacked the oomph to blow a whistle. Windows rattled as the engine engaged before we limped off once again, creeping ever closer to Lecce and Daniela. As always, just when we reached top speed, the train slowed to a stop while another flashed past. For a system run on rags it worked quite well, even if we were now nearly two hours late.

Patrizia had left us in Pescara, vowing never to catch the train again—until the next time she caught it. Her place was taken by a middle-aged woman heading to Bari to visit her sister. Rita was quiet at first, until I unwrapped a bread roll. Then food became the topic for the next three hours.

'What's in it?' she asked.

'Ham and cheese,' I replied.

'What sort?'

'Sliced.'

I wasn't trying to be rude, I simply prefer eating food far more than talking about it. But I was outnumbered. Hopelessly. The Italian flag is a tri-colour tablecloth to which citizens swear allegiance. Food is Italy's national discourse. More talked about even than football, it manages to become the topic of conversation at casual encounters between strangers: in a lift, with a *carabiniere* at a road-block and now on a slow-moving train. When foreign dignitaries visit Italy, newspapers pay more attention to what they eat than who they meet. I once saw a journalist reporting live outside a parliament building, informing viewers that Bush and Berlusconi were inside sharing lamb cutlets and lemon ice-cream. The worst thing that happens at the Italian diplomatic table is a food fight.

Questions on Italian quiz shows are often culinary in nature. Among other tasty teasers, contestants might be asked who is the patron saint of winemakers, or to list certain dishes in order of origin from north to south. And if food isn't the question it is sometimes the prize. In a Sicilian bar I saw a note on a slot machine which read: '*Le vincite si pagano con buoni consumazione*'—'Winners are paid with meal tickets.' Only in Italy when five lemons come up on a slot machine do you win five lemons.

A dumpy housewife, Rita's knowledge of all things culinary gave her almost celebrity status in our compartment. They hung off her every word and wrote down her every recipe. But it was Renato who intrigued me more than Rita. A thirty-two-year-old bank clerk, whose hobbies were tennis and tits, seemed genuinely interested in the fact a complete stranger thought he had 'been sinning for years cooking cannelloni that way'. What had become of sexist Italy? Wasn't Renato's wife supposed to be slaving in the kitchen while he was in the bar playing cards? But this new-age man actually asked for tips on how to improve his favourite recipes. Silvia and her mother were also enthralled but disagreed with Rita's views on artichokes, saying they weren't best cooked whole but diced and fried in olive oil. 'Extra virgin?' inquired Renato. For a second I thought he was himself again.

Sensing my distraction, Renato did his best to include me by asking what my favourite Italian dish was.

'Risotto,' I replied.

'*Oh signore*,' exclaimed Rita. 'You're going the wrong way. Milan's the place for risotto.'

'Crris is Australian,' Renato informed her.

'*Davvero?* You must be in paradise in Italy. I read an article on the way you cook steak in Australia. Sorry, but your barbecues sound so boring.'

'A barbecue is an excuse to drink beer,' I said. 'Food is of secondary importance.'

Renato and Silvia laughed but Rita looked disappointed, as though I had told her I didn't believe in God. Rita and I had little in common, apart from the fact she could have been Daniela's mother.

While they moved on to meat for the rest of the trip to Bari, I hid behind my newspaper. The international edition of *The Herald Tribune* features a daily four-page supplement of Italian news in English. I discovered the paper at the airport on my way back from England and have been a devoted reader ever since. To its 'In Brief' column in particular, whose headlines, while often tragic, read like the stuff of comedy. A few examples:

New shirt automatically rolls up sleeves when hot. Apparently the sleeves shrink in high temperatures. It's only available in grey and costs about US$7000. I wondered if trousers would be the company's next invention, though buyers would need to carry a change of shoes around with them.

Foggia witch is arrested after failed hex. The sorceress from Foggia, a city we were currently passing on the train, had put a curse on a woman who refused to pay €500 because the spell that was supposed to make her husband desire her like before they were married hadn't worked.

Court sees no crime in postmarked pythons. 'Couriers don't take live animals,' said the defendant's lawyer. Sadly for the snakes, he won the case.

Kurdish man caught in lover's suitcase. Customs officials became suspicious when the woman was seen struggling with the weight of her case. He was put on the next ferry back to Greece, not in the suitcase I presumed. She was arrested for illegal immigration.

Italian university to offer 3-year degree in bathing. Where do I enrol?

Elderly Sardinian fires at alleged denigrator. 'I was sick and tired of being made fun of only because I'm Sardinian,' said the accused.

Loud snorer is told to find new home. His neighbours took

him to court and the judge gave him two months to either shut up or sell up.

Art dealer found murdered in Bologna hotel room. Not really, but dozens like it.

Bari–Lecce

I had heard bad things about Bari. The man in the queue at the Italian embassy in Sydney had told me to watch my wallet if I ever went there—'Full of pickpockets and petty thieves.' They would have had to be the best in the business to pick my pocket given I was sitting on it the whole way through town. We held on to our personal possessions but lost several other things in Puglia's capital, including twenty minutes, the last four carriages of the train (to which an engine was attached that would tug them to Taranto), Rita, top-heavy Silvia, her mother, the turtle, and lastly, the colour green.

A satellite image of Italy shows the boot to be green but the heel brown, the colour of baked earth, hence the name *terroni* for those who call it home. The change occurs in the blink of an eye as you enter the scorched Salento. Grass turns to rock, cypress tree to olive grove, and stone villa to whitewashed dwelling—the signature of southern Italy. Industrial-scale agriculture shrivels to subsistence farming. Fields appear less fertile and their farmers more unkempt, many resembling their scarecrows after a life spent in the sun. This is the south of the south, the Mediterranean, where that part of me that loves Daniela will always feel at home.

It's another era. Tractors are old and rusty, make more noise and emit more smoke. A plough is pushed by hand and fails to work unless the farmer operating it has a cigarette between his lips. Broken tools are repaired rather than replaced. Fishing nets are darned by grandma. Widows dressed in black pull chicory from the earth. Men with leather skin pile potatoes into hessian sacks. Dogs are chained up and tossed a meal once a day, if they're lucky. Roads are strewn with rubbish. Stone walls tumble down. There's a crucifix on a hilltop, an olive tree by a beach, an abandoned house with prickly pear on its roof and a washing machine in a dried-up creek. Puglia's peasant beauty is enchanting, weather-beaten and raw, but its pockmarked landscape can assault an eye fond of order.

It was dark when we passed Brindisi, the smoke from industrial chimneys like ink stains in the sky. I watched the lights of a plane departing the airport where I had first arrived in Italy. Daniela had been waiting for me then as she would be for me now, but the prospect of seeing her was more exciting this time round. I loved her differently after a year together. We had history, if not a future.

The only remaining passengers in our compartment, Renato and I had been travelling for eleven hours. Others had come and gone but we had been there since the start. Now we savoured the finish as though running a marathon. The beauty of the Adriatic Express is that it turns the average destination into El Dorado. The delay made our arrival cause for celebration, as though the war for which we had left had been won while we were travelling.

But just when we thought the discomfort over, the lights went out and we travelled the final kilometres in darkness. The blackout seemed confined to our carriage, prompting Renato to suggest we had taken a tunnel with us. When we finally crept into Lecce over two hours late, the platform was a scrum of short sleeves and smiles. And there among the crowd with her hair cut short for summer was the suntanned girl who had left me pale in Milan. Three days had passed since then. One of them on a train. Her eyes alone were worth the trip.

We were kissing in the car when my mobile rang. '*Pronto*. My name's Giovanni. I believe you've got a parcel for me.' Desire took a detour as we delivered a soldier his mother's cooking. I hope he didn't notice that some of the biscuits were missing.

The piazza by the sea

From fast asleep to wide awake in one blast of a home-made megaphone. *'Meloni meloni meloni!'* Nothing had changed in Andrano. Signor Api pumped petrol in a grease-stained shirt, fruit and vegie sellers flushed buyers from their homes, and a stray cat sought refuge under Pippo's Fiat, which, as always, was parked across Daniela's gate. Fishing boats returned to port, farmers toiled in fields, housewives hung washing on rooftops and children stole tomatoes from trailers. A man on a motorbike flashed past the castle balancing a watermelon on his fuel tank. A black widow pedalled across the piazza ferrying a fresh bunch of flowers to the cemetery. The whitewashed village outshone the sun as its bell struck nine o'clock. Thirty degrees already. Summer had returned to Andrano.

'Meeeelanzzaaaneeciiicooooorie!' This time I understood the spiels that stirred me from sleep. A year ago they were indecipherable, now they were crystal clear. My second home and second language had become second nature. I was self-sufficient finally, and could bargain the price of an artichoke even lower than Daniela. I stood on the street in swimming shorts and signalled the drivers to stop. All the sellers knew me, the only Australian in town. *'Il Canguro!'* they called out, before turning off their engines for a sale and, more vitally, a chat.

My return to Andrano was emotional. I had been a resident for over a year on paper but hadn't realised the affection I felt for the town until the town showed its affection for me. Friends beeped as they drove by the house. Others called in and offered presents such as home-made pasta, gnocchi and vegetables they had grown in their gardens. Daniela bought me a Vespa, Valeria baked a cake and Franco stared through me and smiled. But it was Signor Api who made the biggest fuss. '*Whey!*' he shouted as we pulled into 'California'. '*Bentornato Arrison!*' Then he circled the car, peering in the windows and yelling: 'What? No baby? Why not? You've had a year!'

Daniela's father looked feebler, less sure on shaky legs, but he was as stubborn in ill health as he had been when well and refused to go down without a fight. A week after my arrival, Francesco flew down and drove Valeria and Franco to Sicily, leaving Daniela and me alone in Andrano for the duration of her two-month school holiday. The summer was ours to enjoy and we planned to swim, read and unwind. But a chance occurrence on our way home from a walk one evening turned what should have been a relaxing break into the most hectic holiday of my life.

Passing the home of Riccardo, the police chief who'd helped with my documents, we noticed he'd left on his car headlights. One good deed deserved another so we called in to let him know. The buzzer on the gate was answered by his stunning wife, Maria, who covered us with kisses in between screaming at her Dobermans to shut up. Before being given time to say why we'd called, Maria had ushered us to the back garden, where we found Riccardo, sleeves rolled up, standing over the corpses of two headless chickens. Still alive and riotous after witnessing the murder of its mates, a third bird was about to be executed. The police chief placed a brick over its head, another on its feet, and with one 'fowl' swoop of a kitchen knife the headless hen fell silent. Oblivious to the fact their father was preparing their pets for dinner, Riccardo's two young daughters played with friends across the street.

'Look who's here,' exclaimed Maria, distracting her husband, whose face lit up when he saw Daniela and me—indeed he was so excited he ran towards us with the knife still in his hand.

Riccardo was an enormous man, though agile despite his size and exuberant like a child. And his tongue was as frenetic as he was, firing off questions without awaiting a reply. How he interrogated suspects I'll never know.

'My dear friends. How are you? How's your father, Daniela? Have you got plans for tomorrow night?'

'More plans than those chickens,' I said, answering his last question first.

'Come at nine-thirty. There'll be loads of us and we're going to eat these.' He indicated the collection of corpses. 'I raise them myself,' he continued, pointing to an enclosure in which a dozen hens strutted about death row. 'They're delicious. Come tomorrow night and you'll see.'

We shared a drink and were showered with questions, most of which we didn't get a chance to answer. It was always like that with the police chief, you felt as though you'd been celebrated and ignored at the same time. Then, with the same fanfare with which we had been received, we were escorted back to the gate. Only when we got home did we realise we had forgotten to tell Riccardo about his headlights.

'I'll phone him,' said Daniela.

'No, leave it,' I said, smiling. 'Those chickens deserve some sort of justice.'

The following evening, together with twenty madcap Italians and their children, we relaxed in Riccardo's garden eating and drinking until well after midnight. I had no idea who belonged to whom. Girls were told not to eat with their mouths full by several mothers, and boys to quit cutting their watermelon into rude shapes by as many fathers. Severgnini was spot on with his Terrazza Law: dining under a clear sky surrounded by good people and great wine dissolved Italy's daily disasters. Berlusconi could have had his hands in the till at that very moment and we wouldn't have cared.

I couldn't help feeling that the hens had died in vain. Fourth in a five-course feast, by the time the chicken arrived we had

no room left to savour its taste. But I pushed in a few mouthfuls
when I saw Riccardo coming over to chat.

'*Allora?*' he asked. 'How are they?'

'*Buonissimo*,' I replied, holding a burp at bay.

'*Complimenti*,' gasped Daniela, equally stuffed.

'Glad to hear it,' said Riccardo. 'But don't say anything to the
girls. They spent the entire morning trying to count the chickens
who luckily wouldn't stand still long enough for them to realise
three were missing. I confessed to killing one but the butcher
brought the other two, okay?' You know you're in southern Italy
when the policeman is getting his story straight with the witnesses
rather than vice versa.

The perfect host, after the meal Riccardo arrived with a trolley
of liqueurs and insisted I try an *amaro*—a digestive drink that
could pass as herbal if not for its 30 per cent alcohol content.
Tables were cleared away and an accordion appeared. Children
danced, parents sang and a stray dog sniffed at the gate. Many of
the songs were in dialect, and I understood little except that a
woman called Adriana loved too many men and had some
choosing to do. Then they moved on to the tarantula, the children writhing and wriggling as though born with the 'trance-dance'
in their blood. We were still singing at 2 am. None of the parents
even considered taking their children home, and those who
nodded off in their chairs were woken at the end of each tune
by the hearty applause of summertime singers.

Most of the group went home around three while the rest
decided to drive to Castro for gelato. Riccardo was among them
but needed a lift because his battery was flat. We drove in convoy
and followed Riccardo's friend Diego, who claimed he knew a
short-cut. Ignoring the presence of the policeman in the car
behind, Diego drove almost the entire way to Castro on the
wrong side of the road, the left-hand side, 'to make the Australian
feel at home' he explained on arrival. In Italy, new friends will
die to please.

The threat of the sun was only hours away. Tomorrow would

be too hot to move so we needed to make the most of the darkness. Only the ringleaders remained: Riccardo, Diego, Daniela, myself, a concert pianist and the local plumber. But what to do next? My suggestion that we head to the port for a swim shocked everyone, not because they were against the idea, but because they considered it certain death. So we digested for half an hour before speeding to Andrano's port. A diving competition was organised from a rock near tethered fishing boats. In underpants we shattered the sea, screaming like children as the water turned white and the horizon pale pink.

The sun was above the horizon by the time Daniela and I got to bed, but shutting the *serranda* made it set again. For the first time we slept through the watermelon seller when he passed on his raucous rounds a little later.

We spent almost the entire summer with this group of teenage forty-somethings, enjoying a calendar of activities so intense that even the bell had difficulty keeping time. Lively nights were followed by lazy days at Andrano's most popular swimming spot—La Botte, so called because the beach was shaped like a wine cask. Much of the Salento's coastline was nicknamed after contours carved by water and time. A few kilometres further south was La Grotta Verde—'The Green Cave', where fishermen threw lines off 'The Pig's Snout' and swimmers dived off 'The Eagle's Beak'. They were all popular but it was La Botte, with its car park and kiosk, that was the most accessible and the most crowded.

Having rolled down the hill to summer homes, Andrano's residents needed a place to congregate. A relatively flat expanse of rock on an otherwise jagged coastline, La Botte was that place—a piazza by the sea. It was as if the town square had been moved to the beach for the hottest months of the year, where the temperature was at least five degrees cooler than in the village on top of the hill. A kiosk replaced the bar, markets were held in the car park, even the priest held afternoon mass by the beach to escape the heat in the church; how could he advertise heaven when it felt as hot as hell?

Packed close like a colony of penguins, the *Andranesi* milled about the beach minding everyone's business but their own. Dressed in swimmers and plastic sandals, rock and *riccio* too sharp for bare feet, they went about their lives as they would have in the piazza, the only variation being that every so often they dived into the sea to cool off. Local politicians debated municipal matters, waving arms to make a point as though in conference at the town hall. The headmaster told a mother why her son was struggling with maths. The mechanic informed a client why his car wouldn't start. The young exchanged amorous glances and the elderly idle chat. Music blared from the kiosk, where teenagers danced the Chihuahua and The 'IMCA'—there's no Y in the Italian alphabet. Elderly men played cards and drank bright red *aperitivi*. Like most Italian beaches it was a carnival atmosphere, more ice-cream than sun-cream and a sea made of glass.

The view from the beach was spectacular. To the north the town of Castro—whitewashed houses hugging the headland, classically Mediterranean. To the south an olive hillside crowned by Torre del Sasso—a crumbling lookout tower. And across the sea—Albania, hidden by heat haze but close enough for its inhabitants to see how much fun we were having and risk their lives to try and join us.

Behind the beach was a shaded footpath joining La Botte with Andrano's port, the haunt of adolescents too cool to sit with parents. They chatted, shouted, smoked, spat, swore, sent each other text messages despite standing side by side, and saluted friends darting by on Vespas, if they could recognise them, that is. The new helmet law was ruining one of Andrano's most popular pastimes—the drive-by greeting—at least when the *vigile* was on duty and the law was partially obeyed. 'This helmet law is rubbish,' said Daniela's friend Patrizia. 'I can't recognise people when they beep me anymore.' Benefits of modern laws are slow to catch on in ancient towns which put socialising before safety. I can think of few worse jobs than being a *vigile* in an Italian village, where enforcing the law makes you a party-pooper rather than a policeman.

Back on the beach, four generations of one family shared the shade of a beach umbrella, the hole to keep it upright drilled into rock by the father and son team who ran the kiosk. If you wished to find one of these holes vacant, or to spread your towel on a smooth stretch of stone, you had to either arrive early or after 1 pm, when the beach emptied in a matter of minutes as hungry tummies headed home for spaghetti.

After a late night, Daniela and I would meet the gang at La Botte around eleven, when the sun was too hot for sunbathing and the sea more crowded than the beach. Friends would see us coming and start the celebrations, as though we'd been apart for six years rather than six hours. We dropped our towels and joined them in water warm in parts and cool in others, not because of a lack of toilets on the beach but due to submarine springs that jet freezing currents into a sun-soaked sea.

Just as townsfolk chatted in the piazza, at La Botte they trod water while exchanging pleasantries. They didn't go there to relax, they went to gossip while tanning. La Botte was where they discovered what was happening in their village. Daniela's neighbour once arrived for his morning swim to learn that his brother, who lived above him, had been taken to hospital during the night. Still in his swimmers, Umberto rushed to the hospital at such a speed it was a miracle he didn't get himself admitted.

It was because La Botte resembled the piazza that Daniela's father had refused to go swimming there, arousing criticism among friends who accused him of snubbing them. Every year, the woman who ran the *tabaccheria* would ask Franco why he was so *antisociale*, and every year she would receive the same reply: 'Why would I want to spend my holidays with the same people I spend the rest of the year? And why would I go to a beach to hear people tell me I've got a fatter stomach and longer feet than last year? I want to relax, not hear that I'm ugly.' Almost every anecdote Daniela told me about her father made me wish I'd met him earlier, when he could have told me them himself. He sounded delightfully irreverent, an *anti-conformista* in the traditional south.

Franco took his family to Sicily each year as much to avoid La Botte as to enjoy Valeria's hilltop hideaway. He simply didn't wish to sunbathe next to his students, his lawyer, his doctor, his dentist, the man who'd painted his house and the woman who'd poisoned his dog. He found it impossible to escape daily life when surrounded by its protagonists. For some La Botte was paradise, while for others, like Daniela, who took after her father, it was the last place to unwind. During my first summer in Andrano she took me to almost every other beach along the coast, for privacy more than anything, to avoid people gossiping about her Australian boyfriend. But now that I had my own friends, for whom La Botte was synonymous with summer, I dragged Daniela there each morning, at least until the novelty of belonging to the town wore off, or until someone told me that my stomach was bigger than last year.

After a swim we sat with the group and spent the morning organising the evening. Provided we stuck to food and religion, we didn't have to search hard to find entertainment in the Salento during summer. We revisited the smorgasbord of *sagre*—the food festivals, at which we ate enough to raise the sea level by a couple of inches next time we went for a swim. And to thank her for another year's good graces, we attended Andrano's night of nights, *La Festa della Madonna delle Grazie*. Once again the piazza resembled Las Vegas, and once again Daniela prayed for a hailstorm which didn't show.

On the evening of August the tenth we gathered at La Botte for an all-natural fireworks display. According to religious legend, the shooting stars represent the tears of Saint Lawrence, a Roman

Catholic deacon martyred in the year 258. According to scientists, not the most popular people in Andrano, the 'tears' are actually shards of the Swift-Tuttle comet colliding with the earth's atmosphere at around 230,000 kilometres per hour. Whichever explanation you prefer, *La Notte di San Lorenzo* is a pain the neck. Quite literally. Two years in a row now I have spent the night with my eyes fixed on the heavens, and the only thing I have seen flash across the sky is the late flight from Rome to Athens.

A few evenings later we returned to La Botte to watch a religious procession with a twist. A fleet of fishing boats sailed slowly past the beach, giving praise to Saint Andrea—Andrano's patron saint. The lead boat carried clerics and an effigy of the saint, so lifelike it could have suffered from seasickness. A brass band followed in the second boat, doing its best to play on a floating stage but straying out of tune every time a wave arrived. Smaller runabouts brought up the rear, packed with pilgrims riding the tide of goodwill. The statue was ferried to the port, blessed in the car park and then carried up the hill to Saint Andrea's church. Simplicity made the occasion special. To a town founded by Cretan fishermen, a dozen lazy fishing boats are far more symbolic than a kitsch arrangement of neon lights.

The following evening we held a *Scopa* competition on the kiosk's uneven tables. Ten couples competed vociferously for a worthless tin trophy in what became known as the 'Andrano International Scopa Competition', international because of an Australian competitor. I almost won it, I might add, and probably would have if bloody Daniela hadn't played the wrong card in the semis. Riccardo and Maria eventually took the title, although the police chief was accused of cheating in the final.

After the match we left La Botte and drove up the hill towards town. Halfway there we took a country lane leading to a church in a clearing overlooking the sea. Like the church, the evening was dedicated to *La Madonna dell'Attàrico*, the saviour of a baby whose mother prayed for help in curing her inability to lactate and nourish her child. Andrano folklore has it that the Madonna of the *Attàrico*, a word which may come from *allattare* meaning 'to breastfeed', appeared as a vision in the mother's dream and awakened her to the presence of a snake that was drinking her milk while she slept, leaving her dry come morning when the baby looked to suckle.

Daniela had wanted to show me this sacred site for some time, not the church—a modern structure resembling a whistling kettle—but the underground shrine where the legend was born. A flight of steps led to a cave, the entrance to which was a mosaic wall of stones with an opening in the shape of the cross. On the far wall was the palest of frescos of the Holy Virgin nursing a child, barely visible after centuries in a cave that floods with water when it rains. In his book, *What The Stones Could Tell You*, Andrano's priest, Don Francesco Coluccia, says the legend which arose from the painting can be read as social allegory given that at the time it came about, Andrano's landowners 'milked' the peasant labourers dry, just as the snake reduced the mother to praying for her baby's nutrition.

Don Francesco suggests the artists responsible for the fresco were Byzantine monks, who fled to what are now Italian shores to escape religious persecution in the Orthodox orient during the eighth to tenth centuries. He believes they sought refuge in the cave because of its safe position and superb panorama. The fleeing monks brought more than their artistry to the Salento. Among meagre belongings they also packed the seeds of a species of oak called *La Vallonea*, a tree not native to Italy but which now grows in modest numbers in and around Andrano. The most impressive of these was planted in the twelfth century, now a monster on the edge of Tricase.

Andrano's history is visible in its landscape, audible in its dialect and personified in the religious figures who comprise its legends. Legends like that of *La Madonna dell'Attàrico*, the reason we had come to the clearing that night. Indeed most of the town had turned up and the party was well under way. There was a band, a barbecue, an Albanian selling belts, a *vigile* directing traffic and a donkey tied to a tree.

'*Poverino*,' I said to Daniela, indicating the tethered animal.

'Oh, I wouldn't worry about him,' she replied. 'Donkeys are born tied up.'

I loved it when the most stylish woman I had ever met spoke her stark country wisdom.

Although I was a resident, the group treated me as Andrano's guest. I wasn't given the keys to the town, if only because no one locked it. They insisted I taste *servola*—a pork sausage which has become traditional fare for the occasion, refilled my wine glass at every opportunity, and explained the history and significance of the evening. They stopped at nothing to showcase their village; Diego even ventured into a dark field to find a species of wild grass which I was instructed to suck for its aniseed. That's the problem with being the guest of honour: it's nice to be celebrated but you have to do what they ask of you, including sucking things you'd rather not and pretending to have enjoyed the experience. Tell them you don't like it and you risk disappointing an entire community.

By mid-August I was nocturnal and so tanned it looked as though I'd fallen in Daniela's 'black well'. I heard the bell strike four in the morning more often than four in the afternoon, when I was wrapped in the warmth of Daniela and siesta. An afternoon nap was vital to find energy for the evening, plus it meant avoiding the hottest part of the day. When it was too hot to sleep in the bedroom, we put our mattress in the corridor and opened the front and back doors, hoping to at least catch the Z in breeze. This worked until I was woken by a stray cat padding over my chest, so we resorted to sleeping in the cellar when the mercury nudged forty. At five we arose for the second half of the day, charged our batteries with fruit from the fridge, before either returning to the beach or doing any chores that couldn't wait until September.

In the evening, if nothing was organised with Riccardo's group I went to the tennis club in Tricase. Italians are hard to organise at the best of times but in summer it's even more difficult. Arranging a game of doubles with Renato and his mates was more of a challenge than the actual match. Either three or five players would turn up to play but rarely the required foursome. When we did get the numbers right someone would be late, Renato usually, whose forehand was more accurate than the hands of his watch. But I enjoyed his excuses as much as his company. 'Sorry I'm late,' he said one night. 'I had to bake a cake for my mother.' I wondered if he got the recipe from Rita on the train. We would play until after midnight, drinking a beer at the end of each set. Then girlfriends arrived and we headed for Renato's, where he cooked and served dinner approaching a time when I used to eat breakfast.

Given the southern Italian tradition of loyalty to particular beaches, it was quite a feat to convince Renato and his girlfriend to desert 'their' beach and join us at La Botte one morning. But I couldn't have chosen a worse morning to recruit bathers to La Botte, for when our visitors arrived, few people were swimming because of police boats searching for two Italian policemen and an Albanian, missing presumed drowned. Coast Guard helicopters hovered above the water in what looked more a scene from Hollywood than a summer's day by the sea. Short of strapping on a snorkel and joining the search, there was little we could do other than buy ice-creams and watch. The men had been missing since three in the morning and nobody expected good news.

Calm seas and a clear night had provided perfect conditions for people-smugglers to ferry their human cargo across the shortest stretch of water between Albania and Italy. In the vicinity of Andrano it's a mere 75 kilometres across and, depending on which Mafia you do business with, costs around $3000. Speedboats depart Albania after midnight and enter Italian waters soon after, where the Coast Guard and *La Guardia di Finanzia* do what they can to track them.

My own experience of entering Italy shows that border controls are lax even at airports. On one occasion, returning to Rome from Prague, I found the immigration booth unattended. Knowing the airport well by then, I went to a nearby office where I disturbed three policemen huddled around a tiny TV. I held up my passport but the officers weren't interested. 'Go on through,' said one. 'Schumacher's about to be world champion again.'

Given the slack situation at airports, people-smugglers are hardly afraid of deserted beaches under cover of darkness. Once ashore the *clandestini* beg, borrow or steal to move north. But the good fortune of finding a ride is not always a guarantee of success, as the bodies of six Kurdish men on a Salento roadside demonstrated. The illegal arrivals had stowed away in a Greek truck bound for Milan, but their hiding place wasn't insulated from the exhaust and all six died from asphyxiation. When the driver realised what had happened, he left the main road and unloaded the expired cargo in a stopping bay, one on top of the other, like bags of cement.

But more people perish before reaching dry land, as passengers are sometimes thrown overboard before nearing the coast, allowing smugglers to avoid being detected by police. When boats are spotted, crews have been known to toss a baby in the water so police have no alternative but to call off the chase and attempt rescue, by which time the bandits are back in Albania. Where pursuit does occur, a desperate tactic is to ram the police launch, which is precisely what had happened the morning Renato and his girlfriend came to sample La Botte. The impact had thrown three Italian officers and one Albanian overboard. One of the Italians was rescued but the other three bodies were never found.

The Mediterranean is becoming something of a cemetery, with around 2000 people drowning annually in their attempts to enter Europe's back door. Not only in small boats but in large, overloaded and unseaworthy ships which either run aground, are abandoned by crews or simply come unstuck in rough seas. From television news it seems that rarely a day passes in summer without a rusty old freighter found drifting in Italian waters, its engines destroyed by crew who then hide among the passengers, leaving Italian authorities no alternative but to tow the hopeless vessel to land. To benevolent Italy: often criticised for its head but rarely complimented for its heart.

They searched the sea off La Botte for days, long after Renato and his girlfriend returned to their beach vowing never to stray again. But Daniela and I remained loyal to the piazza by the sea, enjoying a life the less fortunate were dying to discover. It blemished paradise knowing that hell lay so close across the water, and was a sobering end to an intoxicating summer.

In the aftermath of the nuclear disaster in Chernobyl, doctors advised children from the radiation zone that the best medicine for their ailments would be some time in a warm climate. Every summer for three years, Andrano hosted thirty Russian children, one of whom stayed with Daniela's family. One night, Daniela heard Olga crying in bed and went to comfort the girl.

'Are you sad because you want to go home?' asked Daniela.

'No,' replied Olga. 'I'm sad because I want to stay and I can't.'

At the end of my second summer in Andrano, it was Daniela who needed comforting as she lay awake in bed, worried about the future and our decision to leave Milan. I calmed her as best I could by saying that her village had become my second home and that I was enthusiastic about my decision to remain, for a while at least. I wasn't sure if I was telling the truth, but I thought of all the people who would give everything to live in Andrano, and vowed to give life in the town my best shot.

The local foreigner

When I had telephoned from London, Daniela's mother told me I was more Italian than her daughter. When I returned to Andrano, I realised she was right. Not because I couldn't go without coffee in the morning, pasta for lunch or siesta in the afternoon, but because a panel beater suggested defrauding the insurance company to fix our car and I told him to go ahead.

The first thing to do when you move to Italy is memorise the panel beater's phone number in your mobile to save looking it up all the time. No matter how good a driver you are, you *will* have accidents. They are part of the learning curve which, like most curves in Italy, is taken at high speed. Becoming Italian means talking with your hands and driving with your feet. But it's not how you drive that makes you one of them, it's how you go about repairing your car.

My first accident happened less than a month after arriving in Italy when a car in Tricase's chaotic Piazza Cappuccini reversed into my path. I collected the Opel Corsa, whose driver accepted blame but urged Daniela not to waste time, money and patience on an insurance company. Instead he offered to call his cousin who was 'good with cars' and would fix the damage quickly. We were even offered a courtesy vehicle—the one we had hit presumably—while ours was off the road.

Daniela, who had years of experience with Italian insurance companies, was most interested in the offer. But I most certainly was not. Fond of official avenues, I thanked the man for his generous proposal, instructed Daniela to take down his details and then took her by the arm and led her back to the car; the fact she was considering the offer meant she was obviously concussed.

The result of my arrogance was months of phone calls and faxes, on top of the mountain of immigration documents we were working on at the time, to complete the simplest of claims which the insurance company only paid four months later when Daniela involved her lawyer. Had the nervous Australian not confused the issue, Daniela and the cousin might have straightened out the problem—and the bumper bar—in a couple of days.

My second accident occurred on the road from Milan to Lake Como when a cement truck changed lanes without indicating, destroying our right-hand front tyre, the panel above it and leaving the bumper bar hanging by a thread. As good a Samaritan as he was a driver, the truckie decided not to stop. So we limped off the *autostrada* and found a mechanic who replaced the tyre with a re-tread, straightened the damaged panel with a hammer, and re-attached the bumper bar with a drill and some rivets; I bet he was good at jigsaws.

Despite a garage full of cars, the mechanic dropped everything but his grease-stained overalls to assist. 'What a turd,' he said of the truck driver while bandaging our sorry Lancia. He worked on the car for over forty minutes and refused any form of payment other than the chocolates we had in the boot. Who said the Italians are a predictable bunch? In the same afternoon our car was damaged by a 'turd' it was repaired by an angel for the price of chocolate.

Because the truck hadn't stopped, we had no way of making more permanent repairs without paying a huge excess, an unfair scenario which a petrol station attendant in Milan later offered to remedy. Noticing the temporary repairs while filling our car with petrol, he said his brother was a truck driver whose insurance allowed him to have as many accidents as he liked without increasing his excess—now there's a safety incentive. Whether he had taken a liking to Daniela, or simply because he deplored injustice (I believe it was the former), he said his brother would be happy to declare his truck guilty of the damage and for his insurance to cover the cost of repairs.

'Go on,' said Daniela, sensing a significant saving. Go away, I thought, sensing a situation more dangerous than the actual accident. Daniela took the man's phone number and probably would have called had I not insisted once again on a more honest approach. I was still playing a dirty game by clean rules. And I was still losing. I failed to realise that the ease with which they spoke of committing fraud reflected the frequency with which they suffered it. Drivers were driven to dishonesty by insurance companies which, according to the ombudsman who called an investigation, had been swindling motorists for years by collaborating to raise premiums across the board, destroying competition and making every-buddy richer.

Like my car, my principles were smashed to pieces when I left the apartment one morning to find a tail-light destroyed, the bumper bar bent and the boot flapping open. A wayward motorist, probably one of few Italians receiving the blind benefit justifiably, had collected the stationary obstacle before fleeing the scene once again.

Enough! It was time to fight fire with fire, which was why I said an immediate 'si' when an enterprising panel beater devised a plan to repair the damage free of charge. He would invent an accident with the car of another client who had suffered similar injustice and been waiting for a red car with damage in the right place. Our Lancia matched the description perfectly: it was red and damaged in the right place, in fact it was damaged in every place.

Initially, I simply couldn't condone solving a problem by breaking the law—the cause of most Italian car accidents in the first place. But then I realised that adapting to a foreign environment meant playing by its rules, unwritten or otherwise, and that there was a difference between a good decision and the right decision. Survival was more important than scruple, and an ulcer was not the sort of souvenir I wanted to take home. I had been swimming upstream for a year, exhausting myself to go nowhere. Now it was time to go with the flow. And I would justify my disobedience as retaliation, that age-old Italian excuse for injustice committed due to injustice suffered. The insurance company had diddled us, now we would diddle them. It was like a game and this would merely be one for us in an everlasting stalemate.

I needed little convincing when the panel beater outlined his plan in further detail. Thousands of euros in repairs would cost just a little pride and perhaps a bottle of scotch for the panel beater's pains. But just when we had worked out the details of the accident, including the little diagram, an obstacle arose. An unexpected one—Daniela. The scheme was too far-fetched for machination's mistress herself. We had both changed our attitude, it seemed.

Over the course of one year, more than learning to live with each other, Daniela and I had switched roles. In the beginning we had fought because she was too willing to flirt with the law. Now we did so because I was. My caution had surrendered to her cunning and her cunning to my caution. And it was not just in regard to the law that we had both turned full-circle. I now wanted a hot meal for lunch while Daniela was content with a sandwich, the rubbish on the street bothered her more than me, and after spending months training her to wear her seat-belt, I now had to be reminded to do so.

After much deliberation, heated at times, we told the panel beater to go ahead with the repairs but to expect payment from us rather than the insurance company. 'It's probably just as well,' he replied. 'Not because they might have smelt a rat, but because the last time I went through your insurance company someone at the agency made off with the cheque.' It was almost enough to make Daniela change her mind. Almost.

If fixing the car had made me a local, fixing the bikes made me a foreigner again. The squeaky antiques were our sole means of transport while the car was off the road, and were themselves in need of repair after a year in Daniela's cellar.

Daniela phoned a man she called 'Compare'—an affectionate term similar to 'godfather' awarded to a man close to the family. Daniela had many compari in Andrano, including Signor Api, who had chosen Franco's sister as his son's godmother. Why that meant Daniela should call him her godfather I wasn't sure. Suffice to say, the tenuous link explained why she called every second old man in her village Compare and every second old woman Comare. Everyone needs a title of some sort.

This particular compare, a stooped man with silver hair, had made bicycle repair his hobby in retirement, although I'm not sure he was flooded with work. No sooner had Daniela hung up than at the gate appeared his Citroen, the old cockroach variety. Into it he force-fed our bicycles, pedals out the window and handlebars blocking the boot.

For someone close to the family, Compare was remarkably distant. He exchanged few pleasantries, didn't want to know who I was, and the furrows on his face suggested his staple expression was a frown. It was the burdened look of many of Andrano's elderly, whose lives revolved around the simple pleasures of family, food and religion. Life looked a trial for these people, a chore to be endured. They hadn't grown up carefree, cavorting on Vespas, chatting on mobiles or seducing the best looking. Health and having enough food had been their goals, and they thanked God for both when the sun came and went. Everything about them said heat and toil, from their snakeskin hands to their sunburnt brows.

A farmer most of his life, Compare was married, had survived colon cancer but lost his son to Italy's roads. The bar in the piazza was his world, where he drank more grappa than his doctor recommended and played cards until the pictures wore off. He smoked, fished, farted and went to funerals, burying his mates until they buried him. That was it really, other than playing *Superenalotto* twice a week, hoping to fluke the winning numbers. I'd love to see what he would do with a few million euros; bet more heavily at cards perhaps.

Daniela didn't know why she called him *Compare*; she had grown up doing so and never thought to question why, something only I found strange. In these remote villages, everyone is connected to someone and someone to everyone else. No matter how long I stayed in Andrano I could never have anything in common with a man like *Compare*. He wasn't effervescent like that other *compare*, Signor Api, and had neither the means nor the inclination to converse with me. We were from different planets. He had no idea where Australia was, nor was he interested in finding out. And we would never share a language. In fact, between the two of us, only I spoke Italian.

Compare conversed with Daniela in a bizarre dialect, discordant and abrupt, in which I recognised certain words but not the overall meaning. It was Andrano's local tongue, an inelegant-sounding slang, like what would remain in the sieve if you strained pure Italian. More guttural than the official language and a great deal more difficult to learn, Andrano's personal parlance is the only means of communicating with men like *Compare*, who had spent almost every minute of his eighty-odd years in the town and to whom Italian was a second language. Daniela even called him *Compare* in dialect.

Italy is known as 'The Land of a Thousand Dialects'. Every village on the peninsula has its own language, a baffling blend of modern Italian and the ancient tongue spoken by the founders, invaders or occupiers of each particular region. In the province of Lecce, for example, the dialect has a strong Greek influence, in Turin the roots of many words can be traced to French, and in Sicily there's a bit of everything—the linguistic legacies of Arab invaders, Albanian settlers and Spanish conquistadors.

Dialect is a linguistic birthmark, a code that ties Italians to their town and its inhabitants. For the foreigner, the difficulty in learning these codes is that it is not simply a question of expanding your vocabulary, because dialect is made up of words that don't exist in the Italian dictionary. Consulting a foreign dictionary would be a similar waste of time because the Italians, in adapting foreign words to local tongues, have deformed them through accent and idiom.

Perhaps the best and, I hesitate to say, simplest example can be found in a question I was often asked during my first summer in Andrano and which, come my second, I had finally understood: *Sciamu mare crai?*—Shall we go to the beach tomorrow? In Italian the question would be: *Andiamo al mare domani?* But in Andrano's dialect, *andiamo* (shall we go) becomes *sciamu, mare* (sea or beach) has stayed the same, and *domani* (tomorrow) has been replaced by *crai,* imported from the Latin *cras.*

It's as hard to explain as it was to understand, and to be honest I gave up trying when I realised the utility of such words was restricted to a few dozen kilometres and a few thousand people. I wasn't in love with the tone either. The constant U in words like *sciamu* made it sound primitive, like a pack of monkeys debating whether to go to the beach tomorrow.

Dialect is something you pick up as you go along rather than study. The presence of the odd Italian word meant I at least caught the gist when people spoke their parochial patois. I knew what it was that I wasn't understanding, like staring at a picture that is out of focus. But only Andrano's dialect was vaguely decipherable. Those of other towns and villages were gobbledygook, hence the need to speak Italian if you want to converse with people from other regions. So for a man like *Compare,* who only speaks dialect, a trip out of town is like a trip overseas.

According to *The New Italians,* in 1990 one in seven Italians could only converse in their village vernacular, and this figure might have been higher if Mussolini hadn't pushed the standardisation of the language for the sake of *unità nazionale,* or at least so his soldiers could understand orders. Interestingly, the soldiers' dialects proved a weapon against *Il Duce,* for when they wrote letters home from the front decrying Fascism and the war, censors couldn't understand their coded correspondence.

Thanks to improved literacy and post-war migration, most Italians now speak the official language. Purists say a man like *Compare* is illiterate because he speaks only dialect. Others say he is perfectly literate because, although it's only spoken by a limited number of people, his dialect conforms to a grammatical structure. Whichever is true, a person limited to dialect is today considered ignorant because of an inability to converse with both the rest of the nation and the outside world. But when the outside world consists of the bar in the piazza, that's not a major problem.

Nowadays, in all but extreme cases, the younger generation uses dialect as a fun rather than a functional language. Two residents of the one town, both fluent in Italian, will drop dialect into conversation to give it a parochial flavour; Daniela says it's like adding home-grown herbs to packaged pasta. Dialect is more a password than a language, a key to belonging to the hearts and minds of a village. One little word reveals intimacy and identity. It has the properties of a private joke: amusing to those who get it, meaningless to those who don't. Daniela and her mother will be chatting away in Italian only to suddenly break into dialect, not because they don't want me to understand—I hope—but because certain characters in Andrano lose their personality when referred to in Italian. Like *Compare*, the man you call to fix *''na bici*' rather than '*la bicicletta*'.

With fewer people speaking dialect out of necessity, many fear their unique tongues will die out and are devising ways to prolong the lifespan of their languages. Like the mayor of Malo, a village in the Veneto region, who declared it illegal for residents to speak anything other than dialect for three days. The idea was a success, apparently. That mayor was no fool, threatening Italians, of all people, with silence.

But while there is breath in the bodies of men like *Compare*, who only ever left Andrano to fight a war and who depend on dialect for survival, 'The Land of a Thousand Dialects' lives on. How can such men be considered illiterate? *Compare*'s knowledge of the only language he has ever needed is so extensive that most younger residents of Andrano can't understand him, not because he doesn't speak their language, but because they don't speak his. Even Daniela, university educated, has a smaller vocabulary than this 'ignorant' old man.

Compare didn't bother to tie the boot down with a rope. He wasn't going far, never had, never would. He muttered something brusque, beeped once and took the corner, heading home to repair bicycles as rusty as himself.

'How long did he say the repairs would take?' I asked Daniela.

'I haven't a clue,' she replied. 'Let's give the old guy a week.'

No such thing as common sense

Daniela had wanted to show me Alberobello for some time. In the vineyard hills above Brindisi stands the medieval township of *trulli*—cone-roofed dwellings made from stacked stones which were designed to be dismantled in the time it took the property tax inspector to tether his horse. No house. No tax. Simple.

Today, Alberobello has been declared a UNESCO World Heritage site and the *trulli* cannot be touched. Unfortunately the same cannot be said for Renato's Alfa, which was stolen while we were sightseeing. When we returned to the vacant parking space, Daniela suggested calling the *Carabinieri*. 'Please don't,' begged Renato. 'It's been a bad day. Why make it worse?'

Italy's police may be impossible, but Italians are impossible to police. How can the *Carabinieri* be expected to supervise the *Napoletani*, for example, who, the day after seat-belts became law, were swerving around Naples wearing T-shirts with a seat-belt printed diagonally across them? And how can they avoid appearing nonsensical when enforcing statutes so senseless they invite circumvention? Like the one stating that no funeral can exceed eighty minutes, or another declaring it illegal to take household rubbish to the communal bin other than between 7 pm and 5 am. Such a law should itself be thrown out, at the correct time of course. One forward-thinking politician actually proposed such a scheme: to pass a law obliging parliament to delete one useless law a day. His idea was either disregarded, or was the first law deleted.

In the town of Galatone, just a canter from Lecce, horses

are sold at live animal markets. During the mad cow crisis, sales of horsemeat skyrocketed, leading to a black market in stolen livestock. A law was passed requiring every horse, like its owner, to have identity papers ready for presentation on demand. It was even money as to who looked more foolish on the news reports, the *carabiniere* asking for the horse's passport or the illiterate horse peddler who only spoke dialect and who scratched his head at such a bizarre request. The two parties stared at each other, bemused, gesticulating wildly; a time-old Italian stalemate born of mutual incomprehension. Who was at fault? The *carabiniere* policing the law? The horse peddler evading the law? Or the government passing the law? Daniela suggested they were all to blame and that the only innocent party was the unfortunate horse, whose slaughter would keep all three ticking over.

In an effort to improve their hapless image, every year the *Carabinieri* PR wing issues a calendar featuring acts of bravery similar to those on the station wall in Loritano. It also published a book of stories in which valiant officers substitute hero and heroine of fable and fairytale; kiss an Italian frog and it will turn into a policeman rather than a prince. Despite efforts to dilute the public's derision, the unfortunate *carabinere* continues to replace the Irishman in Italian versions of jokes otherwise word for word. The best way to burn a *carabiniere*'s ear is still to phone him while he's ironing.

When Italians start their cars they hope to avoid two things—accidents and *carabinieri*. A Madonna in the glove box superstitiously protects against the former, but nothing can guarantee safe passage around the latter. Cruising along carefree, radio on, window down, until up ahead a clumsy crime-fighter with a lollipop stick signals you to stop. You've done nothing wrong, but you're in serious trouble.

It was a week after our regrettable day trip to Alberobello when, driving to La Botte for a morning swim, we were ambushed, the dreaded lollipop stick thrust in our direction. *La Madonna della Glove Box* wasn't doing her job and over seventy people had perished on Italy's roads the previous weekend. Another knee-jerk law—headlights on day and night. Ours were on, so why had we been waylaid? I had seen the announcement of the law on the nightly news but, according to the *carabiniere* who leant in my window asking to see my licence, I had misinterpreted it.

'You can only have your lights on during the day on an *autostrada*, a *superstrada* or an *extra-urbana*. Why have you got yours illuminated on an *urbana?*'

I declined to answer, anticipating, incredulously, where the officer was heading.

'Don't tell me you're going to fine me because this is the wrong sort of road to have my headlights on?'

'*Esattamente signore.*'

A dam burst inside me. As if in slow motion, I unlatched my seat-belt, opened my door, climbed from our freshly repaired Lancia, parked my face within an inch of the plump *carabiniere* and fired a year's frustration into his bullet-proof vest. Diplomacy was beyond me as I launched an inelegant but purgative outburst: 'This fucking country is an absolute fucking mess!'

A crow broke the ensuing silence, cawing loudly from its perch in an olive tree beside the road, mocking the gravity of my eruption somewhat.

'And the crow agrees with me,' I added.

I probably have that bird to thank for saving me from an afternoon in handcuffs.

'*Mi scusi, signore?*' said the officer. 'What did you say?'

'I said I won't allow you to fine me for driving with my lights on just because I'm on the wrong sort of road.'

'And how are you going to do that?' asked a thin second officer, wandering over from the squad car carrying a fat submachine gun.

But I kept on ranting as though it were a water pistol.

'By telling you that the report I saw on the news said that

lights must be on at all times on all roads. It didn't say anything about the type of road.'

The officers exchanged a glance.

'And anyway,' I went on, 'if I want to turn my lights on, I will. They weren't on high beam so what can you do about it? Are you going to book me because the stereo was too loud as well?'

The words came fluently, when it might have been better had they not. Regretting my style but supporting my story, Daniela got out, told me to calm down and stood between me and the policemen.

'It's true,' she testified, 'the report said all roads at all times.'

'*Impossibile*,' said the armed one, again looking at his colleague.

'Obviously not,' I blurted, indicating cars filing past, most with their lights on. 'Are you going to fine all them as well?'

'Chris, *basta!*' pleaded Daniela. '*Stai calmo.*'

But I was an avalanche gathering mass and momentum.

'What a backward system. A million laws only nobody tells the police what they are.'

'And I suppose things are better in Australia?' said the lollipop man, recalling my nationality from my licence, which he may have been about to cancel.

'Well at least we don't need a confusing law telling us on what type of street we need to turn on our lights.'

'So who tells you to turn them on half an hour before sundown?'

'Common sense.'

The pair looked mystified.

'And when it's foggy and visibility is reduced?' asked the machine gun. 'Surely you need a law to say drivers must turn their lights on?'

'No, you need drivers who'll turn their lights on because common sense tells them that if they don't they won't be able to see.'

Daniela had stepped aside, sensing the situation was no longer deteriorating.

'In Italy there's no such thing as common sense,' said the plump one, taking off his hat and tucking it under his arm—his off-duty pose. 'If you heard the excuses I hear for not wearing a seat-belt you'd agree.'

'Undoubtedly.'

'This morning a man told me he was allergic to it and the strap gave him a rash across his shoulder. I felt embarrassed telling him to put on a T-shirt.' He threw his arms in the air. 'What am I, a doctor?'

His mate joined in.

'And the most common excuse we hear for not wearing a helmet is because it messes up their hair. What can we do with people like that?'

'Fine *them* instead of me.'

Daniela stifled a laugh.

The situation had lost its tension. I was no longer the one complaining and, more importantly, my 'infringement' appeared to have been forgotten. I felt sorry for the comical pair in their ludicrous uniforms: striped trousers, knee-high boots and hats too small for their heads. Perhaps some *carabinieri* deserve sympathy rather than scorn. Only by policing fools have they become foolish.

'You preach well,' said the fatter one, tucking his lollipop into his boot. 'Did you come here to be a priest?'

I put my arm around Daniela.

'With a beautiful woman like this? Only in Italy could I do that.'

The officers laughed and Daniela leant against the bonnet, breathing easily for the first time in minutes.

'Have you ever been to Australia?' the thin one asked her. His goatee beard had been painstakingly pruned.

'*Si*,' she replied. 'A few times.'

'And is it like your boyfriend says?'

'It's different,' said Daniela, choosing her words more carefully than I had. 'This sort of confusion wouldn't happen there. My boyfriend is angry because here we have many more laws but we behave as if we didn't have any and our roads are so dangerous.'

'This is nothing,' said the fat one. 'Has he been to Naples? *E' anarchia totale!*'

'Why do you stay here when you could go to Australia?' asked the thin one, cleaning aviator sunglasses on his shirt.

'I'd love to go to Australia,' interrupted the fat one.

'So would I,' said the thin one, turning his attention to me. 'What are the women like?' he asked, before remembering Daniela and excusing himself.

'What's the food like?' inquired the fat one. First things first.

Cars rolled by on the sun-drenched street, most of them driven by friends. They beeped when they saw us, their second infringement if you count the headlights. We waved while fielding questions on Australia from two policemen, who ignored the lawbreakers heading for the blue of La Botte.

Is there another country where a confrontation with police can begin with insults and end with waistlines and recipes? Where one treads the precarious ground between madness and happiness with such wonderful and exasperating regularity? Not in a world of common sense there isn't.

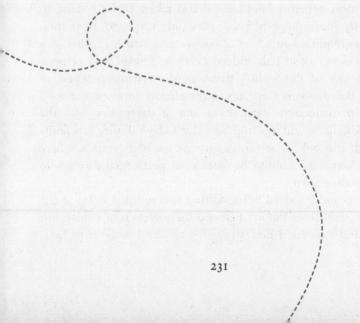

Freccia

Having strayed from formation to perform solo stunts, an air force jet streaked across the sky, loud, low and close above the heads of two lovers kissing passionately in waist-deep water, their tongues tangling in formations of their own. Air show? What air show? There's no distracting some Italians from summer pursuits.

The rest of us couldn't take our eyes from the sky. Thousands of spectators had ignored posters declaring it immoral to be entertained by 'machines of death', gathering on the beach at San Cataldo near Lecce to watch the aerobatic team of the Italian Air Force, *Le Frecce Tricolori*—The Tri-Colour Arrows, give an afternoon display of precision aerobatics and balls-out speed.

Myself a qualified aerobatics pilot—unfortunately one of the world's most expensive hobbies—I had taken Daniela along to the display in the hope of being pleasantly surprised. Formation aerobatics requires a mind-set of cooperation which I hadn't seen much evidence of in Italy, indeed *Le Frecce Tricolori* were responsible for one of the world's worst air show disasters when, in 1988 at Ramstein in Germany, three aircraft touched during a formation manoeuvre, catapulting one of the planes onto the crowd, killing 70 and injuring 400. But today's display was faultless, with the only near-misses on exit roads afterwards, where cars and Vespas, in a bid to be first home, performed daring solo stunts of their own.

Daniela and I arrived home to find two unusual sights at our gate: the absence of Pippo's Fiat and the presence of a shivering, scruffy and emaciated dog, struggling to stand with its pathetic head bowed as though resigned to a falling guillotine. A breeze would have toppled this half-dead hound, and shooing it away would have been useless given it was too weak to do anything except fall into my arms.

Despite being a medium-sized dog it couldn't have weighed more than a couple of kilos, much of which was fleas and ticks. Even today I can't help but flinch when I remember the sight of that moribund mongrel: a frail female, tongue dangling from the side of her mouth, eyes sealed with discharge and nose clogged with a glue-like muck. She was a slow-breathing skeleton, patchy fur falling out in clumps, ribs and hips poking through shrunken flesh, and spine sticking out like the handle of a bag with which to carry her to the vet first thing in the morning, assuming she didn't die overnight.

I carried the featherweight inside the gate and laid her on a towel by the back door. Each laboured breath seemed her last and I have to admit I hoped it was. She was uninterested in food and water as though she'd forgotten what they were, but I left some by her side just in case she remembered. She looked as uncomfortable lying down as she did standing up, so when Daniela wasn't looking I snuck her a pillow from the spare room. We called her *Freccia*—Arrow, after the Tri-Colour Arrows we had watched that afternoon, although we felt sure she wouldn't live long enough to learn the name.

Mahatma Gandhi said a nation can be judged by the way it treats its animals. Looking at Freccia, he would have judged Italy harshly. I can tolerate the Italians tossing their rubbish on the street, but not when that rubbish is alive. Freccia was the trash of self-obsessed dog-owners capable of abandoning around 400,000 pets each summer for the sake of a care-free vacation. Dogs and cats are disposable items to many Italians, who leave four-legged commitments under bridges, in bushland, or tied to guardrails on the side of the road. It doesn't say much for man when his best friend is left to starve.

As usual, the threat of the law deters few holidaymakers, who consider it easier to ditch their pets than take them along or organise temporary care. And given that many Italians believe it pointless to sterilise animals they only intend to keep until the sun comes out, the castaways sire further strays in what become, in the south at least, plague-like proportions. During summer, I often looked across the castle grounds to see two stray dogs collaborating to make six or eight more. Such was Freccia's reckless heritage. She was your classic Italian street dog: conceived on an intersection by a father who bolted and a mother who didn't know what had hit her.

Like the clapped-out whitegoods dumped here and there, mangy street dogs are an integral part of the southern Italian landscape. Their precise numbers would be as difficult to count as the fleas in their fur, but it is estimated, for example, that a quarter of all dogs in Sicily are strays, although 'stray' is the wrong term for abandoned animals. And there are more unwanted cats than dogs, crawling through bins in search of food to survive. The Italian expression for a small town is *un paese di quattro gatti*—a town of four cats, but it's more like four thousand in towns like Andrano.

The strays adopt themselves to places where food scraps fall their way, roaming until they find someone in the village with a heart: the butcher, the barman, even the priest has one 'flock' which comes in the front door to be blessed and another that waits at the back door to be fed. In supermarket car parks, dogs select shoppers by the contents of their trolleys, following them to cars in the hope of being fed. I always bought extra ham which the dogs devoured before licking the packet until the label wore off. One Labrador was so starved he even ate the packet.

Most residents of Andrano can find a better place to put left-overs than in the bin, and once the animals find fertile hunting grounds they remain loyal to them forever. One old woman who lived near the piazza called her house *L'Arca di Noè*—Noah's Ark, and fed as many as eight stray dogs—some with three legs, some with four—and ten stray cats; perhaps they had noticed the statue of Padre Pio by her door and hoped the goodwill stretched to all God's creatures. And if the strays didn't adopt you, you could always adopt them. Each week in the television guide there was a page devoted to homeless animals. One million six hundred thousand of them in shelters across the country. I'd have taken them all if I could. But Freccia only needed me to take one.

I sat with her on the back step until late, patting her while she dozed in the hope her last moments might be memorable. Scores of ticks had sapped her strength and made her anaemic; plump parasites on the shadow of a dog. And swollen teats confirmed the tale of a young boy, our neighbour's nephew, who told us he had found Freccia two days earlier in the castle's dried-up moat, where he had taken her litter away in an attempt to find them homes. The pups had milked their mother dry, making her too weak to resist their removal.

I left Freccia around midnight, returning the next morning to find her ribs still rising, faint but steady, although her food and water hadn't been touched. We put her in the car and took her to three vets, all of whom refused to end her suffering. Yes, she was dying but only of starvation. She had no terminal illness other than homelessness, making her no different from thousands of dogs in Puglia alone. They refused to interfere in the life of the dog, insisting that were she to die she would do so naturally. I had expected logic from men of science.

I appealed for compassion and common sense. Freccia was dying a slow death we would be cruel not to accelerate. What was the point of trying to nurture her back to health for a future which would reduce her to the same desperate state? Nobody was going to adopt Freccia. There weren't enough homes for an excess of healthy puppies offered free in the TV guide and on every vet's waiting room wall. Who then was going to open their hearts to a three-year-old fleabag with a protruding backbone that made her look like a furry coat-hanger? Had she not been abandoned in the first place? '*Caro veterinario*, Italy doesn't want this bag o' bones!'

Daniela called her friend Teresa, who had adopted three strays but had no room for a fourth. 'Whatever you do, don't take her to the pound,' she advised. 'She's better off dead or back on the street.' I had seen exposés of the appalling conditions in Italian animal shelters, with ten or more dogs cramped in concrete cells. As Teresa explained, the shelters were not designed to care for the animals but to get them off the roads where they posed a traffic hazard. It is estimated that street dogs cause over 4000 car accidents annually in Italy, resulting in 20 human deaths and 400 injuries. That's what you get for abandoning them, I suppose.

Meanwhile, I was asking myself the obvious question—the same thing the vets asked me, the same thing Teresa asked me and the same thing everyone I begged to take Freccia asked me—Why didn't I adopt her? The answer was simple. I didn't know how long I would be staying in Andrano. A stray myself, I couldn't offer a home that wasn't mine. Daniela wasn't in the least bit interested in the possibility of my shooting through and leaving a four-legged legacy for her to look after, and putting the dog back in the park in her current condition would have been tantamount to killing her myself. No, the only thing to do was clean her up, reacquaint her with food, give her the medicine the vet recommended and perhaps she might recover. The back step was hers until she either passed on or pulled through. And if she did make it, being a street dog she would probably leave of her own accord. Probably.

Freccia slept for two days after her stay of execution, woken only to be administered antibiotics hidden in Parma ham, the finest in Italy; Daniela's idea to prick her interest in food was a resounding, if costly, success. When the dog finally stirred of her own accord I saw her eyes properly for the first time: two chestnut spheres, sheepish and sorry, saying I was free to do with her what

I willed. She was totally submissive and put up less of a fight than Daniela when I led them both to the laundry sink. Again it was a question of culture. Daniela had grown up with dogs dying outside her gate. She had never abandoned an animal, but she had never adopted one either. That bath was a first for both Freccia and Daniela.

Reluctantly, and with rubber gloves, Daniela held Freccia's head while I scrubbed off a thousand fleas and several layers of Salento dirt. Her wiry fur gradually softened but we had to wash her twice more before arriving at the real Freccia: a black *volpino*, a fox-like cross-breed, with four white paws, a bushy tail and a sleek, smart face. When we took her out of the blood-stained water there was enough dirt to plant carrots and enough fleas to block the sink.

After a week, Freccia was up and about, and after two there was a bounce in her step. Judging by her tail, which bruised my shins when I went out to see her, she was well on the road to recovery—a dog's tail always tells the truth. Freccia had been starved of affection as much as food. Everywhere I went she would trot along beside me before turning abruptly across my path; even being tripped over counted as contact in her book. She made it clear that ham was welcome but company was preferred. Each time I placed food in front of her she would look up at me, down at the bowl and then sidle against my leg. She was sweet for having suffered, smart for having survived, eager to please for having been spared.

Instead of siesta, I would sit on the back step with Freccia stroking her ears or going over them for ticks. One afternoon when the town was sleeping, Daniela shattered the silence by yelling '*Cristoforo Colombo!*' from the living room. That was my name when I was in trouble, so it wasn't just Freccia who ducked her head.

'*Si*,' I replied sheepishly.

'There are fleas in my mother's couch!'

'They probably just want to watch television.'

We ducked again as a shoe hit the back door. It looked like we needed a kennel, for me if not for the dog. The following day we fumigated the furniture, which now included Freccia, a back door mat on which we never wiped our feet.

Our house soon became her hotel. We gave Freccia a meal every evening, leftovers mainly, of which I made sure we had plenty. Then, her stomach satisfied, she would squeeze through the bars of the gate and spend the night roaming with the pack of strays to which she had formerly belonged. Each time I heard her nudge through the gate I thought I had seen her for the last time. But each morning I would find her back on her step, the wanderer returned, her fur a tapestry of bristles and barbs. I'm convinced she deliberately dragged herself through as many prickly predicaments as possible, for she loved the attention when I spent half the morning teasing the countryside from her coat.

Freccia was the larrikin you couldn't help liking, a four-legged Huckleberry Finn, but she had the habit of getting not only herself into a tangle. She once caused me to offend Laura, a close friend of Daniela's mother. Laura was proud of two things: her cooking and her daughter Adele, to such an extent that when she asked me to teach Adele English she offered to pay me with her home-made cuisine—better than cash in Laura's opinion. Thinking she was joking, I agreed to the plan, only to find out soon after that her offer had been genuine. So twice a week I exchanged verbs for vegies and pronouns for pasta, giving a whole new meaning to 'earning enough to put food on the table', although I still haven't figured out how to declare such earnings on my tax return.

Laura's best dish was her gnocchi, well worth an hour's grammar, but one evening we couldn't finish them and the luxury leftovers found their way to the dog bowl. Freccia staggered her meals around her social calendar, eating half before venturing out for the night and the remainder when she returned the following morning. This time, however, she had snubbed the leftovers and gone straight to sleep; perhaps she had eaten with her mangy mates, who thankfully were plump enough not to be able to squeeze through the gate behind her, although several had tried and become stuck halfway.

Laura rose early to prepare her family's lunch and dinner, and preferred to deliver payments for Adele's lessons while they were still hot, ensuring the aroma could be fully appreciated and, of course, adequately praised. She usually dropped by around nine when, in summer at least, Daniela and I were still stirring after nocturnal adventures as intrepid as Freccia's. But today Daniela had gone to the morning market in Poggiardo, so I was alone when Laura's manicured finger pressed the doorbell. Having flopped into bed around four, the last thought in my sleepy head was to check Freccia's food bowl before opening the gate to meals on wheels.

Balancing two trays, Laura was reciting the evening's menu—*maccheroni* and *scaloppine ai funghi*—when she stopped so abruptly that having just woken up I checked that nothing scandalous had poked its head out my pyjamas. But it was her gnocchi she had caught sight of rather than mine, lying dirty in the dog bowl and crawling with ants. Surprise and devastation cracked the thick layer of make-up with which Laura disguised more subtle expressions.

'*Madonna mia!*' she exclaimed. 'You give my cooking to the dog?'

'*Um, er.*' Being lost for words is the same in any language. 'Daniela must have given them to her,' I stammered, cruelly capitalising on her absence.

'Don't tell me,' said Laura, putting her hand up to stop me. 'I don't want to know.'

She handed me the delivery, put on gold-armed sunglasses and stormed out the gate. Oblivious to the damage she had done, Freccia twitched in lazy dream sleep, for the first time in her life without a care in the world.

Laura continued to send her daughter for English lessons, only now Adele brought an envelope with her at the end of each month. Freccia's leftovers returned to their former quality, but my new mate didn't seem to mind. A dog that exists on Italian leftovers eats better than most English people.

Thursday is market day in Andrano, anticipated by resident and stray dog alike. From sunrise to siesta Piazza Castello is crammed with stalls and closed to traffic other than pedestrians and bicycles. Among food and clothing was a caravan converted into a delicatessen under which Freccia waited patiently with her mates, their bodies under the caravan but their snouts sticking out the exact length of its counter. Every so often an off-cut would fall but it rarely touched the ground; Freccia and friends took overhead catches better than the Australian cricket team.

I enjoyed riding through the piazza on market day, offering a casual salute to the people I knew, which by now was almost everyone, and watching the cordon of canines below the mobile deli, their eyes in the tops of their heads on the lookout for ham from the heavens. Regardless of my destination, and even if it meant going the long way, I always went via the piazza. Everyone did; we were summoned there like blood to the heart. The limestone square was the focal point of the town, industrious yet idle, where sellers hawked discount prices and buyers bargained them even lower.

One Thursday, on my return journey across the piazza, Freccia noticed my bicycle and followed it home, squeezing through the gate ahead of me even though I had to open it to get in myself. It was one of the last times she would be able to do so; between Laura's leftovers and the deli's droppings, Freccia was filling out. Daniela's parents were due to return from Sicily in October, and because the gate had to remain closed for Franco, who would roam further than Freccia were it left open, the dog's semi-stray lifestyle was under threat.

As usual it was Daniela who came up with a solution to please everybody. She telephoned *il fabbro*—the blacksmith, yet another stooped *compare*—who removed the bottom section of one of the vertical rungs in the gate. Daniela hoped Valeria wouldn't notice the missing grille but kept it in case she did. Freccia had a new window on the world and was once again free to come and go as she pleased.

A week after opening that window I was forced to cover it with a brick and tie Freccia to the banister on the back steps. The vet due to sterilise her the following day had ordered her stomach empty and if she roamed during the night she might find something to nibble. For a spirit as free as Freccia's it was a night in prison. Her motley mates came by the house at the usual hour, but when she didn't appear they sat at the gate and howled a vigil. When I went out to assure them it was a one-off detention designed to protect us all from further misery, I found the knot in the rope wet from where Freccia had tried to chew her way to freedom. Loyalty can never be measured by the length of a rope or the height of a fence. I was glad; independence was her only hope.

The following morning we took Freccia to a vet in the distant town of Melafano, a collection of whitewashed buildings just south of Bari but worth the long drive because of his discount for strays. Having used him before, Teresa came with us, hoping her introduction would lower the price even further. The practice was closed when we arrived for our 9.30 appointment, so we waited outside a whitewashed house that was identical to others along the street but for a gold plaque stating the vet's name, opening hours and phone numbers.

Half an hour later the vet's assistant arrived and opened the front *serranda*, releasing a fox terrier which scampered down the street at a pace which suggested it had been detained against its will. Perhaps it objected to the waiting room: a metal crucifix, a thirsty plant, dog hair in every corner and a stale smell of animal ailment.

At half-past ten, an hour late, the vet breezed in as though he was early. Ignoring the animals queuing more patiently than their owners, he greeted Teresa and signalled us to follow him to his office, a shrine of Fascist memorabilia. Hanging above his cluttered desk was 'The Benito Mussolini 2000 Calendar', its caption reading: '*Il Duce*, with you in the third millennium'. On a bookshelf stood three dusty bottles of wine, their labels a portrait of Benito boasting the commemorative claret to be 'The Pride of Predappio'—the dictator's birthplace. Everywhere I looked there were souvenirs of Fascism, except in the waiting room, which could be seen from the street.

Where else but southern Italy can you haggle over the price of a hysterectomy? After a discussion more suited to a marketplace, we were led to a room at the back of the practice overlooking an unkempt garden, where a washing line sagged under the weight of towels that had once been white. Like the vet's office, minus some of the clutter, the operating theatre featured a photo of Mussolini, on horseback this time, pointing into the distance at colonies to be conquered; well, to Abyssinia at least. There were preserved organs in jars on shelves and a dead cat lay paws-up on a bench. More a terrorist than a terrier, the vet's dog had returned and mounted a table in the corner of the room where it drank from a tray of surgical instruments, earning it exile to the waiting room where it mounted a cocker spaniel.

What do you do when a Fascist sympathiser is preparing to cut open your most recent friend at a discount rate? In hindsight you invent an excuse and scamper like the terrier under the roller-shutter. But in the heat of the moment, too shocked to protest, we watched ruefully as the vet administered the anaesthetic and slight Freccia slumped asleep. The white-coated assistant then grabbed her by the neck, spun her into position and tied her paws to a table less sterile than Freccia would soon be. Donning a pair of rubber gloves, the vet invited us to stay for the operation; well, he invited me to stay for the operation because Daniela and Teresa had fled at the sight of the needle.

Freccia's tummy was split with the scratch of a scalpel, a small incision into which the vet slipped a chubby finger. Pliant and pink, her flesh tore easily, the delicate core of a tough-skinned dog. In what only he considered an opportune moment, the vet then tried to spark a conversation. 'What the fuck is an Australian doing down this low?' he asked, referring, I presumed, to the south of Italy. '*Turismo*,' I replied, curt and concise, hoping he'd return his attention to my dog instead of me. But he was intent on chat and the questions kept coming, while Freccia's tongue hung limp from her mouth and the terrier, having returned from the waiting room, wandered at his feet licking stains from the tiles.

'How long is the flight to Australia?' asked the vet, his finger up to its knuckle in the dog.

'From Rome about twenty-one hours.'

'*Cazzo!* Don't think I'll ever get there. Aeroplanes frighten the pants off me.'

'Uh huh.'

'Trains too. Cars and boats are my thing. Give me any boat in any sea and I'll get her back to port.'

'Uh huh.'

He fossicked inside Freccia for the parts he required.

'One night I ran out of fuel and drifted for eleven hours in skyscraper seas. It was hairy stuff but I'm still here to tell you about it.'

'Uh huh.'

Fortunately he was interrupted by the phone in the office. Unfortunately it was for him—'Your brother-in-law,' announced the assistant, returning to the room.

'*Chi?*'

'Your brother-in-law.'

'I haven't got a brother-in-law.'

'He said he was "Luigi, the vet's brother-in-law".'

'Luigi?' said the vet to himself. 'I don't know a Luigi.'

His face twisted as he sank his finger further inside the patient.

'What should I tell him?' asked the frustrated assistant.

For a moment I was worried he would take the call, but

thankfully he thought better of it and continued his search for Freccia's ovaries.

'Get his number and I'll call him back,' he directed, 'whoever he is.'

Freccia's cut stretched as the vet exclaimed, 'Where the fuck are they?' and inserted a second finger. He turned his head to the roof and closed his eyes, recalling, I feared, the pages of a textbook. Having dealt with the mystery caller, the assistant returned as the vet declared, 'The buggers are hiding,' and reached for his scalpel to slice Freccia further. The dog whimpered, causing me to do likewise, but the vet assured me she was 'just dreaming of the well-hung lads who'll soon be no good to her.' I winced at the thought, or the way he put it, before realising that was actually the objective.

When a third finger turned up nothing, rather than put his whole hand in the vet called off the internal search and pulled Freccia's insides out where he could sort through them in the light. Her vitals glistened in his gloves. Like a photographer scanning a reel of negatives he scrutinised a length of intestine before laying it on the table.

With no door to stop him doing so, a man in a linen suit strolled into the room smoking a cigarette. I had no idea who he was other than not the vet's brother-in-law, but he must have known the vet well as he didn't wait for an invitation to sit on the bench by the dead cat.

'*Morto?*' he asked, regarding the corpse indifferently.

'Clearly,' replied the vet, terse suddenly—hopefully because he was concentrating.

'What happened?'

'Same as your wife's dog—poisoned.' The vet looked at me. 'It happens a lot here.'

The intruder sucked on his cigarette which slanted upwards and shortened visibly.

'Schumacher got pole for tomorrow's race,' he said, ashing on the floor.

'*Bene.*'

'What a team those boys at Ferrari. *Campioni.*'

I wasn't sure what upset me more: his distracting the vet or his smoking.

Playing the tourist, I asked the vet: 'Can you smoke in an operating room in Italy?'

'*Probabilmente no,*' he replied, raising eyebrows at his visitor who put both hands in the air—Italian for 'Who, me?'—before taking a final toke and flicking the butt out the window. Then he slapped the vet on the arm and made for the exit.

'I'll call you when my wife decides what she wants done with the body,' he said, presumably referring to her poisoned dog.

'*Va bene,*' said the vet. 'And say hi to your mother.'

We might as well have been in a bar.

After a frustrated start, the rest of the procedure was rapid routine. The vet declared that he couldn't find Feccia's ovaries and that his only option was to remove her uterus. He cut three strips of flesh from the jumble of organs on the operating table, tossing them into the bin like a show-off chef with an accurate arm. The patient bled and the assistant dabbed at the wound with a towel from the washing line. The vet then fed Freccia's guts back inside, in the same order in which he had taken them out I hoped, before wiping the wound, sewing it together, spraying his needlework with disinfectant and covering the scar with a swab. Procedure complete, he asked his assistant for some thick sticky bandage, which he used to bind Freccia's midriff twice round, wrapping her like a Christmas present.

'How are you going to get that off without taking her fur with it?' I asked.

'*Tranquillo,*' he replied, tossing his gloves into the same bin as the uterus. 'She won't feel a thing.'

Freccia was untied and turned on her side before the vet and his assistant left the room. While checking his mobile phone for messages, the vet walked to his office and shouted '*Avanti!*' to his next patient. Alone with Freccia and Mussolini, dog and dictator, unlikely company. I patted the patient and gazed at the portrait of the 'Apostle of Violence' as Mussolini crowned himself. What would he have made of the vet's performance? After initial complications, full marks no doubt: clinical, brusque and unmerciful—the hallmarks of the Fascist regime.

Half an hour later the vet returned, poked Freccia's tongue back in her mouth and slapped her awake as though she had fainted. When she reluctantly came round he inspected her bandage, declared it '*perfetto*' and ushered me into his office to settle up. He gave me a discount because Freccia was a stray, which hinted to me that despite his gruff exterior he actually had a heart and was perhaps sympathetic to my cause. Then he asked me a few more questions about Australia, which I did my best to answer over the noise of two barking dogs in the waiting room.

Despite the bumpy road, Freccia slept all the way home from Melafano, oblivious, hopefully, to what had been a painful morning for both me and her. While concentrating on the road, I questioned Teresa's loyalty to the vet, explaining what had happened in the operating theatre.

'Are you sure he couldn't find her ovaries?' asked Teresa.

'That's what he said.'

'If you ask me, he found them but didn't want to take them out.'

'Why?'

'So that she can still go on heat.'

'But she can't go on heat without a uterus,' countered Daniela.

'Yes she can,' insisted Teresa.

'I'm not sure she can,' I said. 'But anyway, why would he want her to go on heat?'

'So that she can have sex, of course.'

'But why would he be interested in a stray dog's sex life?'

'Crris, most Italians believe sterilising animals is cruel because it's not natural.'

'And it's *natural* to abandon them, is it?'

Teresa fell as silent as Freccia.

Antibiotics and Parma ham made for a quick recovery once again, and despite orders to rest, Freccia was roaming with her mates the following evening. She looked ridiculous cocooned in the bandage, and I had to rush out to the castle park one afternoon when I saw an old man trying to unbind her. Worried it would happen again, I wrote: 'Do not remove. I have had an operation' on the bandage, causing the vet to laugh when I took Freccia to have her stitches removed. As I had feared, rather than cut the bandage he yanked it free. 'Just like a bikini waxing,' he said as Freccia yelped. Then he snipped the stitches and inspected the wound by peering over half-glasses, before Freccia and I fled his peculiar premises almost as fast as the terrier had done a week earlier.

As a reward for her stoicism and resilience we gave Freccia a kennel. Sadly, when we went to buy it, we were reminded of how much we were doing for one dog but how little we could do for the rest. Kennels were lined up on the footpath outside the hardware-cum-pet-shop in Tricase. The shop assistant kicked each one we were interested in, causing a stray dog to scamper. Almost every kennel already had a lodger so we chose the only one that didn't, hoping not to deprive the squatters of shelter.

Freccia adored her new premises, a daytime residence only, because in the evenings she remained loyal to the pack which continued to pass by the gate. That was her routine until one morning, about a month after her operation, I went out to find her bowl full and her kennel empty. Two days passed with no sign of the dog to which I realised I had become attached. Her pack had also vanished and I began to think I had been abandoned by the abandoned.

On the third morning of Freccia's disappearance, I was writing in the study when I heard the inimitable sound of her squeezing through the gate and rushed out to find her collapsed in her kennel, chest heaving and paws bleeding. She slept for two days and it wasn't until she surfaced that, while going over her for ticks, I noticed a tattoo in her ear.

A trip to the *polizia municipale* confirmed Daniela's suspicions that the dog catcher from Corsano, a village beyond Tricase, had done his post-summer rounds to clear the streets of this year's walking waste—discarded in June and collected in October. The number of dogs seized in Andrano corresponded to the number of members in Freccia's gang, including its one part-time member. A frail dog can only escape from the pound and find its way 15 kilometres across tough terrain if it has someone to live for. Freccia knew she had me, and that I would be waiting for her like an anxious parent.

I was delighted to see her and bought her a collar to avoid her being taken again. She wore it with pride as though it confirmed adoption. And I suppose it did. The tenacious fleabag who had survived sickness, starvation, the removal of her young, numerous attempts to have her put down, an eccentric vet and now the dog catcher, had won my respect, my admiration and a place in my heart. I think I loved her all the more in the end for having tried not to love her in the beginning.

Without her mates to entice her, Freccia roamed less and less. Only on market day would I spot her around town; under the deli mainly, which she now had all to herself. She became my dog, my mate, and above all, my shadow, following my bicycle wherever it went. And if I ventured further afield than Andrano, she would climb aboard my Vespa, sit between me and the handlebars, and lower her head as though she understood aero-dynamics, a fitting way to ride for a dog called Arrow. She came to tennis, the beach and 'California', but her favourite outing was of course the butcher's, from where she rode home between my arms, wind in her fur and bone in her mouth.

Freccia kept me company for another six months, after which

a vet in Tricase, a gentle young man who I wished I'd met earlier, found a tumour in her stomach and spared her the suffering. I stroked Freccia's ears as he prepared the needle, looking into her eyes as they clouded then stilled. The last thing she saw was a promise of safety and how grateful I was for her sandpaper paws. I had braved many mishaps since moving to Italy, yet Freccia's death was the first that reduced me to tears. But it wasn't only Freccia who broke my heart, it was the millions of other abandoned dogs in Italy who would never nudge their nose through my gate.

When I look back on Freccia, I sometimes think she rescued me as much as I rescued her, given we were both strays in Andrano. Perhaps the person who adopts the stray is looking for a mate as much as the dog. I often felt isolated in Italy, mentally rather than physically. Regardless of how well I adapted, I was different in every way, from my sense of humour to my ability to queue without starting a fight. Socially, culturally, even religiously, I had an unorthodox take on most things. Freccia was the only companion who didn't remind me how foreign I was. I swapped food scraps for a silent bond more valuable than words can describe, for like-minded company that made me feel at home. She even ate toast with Vegemite, the only Italian I could convince of its merits.

Before Freccia stopped by the gate it had been 'me' and 'them'. Afterwards it was 'us' and 'them'. Daniela was my friend but Freccia was my ally. You can travel the world and meet different people but wherever you go the dogs are the same. Give them a pat and a plate of food and they'll follow your footsteps for as long as they live. And for as long as I live I will remember the hungry hound who put friendship before food, the mono-coloured arrow that pierced my heart.

Digging a grave in a stubborn landscape of calcareous rock is next to impossible. After a lengthy search for soft terrain, including several failed attempts which jarred my teeth and bent my spade, we found a patch of ground as suitable as it was spectacular, an olive grove on a headland behind Torre del Sasso, the lookout tower with its view of La Botte and Mediterranean blue. It's a serene spot, where the days are peaceful and the nights so moonlit with the reflection off the sea that Freccia will have trouble telling one from the other, something she was never very good at to begin with.

The sun was setting when we buried Freccia among olive trees that had stood for hundreds of years, and to which we gave that light-limbed rascal for thousands more.

Professore—an unusual Italian

Valeria had spent three months in Sicily, and if only she'd stayed another day she would have been there when her ninety-year-old mother passed away in her sleep. Instead, so soon after unpacking her suitcase in Andrano, she threw another one together and caught the first bus back to Alcamo, where she attended the funeral and kept an eye on her sisters, ensuring they divvied up the hillside according to the final wishes of its owner. Ten days she was gone, during which I cared for Franco now that Daniela was back at work. That was how I came to learn the story of a man who broke his nose trying to step inside the mirror, a mirror in which I saw a reflection of Franco's life, as well as that of Andrano, from whose small-town suffocations Daniela's father had spent most of his healthy life attempting escape.

Alzheimer's is a test of patience for the carer, a quality I never had much of until my ten-day crash course with Franco. Or was it resilience—the ability to remain optimistic while cushioning a condemned man's slow passage to the grave? The indignity of the disease is that it doesn't kill, rather it reduces the sufferer to a vague, wasted and ungoverned body, pleading to die yet breathing like the day it was born. The mystery illness is an agonising wait for the inevitable, for the carers as much as the patient, who do what they can to soothe, knowing too well they cannot save.

Five years after being diagnosed with Alzheimer's, Franco's future was as veiled as his past. Unlike his hairline, Franco's brain cells were receding, giving his otherwise healthy body no choice but to shut down as well. His deterioration had taken a slow but steady course. In the year that had passed since I first met Daniela's father, he had progressed beyond anger and no longer hurled obscenities as he had at the broom tree. His voice was softer, a mere mumble, and his random utterances were almost always indecipherable. His bowels and bladder were beyond his control and his handsome face no longer looked confused; having forgotten how to question, he was spared the search for answers.

Franco's inability to communicate made nursing him guess-work. Was he hungry? Did he have a headache? Did he need an extra blanket? Lighter pyjamas? Another pillow? Did he break anything when he fell down the steps yesterday, other than our hearts and some shoddy brickwork? He needed a psychic rather than a nurse, and Valeria could only hope that her husband's mute misery was relieved by the daily routine she had established for his palliative care, a routine which Daniela and I followed strictly while her mother was away.

Caffeine countered the barrage of tranquillisers needed to shut Franco down. Some mornings he smiled when I opened his *serranda* and gave him his coffee, but usually he was expression-less, staring into space as though rehearsing death. So began the painstaking process of hauling the patient out of bed, washing him, dressing him and, hardest of all, feeding him. The problem wasn't persuading him to take what was on the spoon but reminding him to swallow. His mind would wander, and only by pressing another mouthful to his lips could I induce him to make space for further instalments. Both his bib and his beard needed cleaning afterwards, but his eyes were brighter and his day had begun, identical to yesterday and a clone of tomorrow.

After breakfast I supervised Franco's morning walk outside. Grey hair on the collar of his light autumn jacket, he padded along the porch, sliding his shoes and eroding his soles. The thin man could never walk as far as his mind would take him. He mumbled the cobwebs of a conversation before stopping abruptly and laughing aloud. Rarely was he silent, apart from when he plucked a flower and placed it in his mouth, making me wonder if I'd given him enough breakfast.

Daniela's house stood on the main road leading to the piazza, a busy thoroughfare along which passers-by greeted Franco when they saw him in the yard. Cyclists rang their bells and shouted '*Ciao professore!*'—Franco's title for having taught at the local high school. Motorists beeped, pedestrians waved, and some even reached through the fence to warm his left hand which had turned purple through lazy circulation; he held it to his chest, clasped in a fist as though preparing to punish the gods for his fate.

Passing villagers knew not to expect a reply from Franco, who responded more to voices of his own imagination than to greetings from friends and family. He would often turn his head to salute shadow or silence; I wasn't sure what disturbed me more, seeing him ignore or invent people. Most yelled a greeting and continued on their way, like the postman, who delivered telegrams of *condoglianze* for the loss of Valeria's mother.

Almost all the *Andranesi* acknowledged Franco, but some rushed past the house without looking in the yard, fearful of what they might find. Several close friends had been unable to cope with his mental demise, and preferred not to see him stumbling on the patio chewing garden shrubs. I found this insensitive until one of his dearest friends, the vice-mayor of Andrano, explained their behaviour. 'You're lucky, Crris,' he said. 'Very lucky. You didn't know Franco when he was well. Perhaps if you did, you too would have difficulty seeing him now. He was such an intelligent man. So quick-witted and creative. It's impossible to accept that this has happened to him. I have lost my faith in everything.'

When Franco was born in 1938, Andrano's castle was occupied by the last of its incumbents—the Caracciolo family. Franco's aunt worked as a live-in nanny in the castle, attending to every

need of her young ward—the Princess Ippolita. As his aunt's
guest, Franco spent much of his childhood at the castle, where
he learnt to play a variety of musical instruments including
violin and piano, and had books from the royal library read to
him by an aunt who nurtured her nephew as much as she did
the princess.

The son of pious parents, at the age of twelve Franco was
sent to a seminary in Otranto, a medieval city to the north of
Andrano. There, in stark contrast to a semi-regal upbringing,
Franco was intellectually blinkered and made to wear a tunic
which he could only take off under his sheets or when the light
in his dorm was extinguished. His diary was read and his letters
home censored, but, to please his parents, Franco tolerated the
divine dictators until the day he chased a football into a creek,
muddying his tunic and earning him a slap on the ear which
deafened him for a week. On his next visit home Franco
complained to his parents, who removed their son from the
seminary and gave him a more orthodox education where the
students chose their future vocations rather than the teachers.

When he was eighteen, at a time in Italy's history when most
people who moved away did so to help their families rather than
themselves, Franco moved to Lecce to study at the conserva-
torium of music. He was both criticised and admired for his
selfishness and drive, sentiments he would stir in others for most
of his life. After graduating, he taught music in a hilltop town
near Cosenza in southern Italy, where he met and married the
Sicilian *signorina* who taught at the same school after transferring
there from Alcamo.

Franco felt stale if he spent more than a year in one place, so
the newlyweds moved as often as they could. For several years,
Franco dragged Valeria around the bottom of the boot until the
birth of Daniela and Francesco put an end to their itinerant
lifestyle. For the next eight years the young family lived in a
coastal village of Calabria, until Franco woke up one morning
and declared his feet itchy again.

At the same time Franco decided to move, he received a surprise present from his aunt in Andrano. The prince had given her some land on castle grounds which she in turn gave to her favourite nephew. Although Franco had his heart set on living in Florence, the city of his artistic dreams, he was happy to go there via his home town: to accept the gift and build a house on the land which he would then sell to fund his move north. It was most un-Italian, rash and uncertain, and it excited no one more than Franco.

Franco's mother looked forward to her son's homecoming and hoped it might be permanent. She had lost her husband to lung cancer when Franco was twenty-five, after which she had seen little of her son, in whom the tragic loss of his father had inspired anger and, as always, the desire to flee. On his return to Andrano, Franco expressed his feelings towards his birthplace and family in a poem Daniela keeps on her bedroom wall.

> *Ho perquisito le rughe della mia terra*
> *ed ho scoperto i colori caldi del sud*
> *fra i fiori*
> *che ha seminato mio padre.*

> *E' qui la mia scuola,*
> *su questi campi di bronzo,*
> *dove il silenzio è colore,*
> *dove un lamento è preghiera . . .*
> *mentre la 'torre spaccata'*
> *attende che scenda qualcuno*
> *dal prossimo treno*
> *e poi lascia andare nel mare*
> *l'ennesima pietra!*

> *Un altro treno è passato:*
> *non è sceso mio padre!*

Ho ripercorso le strade della mia terra
ed ho rivissuto l'amore bruciante del sud
fra i fiori
che sta raccogliendo mia madre.

I searched the wrinkles of my homeland
and discovered the hot colours of the south
among the flowers
that my father planted.

My school is here,
on these fields of bronze,
where silence is colour
and complaint a prayer . . .
while the broken tower*
waits for someone
to get off the next train
and cast another of its stones
to the sea!

Another train has passed:
But my father didn't get off!

I retravelled the streets of my homeland
and relived the scorching love of the south
among the flowers
that my mother is gathering.

Franco built his house near the castle, but instead of selling it
and moving to Florence, he has lived there ever since. Daniela

---

* The '*torre spaccata*' or 'broken tower' refers to the Torre del Sasso, behind which
Freccia is buried. Part of the tower has collapsed, and its position on the
headland gives the impression that the loose stones could be dislodged and
sent tumbling to the sea.

and Francesco had made friends in Andrano and refused to be uprooted again. They protested at their father's attempts to relocate and, supported by their mother, they won. But Franco felt trapped, telling colleagues and friends that the village was not his family's home and they were merely passing through. It was as though the 'scorching love' he mentions in the poem would burn his feet if he stood still for too long.

For the next twenty years Franco taught at the local high school, but he despised the quiet life and was rarely happy in his home town. If music were a metaphor for Franco's life, he was a free-spirited soloist rather than a member of an orchestra. He refused to obey the conductor's baton, just as he refused to participate in town affairs, festivals and gossip. Those who tried to recruit a man of culture to their political parties found the same door on which they knocked closed abruptly in their face. And he never went to the bar in the piazza—and if you don't do that in small-town Italy, you will always be an outsider.

Whenever he had the chance, Franco escaped to Rome or Florence to play concerts or exhibit his art. Creatively and intellectually he was unsatisfied in Andrano, a town whose culture was based on tradition. But tradition didn't interest Franco. He saw it as paying homage to survival rather than progress. In all the years he lived in Andrano he never once went to its Festival of the Madonna. It was variety that Franco was after, and the village offered little of that.

The predictable nature of life in Andrano frustrated him the most; routine, a future devoid of adventure. 'We'll come back here in twenty years and Pippo's Fiat will still be parked across our gate,' Daniela recalls him saying when trying to convince his family to pack its bags. I had picked up the same impression on my first day in Andrano. Now that I'd returned, I realised it was accurate.

Franco believed the *Andranesi* found comfort in the fact they could foresee their modest fates, something that frightened him more than an uncertain future. From the day they are born, each resident pays an annual tax to the *municipio* for a grave in the town cemetery, an arrangement which disturbed Franco, who believed that if you knew where you were going to be buried you were already dead. Needless to say, he was behind on his payments.

Daniela's father refused to accept that all life had to offer was a guaranteed grave, small-town traditions and gossiping about the lives of others while one's own life slipped by. He longed for a place with a sophisticated heartbeat rather than a parochial pulse, a place where strangers existed rather than just cousins and *compare*. There was an internal calamity about him, a dissatisfaction with his lot, like a goldfish tired of its bowl or a budgie bored with its cage.

Surprisingly, Franco was not disliked in Andrano. On the contrary, his artistic talents were admired and his paintings bought by many. But his preferred company was that of his students, fertile minds which he encouraged to think beyond the borders of their town. He felt that young people were wasted in Andrano and hoped his own children developed careers that would take them further afield. He was even against Daniela dating local boys for fear they might sway her to stay. That said, for Franco the world started and finished in Italy, and had Daniela declared she was off to Australia to visit a man she had met in Ireland, her father would probably have recruited the boy-next-door to marry his daughter. He encouraged her to roam, but only as far as Rome. Unfortunately, Franco was already ill when Daniela and I met, and we will never know if our relationship would have had his approval or not.

I have often wondered if Franco's desire to control life, his obsession to leave the village and his depression at having stayed, perhaps contributed to an unstable state of mental health which manifested itself as Alzheimer's. Indeed doctors initially diagnosed him as 'depresso' and from there, at fifty-nine, his slide into illness was swift.

At the beginning a series of minor mental lapses was attributed to nothing more sinister than stress, but then the frequency of errors increased and alarm bells began to ring. He forgot what day it was, lost his possessions and lit the wrong end of cigarettes. He got up at 3 am, convinced it was time to go to work, and when driving around Andrano he became lost in its laneways, a maze for the uninitiated, amazing for the local resident.

When Valeria realised her husband was becoming a danger to himself, she hid his car keys, persuaded him to take time off work and took him to a number of doctors, who, after initial hesitation, made a dramatic diagnosis. Franco was told by a specialist in Rome that he would lose both his memory and his mind, a forecast he promptly forgot, confirming it immediately. At home the next evening, Franco remembered his trip to the specialist and appealed to his family for honesty. 'I feel something in my forehead,' he said. 'Something heavy, like a dull weight. Would somebody please tell me what the hell is happening?' But nobody would. Daniela stifled tears, Francesco left the room and Valeria put her head on her husband's shoulder. Their incapacity to help made them as angry as Franco, whose lucid moments dwindled until his life, his language and his loves slipped gradually from his grasp.

It wasn't long before Franco was forgetting his name, soiling his trousers and struggling to perform simple tasks like dressing or brushing his teeth. He was confused, becoming lost mid-sentence and forgetting where the bathroom was. With the help and support of her children, Valeria found the words to convince her husband that it was better he didn't drive, that he take early retirement, and that he sign everything into her name while he could still write his. Then Valeria took early retirement herself and her daily routine began, including the morning walk in the garden, where, for the first time when greeted by passing friends, *professore* failed to respond.

After his morning walk outside, Franco spent the rest of the day shuffling about inside, while I spent the rest of the day shuffling about behind him, doing my best to ensure he harmed neither himself nor the house. He inched from room to room, old terrain a new discovery. Whenever I was distracted and had to leave him briefly, I returned to find him standing in the corner like a child counting to a hundred in a game of hide and seek. I could have counted to a thousand and he would have still been there, trying to figure out why his world had turned white. I spun him around and he was off again, to the sofa next, to pick up a cushion, carry it for half an hour, before placing it down on my computer in the study. During the course of the afternoon he covered every tile in the house. Valeria should have tied the vacuum to him.

The walls of the house were hung with his artwork, paintings and drawings which, like his poems, revealed a reluctant love for his homeland. Familiar features of the local landscape had been distorted and deformed, as though he appreciated their existence but wished they would change. He stopped in front of the paintings and ran his fingers across the brushstrokes, fragments of a whole he no longer understood. Then he closed his eyes, either on memory or the search for it, before turning away from the picture with his hand still painting, until it too forgot its purpose and fell at the artist's side.

I longed to talk with Franco, to ask the meaning of certain paintings and discover the man behind them, to hear stories from his past recounted by him rather than by his daughter. His incapacity triggered frustration in me and at times I wanted to shake him until he snapped out of the trance in which he appeared to be caught, until he screamed for me to stop with the bold voice he once had, until before me stood the genius rather than the fool. I squeezed his arms tight. '*Professore, professore!*' Nothing—except tears in my eyes and the sound of feet shuffling to the same corner of the room from which they had come.

Unable to discern their use, Franco was a hoarder of objects.

His trousers were weighed down with pebbles from the garden, forks, pegs, keys, soap and other sundry items. If we'd lost anything we checked Franco's pockets before searching elsewhere. He amassed so much junk that by the end of the day he could have held a jumble sale in his jeans.

In summer Franco stored his pilferings in his pants, but in winter he cast them into the fire, turning up the temperature in a room where we were doing our best to stay cool. One evening I was reading in the lounge when Franco trudged past, snatched my book from my hands and tossed it into the flames. The cushions in the living room met the same fiery fate, as did a pair of my shoes, Valeria's handbag, numerous phone bills and Daniela's winter coat.

Such antics lent Franco personality when the disease was doing its best to rob him of every trace. But the black comedy stopped when he stood in front of the mirror. Like a newborn baby, which, mentally speaking, the doctors claimed he was, Franco couldn't comprehend that what he saw was a reflection. He objected to the stranger and, when still capable of anger, told it where to go or questioned the chastity of its mother. Mirrors were a doorway rather than a visual echo, and he broke his nose on one occasion trying to take a step inside. Like she did with the open fire, Valeria insisted on leaving mirrors in the house to retain a semblance of normality, but I turned them to the wall when Franco was my responsibility.

As always, Valeria's friends dropped in while she was away, bringing vegetables from their fields or meat from the butcher. It was the Italian way of helping out: putting food on the table of someone who had too much on their plate. Almost the entire town got behind the struggle at number 15. *Il farmacista* delivered Franco's medicine, the cobbler dropped off Valeria's shoes, and a nun called in with a plastic statuette of the Madonna filled with holy water from Lourdes. It was for Franco—a miracle cure, but she might have done better filling it with gin and giving it to Valeria.

I was giving Franco his breakfast one morning when the doorbell was rung by the mayor of Andrano. He had come to present a poster which the *municipio* had made from one of Franco's sketches of the castle balcony and which the mayor intended to use as his administration's motif. Franco's name appeared at the foot of the poster alongside the year 1992, when the artist had no idea that his thoughts would turn as abstract as some of his paintings. I thanked the mayor and rushed back inside to finish feeding Franco, who would no doubt have found it as ironic as I did that a man who had always shied from politics should create the emblem for his town's ruling party.

Nursing Franco was difficult enough at home but the real challenge began when we took him out. I waited for Daniela to come home from school before attempting excursions with her father. Usually we went for a drive along the coast, to watch fishing boats leaving port or sunset over Castro. But there were also chores to be done. One afternoon we stopped at the barber's, a windowless room full of cigarette smoke and hunting magazines. The old men in the queue were happy to let Franco go ahead, but we couldn't coax him into the chair so while he wandered the room the barber cut his hair, pursuing the moving target with his scissors.

Despite a few ragged edges, Franco looked smart when we took him to have his photo taken for his *carta identità* which was due for renewal. Luigi aimed his camera higher than usual so that the hands anchoring his subject wouldn't appear in the photo. It was touching, the way the town made allowances for the man who had drawn its motif.

After ten days Valeria returned, her mother at peace and the hillside in pieces. Without resting after the overnight bus she immediately set about shaving Franco's beard, which Daniela and I had let grow because it masked his lack of expression and made him look mysterious rather than mystified. She then got to work on his dandruff problem by running the vacuum cleaner over his head, guiding the hose with her right hand and combing his hair with her left. For the first time since I'd known him, I believe Franco understood what was happening, the look on his face one of total surrender. I later complained to Daniela, saying that as uncomprehending as her father was, surely Valeria shouldn't Hoover his head. 'It's not because he can't understand,' replied Daniela. 'She did the same to us when we were kids.'

A stubborn, hardy woman, 'Sicilian, not Italian', Valeria recommenced the routine of nursing her dying husband without a whimper. The more I came to know her, the more I considered Daniela's mother the most headstrong woman I had ever met. It was probably her biggest defect, but in the circumstances, her biggest strength. She gave in to nothing. Unlucky to have fallen ill, Franco was lucky to have done so with Valeria by his side. Ten days I had been nursing him and I was exasperated. Valeria had been doing so for five years, with as many more to come perhaps, and Daniela was yet to hear her complain.

But her struggle didn't seem fair, on Franco as much as Valeria. When Freccia was dying of an incurable disease we helped her off to sleep. Yet in English, to treat someone badly is 'to treat them like a dog'. Perhaps 'to treat them like a human' might be more accurate. Is it absurd that a stray dog had more right to a peaceful death than Franco? I remember Freccia looking up at me with trusting eyes as we ended her pain. Did Franco still trust us, given that every morning we denied his plea to rest by dragging him out of bed and drugging him to his feet? We did it because he was human, a privilege, apparently.

Devoting every moment to prolonging the life of someone perhaps better off dead carries its own risk of mental illness; in fact the doctors had warned Daniela and Francesco to look after the nurse as much as the patient. Amazingly, Valeria found the strength to sing while caring for her husband: 'O Sole Mio' and other Italian favourites that kept her spirits up. She had even come up with her own lyrics to help bolster her nerve, like: '*Dio lo vuole così*'—'This is the way God wants it'. It was agony to listen to, but it kept Valeria ticking over. Her courage seemed infinite, but Daniela knew otherwise, and had returned home from Milan for the sake of her mother more than her father. I admired her for that decision, almost as much as I admired Valeria, who, for as long as it was necessary, would honour the promise she had made before God over thirty-five years ago—to love her gypsy husband in sickness and in health. Franco's memory might have wandered, but Valeria's was as strong as her will.

The cruelty of Alzheimer's is that it steals the past as well as the future. We should all have the right to die casting an evaluating eye on whom we loved and what we achieved, on our families and friends, our triumphs and tears. I only hope that death unlocks Franco's memory and gives him back his life: his wedding, his music, his children, his art. That when death finally comes, *professore* finds the paradise he never found during his life, despite constant searching. A place he has never known, but a place he will always remember. Wherever that place is, Franco, may the flowers have the sweetest fragrance, and may your father be on that train.

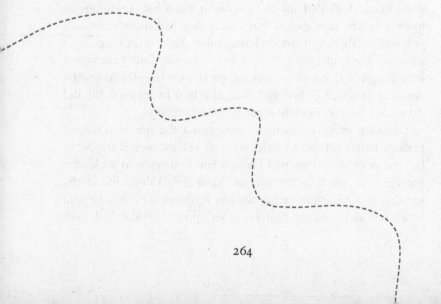

Snowed-in by the sea

Ahh the Mediterranean: sun, sea, snow . . . SNOW?! Yes, snow, and lots of it. Snow on the bell tower, snow on the beach and snow in the branches of sun-loving olive trees. The myth of the Mediterranean is that summer is endless. The secret of the Mediterranean is that winter is as harsh as summer is hot.

It began in late October. Sun weakened and cloud strengthened. Days shortened and nights lengthened. White smoke swirled from whitewashed chimneys, dancing on wind before disappearing. Autumn storms dishevelled the sea and boats were fished from a choppy port. Only the olive trees retained their leaves, while the Vallonea oaks thinned to gnarled nakedness in a matter of weeks. Tourists and northern numberplates vanished, siesta was skipped, shops changed trading hours from *ora solare* to *ora legale*, La Botte emptied and the piazza filled. The temperature dropped dramatically, but it wasn't until it neared freezing that Signor Api's grease-stained shirt was replaced by a jumpsuit and woollen hat with flaps on either side, as limp as a Basset Hound's ears, to cover his own frozen lobes. Not even his home-made wine could protect the old man's extremities from a Mediterranean winter, which was colder, longer and bleaker than I had ever imagined.

While the sights might change, it's the smell that signals the onset of winter on the heel of the boot. The agricultural calendar comes to a close at the beginning of November, when crops are picked, pickled, sun-dried and salted for consumption during the cold months ahead. In overloaded *ape*, farmers transport their produce home to housewives, who drown eggplants and onions in vinegar and douse peppers and anchovies in salt. Like last year, the bow-legged man across the road rolled his grain on the side of the street, his wife following behind picking out imperfections. Andrano's streets channel smell as effectively as they do sound, aromas finding their way to every nostril in town, including those of stray dogs, hypnotised by hunger in the salt-and-vinegar breeze.

Plump, full of sunshine, olives are also harvested in autumn. Wielding broom-like contraptions that dislodge without damaging, farmers shake them from their branches into nets whisked away to waiting trucks. The olives are then taken to a *frantoio* where they are selected, washed, ground and kneaded before their oil is extracted and left to decant. Puglia's olive trees produce an extra-virgin oil that 'tastes like sunlight' according to Daniela. The smell of olives being pulped is agreeable but the stench of their pips being burnt is revolting. Fortunately the production of olive oil in Andrano is small scale, but I gagged every time we drove past the industrial chimneys on the road to Lecce.

Competing with the smell of olives is the stout smell of grapes, red and green, delivered in truckloads from vineyards near Brindisi—a city whose name means 'to raise a toast'. Tip-trucks unload into cellars throughout the Salento, where home-made wine is produced by the barrel. From when they are picked in September until the wine is ready in November, Andrano is intoxicated by the acrid aroma of fermenting grapes.

On the eleventh of November at *La Festa di San Martino*, named after Saint Martin, patron saint of wine-makers, the *vino novello*—new wine—is sampled. Most of the *Andranesi* make their own vintage, which they taste for the first time on *San Martino* and which better be good as it has to last a whole year. Signor Api declared himself delighted with his drop. As did our bank manager, Errico, with whom we spent *San Martino* singing along to a banjo, which he strummed skilfully until draining his fifth glass of backyard Bordeaux, after which his chords became as casually formed as the queue in his bank.

Other than *San Martino* and the occasional religious festival, revelry is rare in winter, when towns like Andrano hibernate. During the cold months, the *Andranesi* work and wait for the warm months, counting the days until the sun returns to the Salento. The Mediterranean lifestyle revolves around heat and the outdoors. When ten centimetres of snow fell in twenty-four hours in mid-December, we had no skis or sleds to make the most of it and had to get our kicks by throwing snowballs at the *vigili* and building a snowman with olives for eyes.

At the end of summer, friendships faded like suntans, with many *Andranesi* returning to far-flung jobs or university. Our summer group lost its ringleader, Riccardo, transferred to fight crime in an infamous Mafia town near Palermo; rather him than me. Those who remained kept to themselves. The only friend I saw regularly in both summer and winter was Renato, who deemed any weather suitable to beat me at tennis.

I found it incredible that, in a town of 5000 people, we could pass almost the entire winter without bumping into friends with whom we had spent the summer—excluding those who had moved away, of course. Perhaps it was because, in a certain sense, we had ourselves moved away, preferring to rent a house on the seafront rather than up the hill in town. We had returned to Andrano to help Valeria with Franco but that didn't mean living under the same roof. If I was going to live in a southern Italian fishing village, I was going to live by the sea, regardless of wild weather, salt spray and waves that reached the road.

So as the cold braced Andrano and residents packed their cars and drove up the hill to homes built for winter, Daniela and I packed our car and rolled down the hill to a house built for summer. Tongues wagged of course, as they always will in Italy when you do something against the grain. We were pronounced foolish, and Daniela was said to be doing things she would never have done before her Australian boyfriend arrived. I was viewed with suspicion and taken for a madman because I swam in the sea when the swell was up, *and* within two hours of food. But neither of us could have cared less; extreme living sparked a solidarity that made us friends first and lovers second.

We found the beach house through that most effective Italian classified—the grapevine. A friend of a friend heard we were looking and offered us his three-bedroom villa overlooking La Botte for the equivalent of $60 a week. A two-storey dwelling with whitewashed walls and red shutters, like most houses along the beachfront it was designed for temporary summer living. What furnishings it did have were of modest comfort and we spent the first day of our tenancy repairing beds, replacing mattresses and sealing windows and doors so that winter remained outside. Decorations were religious kitsch. After making a mental note of their positions in order to return them to their rightful places at the end of our stay, we removed the crucifixes, the tapestry of the Last Supper and a two-foot ceramic statue of the Madonna.

The beach house wasn't heated but a fireplace at least warmed the living room. Position and panorama were more important than comfort, however, and French doors on an Italian balcony afforded us priceless views for a pittance. To the left was glistening Castro, its ruined castle illuminated at night and fishing trawlers heading out to sea in any weather, spiteful or serene. To the right, the olive headland crowned by Torre del Sasso, and across the white-capped Mediterranean, the snow-capped Albanian mountains, distant but distinct in the absence of summer heat haze.

We ate breakfast watching red-hulled tankers creeping up from Africa and Greece to Italian ports like Venezia and Trieste. Daniela bought me a pair of binoculars to read the names of passing ships by day, and I bought her a telescope to watch the stars at night; there were few lights down at the port in winter, making it perfect for stargazing. It made a welcome change from the apartment in Milan, with claustrophobic views of rat-racers in their bathrooms.

I still don't know what the address was. The name of the street was painted on the mosaic of local stone that comprised our front wall, but some letters had faded and the words were illegible. The house didn't have a number, which mattered little given the postman didn't deliver to such a lonely location. All our post went to Valeria, who more than compensated for our not having an address by recently acquiring three of her own; someone from the *municipio* had travelled the town putting a number on every door that fronted the street. Even her garage had a separate address.

There was no water or sewerage connection but a water tank and *pozzo nero* under the house, separated, fortunately, by a thick concrete wall. One truck came to deliver water, another to take away sewage. They were identical-looking trucks; only the nose could tell them apart. The driver of the water truck was the father of a former student of Franco's, so we received a sack of potatoes from his fields with every refill. On really cold days he heated the tube before pumping water through, ensuring it didn't freeze between his truck and our tank.

I never saw the driver of the 'turd truck', who did pick-ups at dawn to spare neighbours the smell, a gesture he needn't have observed with us since our only neighbours were two lovers who used the apartment above ours twice a week. Every Tuesday and Thursday, a pot-bellied architect and his shapely young mistress turned up in separate cars ten minutes apart, arriving after dark and parking behind the house to hide vice and vehicle from view. They stayed for about an hour, sometimes more, sometimes less depending on the architect's stamina, before returning to their cars ten minutes apart once again. When spring brought people back to the port, the architect suspended his lease and his love affair, until autumn returned, the port was deserted and both were reinstated.

Other than the nocturnal neighbours, the beach house came with more stray animals than functional electrical appliances; cats mainly, which the summer tenants had fed and which came to the door each day, meowing plaintively until their mouths were filled. There was also a puppy, unmentioned in the lease, who'd been abandoned behind the house and who I called Olive because I found her under an olive tree. How anyone could have discarded her was beyond me. She was superb: a cream cross-breed with green eyes and a pink nose that had become dirty from scrounging for food.

Although we already had Freccia up at Valeria's, there was room for one more in the ark, so we adopted Olive, or vice versa, and gave her some food and the run of the yard. The irony of renting a house on a hillside of stray animals was that pets were forbidden in the lease. Our landlord had the habit of turning up unannounced to work on the garden, and at times I was forced to hide Olive like the Resistance hiding Jews from the Nazis. Much of this book was written with her curled on my lap in the study, my hand around her snout so she wouldn't bark and give us away. Eventually I gave her to a trusted colleague of Daniela's, who despite vowing to have her de-sexed at six months is still looking for homes for a litter of eight.

When we inspected the house there was a washing machine. When we moved in there wasn't, only a space where it had stood. 'Never was one,' insisted the landlord, a man with hunched shoulders and decaying teeth, the consequence of his smoking like a chimney, a feature which the house thankfully had both before and after we took up residence. When he did finally admit to the missing machine, he claimed to have misunderstood during our inspection of the property. Apparently, when Daniela had pointed at the rusty appliance asking: *'Funziona?'*—'Does it work?', he thought she was referring to the power point to which it was attached. Of course. Rather than buy a washing machine we took our dirty clothes up to Valeria, who still refused to wash underwear of a certain colour.

Among the appliances that did remain after our inspection, the water pump was the most defective, supplying a constipated trickle which, when standing under it, felt more like water torture than taking a shower. And the few drops that did fall were cold due to the boiler being equally defunct. I'd seen more modern machines dumped on the side of the road. Calling a plumber to come and fix faulty appliances can be frustrating in tiny towns like Andrano. With little or no competition for miles around, you must invariably summon the same bandit who installed the machine, either him or his son or grandson, who inherited the family business through birthright rather than brains. This person will usually be a *compare* or second cousin, who gives priority to the bigger jobs which pay and leaves *favori* for the future.

Daniela called a plumber who was as lazy as our water supply. 'The wife's got friends from Palermo', he pleaded, 'don't make me come now and upset her. I've only just got back in her good books.' After a week of similarly lame excuses he finally showed up, said he didn't have the parts to fix the boiler but that he should do in another week.

A week later our boiler was working, although when in use it sounded as though a Vespa was loose in the house. The problem now was that it didn't have any water to heat given the pump was still spluttering and would continue to do so, explained the plumber, until expensive repairs were made.

Despite its technological imperfections, the beach house was charmingly simple. Far from home yet close to Daniela, I enjoyed the Mediterranean winter in a house designed for summer. Some central heating wouldn't have gone amiss, but like the come-and-go tenants above, we were rarely cold for long. Especially when snowed-in by the sea.

Global fishing village

Winter meant work, for both Daniela and me. Daniela had been back at school since early September having been transferred to her former primary school in Tricase. She had missed her students, who had grown dramatically in her absence and were now at that whimsical age when their teeth remained in the fruit they ate for lunch. And the students had missed her as much as she had missed them. The boy who justified tears over Daniela's departure by saying he wasn't a robot suggested they celebrate her return by declaring it 'Daniela Day'—a special holiday to be observed every year with a day off school. Cunning at the age of ten, another southern Italian landlord in the making.

If Daniela's job was secure, my prospects were somewhat precarious. But thanks to Mary on the Adriatic Express, whose contact proved easier to find than her art dealer boyfriend, I had teed up an interview for a part-time teaching position at an English school. Daniela came with me to the interview, which took place on a Saturday evening at the owner of the school's apartment in Lecce's historic centre.

Claire was English but had lived in Italy for fifteen years where she had married an Italian she later divorced. A short, cheerful woman, she had two children, three birds, two dogs and a turtle, all of whom were present at the interview—an unlikely panel of judges. We sat in her kitchen with its low-arched ceiling while the children played on the adjoining terrace, lowering string over the railing to the bar below like fishermen tossing lines over the side of a boat. Using the pegs supplied, the *barista* attached various goodies to the string—potato chips and chocolate bars—which the children reeled in while giggling hysterically. '*Grazie*,' they yelled downwards, cupping mouths to lengthen voices. '*Prego*,' came a faint reply from the deep.

The questions at the interview weren't quite those for which I had prepared. 'Do you like Italy?' Claire asked, fetching me another beer. It was a question I was often asked and which I dodged if at all possible, not because I was undecided but because most people who asked were Italian and expected a positive answer. But Claire was in my shoes, meaning I could be blunt without the risk of offending national pride. 'I find life in Italy brilliantly bad,' I replied. It felt good to be in the company of someone who knew exactly what that meant and, better still, agreed. I could have spent the entire evening trying to explain what it was—other than Daniela—that kept me in a country as frustrating as it was fun, but needed to look no further than the evening itself. Italy's unforeseen pleasures; that a man in search of a part-time job finds a full-time friend.

I told Claire about the feeling of displacement I had experienced on trips to England and Australia. Of that sense of resented privilege—being lucky enough to know two worlds intimately while feeling totally at home in neither. Claire smiled. 'It only gets worse,' she said. 'When I'm here I miss home and when I'm home I miss here. I'm starting to think I'll never leave. For all its faults, Italy keeps me young and on my toes.' For a woman as short as Claire, finding a country that kept her on her toes seemed reason enough to stay on its own. But I found it interesting that, even after fifteen years, she still used the word 'home' to describe England rather than Italy. If home is where the heart is, it suggested hers lay elsewhere. But she had stayed in Lecce even after splitting with her Italian husband. I couldn't imagine staying in Andrano if Daniela and I went separate ways.

Like most conversations about Italy it moved swiftly on to food, Claire's next question researching my culinary rather than my professional experiences. For some reason she was interested in my opinion of Italian cooking; maybe there was a canteen at the school which she wanted to be sure I would like. I said I adored Italian food but missed variety, Asian cuisine in particular. Claire felt the same way and invited us to dinner the following weekend, promising to cook sushi and invite her English friend. She gave me the whereabouts of a shop in Lecce that sold soy sauce and peanut butter. She didn't know if it stocked Vegemite, but was sure it sold Marmite—the same thing in Claire's opinion. It was the first time we had disagreed all evening.

My CV lay unread in Daniela's handbag while Claire asked if I could teach the following Tuesday; the fact I spoke English seemed good enough for her. I would be covering one of her classes, as she had promised to take her children to Bari to watch the arrival of a famous warship. I was given the school's address and a textbook from which to teach. Italy had rubbed off on Claire, who preferred to give things a go and see how they worked out rather than plan them in advance. We didn't even strike a verbal agreement yet I knew the job was mine. How would I ever survive more formal interviews in the world I had known before Italy?

As winter progressed I saw Claire more often as a friend than as a boss, not because she had no work on offer but because I was too busy to accept it. The sports magazine for which I had written before moving to Italy commissioned various stories from Europe, and thanks to the World Wide Web I could research and write them from Andrano—a global fishing village. A year ago, somewhat reluctantly, we had moved to Milan so that I could find work, when all the time I could have done so from the Salento.

An avid reader, I had been worried about the effects of the internet on the printed word. Yet here was the internet helping the printed word, allowing me to write stories that would have been impossible without it. On one occasion, through a London media agency on behalf of an Australian magazine, I arranged an interview with a Swedish motorcyclist for an upcoming race in the Czech Republic, all from an Italian village where even the locals couldn't find work. Another time, the editor of *Inside Sport* emailed me an urgent request for photos to accompany an article of mine going to print. In less than an hour, from a beach house on the heel of the boot, rug over my knees and laptop over both, I tracked down a photographer in London who forwarded me a selection of images which I in turn sent to Sydney at the touch of a button.

The internet only shrank virtual borders I then had to physically cross to get the story, but that was all the fun. Over the course of the winter I visited Sweden, Russia, the Czech Republic and Austria, to report on speedway, aerobatics and the Olympics. One morning, leaving Andrano on assignment, I stopped for petrol at 'California' where I explained to a man who had never sent an email how the internet allowed me to work from a house with no postal service. I was on my way to Brindisi to catch a morning flight to Rome, where Sandro Donati, Head of Science and Research at the Italian Olympic Committee, expected me for an afternoon interview. Signor Api listened intently as I told him how I would fly to Rome, do the interview, fly back to Andrano, write the story, then send it off to Australia in less time than it took him to fill my car with petrol. 'That's technology,' said Signor Api. 'Man's biggest waste of time.' I should have known he would have his own take on things.

It was too early in the day for his home-made plonk to have polluted his opinions, so he obviously felt strongly on the subject.

'Technology takes us forward, Signor Api,' I protested.

'Rubbish,' he rebounded. 'It takes us backwards.'

Here we go.

'I can understand your use of the internet, but when I see cars pulling up with television screens built in, I wonder where it's all going to end.'

The orator was away, raising voice and arms to address the street.

'Man disgraces himself by believing technology brings happiness. Technology has no conscience. It distorts what we need. A television in a car! What the hell for? There's this need to have everything immediately these days, but little left worth having immediately.'

'What about medical care?'

'Drive carefully and you won't need it.'

Signor Api closed my petrol cap and waved me on my way.

One of the few machines Signor Api owned was the bowser on his driveway, allowing him to make a living and lead a generally simple existence. What gave him the right then to pontificate on technology, hailing from a village that spent more on religious festivals than infrastructure? And what gave him the right to be so damn incisive? I belonged to a modern world, Signor Api to an ancient one. I saw technology as inevitable, Signor Api as a choice. Had I misjudged the *Andranesi*? Was it short-sighted of me to think them short-sighted? They could afford decent roads if they wanted. They could even paint lines on them if they went overboard. They simply chose not to, having different priorities that embraced the past rather than the future. And that, while unenlightened, was also uncomplicated and refreshing.

When I first moved to Italy I had never imagined chatting freely with the likes of Signor Api, much less interviewing an Italian Olympic Committee official for four hours in Italian; it wasn't so long ago I was ordering a kilometre of sausages. Sandro Donati had devoted his career to exposing widespread corruption in international sport. At the World Athletics Championships he blew the whistle on judges recording long jump distances for one competitor *before* he jumped, ensuring the favoured athlete won a medal. Donati's position made him privy to sensitive information, like the fact that a number of the athletes who competed at the Sydney Olympics had exaggerated levels of human growth hormone, some as high as sixty times the level found naturally in the body. Unmasking champions as cheats had made Donati's desk a sea of summonses. He had faced ten law suits since Sydney alone, seven of which he had won and three pending trial. In my editor's opinion it was Donati who was the real champion.

Returning from Rome later that night, I beeped as I drove past 'California' on my way to our seaside hideaway. I was eager to freshen up after such a long day, heading straight for the shower while Daniela prepared *spaghetti alle melanzane* in the kitchen.

'I forgot to tell you,' she shouted over the blow-heater as I undressed in the bathroom, 'the landlord fixed the water pump while you were away.'

I turned on the tap with high expectations, dashed instantly by an explosion under the house which caused the water to stop running, the blow-heater to stop blowing, and the lights to weaken briefly before returning fitfully.

'That tight-fisted bugger fixed the pump himself, didn't he, Daniela?'

'Er, no,' she replied sheepishly, another polite little lie aimed at protecting me, or the landlord *from* me.

Technology can bring happiness, Signor Api. It may not be televisions in cars as you say, but there are some things worth having immediately—like hot water for instance. When I said the simple life was 'refreshing', I wasn't referring to cold showers in winter.

Early afternoon, mid-winter, the day after my return from Rome. I was working on my story in the beach house when a car pulled up outside. It was too early for the lovers, so I went to the window to see who else was foolish enough to be down at the port in such rotten weather. I recognised the driver of the silver Audi as Carlo, a friend of Daniela's family, and welcomed him into the house, offering him a glass of whisky for the warmth that was in it. The temperature gauge by the door registered 3°C and I had put out the fire because a gale off the sea was blowing smoke back down the chimney.

A tall man with a thick moustache and thinning black hair, Carlo drained his whisky glass—a recycled Nutella tumbler—in one gulp, either keen to explain his visit or escape my simple surroundings. He had come to invite Daniela and me to dinner that evening and wouldn't take no for an answer. Anticipating his central heating as much as his company, I said we would be delighted. But I suspected a catch of some sort. Another translation most likely, an urgent one to have dragged Carlo, a lover of his leather armchair, down to the port in winter.

Dinner was delicious: *pasta al pomodoro* followed by some sort of local fish baked in salt. Carlo had spent his afternoon preparing the meal. Having retired on a government pension at the ripe old age of thirty-seven, he had become something of a house-husband, while his wife Rosaria worked in an office in Lecce. After Rosaria had cleared the plates but left our glasses, Carlo whispered something to his son Roberto, who left the room briefly before returning with a bunch of papers—time to earn my dinner. It wasn't a translation but a job application, for a position in Rome with a company that controlled the movement of satellites in space, or at least that's what Carlo told the town. The form needed to be filled in English, a language neither Roberto, nor his parents—nor anyone else in Andrano, it seemed—could command.

Despite the fact that Roberto seemed content riding his Vespa around town all day, Carlo was desperate to get him out from under his feet—and his wallet—into employment. So desperate that he wasn't in the least deterred by the minor obstacle that Roberto was totally unqualified for the position. After reading the form I expressed reluctance to continue, pointing out—as politely as possible—that Roberto hadn't a hope in hell. Carlo, however, moustache tinged with tomato sauce, instructed me to write the most desirable answer to each question, to declare his son a doctor if that's what the company wanted to hear. I took a gulp of *grappa* and did my best to explain to Carlo and his ugly duckling son that if I declared Roberto to have an Engineering degree and to be fluent in English, the company would at least expect him to be capable of reading the lies on his application when they called him for interview.

Realising I objected to being a party to blatant lies, Carlo was quick to assure me that Roberto would learn English before the interview. 'Look how well you've learnt Italian,' he said. 'How hard can it be?' When I suggested this unlikely, Carlo grew impatient, pulled a piece of paper from his top pocket and held it up dramatically the way a football referee displays a red card. 'You see this, Crris?' he went on, slapping the paper down on the table and tapping it twice as though performing a magic trick. 'With these Vatican contacts, that form you're filling out is a *formalità* which will probably never be read.' His laugh became a cough as he lit another cigarette, having finished his previous puff only minutes before. 'In that case why doesn't Roberto fill it out?' I asked defiantly, surprising everyone at the table, especially Daniela, who was beginning to fear for the mood of the evening.

Meritismo meant nothing to this idle man, for whom getting a job was based on who *he* knew rather than what *his son* didn't. Two worlds collided at Carlo's dinner table. He had cooked me a meal, plied me with *grappa* and complimented my Italian. What more could he do to get me on board? Instead of educating his son, Carlo tried to educate me. 'This is Italy, Crris,' he said. 'What I'm doing is nothing. There are people here who pay to get their jobs.' Better get your chequebook out then, Carlo.

Carlo's situation reminded me of a cartoon I had seen in an Italian newspaper. The 'before' and 'after' illustrations accompanied news of the abolition of compulsory military service and the intention to replace a conscripted army with a professional, well-paid military. The 'before' cartoon, referring to when military service was mandatory, showed the father of a dorky-looking boy offering a general a bribe and asking if he could see to it that his son *wasn't* selected. The 'after' illustration pictured the same scene, only this time the father asked the general to see to it that his son *was* selected.

In the south of Italy, where jobs are as thin on the ground as grass, concerned fathers like Carlo will do whatever it takes to get their children into the workforce. It made me appreciate how lucky I was to be able to teach in Lecce or write from Andrano. The heel of the boot has been something of an Achilles heel for Italy's government. And if the situation was bad in Puglia, in Calabria it was dire—the toe of the boot holds the dubious honour of having the highest unemployment rate in Europe. Barren fields sow desperation. In a remote Sicilian village a council worker employed by the *municipio* on a casual basis murdered the mayor and four other administrators when his request for full-time work was denied.

Ironically it was Carlo's generation that made life difficult for Roberto's. The Christian Democrat government, which held power in Italy for almost forty years after the birth of the Italian Republic, albeit jumping from one feeble coalition to the next, secured a stronghold in the south through a practice called *clientelismo*—the offering of public service jobs in exchange for votes. In 1976, Palermo had more than 2500 dustmen!

To free up state positions, which were swapped for political loyalty, the government retired workers early by lowering the return of service from thirty-five years to nineteen years six months and a day—although most workers took that last day off. While this helped the Christian Democrats win power in the south, it also crippled the treasury by paying generous government pensions to fit and able thirty-seven-year-olds.

Roberto inherited the consequences—and the bill—for his father's early retirement. He can't find a job in the public sector because positions are scarce now that the return of service has been lengthened, and any job he might be lucky enough to land in the private sector, with or without his Vatican contacts, would make him a slave to Italy's paralysing tax rates which a lawyer student of mine in Milan described as '*volgare*'. But someone must pay for Carlo's existence: put out to pasture while still a pup, tomato sauce in his moustache, cigar between his lips, free to worry about his son's future from his favourite leather recliner.

Daniela kicked me under the table and cast me a glance that begged I collaborate for the sake of her family's friendship with Rosaria more than to help Carlo. But how could I write that their son had a university degree when he had in fact left school before the bell rang? I skipped to the section asking for details of the applicant's current situation. Roberto thought it unwise to say that he was pouring cappuccinos two mornings a week at a local bar as it probably wouldn't interest a company which operated satellite guidance systems. It was the first intelligent comment he had made all evening. Too bad he hadn't made it in English. Carlo suggested I write that Roberto was doing two courses, one in multimedia and the other in French. When I protested he reminded me of the form's irrelevance, held up his trump card once again, and hurried me to the section asking for references, where he instructed me to write all seven Vatican contacts in a box with space for two. Lucky Carlo was a religious man or his son wouldn't have had a prayer.

I put down the pen and looked up at Carlo, who, as though ashamed, had disappeared behind a cloud of cigarette smoke; if I hadn't heard him cough I would have sworn he'd vaporised. Despite the cold I was delighted to return to the solitude and stars of the beach house, where I poured myself a nightcap and returned to work on my article about the corruption of sport, an abandoned dog on my lap and the architect testing the foundations of the building with his mistress on the other side of the wall. Were there any honest folk left?

Roberto got the job in Rome. I still don't believe it was for the company Carlo boasted. But just in case, beware of falling satellites.

Nights shortened and days lengthened, sea calmed and sky cleared, buds formed on branches, chimneys quit smoking, and Signor Api emerged from under his woollen hat, although the jumpsuit would stay for a month or two yet. Andrano returned to life among the sounds and smells of springtime: poppies, robins and the whistle of a passing cyclist.

The bookends of winter were two festivals, one religious, the other pagan, thank God. *San Martino* had signalled the coming of the cold, now *Carnevale* celebrated its passing. In late February the *Andranesi* gathered in Piazza Castello for the fancy dress event, which Italians say 'rejoices the victory of the light of spring over the darkness of winter'. Many residents hadn't seen each other since the wine festival, and although reunited their identities remained secret, for disguise was obligatory at this anonymous romp.

The motto of the mayhem was simple: '*A Carnevale, ogni scherzo vale*'—'At *Carnevale*, anything goes'. A grisly-looking group of devils, trolls and witches, pranced around the piazza spraying each other with shaving soap and water pistols. Prior to the party a parade of floats had toured the streets, towing papier-mâché parodies of Berlusconi attached to a lie detector and Michael Schumacher standing on a Ferrari showing off a trophy.

Andrano throws a party for one night only, but *Carnevale* lasts a week, a time when friends all over Italy play practical jokes on each other. Francesco sent a mock letter from the office of births, deaths and marriages to Antonio and Adele, informing them that it was illegal to name a child after a geographical place and giving them ten days to change their daughter's first name. Antonio confessed to being concerned for a moment, until he realised that only a year had passed since Asia was born, far too early for an Italian public office to take action.

Daniela had fond memories of *Carnevale* because of her mother's antics more than her own. Some years ago, together with a fellow teacher, Valeria had dressed up as a fat man and strolled through the piazza telling her students to '*andare a fare in culo*' or 'go fuck themselves', an indelicate phrase to level at children but far more playful in Italian than it sounds in English. The vulgar duo stole the show and for weeks after *Carnevale* the town was gossiping as to their real identities. Valeria had donned the disguise at a friend's house in Marittima, and not even Franco knew it was his wife who was the talk of the town. He was livid when Valeria finally confessed a month later. But she defended her prank, saying, as Daniela recalls: 'My students are rude to me every day. It was time to get my own back.'

Over a decade later, Daniela and I took Franco, now incapable of anger, to the window to watch the parade pass by the house. Other than the floats, the streets were closed to traffic and were policed by the *vigile*, the only partygoer dressed normally, although some smart-arse had stuck horns on his hat. Recognising no one in a town where everyone knows everyone is unnerving and bizarre. But Andrano was clearly having a wonderful time not being itself, masquerading as a menagerie of ghouls and gremlins. The Incredible Hulk swung from a tree and a devil thrust a papier-mâché pitchfork at a nun. A scantily dressed nymph in a monster mask ran screaming down the street, followed closely by a lecherous priest, his hands groping for her chest.

I enjoyed watching the woman in the tight skirt and top, not because she was attractive, whoever she was, but because if she was wearing a costume so brief then another long summer couldn't be far away. And that was definitely worth celebrating.

Vero o falso?

In his book, *L'Italia del Pizzo*—The Italy of the Backhander, Franco Cazzola, a sociology professor from Torino, claims the most common form of corruption in Italy is a bribe to secure a driver's licence. I discovered why when my international licence expired and, regardless of the fact I had been driving for twelve years, the last of those in Italy, I had to qualify for a European licence at an Italian driving school. It should have taken a few weeks. Instead, it took three months.

On the advice of Renato from the tennis club I chose a driving school in Caritano, a dusty collection of concrete inland from Andrano. A simple two-room house, the school's only distinguishing features were a sign on a whitewashed wall reading *Autoscuola*, as well as 'stop' and 'no entry' stickers on a glass front door. But I failed to heed such warnings and took a step inside I would regret.

A frumpy, freckled brunette, the school's secretary, sat at her desk in the waiting room smoking a thin cigarette. Hanging on the wall behind her was a 'No Smoking' sign—a fine first impression for a place preaching compliance with rules. When I explained my circumstances to the girl she screwed up her face, blew a stretch of smoke into mine, and yelled *'Vieni Michele!'* towards the doorway of the adjoining room.

Michele was the school's owner, tall and elegantly dressed, with the skeleton of a beard—a rather finicky bit of fluff—tracing the length of his jaw. Prematurely grey, from a career of near-misses no doubt, he strode into the room where we struck a deal which took into account the fact I had been driving almost as long as he had. I agreed to attend the first week of his four-week course, 'just to run through the street signs and be sure you know what they mean,' after which he would book both my theory and driving exams in Lecce. It sounded simple.

The following evening I returned to the school to complete an eye test with a medical officer. A week later, after paying €50, I was given my *foglio rosa* or learner's permit, without passing a theory test. This was standard procedure and not because of my special circumstances; in Italy you start driving *before* learning the rules of the road.

Michele's course went from 6.30 to 7.30 five nights a week. On the opening night, students from Caritano and surrounding towns smoked cigarettes in the courtyard while waiting for class to begin. They watched on intrigued when I pulled up and reverse-parked with one hand before strolling into the school with a driving manual under my arm. Italy had thrown many bizarre situations my way, but none more peculiar than driving myself to driving school to get my driver's licence.

In a humid room with chalky walls and a low, cross-arched roof, Michele made a grand entrance and took a seat at an even grander desk. His audience was twenty teenagers, plus one mature student. The boys seemed to have spent more time on their appearance than the girls. One had even trimmed his eyebrows into a ripple effect; this was a chance to pick up women rather than driving tips. We sat on university-style chairs with fold-out table-tops, on which we rested our 207-page driving manual titled *Auto e Moto su Strada*, containing information on everything from the meaning of a red light to the workings of a diesel engine.

On the wall behind Michele was a blackboard, a television screen, a traffic light and an eye-chart. High above his head were two placards, close to actual size, of the front and rear ends of a Fiat 500, complete with functional lights, indicators and number-plates. Next to the car, which appeared to have crashed through the wall, was a poster explaining the meaning of every dial and button on its dashboard.

Along the sides of the room were an assortment of car parts mounted on rickety stands, including an engine—antique enough to belong to the Fiat—brake systems, fuel lines, gear boxes and a variety of cylinders and pumps. An entire car appeared to have been dismantled in the classroom. The only missing parts were wheels and fuzzy dice.

The walls were decorated with posters displaying road signs, correct use of seat-belts and first-aid techniques. The poster nearest me was titled 'The most frequent causes of accidents'. One of the reasons cited was 'driving too fast for the conditions', illustrated by a sports car failing to negotiate a hairpin bend in the road and plummeting into a ravine. Beside the charred remains of the car was the word 'No' in red print, meaning, presumably, 'don't do this'.

Michele called the class to attention and struck a key on his computer. A traffic light appeared on the TV screen behind him which, at the touch of another button, turned green to signal the start of the course. Nice. Michele's teaching technique was to display the contents of the driving manual, road sign by road sign, on the television linked to his computer. After explaining the meaning of each sign, he asked a series of true or false questions to test our understanding of his explanation. In theory it sounds impressive. In reality it was a waste of time. Not because of our dodgy answers, but because of his senseless questions. A few examples:

Q: 'The pedestrian crossing is that part of the road reserved for pedestrians to cross the street and at which cars must stop and give precedence to pedestrians,' stated Michele. '*Vero o falso?*'

A: '*Vero,*' replied the class in unison.

Apart from the fact I am yet to see a motorist other than myself stop at a zebra crossing in Italy, the answer was indeed 'true'. Even if none of the students would ever respect the rule, they had clearly understood the sign's meaning. But Michele wasn't convinced.

Q: 'You must only stop for pedestrians crossing from the right.'

A: '*Falso*,' the class agreed.

Q: 'You must only stop for pedestrians crossing from the left.'

A: '*Falso*,' came a lethargic chant.

Q: 'You must only stop for children.'

A: '*Falso*.'

Q: 'You must only stop for animals.'

A: '*Falso*.'

Lucky Michele had cleared that up or we'd have been mowing down people while giving way to their pets.

He struck a button on his keyboard, the next road sign appeared on the monitor, and after a lengthy explanation the interrogation continued.

Q: 'You must give way to buses.'

A: '*Falso*.'

'Exactly,' exclaimed Michele. '*Bravi*. Because this is a sign for a level crossing for trains, and buses don't use train tracks, do they?'

A: '*No*.'

The room rolled its eyes.

Q: 'This sign tells you that it rains a lot in the area.'

There was a pause, the time it takes for twenty teenagers to crease their brows before one of them utters a speculative '*falso?*'

Our attention had started to wander. One boy sent a text message on his mobile. Another complimented the girl next to me on her earrings.

Q: 'This sign indicates that you must turn around and go back the way you came.'

A: The majority replied '*falso.*' One girl squeaked a hesitant '*vero*'. The rest remained silent.

Now he was really confusing them. If a sign indicating a two-way road could be taken to mean you must turn around and go back, then, extending such logic, a sign indicating a roundabout would mean you must drive around in circles. The clock on the wall ticked ever so slowly.

Q: 'No entry for motorcycles.'

A: '*Scusa?*' replied the class, confused.

Q: 'No entry for motorcycles,' repeated Michele.

A long pause.

A: '*Fal-so,*' said a sarcastic boy from the back of the class. Me.

'*Si, falso,*' said Michele, pleased he had stumped them. 'Because a motorcycle is less than 2.3 metres wide, and this sign prohibits entry to any vehicle wider than 2.3 metres.'

It was fourth division Mastermind.

Up flashed the least observed road sign in the country, on display at the entrance to every town and city. Invariably attached to another sign bearing a town's name, it is either rusted, bent or, in the case of Andrano Porto, riddled with bullet holes. The sign prohibits, as Michele explained, the sounding of horns other than in case of emergency, excluding weddings, of course, and victories by either Ferrari or the *Azzurri*—the national football team. It's an idiotic instruction because Italians can't drive for more than a hundred metres without honking their horns, as if getting from A to B first means letting B know you're coming.

Despite the sign appearing at all five entrances to Andrano, few motorists can resist a musical greeting when they pass a friend around town, and late-night winners of Vespa drag races cannot deny themselves a victory salute on high-pitched horns. Meanwhile the signs declaring such frivolity illegal rust silently on the edge of town. Even Michele, a lover of worthless explanations, didn't bother to waste time on this one. Deprive the Italians of oxygen before denying them their right to make noise.

After studying signs we moved on to signals painted on the road. Michele informed us that such signals were always white, information which you would think excluded the remaining colours of the spectrum. But our instructor wanted to be sure.

Q: 'Painted arrows on the road are red.'

A: '*Falso.*'

Q: 'Painted arrows on the road are blue.'

A: '*Falso.*'

I'm not going to strangle him, I'm going to run him over. Apparently you can if he's crossing from the left.

The only logic I could find in Michele's approach was that

if a student knew what a road sign *didn't* mean, they would perhaps better remember what it *did*. But telling someone they can only cross a drawbridge when it's closed denies them common sense. Michele's course did little other than anger me and confuse my classmates. Their answers to the quiz at the end of week one showed they were perplexed rather than prepared. One girl thought a distance to destination sign reading 'Venezia 4' meant move into the fourth lane for the exit to Venice. But it was the teacher's mistake rather than the student's. She could never have conjured such a fanciful answer if Michele hadn't helped her contrive it. The young woman would sit the licence test in three weeks, and it was beginning to look as if she'd be walking those last 4 kilometres to Venice rather than driving them.

After class on Friday, I approached Michele and explained that after twelve years behind the wheel, I was confident I knew the colour of the arrows on the road and could he please book my exams as promised. He assured me he would do so but first wanted to examine me himself to make sure I would have no problems come test day. I agreed to what seemed a good idea and fixed an appointment for the following Monday. We also scheduled a test drive for Tuesday to ensure I was ready for the driving exam.

I arrived five minutes early for my Monday appointment, hoping the second week would be more productive than the first. Half an hour later Michele was still occupied in the class-room with a group of students. When finished, they invited him to the bar for an *aperitivo*. Michele accepted before spotting me in the waiting room and remembering our meeting. Realising himself double-booked, but not wishing to break either engage-ment, he attempted to combine the two by inviting me to the bar. When I declined, saying I had a student due for an English lesson later, he told me to wait and he'd only have one drink. I laughed and suggested it would be unprofessional for me to be late for a student. But Michele couldn't spot irony. Not even if you held up a road sign saying 'Irony Ahead'.

Realising the evening was lost, I suggested doing the theory check after my mock driving test the following evening, if he hadn't forgotten that appointment as well. He hadn't, but needed to cancel due to an engagement in Lecce.

'Shall we say next Monday at seven-thirty?' he proposed.

'That's a week away!'

'*Allora?*'

The following Monday, bang on time, I walked into the classroom to surprise Michele beginning a lesson with a group of student truck drivers. Each of them was overweight, as though that were a prerequisite for the licence.

'You forgot again, didn't you?'

'No no. Come in. Sit down. Let's do it.'

Though loath to admit it, he had indeed forgotten our appointment. Nevertheless, instead of rescheduling once again, he quizzed me for half an hour in front of his students, none of whom objected to making a detour. Munching on plum cakes which someone had brought to class, they seemed highly entertained by an Australian negotiating his way around Italy's street signs, applauding correct answers and shouting '*Bravo, bravo!*'

During a pause in proceedings I asked Michele what the alcohol limit was in Italy. I had wanted to know for a while but neither Daniela nor the driving manual could help me.

'*Zero virgola tre*' (0.3), he said quickly, a speedy reply suggesting an accurate one.

My spectators stopped munching their plum cakes.

'*Non è vero,*' objected one, bearded, burly and begging to differ. 'It's *zero virgola quattro.*'

'It's two beers in an hour,' said another, spraying a mouthful of crumbs on a classmate.

'No, it's three,' said a third, who had taken off his shoes and was rubbing his feet.

'*Zero virgola tre!*' shouted Michele, thumbing through the manual in search of proof to his claim but finding only what I had, the vaguest of explanations stating that anything over half a litre of 'light wine' a day would remain in the bloodstream. I later discovered that both Michele and his students were wrong. Originally 0.8, the legal limit had been reduced to 0.5 in 2002. But such trivialities matter little to Italians, who thankfully don't drink all that much. One wonders what their road toll might be if they did.

After half an hour, and two packets of plum cakes, Michele suggested I return the following Monday to continue the quiz. When I asked about the driving check he said we'd do that the following week as well. Frustrated, I agreed to return on the condition he book my exams; booking the damn thing would turn out to be more of a challenge than passing it.

Michele wasn't around when I arrived the following Monday. 'Delayed in Lecce,' according to his secretary. 'Come back tomorrow.' The following evening I showed up at the same time and passed Michele in the waiting room buttoning his coat and heading towards the school mini-bus. 'I'll be right with you,' he said. 'Just have to drop a few students home first.'

The secretary, who either felt sorry for me or was tired of my company in the waiting room, said her boss would be at least an hour by the time he had dropped each student home. Tired of forgotten appointments and broken promises, I ignored the stop sign on the door and stormed out of Caritano's *autoscuola* for the last time. It had taken a month to go nowhere, and to discover that the only thing disciplined about Michele was his beard.

Giovanni most welcome

When Daniela had done her driving course twelve years earlier, she spent more time at the beach than in the classroom. Her unorthodox instructor, Giovanni Benvenuto, who worked at an *autoscuola* in Castellano, preferred to hold summer school at the seaside. Daniela recalls how Giovanni would collect her from home, together with a carload of other students, take them to La Botte, then supervise a few hill starts in the car park before instructing them to dive rather than drive. His wife Rosanna made pasta with the mussels and clams they prised off rocks, a seafood marinara her husband shared with students while explaining the rules of the road.

As soon as she heard I had to get my Italian licence, Daniela suggested I contact Giovanni. Foolishly, I hadn't listened. I believed that the process would be straightforward and simple, plus I wanted to prove it possible to get something done in the south of Italy without knowing someone. On the road to Castellano two months after that naïve decision, Daniela sat quietly in the passenger seat, too sweet to say 'I told you so'.

The *autoscuola* where Giovanni worked was situated in a cramped laneway, so cramped that leaving the car outside meant ignoring every rule of parking learnt inside. The walls of the school were peeling, red roller shutters had faded to orange and the sign above the door was smashed, its neon tubes exposed and blinking intermittently. From a crisp February evening we opened the door onto smoke and raised voices. Round two had begun in a similar fashion to round one.

A long-legged young secretary welcomed us before returning to a pile of forms on her desk. On the wall behind her, other than the obligatory crucifix, was a gallery of framed certificates declaring the school to be licensed. Decades old, each jaundiced certificate was decorated with a mosaic of colourful tax stamps which kept them current. Everything else in the room seemed to have expired, including an old woman on the couch and the cigarettes of two youths talking on mobiles. The floor was uneven and the tile cracked, but the secretary's scarlet lipstick redeemed shabby surroundings.

Daniela introduced herself and said she had come to see Giovanni. The secretary replied that she would have to wait. When Daniela asked how long, a booming voice from the other room gave the answer: 'Is that Daniela from Andrano I can hear?' Not long. Through a low doorway darted a short, stout, middle-aged man, racing towards Daniela with arms outstretched, a fitting reception from someone whose surname literally means 'welcome'. 'Giovanni!' exclaimed Daniela, kissing his sunburnt cheeks; he too had fields he worked on weekends. Their paths hadn't crossed for years and they spent several minutes catching up on news. Daniela then introduced me—*il ragazzo australiano*—and Giovanni shook my hand with such force that I had to widen my stance to stay put.

Clownlike and exuberant, Giovanni had a shaggy crop of hair on both sides of his head but nothing on top except sunspots. He wore corduroy pants and a flannelette shirt with a button on his belly gone missing—burst by the look of things. He spoke as jerkily as he moved. Dialect mainly. I could hardly understand him, yet couldn't help liking him. He was more down to earth than Michele, and although he resembled a scarecrow more than a driving instructor, I knew he was the man for the job.

Giovanni hurried me into the adjoining room, where the same medical officer with whom I had done my eye test at Michele's sat behind a wooden table. He visited all the driving schools near Lecce, which is why you had to wait so long for an appointment.

Vaguely remembering me, he narrowed his eyes and said: *'Canadese, vero?'*

'Australiano,' I corrected.

'What happened in Caritano?'

'Things didn't work out,' replied Daniela.

The white coat smiled, said he was sure I hadn't gone blind in two months and that I could skip the eye test. Then he copied my name—incorrectly once again—from my identity card onto his form.

When the medic had finished with me it was the turn of the old lady in the waiting room. Still independent at eighty, even if Giovanni had had to pull her out of the couch, she rested her weight on a walking stick, squinted behind oval spectacles, and in a breathless voice recited the letters on the placard—*'pee, zeta, esse, acca, kappa.'* She passed with ease, although Giovanni said she had been doing the annual check at the school for so long that she had no doubt memorised the chart. The ancient woman then hobbled back to the waiting room and handed the secretary her licence: a faded, ragged, fragile piece of paper issued by the Ministry of Transport and Civil Aviation forty years earlier.

Inside the front cover of the concertina document was a black-and-white photo of the woman in her youth, which now resembled the secretary more than the licence holder. On the back cover was a patchwork of tax stamps. Until a few years ago, Italians had to pay 70,000 lira annually for the privilege of having a driver's licence. Like most taxes levied on such documents, proof of payment required a *bollo* to the value of the tax—available from any tobacconist—to be attached to the licence. With four drivers, Daniela's family had to pay 280,000 lira a year in licence tax alone and so decided to buy just one stamp and leave it with the car keys. Whoever took the car took the tax stamp as well, attaching it temporarily to their licence. When they returned they hung the keys on the nail and put the stamp on the table, ready for the next person who needed both.

Daniela's wasn't the only family to lick its way around the

law. Stories abounded, invariably originating in Naples, of the best way to stick the stamp in a licence to make it appear a permanent feature. *Carabinieri* booked motorists for inadequately adhered tax stamps and it became the typical Italian stalemate between citizen and government. The tax was eventually abolished and drivers were spared the unsavoury routine of licking stamps before starting engines.

Her licence renewed, her legs far from it, the woman staggered out the door which Giovanni held open. '*Buonasera*,' she muttered to no one in particular, a southern Italian custom when leaving shop or office. '*Buonasera*,' echoed the room half-heartedly. While the secretary completed my second *foglio rosa*, Giovanni ushered us into his office where he explained that foreigners wishing to get their Italian licence needed a letter from their embassies requesting permission to do the test orally. I protested when he told me I had to get the form in person, meaning a trip to either Rome or Milan. But Daniela insisted Giovanni knew best and I wasn't going to ignore her advice a second time.

To give an idea of what the embassy should write, Giovanni offered to photocopy a similar letter which an Albanian student had successfully used. When he called out for the secretary to get him the photocopy, she responded angrily: 'One thing at a time, Giovanni! Do you want me to finish the *foglio rosa* by tonight?' Giovanni sank his head into his neck like a schoolboy who'd thrown a stone where he shouldn't. 'She's Swiss,' he whispered. 'Very precise. The school used to be open from when it opened until when it closed. Now it's open from five-thirty until eight-thirty.'

After an *aperitivo* at a bar nearby, Giovanni excused himself, saying he was late for an appointment in Lecce. After he left, we returned to the school where the secretary gave me my second *foglio rosa* and a bill for €250 which covered both of the coming exams but which shocked me nonetheless.

'I thought Giovanni was a friend of yours,' I said to Daniela on the drive home.

'Leave it to me,' she replied calmly. 'We won't pay that much.'

The following Monday I flew to the Australian Consulate in Milan rather than the embassy in Rome, profiting from the inconvenience to catch up with old friends and colleagues, and to take some horsemeat, Francesco's favourite, which Valeria had prepared for him. Just once I'd like to travel in Italy without having to ferry food to someone. 'What's in your suitcase, sir?' 'Half a horse, if you must know.'

By Wednesday I was back in Andrano, and on Friday we returned to Castellano to give Giovanni the letter and do a quick oral test to make sure I would pass the exam. I did the test with the secretary, who spent less time examining than seeking solidarity in the fact I was foreign. Married to a man from a nearby village, she disliked the south of Italy and claimed— as Danny had about the north—that it was 'the Third World'. She loathed the Italians for their *menefreghismo* or 'fuckyouist' approach to life, the rubbish for its ubiquity, the government for its corruption, the *carabinieri* for their stupidity, her boss for his disorganisation, the hospitals, the schools, the banks . . .

I wouldn't have objected to her diatribe had it not been voiced in front of a group of local lads waiting for Giovanni. Sucking on cigarettes, they stared at the secretary as she reinforced their stereotype of the stuck-up Swiss. I felt uncomfortable because she expected me to agree with her, which I did on many counts, though with less venom. When she said she intended to return to Switzerland the following year, Giovanni overheard and asked why she didn't go to Albania instead, which he suggested to be more advanced than Switzerland; he had turned baiting her into a sport. His jibe had the desired effect, incensing the secretary, who told Giovanni it was precisely people like him who made Italy so mediocre. Giovanni laughed, the secretary fumed, and I did my best to side with both when all I really wanted was my fucking driver's licence.

Having passed the mock test, I would undertake the real thing at the motor registry in Lecce. Giovanni said he would book me in for the next oral examination day two weeks hence, some two and a half months after I had first set foot in Caritano's *autoscuola*. Before leaving, and deliberately in front of Giovanni, Daniela told the secretary she had misplaced the bill and asked what the total cost was again.

'Two-fifty,' replied the secretary.

'One-twenty-five,' interjected Giovanni. 'Taxes only. Nothing for me.'

'*Molto gentile*,' said Daniela, paying him in cash immediately.

The secretary was livid, having found another reason to go home. Daniela was masterful, giving me another reason to stay.

Daniela took the morning of my theory exam off work and we collected Giovanni from Castellano before heading to Lecce. I drove, Daniela sat in the back and Giovanni rode up front, my driving instructor's seat-belt hanging limp by the door. Bang on nine we arrived at the motor registry, a large building in a compound outside the city centre. After hunting out a spot in the car park, which was like inserting a piece in a jigsaw, we found three spare seats in a waiting room crowded with foreign faces: African, Albanian, Chinese and one Australian. It was oral exam day, reserved for *stranieri* with a permission slip from their embassies.

Every fifteen minutes or so a door opened at the top of the room and a voice called two surnames, or attempts at two surnames as they were foreign tongue-teasers. A regular at the registry, Giovanni disappeared for several minutes and returned with good news: the examiner on duty was a man he knew well, a certain Signor Pozzo from the same village as Giovanni.

'Ah,' exclaimed Daniela, 'not Paolo Pozzo? He's a family friend, I think. I'm sure his wife went to school with my mother.'

'*Perfetto*,' said Giovanni, smiling.

It seemed I had passed already.

Two hours later, the door opened and a voice called 'Arrison', as well as the surname of a young Frenchman who followed me into the examination room. On a raised platform at the end of the room, which appeared to be a lecture hall, sat a man in a beige suit behind a desk stacked with manila folders. '*Prego*,' said the examiner, taking the top two and offering the Frenchman and me seats in front of his desk. Giovanni helped himself to a seat in the first row of chairs; it was a public exam and he was free to spectate.

While Signor Pozzo flicked through my file, Giovanni summarised my situation—and made the issue of my licence appear a formality—by saying I was Australian, I had been driving for twelve years, and after a year in Italy needed an Italian licence.

'*Australiano?*' repeated the examiner. 'What the cabbage are you doing here?'

Before I could reply, Giovanni did so for me, not for the last time that morning.

'Crris is the boyfriend of a young woman from Andrano who knows you and is waiting outside to say hello. Shall I call her in?'

'*Certo.*'

'Daniela!'

It was the only Italian name called through the door that day.

'*Buongiorno*,' said Daniela, striding elegantly into the room.

'*Buongiorno*,' replied Pozzo, descending his throne and shaking her hand.

'It's an enormous pleasure to see you, Signor Pozzo. How are you?'

'Very well. And you? Your family?'

'Extremely well. And your wife?'

I couldn't help but smile while watching Daniela and Giovanni smother the examiner in flattery and friendship. It wasn't that they thought I couldn't pass on merit, it was simply the way things are done in a country so inefficient that having someone on side can make all the difference. The trick was to make the man feel special. Daniela's sweet but subservient smile was as good a guarantee of passing as learning the driving manual by heart.

Having buttered the examiner, Daniela left the room and my test got under way, beginning with 'who goes first' diagrams. Pozzo held up a placard of crossroads, put his finger to a picture and waited for me to direct traffic.

'*A, E, V, H, C,*' I recited.
'*Bene,*' replied the examiner.

'*Tram, B, A, C.*'
'*Esattamente.* Always let the tram go first unless it's got a red light.'
'*Bicicletta, S, P, N.*'
'*Si.*'
'*Ambulanza, T, R, D.*'
'*Si.*'
'*G, D, Autobus, B.*'
'*Bene.*'
The Frenchman then performed point duty before the questions grew obscure.
'What type of licence must you have to drive a truck weighing over 3.5 tonnes?'
'One that we don't need,' rebounded the Frenchman.

Pozzo smoothed his moustache and gazed out the window, pondering our punishment perhaps. Impertinence had ruined the easy mood which Daniela and Giovanni had painstakingly aroused. The Frenchman failed to realise that whether we knew the answer or not, we were better off congratulating the examiner on his choice of question rather than antagonising him for its irrelevance. He was either new to Italy or didn't have as good a mentor as I did.

While Pozzo and the Frenchman discussed the question, Giovanni made a hissing noise to gain my attention. I thought I was imagining it at first, and did my best to ignore it once I realised I wasn't. Only when a colleague came in to consult the examiner did I risk turning from my chair to find Giovanni leaning forward in his, head bowed and face strained, whispering the answer through clenched teeth in a substandard display of ventriloquy. '*E*,' he squeaked. '*Patente E.*'

Having drawn a blank from the Frenchman, when his colleague left the room Pozzo turned his attention to me. 'Well,' he said with diminishing patience, 'what type of licence do I need to drive a truck weighing over 3.5 tonnes?' It was an absurd situation. I was sure the examiner had seen Giovanni whispering the answer, yet at the same time I realised my instructor was a wily old veteran who knew what he could get away with. I wasn't sure what to do. Perhaps it was a trap to see whether I would cheat or not.

'*Allora?*' pressed the examiner.

'*E*,' I said meekly.

'*Mi scusi?* I didn't catch that.'

I cleared my throat and found my voice.

'*E. Patente E.*'

'*Bravo*,' praised the examiner.

The Frenchman and I shared a glance of disbelief.

Pozzo's next question made me wish I had confessed ignorance rather than borrow Giovanni's knowledge.

'And for how long does an E licence last?'

My eyes widened. The Frenchman had shut his.

'Five years,' squeaked Giovanni.

Pozzo studied my file as though turning a blind eye.

'Five years,' I said confidently.

'*Bravo,*' he praised again.

The questions became even more left field. Perhaps Pozzo realised he was actually testing my instructor and wanted to see what he was made of.

'For how long can you leave your car in the SOS bay on an *autostrada*?'

Even Giovanni was silent. The examiner had stumped student and teacher.

'Until they come and tow it away,' said the Frenchman, stubborn but realistic.

Pozzo cocked his head towards me.

'It depends on the nature of the problem,' I said, shoulders shrugged.

'Three hours,' announced the examiner, proudly answering his own question.

'And what if it takes more than three hours for help to arrive?' asked the Frenchman, perhaps speaking from experience.

The examiner slapped his hand on the desk like an auctioneer closing bids.

'Three hours is the maximum time you can leave your car in the emergency bay,' he barked. That was the rule. He wasn't interested in reality.

'Does it say so in the driving manual?' challenged the Frenchman, convinced it didn't. He had given up on passing and taken to proving a point.

The examiner cast a stern glance over Armani half-glasses. The question was ignored. The effrontery was not.

To a moan from the Frenchman, Pozzo posed his next question: 'How fast can a petrol tanker drive in a town centre?' I had no idea why he continued to ask questions pertaining to a licence for which we were not applying. I looked around at Giovanni while the Frenchman fired shots in the dark—'fifty, sixty, seventy?'—but even my instructor's shoulders were shrugged. 'Thirty!' declared the examiner, silencing the Frenchman who had arrived at a hundred.

It was fast becoming a lesson rather than a test and continued in that vein for another five minutes. Then, more frustratingly, Pozzo began asking questions of a medical nature. We were asked how we would treat a blood haemorrhage at an accident scene; were Pozzo involved I would let him bleed to death. What were the different types of haemorrhage? How can you tell them apart? How should each one be treated? And so on. Although my own blood had started to boil, I attempted a response, stating—in all honesty—that I would probably just call an ambulance rather than make matters worse. Unsatisfied, the examiner began asking questions of our instructor rather than us.

'Surely they studied these things at the driving course, *istruttore*?'

'Of course they did,' fibbed Giovanni. 'They know what to do, they just have trouble describing it in a foreign language.'

Apart from the fact I hadn't done his driving course, which, I believe, is what the examiner was trying to prove, I had failed to answer because I had no idea how to stop a haemorrhage in English let alone Italian. I even had to look the word up on the spell check before getting it right here, and chances are that if I can't spell a haemorrhage, I won't be able to stop one.

Our hypothetical victim bleeding to death, the examiner declared the exam finished and we were free to leave the room. Having maintained my composure for the entire farce, I lost it now as I stormed outside where I told Daniela that I had surely failed because the examiner seemed to think I wanted to steer a petrol tanker around the streets of Andrano rather than a car. She was shocked, approaching Giovanni when he appeared a few minutes later, my file under his arm and a smile across his face.

'Did he pass, Giovanni?'

'Daniela? What a question. Of course he passed.'

'*Non è possibile,*' I said.

'*E' possibile,*' insisted my instructor.

'What about the Frenchman?'

'He passed as well. *Andiamo al bar.*'

It wasn't until Giovanni showed me my file marked *promosso* that I believed him, by which time we were well on the way to a bar in Castellano to share the caffeine conclusion to a morning in a public office. But the experience had left me furious and perplexed, more so than any other since moving to Italy. I had wanted to pass on merit, not because the wife of Signor Pozzo had gone to school with Daniela's mother. It was almost as if the examiner had asked obscure questions so that my licence would be awarded because of his generosity rather than my ability, making him special in Daniela's eyes.

While grateful to Giovanni, I felt the need to challenge his role in the morning's charade and, like Pozzo, fired off questions their receiver found irrelevant.

'Would I have passed that test if you weren't friendly with the examiner? You even gave me the answers to some of the questions. What would have happened if he had seen you? In fact, I'm sure he did see you.'

'He's a friend,' defended Giovanni. 'And it's a public exam.'

'Surely that means you spectate, not participate.'

'You passed, didn't you?' he shouted, surprising Daniela whose eyes widened in my rear-view mirror. 'What do you want?'

What *did* I want? There was no point blaming the maze on the man who helped me through it. Fifty-five people had died on Italian roads the weekend prior to my exam—a disaster and a disgrace. But was that Giovanni's fault? I dropped the subject and drove. I had what I needed and that was all that mattered. 'Fuckyouism' starts there sometimes, in hopelessness rather than selfishness. My passengers had already forgotten the exam. Giovanni chatted about his holiday home in Calabria and the conversation turned to more important things, like enjoying rather than educating Italy.

'If anyone at the motor registry asks why we requested an urgent exam, say you need your licence for work,' advised Rocco, Giovanni's colleague and my driving instructor. Sitting in his dual-controlled Fiat on the first of two trial drives to prepare for my test, I had reached the final stage of the three-month saga. Giovanni's job—the theory—was complete. Now I was in Rocco's realm—the practical.

A plump man in his early forties, not fat but roly-poly, Rocco had the chocolate skin I lay on the beach all summer to achieve but which came naturally to this southern Italian. He spoke as fast as Giovanni and drove even faster, but now it was my turn to take the wheel. Before starting the engine I asked Rocco if he intended to put on his seat-belt. Having never heard such a request, he cast me a mystified glance.

'*Scusa*,' I explained. 'I'm only asking because if you don't ask in Australia they can fail you for not ensuring the safety of your passengers.'

'As the instructor,' he replied, 'I am required by law not to wear a seat-belt in case I have to lean across and grab the steering wheel.'

'Oh. Does it happen often?'

'Often enough.'

Following orders—left here, right there—I drove around the dusty lanes of Spongano, the town near Andrano where Rocco lived. It was lunchtime, mid-spring, the sun hot and high, and like every whitewashed village in the Salento, Spongano was a ghost town under the sleepy spell of siesta. But for a child kicking a football and a few mangy street cats, the place was deserted; we couldn't even find a car behind which to practise a reverse park.

'You're driving way too fast,' declared Rocco.

'I haven't gone over sixty.'

'It's too fast for the exam. You have to crawl.'

I put the engine near a stall in third and Rocco relaxed in his bucket seat.

'I know you've been driving for a long time but you can't drive normally in the exam. It's too fast. You have to try and go back to basics.'

Easier said than done when you've been driving for twelve years. When you're in the habit of breezing into reverse parks with the open palm of one hand, it's suddenly very difficult when told to use two. My arms became tangled and I scraped the gutter for the first time in years, a problem in Spongano given the gutter is the wall of a house. I needed to eliminate bad habits which come with experience, like selective use of indicators, faith in wing-mirrors or steering with one hand while resting the other on the window. It was almost as difficult as learning to drive in the first place and, as Rocco said, I risked being failed for being too good a driver.

A few days later we did a second test drive in which I didn't threaten fourth gear, indicated to dodge a dozing stray dog, and stopped for an orange light rather than speeding up—I was ready to take the test. The next morning Rocco picked me up early and launched me to Lecce, the man who had preached sluggishness racing like a bullet taking leave of a gun. When he overtook an Audi while playing chicken with an oncoming truck, I was tempted to stand on the dual brake pedal at my feet.

When we arrived at the motor registry I followed Rocco around the building on his search of unmanned offices. I was used to feeling invisible in an Italian public office, but this time it was the staff who had gone missing. When we finally found assistance we were told that today's examiner—thankfully not Signor Pozzo, who would probably have had me mow down a pedestrian to see how I dealt with a haemorrhage—was out conducting a driving exam. Returning to the car park, we waited with seven other instructors and their nervous charges. An intense April sun prompted something of a striptease, jackets giving way to jumpers, then jumpers to short-sleeve shirts. '*Vestirsi a cipólla,*' Daniela calls it—'to dress like an onion'.

Driven by a careful student, a Fiat Punto limped into the car park. There was no sign on the car's roof to warn of the apprentice at the wheel, instead its doors were decorated with magnetic *autoscuola* plates, one of which was upside down. When the car stopped to let out the examiner, seven driving instructors descended upon it like paparazzi, surrounding a young woman— the *esaminatrice*—who emerged from the back seat like a film star on opening night. 'I have no preferences,' she shouted at the barking pack. 'Work the order out among yourselves.'

The woman made her way to the car of one instructor who had seized her by the arm and given her little choice. This display of democracy prompted the others, Rocco included, to race for their cars while calling students to follow. By the time I closed my door Rocco had performed a hasty three-point turn, muscling his way into second position in a queue of seven cars snaking its way out of the registry; it reminded me of the days when competitors scrambled to their motorbikes at the start of a grand prix. An irate voice from behind yelled: 'What the fuck's going on? I was here first and now I'm fourth. What sort of system is this?' I couldn't have put it better myself.

Passers-by must have thought our procession of *autoscuola* cars a funeral for someone at the motor registry. Rocco tailgated the leading car to avoid being overtaken and losing a precious second place, a tactic which almost backfired when the driver under examination rode a speed-hump in too high a gear, stalling the car which rolled back towards ours. The instructor sitting alongside obviously hadn't had time to press the dual-control clutch, something Daniela claimed Giovanni had been known to do during driving tests; his assistance wasn't confined to the theory exam.

'*Cazzo!*' exclaimed Rocco, standing on the brakes. Bonnets bowed behind us as the procession did likewise, doing little to calm the nerves of the student driving the leading car, who realised he had almost caused a seven-car collision before leaving the registry. When I asked Rocco if the examiner would fail the boy for his stall, he replied that she would have been too busy flirting with the instructor to have noticed. 'She's on heat, this woman,' he said with a sleazy smile. 'Just drive slowly, don't have an accident and I'll do the rest.' But the driver was hardly given time to make another mistake, for a couple of minutes later, after only just reaching Lecce, he stopped on the shoulder of the road where his exam met a swift and successful conclusion.

While the examiner completed the boy's documents, taking longer than the test itself, Rocco and I switched places in preparation for my test, which I hoped would be as brief as the one I had just watched. Our motorcade blocked the lane of a busy street, and motorists trapped behind hurled abuse and honked horns. Amplified by apartment blocks lining the road on both sides, the commotion brought shopkeepers onto footpaths and housewives onto balconies. The theatre of daily life continued, only now the spotlight was on me.

Rocco waited by the first car for the examiner to finish her paperwork. When she had done so, he opened the door and escorted her towards his Fiat, disguising concern that another instructor might beat him to her as an act of chivalry. Distracted by the horns, the woman looked along the street and noticed the queue of *autoscuola* cars holding up traffic.

'Don't tell me you all followed me?' she exclaimed.

'Don't worry yourself with what they're up to,' replied Rocco, dismissing queue and question; he spotted an early finish and didn't want to be sent back to the motor registry. He changed the subject by telling the woman she looked gorgeous, while unceremoniously pushing her into the back seat of his two-door Fiat, a manhandling which met only playful protest.

It soon became apparent that Rocco's description of the woman as 'on heat' had been accurate. It was the examiner who wanted to be examined.

'Why can't you buy a four-door car, Rocco?' she complained,

arranging curly hair. 'I can't squeeze into hatchbacks anymore. I've put on weight. Look.'

She ran her hands along thighs suffocating in tight jeans.

'*Sei perfetta signora*,' assured Rocco, closing the door. '*Assolutamente perfetta.*'

In truth the inelegant thirty-something was nothing if not plain, but as far as Rocco was concerned, while in his Fiat she was Sophia Loren. When she asked who I was in a less than polite tone, I thought she was objecting to my presence now that she had taken off her coat and built a nest in the back seat. But then I realised she was holding a list of names and genuinely wanted to know.

'Chris Harrison,' I replied, foolishly putting the H in front.

She scanned her list.

'*Mi scusi?*'

'Crris Arrison,' I said, deforming my own name.

After a brief search she found my folder, stared at my photograph, then leant forward between the seats to do the same at me.

'Would you take your sunglasses off, Crris,' she asked, adding 'did I get your name right?'

'*Perfetto signora.*'

She sat back in her seat, satisfied I was me.

'Let's do a three-point turn,' she instructed, 'to head back the way we came.'

I performed a slow and studied about-face, complete with indicators for the first time in years. The five remaining driving school cars frantically followed suit, a formation manoeuvre which, to spectators on their balconies, must have looked beautifully choreographed. Without realising it, the examiner had reversed the pecking order, and the car that had been next was now last and vice versa. This resulted in another furious burst of horns, which I did my best to ignore as I crawled off down the street.

My test lasted all of two minutes, and for most of that time

I was stopped at a traffic light. After a left turn and a reverse park—Lecce is so flat you can't do a hill-start—at the examiner's request I pulled over and parked, remembering to indicate first, of course. While scribbling on my forms, the woman explained that it was the theory exam that mattered in her opinion and if I'd passed that then I deserved my licence—a bizarre comment from a driving examiner. Rummaging through her handbag, she pulled out a wad of plastic cards bound together by a rubber band, before handing me my photo licence which I signed on the dashboard. The date on the licence was the date of the test. Not sure what would have happened had I failed.

She wished me 'happy highways' before accepting Rocco's hand and climbing from his Fiat. He and I swapped places and with brusque acceleration, the sort that decorates a road with rubber, left her standing on the street where she was fought over by a scrum of instructors.

I had expected the ordeal to end with an interim licence and a further three-month wait by the mailbox until the real thing turned up. But Italy is full of surprises. Racing to a bar Rocco knew, I slipped the card into my top pocket, took a deep breath, and months of frustration were forgotten in an instant. I was proud of myself—an Italian driver's licence without bribing anyone.

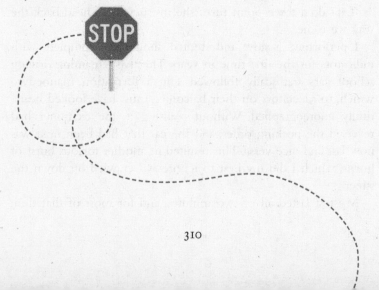

A well-connected leg

Daniela remembers her father by imitating him. When she sees a performer of dubious talent on television she whispers '*raccomandato*' under her breath, implying the performer would still be in a low place had they not been friendly with someone in a high place. 'Recommended people drove my father mad,' Daniela once said, before spotting the sad implication.

'It's not what you know it's who you know' is valid the world over. Italians are not unique for exploiting friendship to get a foot in the door. What sets them apart is the fact that without networking it is difficult to perform even mundane tasks like organising a driving exam. It took a 'recommendation' from Giovanni to finally get my driver's licence, and when my *permesso di soggiorno* came up for renewal after two years in Italy, with one call to Riccardo the police chief it was ready in a couple of days, while queuing Africans, connected to no one except far-flung families to whom they posted a pittance, were waiting up to six months for their documents.

The only friend more valuable than a *poliziotto* is a *medico*, someone to help jump queues in overcrowded public hospitals. As usual, I discovered this the hard way when I needed medical attention after hurting my hip playing tennis; I was beating Renato for the first time when a string snapped in my body rather than my racquet. Thanks to my residency I was entitled to free public health care. I even had my own *libretto sanitario*—a savings account style booklet to keep a record of my ills. I was carrying this *libretto* the stifling spring morning Daniela drove me to Soldignano, where I limped into the waiting room of Dr Nino, the man who had drowned me in home-made *limoncello* at my medical examination two years earlier.

Thirsty pot plants, a cross-arched roof, peeling paint and body odour. How many times had I waited in expiring rooms like this one, public offices in provincial outposts, minding my own business and being stared at like an extraterrestrial. In small-town southern Italy, where everyone knows everyone, a foreign face is almost enough of a shock for the locals to require medical attention. In this case it was close at hand, or might have been if Dr Nino gave his patients appointment times. Instead it was first-in-first-examined, giving us plenty of time to peruse the catalogue of self-praise with which he adorned his walls, testimony, I hoped, to years of conscientious study rather than a friend in the right place.

An hour or so later a voice from the next room called '*Avanti!*' and it was our turn. Passing from the waiting room to the equally stuffy consultation room, the smell of body odour was replaced by the stench of cigarette smoke. Perched behind a laptop computer, a modern trinket in an antique room, was a bearded Dr Nino, cigarette between his fingers and smile across his face. '*Canguro!*' he exclaimed, sighting my limp. 'Did you get hit by a car?' A man who smokes while telling patients not to needs a keen sense of humour.

Unconcerned that his waiting room was bulging at the seams, Nino chatted awhile before examining my hip and suggesting I'd played the wrong shot. After freeing up his writing hand by stubbing out his cigarette, he wrote me a referral to see an orthopaedic surgeon at Falese Hospital. Having anticipated my needing to see such a specialist, Daniela had made an appointment for the following Monday. Hearing this, Nino warned us to be careful, saying specialists and their staff had called a strike for Monday and that consultation rooms would be operating at half-mast if at all.

Rarely a day passes in Italy without some form of industrial action, syndicates squabbling with government over the renewal of public contracts. During my time in this litigious country I can remember strikes by postal workers, journalists, judges, teachers, doctors, nurses, pilots, air traffic controllers, cabin and ground crew, baggage handlers, bus drivers, train drivers, cooks in public schools, Formula One commentators, toll collectors, service station attendants—Signor Api excluded—audio and video technicians, truck drivers, ferry staff, as well as two general strikes and the cancellation of the national lottery. Indeed the only workers I am yet to see strike are Italy's indefatigable housewives, which would no doubt be the only stop-work that a majority of Italians would notice.

Overutilised to the extreme, strikes have become routine, just another inconvenience to the Italian way of life. In one twenty-five-day period there were no fewer than thirty-seven protests against the government. Calling a strike is as common-place as 'chucking a sickie', the difference being you don't need a medical certificate to justify a strike. And now medical staff were 'crossing their arms', as the Italians term a stop-work. Rather than risk disruptions, we scheduled a visit for later in the week.

An hour's drive from Andrano, Falese's *ospedale* stands in the centre of the small city and is as difficult to find as a doctor once inside. After weaving our way across the city's patchwork asphalt, with similar confusion we navigated a maze of corridors in search of the *ambulatorio*—the specialists' consulting rooms. Two people we asked gave us directions leading back to where we had started, a third led us to a vending machine, while a fourth at least put us in the vicinity for a fifth to finish the job.

Ask an Italian for directions and you'll receive an intricate trail which, when followed, often gets you more lost than you were when you started. It's not ill will but the complexity of the answer, the hypnotism of the hand signals and the eccentric appraisal of pertinent detail. Lost on her way to a meeting, Daniela once asked an elderly woman for directions to a school in

Spongano. 'Continue on this road,' explained the woman, 'then turn left when you see a Fiat 500 parked outside a bar.'

'What if someone's moved it?' asked Daniela, referring to the car, not the bar.

'They better not have,' replied the woman. 'It's mine.'

After paying a €20 'ticket', the price of seeing a specialist, Daniela joined me in the waiting area for the *ambulatorio*. This was a corridor outside a series of rooms with signs above their doors: *orthopedia, pneumologia, dermatologia,* and situated cleverly next to the toilets, *urologia*. Despite rows of chairs lining both walls, patients preferred to wait in scrums outside each door. Knowing where to join such 'queues' is as much of a challenge as keeping your place.

As we crowded the doctor's doorstep like seagulls disputing a potato chip, I noticed that every decoration had a religious tone, from crucifix to advertisements for prayer groups. Falese Hospital is run by a group of nuns whose iron will, according to Daniela, distinguishes it from other hospitals in the area for its cleanliness and smooth operation.

Many Italian hospitals, particularly in the south, are as unhealthy as their patients. In the words of the Health Minister: 'Half Italy's hospitals should be closed. They are old, outdated and no longer capable of responding to the citizens' needs.' Then come the doctors: famously gifted or infamously incompetent. An Australian surgeon who worked in Italy for several years told me that for every talented Italian *medico* there are twenty who shouldn't be practising. He had worked in the north of the country with a surgeon who repaired botched operations, of which one patient had undergone no fewer than fifteen. Tales of *malsanità* or 'medicine gone wrong' abound in Italy; stories of patients going into hospital for minor operations and losing far more than their appendix.

Waiting lists for medical procedures are painfully long, something I found out personally when the 'queue' finally cleared and my turn came around. The surgeon ordered me to undergo an

MRI scan, but when Daniela called to book she was told that the earliest appointment was in six months' time. So with the help of a friend, himself a surgeon at Falese Hospital, a plan was devised which would see me wait just a week. But to justify the urgency of the test I would need to feign severe pain and undergo what Italians call a *ricovero*—to be 'recovered' or admitted to hospital. Unfortunately, the only available bed would be in the urology ward, which, due to the anatomy on display there, I imagined to be the last place I'd find a nun ensuring things ran smoothly. But it was either that or wait six months, so I decided to put my faith in the sisters and my well-connected leg under the microscope.

A week later, my hip still hurting, if not as much as I had been told to let on, I was packing an overnight bag in the bedroom when Daniela called out from the kitchen: 'Don't forget to take cutlery, toilet paper and drinking water.' So began my *ricovero* in a southern Italian hospital, which despite being one of the better hospitals in the Salento, left me thankful I wasn't actually ill.

At 7 am on a warm Wednesday, my stomach empty, my limp dramatic and my arm through Daniela's, I arrived at the admissions counter of the urology ward. Always punctual, we were first in a queue of short men and round women, patients and escorts, husbands and wives, each holding a suitcase containing pyjamas, slippers, and as I would later discover, cutlery, toilet paper and drinking water.

During check-in, as Daniela handed over my *libretto sanitario*, the sister behind the counter appeared to grow suspicious: 'Why exactly is *Il Signore* here?' she asked.

Unprepared for such a question, Daniela improvised: '*Per analisi urgenti.*'

'But there aren't any details of these urgent tests in the register.'

Again Daniela thought on her feet. 'I'm sure the doctor has all the details,' she said.

'Then let's wait for him to arrive before admitting the patient,' snapped the sister, antagonistic more than angelic. 'You can wait in there,' she added, indicating a makeshift chapel across the hall, the perfect place for those with something to confess.

The shrine comprised icons of the Madonna, a silver crucifix, pot plants, a Bible on a wooden lectern, several chairs occupied by patients in pyjamas and a woman in an apron feather-dusting the icons. 'That's the boss,' she whispered as we sat down. 'Everyone assumes these nuns are sweet but they're actually as hard as nails.'

A bell rang loudly. I thought it was the fire alarm until spotting a priest calling patients to prayer. Several old men in slippers shuffled into the shrine, along with the sister who, unlike the patients, recited the prayers without the aid of a photocopy. As usual I was stared at by all, especially the sister, who wondered why I wasn't praying. In actual fact I was, if only for the arrival of my specialist.

By nine o'clock, when the other new admissions had already filled specimen jars and the better beds by the window, I was still slouched in the chapel reading about the Pope's summer holiday. Daniela called her school to say she would be later than first thought. Sleepy and starved, I had been told to fast for blood and urine tests which all new patients had to undergo. I didn't need them, but had no choice other than to cooperate, lest I draw attention to a ruse the shrewd sister had already sniffed.

When the urologist—the man with whom Daniela's friend had masterminded our plan—finally arrived at half-past nine, the sister tore into him with a ferocity that surprised me. 'Dottore Pinola!' she challenged. 'You haven't put any information in the register as to why we need to admit Crristoper Arrison.' The doctor begged the nun's forgiveness, saying I needed an urgent scan and other tests. 'But does he need to be admitted to do these tests?' pressed the nun.

'The sooner the better,' insisted the doctor. 'He's in a lot of pain.'

I was going to wince from the chapel but then thought better of it. The nun stared at the doctor who looked everywhere but at the nun, and just when I thought he was going to crack, Daniela's friend, the surgeon responsible for the scheme, breezed into the room declaring: '*Fate presto!* They are ready downstairs for Crristoper's MRI.' He may have been late but his timing was perfect.

I followed the surgeon to the ground floor where he handed me over to the team in the MRI lab. Fascinated by my nationality and my reasons for living in the Salento, the technician fired an array of personal questions, hoping to get as detailed a picture of my background as his machine would of my hip. Positioning me on the slide, he recounted the tale of his cousin who emigrated to Australia twenty years ago and hadn't returned. 'Australia is the country of my dreams,' he said. 'All that space must be amazing.' When he then slotted me into a claustrophobic tunnel, I realised he had a point.

After forty minutes listening to deafening sonic alarms—some ear plugs wouldn't have gone astray—I was slid from the doughnut and helped to my feet by the technician and a doctor I hadn't yet met. They stood shoulder to shoulder as though blocking my passage. 'This is the Australian,' said the technician to his colleague. Then he moved his finger backwards and forwards between himself and the doctor, inquiring: 'Which of us is the younger do you think?' My stomach making noises similar to the machine I had just exited, I had difficulty hiding the fact I couldn't care less and picked the technician, who burst into applause. 'Ha ha,' he mocked, punching the doctor's arm. 'Dye your hair, old man!' It was the sort of bedside manner that suggested not only the patient had been 'recommended'.

After a routine cardiogram and blood and urine tests, all of which confirmed I was healthier than the doctors, I was shown to the bed where I would spend the next twenty-four hours lying low to avoid the nun who knew I'd had the better of her. Mine was the last in a row of four beds in a room designed for three, a mirror image of the room opposite, separated by a toilet and a common entrance. Other than the beds, the only furniture in the room comprised four lockers, a chair at the foot of each bed, a crucifix on the wall and three bedside tables. The window was shut and the smell atrocious, a mixture of body odour and blood. The men in the room opposite had been operated on that morning, while those in my room, who muttered an automatic *buongiorno* as I entered, would each encounter surgeons before sundown.

Lunch had been delivered while I was doing my tests. Lifting the cover on the tray revealed a bowl of minestrone, a bread roll, three potatoes and some slices of lamb; the saving grace of Italian hospitals is that you eat well. The only thing missing was cutlery.

'I told you to pack some.'

'I thought you were joking.'

After rushing to the nearest supermarket to buy me a plastic knife and fork, some toilet paper and a bottle of mineral water, Daniela dashed off to work promising to return as soon as she could, leaving me in the company of three prostrate men with prostate problems and loyal ladies at their feet.

With no curtains between the beds, I ate lunch watching the man next to me being prepped for theatre. The pensioner, whose name was Rocco, was rolled onto his stomach, his gown opened and a needle thrust into his snow-white behind. Like the rest of the room I pretended not to look at his buttocks of solid muscle. For an old man he was in fine shape, one of the Salento's tireless farmers, his wife informed me during the conversation which ensued while her husband was under the knife.

The lack of privacy added insult to our injuries, but, like the Adriatic Express, the hospital's shortcomings united those who suffered them. When Italians are in discomfort the conversation sparks like kindling. For the foreigner, however, a chat with homespun types can lead to a dead end. These were southern

Italian peasants in the true sense of the word; farming families, sunburnt and simple, who spoke a mixture of dialect and Italian and for whom Italy's frustrating but free public health system was more of a godsend than the nuns who ran the hospital. They were people who had never left Puglia and whose questions were polite but unpolished—like what language did we speak in Australia. It takes practice to field such a question without showing surprise, but practice I got plenty of during my time among these intriguing people, whom it would have been small-minded on my part to assume had nothing to teach me.

'Where is Australia?' asked Uccio from the bed by the window.

'Near America, isn't it?' speculated his wife, looking at me for confirmation.

'No, it's . . .'

But my attempt to explain was interrupted.

'Italy's the best country in the world,' asserted Rocco's wife, who had begun crocheting a doily. The frail woman had never ventured north of Bari, yet could make such a claim in an unofficial language to a well-travelled Australian who spoke better Italian than she did. There's something delightfully patriotic, yet at the same time frustratingly ignorant, about people with no comparison declaring their country to be the best. They were people who had no relationship with the outside world beyond their televisions. Beautifully naïve, like the friend who tried to send me a postcard in Australia only to have it bounce back because it didn't have enough postage to travel further than Marittima. But where else would you want it to travel when your whole world's the Salento?

But if Italy was the world's best country, why were they criticising everything in sight, from lunch and the lack of toilet paper to the smell and a broken chair? *'E' una schifezza!'* they exclaimed repeatedly. 'It's a disgrace!' Why? Because Italians lament what they love. Had I criticised the lack of toilet paper they would probably have become defensive, saying inconvenience made them wonderful improvisers; at least then we would have agreed on something. But what was the point of criticising, in arrogantly asserting the hospital to be the worst I'd ever seen, when for them it was the pride of the district? My reality was beyond their experience and theirs was beyond mine.

We had little in common and my presence was soon forgotten, but I learnt more when they chatted among themselves. They were quick to know each other because they were such similar folk, senior citizens with the south in their blood. They quizzed each other on which dusty corner of the Salento they called home, and when they realised that most could have gone to closer hospitals, they wanted to know why they had journeyed to Falese. Raised eyebrows suggested the question was rhetorical, and Rocco's wife, with more tact this time, said: 'We have faith in the doctors here.'

I wondered whether she questioned that faith when her husband was wheeled back into the room, more like a child in a shopping trolley than a sick man on a stretcher. We watched on in sympathy as his bed was shoved against the wall, his gown parted and his blood-stained privates made public as the nurse checked their progress. Then a sheet was cast over him and he was left to sleep off the invasion that would hopefully improve his twilight years.

The nurse soon returned to collect Antonio, two beds from mine and one from the window, whose turn it was to be operated on; they were queuing for the first time in their lives. He was prepared in the same cavalier manner, a dart cast into his rump, but to wheel his bed from the room the nurse had to push mine against the lockers and Rocco's against mine, blocking me against the wall. This woke Rocco, who expelled a yelp of pain.

'Oh shut up, sleepy,' said the nurse. 'It can't be that bad.'

'It wasn't until you moved him,' said Antonio, assuring himself similar mistreatment.

'We'll leave the beds like this,' the nurse told me. 'Otherwise we'll just have to shift him again when we get back.'

I hoped the operation was a quick one, as my only passage to the toilet was across Rocco's bleeding genitals, which, through no fault of his own, did little to freshen the room.

An Asian woman with a hopeful face, one of many *extracomunitari* in the south of Italy, walked into the room with a tray containing watches, cigarette lighters, trinkets and toys. While street-sellers are commonplace at traffic lights, I was surprised the sisters had allowed one into the hospital. Had she stocked cutlery she may have made a sale. Instead she was dismissed by all. She couldn't have been in Italy long as she had yet to grasp the gesture for 'not interested in the slightest'. Indeed she was so insistent I feared she would wake Rocco, who had just had his prostate pruned, to see if he wanted to buy a key ring. Eventually she was shooed from the old man's bedside by his wife, who had escaped the smell in the room by crocheting in the corridor, returning at regular intervals to adjust her husband's pillows and apologise for his snoring in my ear.

I was trapped against the wall for over an hour before Antonio was wheeled back in and our beds were straightened. Unlike Rocco, who had undergone a more complex procedure, Antonio was wide awake and still abusing the staff. Like soldiers in a military hospital we celebrated his return, with patients in the adjoining room wandering over to see how he was. An indelicate man with three teeth in his mouth—he needed a dentist more than a urologist—instead of telling his visitors how the operation had gone, Antonio pointed to a jar on his bedside table containing a pebble in a pink solution. Pained but relieved, he declared: 'The little bastard's finally out.'

'Not so little,' said Uccio, holding the jar up to the window. 'Where was it?'

'Where do you think?'

'You poor Christian. I pick things off my olive trees smaller than this.'

Dinner was dealt with early to facilitate visiting hours from six-thirty to eight. Signs around the hospital spelt out the rules for calling on the ill. Children under eight could only visit on Sundays and public holidays, while a maximum of three people were permitted to stand by the bed of a patient at any one time. Fortunately, nobody paid a grain of attention to these rules, and at six-thirty a crowd of well-wishers stormed the ward. I say fortunately because the crush of people meant there was little chance of my being missed by sneaking out with Daniela for some real medicine: a pizza and a couple of beers at the nearest bar. After negotiating my way around the nun, all I had to guard against was the hospital tag around my wrist shooting out my sleeve as I raised my Heineken bottle, just in case a doctor was taking a similar break.

At eight-thirty, as visitors left the building, I kissed Daniela goodnight and sidled past the sister on my way back to bed. Night fell, corridors quietened, and Uccio by the window, who in my absence had undergone a colonoscopy, muttered '*mamma mia*' repeatedly. As if having a camera inserted into your colon isn't traumatic enough, for some reason at Falese Hospital the procedure is performed without anaesthetic. So Uccio had been fully conscious while a two-inch *telecamera* was shoved through the length of his large intestine, preceded by an injection of air that distended the colon to accommodate the camera. That air was now exiting his bowel in a noisier manner than it had entered. At times abrupt, at times enduring, Uccio's smelly symphonies were invariably concluded by a sigh of relief from their composer, who had been cleverly placed by the window. My heart went out to the man who described the procedure in one word—*tortura*.

When the priest rang his bell to promote evening prayer, Uccio cursed just about every religious character from Abraham to Zachariah. Saving their strength for the football friendly between Italy and England, few patients made their way to the chapel. I wondered if the priest would have lamented the low turnout had he witnessed the touching show of solidarity with which patients later helped each other to the TV room, pulling drips and pushing wheelchairs so that room-mates could watch the match. A 2-1 Italian victory was the best medicine for those men, whose bedpans were forgotten in the cheer of the final whistle. After the match a united group went separate ways, returning to individual beds, water bottles and toilet rolls. The only common property is the national football team.

Lights out was accompanied by a shift change, with the new nurse performing what she hoped would be a lightning check on patients before leaving them to sleep. '*Porco mondo*,' she swore, discovering empty drips and full bedpans. 'I'm tired of this.'

'You're tired,' provoked Antonio. 'What about us?' And what ever happened to that wash I was promised? I want a shower and a shave now!'

'If you close your mouth you might just get one,' retorted the nurse.

'*Vaffunculo*,' volleyed Antonio, realising he would receive neither.

The nurse ignored the insult, if only because she was too busy tying up loose ends left by lazy colleagues.

Glancing at the chart at the foot of my bed, the nurse inquired: 'Have they given you something for the pain, Signor Arrison?'

'Just my usual medicine,' I lied. 'Plus a few beers in the bar down the road,' I added, when she had left the room.

'Is that where you went during visiting hours?' asked Antonio. I put my finger to my lips.

'*Capito te*,' he marvelled. 'Good for you. Take me with you next time.'

But drinking with Antonio sounded like a way to get myself back into hospital.

Approaching 11 pm the ward was serene and still. Even the nuns had knocked off. The only sounds were of distant snoring and Uccio's colon shrinking to its former size. Having dozed in the afternoon, I wasn't tired enough to sleep. But there was little else to do. I couldn't read because the room was designed for three and there was no lamp above my bed. Rocco turned his on for me but I realised it was too bright for his eyes and pretended to have changed my mind. 'Why don't you try dimming the light with some newspaper?' suggested Antonio, who, before waiting for my response, bellowed: 'Nurse, we need some newspaper!'The snoring promptly stopped in the adjoining room.

To my surprise the nurse arrived with a newspaper, admonished Antonio for shouting, and drew his attention to the call button before returning to her late-night film. Noticing my difficulty attaching the newspaper to the lamp's perspex cover, Antonio ignored the nurse's warning and opened his lungs once again. To his credit, he at least pressed the call button while yelling: 'Nurse, we need some sticky tape!' Again to my surprise the nurse delivered the tape. It seemed his requests could get Antonio anything except a bath.

One by one my room-mates nodded off, making more noise asleep than they had done awake. Uccio fouled the air further by farting all night, while Antonio and Rocco snored in patterns whose predictability grew soporific. Around 1 am, serenaded by an orchestra of orifices, I finally fell asleep.

A single shaft of light snuck through a hole in the *serranda,* illuminating the crucifix on the wall above our heads. *Il Signore,* as the Italians call Him, had kept an all-night vigil over the four of us, two of whom were bleeding internally while a third filled the room with enough gas to fly a hot-air balloon. As he stirred, Uccio apologised for his thunderstorm bowels, saying it was the only way he could get some relief. '*Non c'è problema,*' replied Antonio. 'You fart as much as you like. But for the love of God open that window.'

The most mobile of the four, I volunteered to open the roller shutter, filling my lungs with another sultry Salento morning. The ward awoke with yawns, stretches, the occasional belch and a frugal breakfast of coffee and a croissant. Word had travelled about the size of Antonio's kidney stone, and patients from nearby rooms attended his bedside to examine the emission, making its owner proud of something he had cursed for so long.

To clean his bleeding bladder, the nurses had told Rocco to drink plenty of water, overlooking the fact he had none. He could have drunk tap water but that would probably have kept him in hospital. I gave him what was left of my bottle, hoping Daniela would be along soon so we could sneak off to the bar for more coffee.

'Who wants a thermometer?' asked a nurse who had recently come on duty.

'*Io*,' said Antonio.

'Me too,' said Rocco, raising his hand like a schoolboy.

Surely the nurse should have been the judge of who needed a thermometer, instead she distributed them like a stewardess handing out headphones. It was the same with the blood pressure test—you only got one if you rolled up your own sleeve. The nursing staff appeared indifferent to their jobs, performing an unenthused minimum. They were brusque rather than unkind; casual, hasty and slightly aloof. Given the strictness of the sisters, I had expected otherwise. But cleanliness is next to godliness and the cleaner was far more thorough, noisily scattering beds and chairs as he mopped the floor. 'Can't you do that quietly?' shouted Antonio, whose dental debacle was surely the result of having ordered people about once too often.

Shortly after nine o'clock, three doctors and a nun came by pushing a trolley containing a file for every patient, including the four of us in room 205, new-found friends who would never meet again. Uccio was told he could go home that afternoon, Antonio heard that he would be detained until tomorrow, Rocco discovered that a nurse would be along soon to flush his bladder, and I was told that my MRI had found nothing that time and a break from tennis wouldn't mend and my dismissal was being prepared. I was delighted. Even when you're not really ill, being told you can leave hospital is wonderful news.

I thanked nun and nurse, and bade farewell to a group of men whose company had been the highlight of my *ricovero* in a southern Italian hospital, a 'recommendation' I would make to no one, especially the sick.

The Italian inquisition

When you've no idea where your life is going, it's perhaps the wrong time to ask someone to spend the rest of it with you. But after two years with Daniela, I knew one thing for certain: I could take or leave her country, but I could never leave her. So when Don Francesco read the statistics for births, deaths and marriages at midnight mass later that year, one of the marriages was Daniela's and mine, and one of the deaths was very nearly her mother's.

Despite our obvious differences, as well as having no idea in which hemisphere we would settle, on the whole I considered Daniela's and my marriage prospects promising. We had been living together for almost two years and spent all but a few days of that time in each other's pockets. Marriage would surely change little, other than emptying those pockets to pay for a wedding. My documents to remain in Italy would become automatic, and anything that meant less time in stalled queues and smoke-filled offices had to be a positive step. Tying the knot would also silence town tongues, which had branded us as living in sin since the day I arrived. So even though we had no idea where that future would be, when I asked Daniela to share it with me regardless, she smiled, burst into tears and said *'Si, si, si!'*

I've never understood long engagements. I asked Daniela to marry me because I wanted her to do so as soon as possible. We intended to tie the knot during the coming summer but found it impossible to get a weekend booking at a good reception venue for at least twelve months. Not only on Saturdays were things booked out. Italians get married on any day of the week except Tuesday and Friday, when it is considered bad luck according to the proverb: '*Di venere e di marte, non si sposa e non si parte*'—'Friday and Tuesday, no weddings or departures'.

Italians are reluctant to challenge such proverbs. For a population regarded as relaxed and inexact there are rules and regulations for almost every situation. To guard against an unfaithful partner, for example, a superstitious Italian will hesitate before accepting *two* of something—*two* being the number of horns on a cuckold's head. Those careful to avoid *two* must remember not to choose *four*—the number of pallbearers at a funeral. I once served Daniela four strawberries with her ice-cream, only to see her pick one out and put it in my bowl. 'You're lucky I'm not from Naples,' she said, 'where they actually believe this rubbish.'

Turning a chair on one of its legs will also bring bad luck, as will sitting at the corner of a table; we had a round table in our beach house so this wasn't a problem. Shape is no guarantee of safety, however. If you're the youngest at a table of thirteen people—square or round—you will die before the others. Food poisoning perhaps? Other omens threaten marital happiness. If someone's sweeping and they touch your foot with the broom, you will never marry or if you're already married you will soon be divorced. At least you'll have a clean floor to cry on.

Southerners are more superstitious than northerners apparently. Sicilian folklore tells the story of a man from Palermo who lived alone—you'll understand why when you hear his story—and believed the month of March to bring bad luck; possibly, the author suggests, because Julius Caesar was slain in March. Whatever the reason, the man locked himself out of harm's way in his apartment until midnight on the thirty-first of March, at which time he went out onto his balcony, lowered his trousers and peed on the piazza. 'March, you evil bastard,' he shouted. 'I've pissed on you again!'

Daniela had been suffering a curse of her own since the start of our relationship: juggling the traditions of her family with my indifference to those traditions. The latest flashpoint was that I didn't mind where we tied the knot, and when bookings proved difficult to come by in Italy, I suggested eloping to a tropical island, with Pina Coladas for priests and Black Russians for bridesmaids. Daniela was both excited and appalled by the idea; there was her family to think about. When I then suggested a low-key wedding in Italy with just family, Daniela quickly did the sums and said: 'Great, that's seventy-five people not counting my mother's side.'

The situation demanded a rethink. How could I deny some tubby Sicilian aunt, with few joys in life other than minding other people's business, the spectacle of witnessing her niece tie the knot? Daniela was right: certain traditions were avoidable but others were not. So I backed down. Or compromised rather. No tropical island wedding, but no waiting twelve months for an Italian one either. There was only one thing for it: to get married on a *venerdì*, a fearsome Friday, a quiet day for reception venues to say the least.

We found a booking with ease and planned our wedding for the last Friday in June, leaving only a few months to prepare. It would be the perfect time of year—the beginning of school holidays, with two summer months for an extended honeymoon. And the weather should be ideal—neither too hot nor humid. We were delighted. We had thought of everything and everyone. We had also caused the first of many scandals.

'*Venerdì?*' exclaimed Valeria when we told her the news. 'You can't get married on a *venerdì!*' And it wasn't only Daniela's mother who was shocked. When our wedding date was posted on the town notice board, much of the village had something to say. As though it were their business, they aired their opinions in the piazza and at the supermarket. To many it was simply reconfirmation that I would always be an outsider and that Daniela's and my relationship would be doomed by differences. '*Moglie e buoi dei paesi tuoi*' goes yet another local maxim. 'Choose your wife and your cows from your own village.' I got the blame for the decision, of course. Daniela would never have chosen a Friday were she marrying the boy next door.

My parents on the other hand were delighted by the news and didn't care which day we got married provided we gave them enough time to fly over and attend, as well as discover where I'd been hiding for the past two years. Experienced travellers, they immediately had their noses in phrasebooks and guidebooks, aiming—as always—to get under Italy's skin rather than scratch its surface. They were sixty-five going on forty. I have always admired them.

Though initially upset by the day we had chosen, Daniela's mother was also thrilled, offering to build an apartment on top of her house. When we declined, she said the extension would have its own private entrance. That would give her house four addresses! When we still said no she dropped the subject. What mattered was that we would marry in church. This was Catholic southern Italy, where weddings were strictly religious affairs. Some rules even I couldn't ignore. Or couldn't I?

After asking Daniela to marry me, I had also asked where she would like to marry me. When she stopped crying, she replied that she had always liked the idea of getting married in the famous cathedral in Otranto, a medieval port city to the north of Andrano. Built by the Normans in 1080 and elaborated upon in subsequent centuries, the impressive basilica stands at the centre of the ancient city on a small, sloped piazza adjoining the seminary where Daniela's father had studied. Other than its Renaissance rosette, what Daniela liked most about the church was its massive mosaic floor, one of the largest in the world, which covers the entire cathedral and tells the story, piece by piece, of the religious history of human life.

The history of Otranto is interred in the walls of its cathedral. When Turks invaded from the sea in 1480, firing cannonballs which today line the city's streets, the Christians courageously defended both their city and their faith from Muslim siege. But after a bloody struggle which lasted fifteen days and razed much of historic Otranto, the city was seized and the locals ordered to renounce their religion. Anyone resisting was beheaded. When the city was eventually recaptured by Christian forces, the skulls of the martyrs were placed in seven glass cabinets in the walls of the cathedral. Today the stunning beauty of the 'Tree of Life' mosaic is sombrely balanced by the grisly faces in the Martyrs' Chapel, a macabre memorial which, to my mind, tipped the scale back in favour of a tropical island.

After Daniela called my Ukrainian mother to ask my religion—I would have told her myself had I known—she phoned the rector of Otranto Cathedral to ask if he would marry a non-practising Catholic to a forgetful Ukrainian Orthodox. He was happy to grant Daniela her wish, provided we filled his collection box and attended a marriage preparation course for the Catholic faith. Had I been Catholic we would still have had to attend the course, which is designed to 'prepare for the demands of a shared life', under the instruction of a priest who has never experienced a shared life, but that was irrelevant according to Valeria. As she put it, we needed to be ready for the commitment of marriage in the eyes of God. And a certificate to prove we were ready.

Due to marry fiancé Stefano a couple of months before our wedding, Daniela's cousin Federica suggested the four of us do the course together with the priest in her home town. So every Monday for six weeks, with a group of seven other couples including Federica and Stefano, we were to meet at Don Filippo's house in Soldignano. Differentiated from other houses by a neon cross on its front wall, Don Filippo used his front room for the marriage course in the evenings and as a classroom for orphaned immigrant children during the day. The walls were adorned with children's paintings, elephants and giraffes, while in the centre of the main wall, pride of place, were portraits of the Pope, Mother Teresa and some other famous cleric, not painted by the children of course.

'Whatever you do, don't say we live together,' instructed Daniela on our way to the first meeting.

'And where else in Andrano am I going to live if not with you?'

'With my parents.'

Of the seven couples, Daniela and I were the only pair living together out of wedlock. We could have told the others far more about the trials and tribulations of cohabitation than any priest either guessing or quoting scripture. Yet we were the ones who were shunned—or who would have been, had we let our sins slip. Federica too was sworn to secrecy and had covered for her cousin several times in the past. When Daniela and I went skiing in the Dolomites, Daniela realised she had left a box of contraceptive pills on the bathroom cabinet at home. One call to her cousin and the pills disappeared. Valeria suspected nothing. How nice of her niece to pay her a casual visit.

After welcoming us to the course, Don Filippo distributed a red, hard-back copy of the Good Book to each couple before holding his own above his head. '*Questa è la Bibbia,*' he said. 'This is the Bible. I'm sure many of you have never seen one before.' He asked us to turn to Psalm 46, and when most of us flicked to page 46 he had all the evidence he needed. But he knew Federica's face from mass and asked her to help the heathens out. 'What page is Psalm forty-six on, Federica?'

'*Quattrocentoquaranta,*' replied the teacher's pet.

When Don Filippo asked a shy young man to read aloud, the man's face turned as red as his Bible. He was *analfabeta*—illiterate. I had read about high illiteracy rates in the south but until now hadn't seen much evidence of them beyond the average Italian's inability to read a stop sign. This particular man was a farmer and both he and his plump fiancée had ruddy faces and broken fingernails. Their stained, simple clothes were in stark contrast to those of the couple beside them, she in Versace slacks with a gold D&G belt buckle, he in an Armani suit perfectly matched with tan leather shoes. The two couples reminded me of a tractor and a Mercedes parked side by side on a potholed street, an everyday sight in Andrano. They personified the south of Italy: the haves and the have-nots, the gaudy and the grubby, the white-collar and the dirty-collar.

After a brief but awkward silence, the man's fiancée read for him. Then, perhaps deterred by the experience, Don Filippo closed the Bible and preached on the concept and commitment of marriage. I enjoyed listening to him speak when he used his own words rather than those of the manual. A short man, thin and bespectacled, he had a soft and pleasant voice which he could project without raising, a prerequisite of the job, I presumed.

Don Filippo had tried to drag his church forward with humour and self-irony, a last-ditch effort to make it attractive to youngsters. And in a certain sense he had succeeded, although livening up a tiny parish in Soldignano was a long way from reforming Christendom. He spoke openly on sex, telling his listeners, whose ears had all pricked up, that sex after marriage was different because spare time had to be created in a life of new-found responsibility. He was talking to people who had never lived anywhere other than at home, and who, on their wedding night, would move into a new house with their partners for the first time. When he then asked the men to make a *wife* of their fiancées rather than a *housewife*, Daniela playfully stared at me and nodded her head.

Aware that most of the women present would be pregnant by the end of the summer, our instructor told us to love the gift of children that '*Il Signore* may or may not grant you,' and to cherish that gift, be it male or female. 'A child is the greatest gift of the holy blessing that God can give,' said Don Filippo. 'Girls are not excluded from that.' He was attacking the shameless Italian preference for male children. Where else in the world do you wish somebody luck by saying: '*Tanti auguri e figli maschi*'—'All the best and may you have male children'?

Since Don Filippo was expected to preside over most of the couples' ceremonies, he took a few moments to run through the logistical side of wedding day. Punctuality was most important, he said, and if we were late we would find him the same colour as his Bible. He begged us to please not waste too much money on flowers, saying they died quickly in summer and we would have already spent a fortune on the bride's dress. We were also requested to find a photographer who understood the difference between a church and a football stadium. 'The priest has a difficult job,' said Don Filippo, 'which is made harder by a flash going off in his face every five seconds.' Moving on to music, he said that other than the organ, stringed instruments, 'with the exception of electric guitars', were most acceptable. However drums of any type were not suitable for a church. 'I don't know if Australians are in the habit of playing percussion instruments at a wedding,' said the priest looking at me, 'but I have to tell you that in Soldignano it is strictly forbidden.'

Nothing happens in Italy without the correct *documentazione*, so he next ran through the forms that would keep our love legal. The first of these was the provocatively titled *Posizione Matrimoniale*, which caused sniggers among the congregation. 'Don't get excited,' said Don Filippo. 'This is not the *Kama Sutra*.' It was in fact a questionnaire regarding the personal details of bride and groom, their last chance to declare anything for which their partner could annul the marriage, 'like sterility, rare diseases or children sired on military service in Africa', we were told.

Daniela cast me a concerned glance.

'Don't look at me,' I said. 'I did military service in South America.'

'Did you?' inquired Federica. Bless her.

The next piece of paper was the Italian version of the banns: an announcement of the union to be displayed both at the church in which the wedding will take place and the town hall in the couples' villages. This allows people with grounds for objection to voice their reasons. But if the banns are designed to save marriages an adulterous end, it would appear the procedure is now redundant. Well, in Bari at least, where a judge ruled that adultery can be committed *before* marriage. Does that mean a pre-nup can be finalised *after* the wedding?

At ten o'clock, Don Filippo decided to leave his sermon on the religious side of the ceremony until the following week, disappearing into his kitchen saying he was sure he had a bottle of *spumante* and some cake. Like the others, we stayed for as long as politeness dictated before taking leave of a priest who would never run our wedding day. And neither would any other man of the cloth. One meeting of the marriage preparation course had been enough for me to realise why I hadn't been to church for twenty years—apart from when the Sydney Swans made the AFL Grand Final in '96 and I snuck in for a quick prayer. It didn't help.

Nothing personal against Don Filippo, whom I admired for giving orphaned children his care and attention. I simply didn't want someone reciting verses I couldn't relate to on the most important day of my life. I realised that marrying out of church would cause a bigger scandal than marrying on a Friday, but I also knew my wedding day had to make us, rather than the village happy. While I was prepared for the responsibility of marriage, I wasn't prepared to have a religious wedding. But how to tell Daniela?

Miles from anywhere but close to each other, back at the beach house Daniela and I lazed on the carpet in front of the fire. These were among my most treasured moments in Italy: a deserted port, the sound of the sea, dancing fire and Daniela. Gazing sleepily into the flames, she had sensed my mind was a thunderstorm and was waiting for me to speak.

'*Amore?*'

'*Si.*'

'I want to marry you more than anything in the world . . . '

'But.'

' . . . but I don't want to get married in church.'

A surge of flame illuminated her face.

'So where do you want to get married?'

'A princess should get married in a castle.'

Daniela laughed.

'A civil ceremony?'

'An original ceremony. Our way. Our words.'

She lay her head on my chest and spoke to the fire.

'It's a wonderful idea, *amore*. And we'll do it. But don't expect my mother to be as excited about it as we are.'

'Whose day is it anyway?'

'My father is dying, Chris. I can give my wedding day to my parents if I have to.'

'I want to give them something special too. But it should be something honest. From us.'

Heat and shadow flickering across her, Daniela raised her head, kissed me, and then challenged Don Filippo's theory that marriage stifles sex.

Thirty per cent of Italian marriages which end in divorce do so because of the mother-in-law. But my mother-in-law refused to be included in that statistic, for she almost caused the end of Daniela's and my marriage before it started. This is possible according to a judge in Bari.

Voicing her concerns over Sunday lunch, Valeria said she was troubled by our decision to marry out of church. Her disappointment was directed at me mainly; she felt certain I had changed her daughter's mind on the matter. I said I had consulted rather than convinced Daniela, stressing that I had sought her opinion on whether our plans would put her in a difficult situation.

'And what did you say?' asked Valeria, surprised.

'I said no,' volleyed Daniela.

Once again Daniela was trapped between me and her mother, and once again she did her best to please us both. What was said over the lasagne is not important, suffice to say that Valeria felt it her right to question her daughter's decisions. This didn't surprise or upset Daniela. What did hurt, however, was her mother's refusal to consider our marriage blessed if it took place in the castle. Valeria needed a concrete God at the wedding, or at least a porcelain one with a beard and sandals. This caused Daniela and me to argue back at the beach house, as I attacked her mother's short-sightedness. Daniela agreed but begged me to at least try and understand Valeria's provincial point of view.

Daniela's and my relationship had come as a shock to Valeria, who had expected her daughter to marry the boy three doors down. Daniela had dated Tommaso for seven years before heading to Ireland and bringing me back as a souvenir. In a village like Andrano, where a northerner is a foreigner, an Australian is the next best thing to an alien. Yet Valeria had welcomed that alien into her home despite knowing his relationship with her daughter might leave her lonely in old age. Her husband was dying, her son called Milan home, and then Daniela began talking of one day moving to Australia. But Valeria never spoke of her fear or her pain. She nursed Franco with a crippling arthritis that twisted her fingers like the branches of an olive tree. Yet from the shadows of that hardship, all she ever prayed for was the happiness of her children. Ironically, while she considered me irreligious, I considered her a living saint.

When Daniela and I had moved to Milan, leaving Valeria alone with Franco, mother encouraged daughter to find her feet in the city. In the same situation, Daniela assures me, many Italian mothers would have begged or perhaps even blackmailed their daughters to stay. Despite selflessness, it was difficult for Valeria to see beyond the stone walls of her town. Survival in Andrano means thinking like the *Andranesi*, being one of the clan, something Franco had found impossible. Valeria knew that Daniela and I would never live above her, yet it was natural for her to offer and to hope we would accept. And it was the town talking again when Valeria challenged our decision to marry out of church.

In her solitary situation, Valeria was susceptible to the opinions of friends, most of whom hailed from small-town southern Italy. And her sister-in-law, Daniela's Zia Francesca, just happened to be a nun. Hardly the person to have on the devil's debating team. Daniela knew when Zia Francesca had phoned because her mother's objections to the wedding were more assured. But she forgave her mother's intrusions, knowing the town and her aunt were behind them. Accustomed to 'hands-off' parents, however, I was at odds with Valeria's guidance, both parental and spiritual, placing further strain on what had been a precarious bond from the start.

Valeria had loved me like a son from the moment my burgundy underwear ruined her washing. 'Figlio mio,' she called me. 'My son.' A mother's love has its advantages like security and spaghetti, as well as disadvantages like suggestions and interrogations. While Valeria was consistent in her new-found role, I was inconsistent, reaping the advantages but resenting the disadvantages. I was happy for her to wash my underpants but didn't care for her opinion on what colour they should be. Perhaps she wanted a second son more than I wanted a second mum. I sought the camaraderie of friendship rather than the commitment of family, the pasta without the prying.

Tense but comic situations characterised our relationship. Before our telephone was connected in the beach house, every morning I strapped my laptop over my shoulder and rode up the hill on my Vespa to check my email at Valeria's. And every morning I spent less time on the internet than I did on the grapevine, hearing what was happening in Andrano: who the funeral bell was tolling for this morning, who had been taken ill, who was getting married and who was getting divorced.

By the time I untangled myself it was usually late morning, with Valeria insisting I take some culinary cargo home for lunch. Telling her I had arrived by motorbike failed to deter and, on one occasion, in her apron, she followed me out onto the driveway carrying a saucepan of beans in a basil and tomato sauce. Freccia was still with us at the time and raised her spirits and her nose as the saucepan appeared. After I mounted the *motorino*, Valeria thrust the saucepan in my direction, saying: '*Buon appetito*.'

'They smell lovely,' I replied, 'but I can't take a saucepan on a scooter.'

'What about here?' she suggested, putting the beans between my feet.

'They'll spill.'

'And on the seat between your knees?'

'They'll still spill.'

Freccia realised the beans weren't for her and returned to her sun-drenched corner of the courtyard.

Valeria's eyes lit up as they spied the perfect spot for the saucepan: on the dash between the handlebars right over the speedometer. Italian blood in her veins, she obviously considered it the most redundant part of the bike.

'How will I balance it there, Valeria?'

'You've only got to roll to the bottom of the hill!'

Sicilians are as persistent as they are generous, and despite further protests I crawled home with a saucepan on my speedo. What I love about Andrano is that I turned no heads doing so, apart from that of the *vigile*, who was standing in the piazza and whose nostrils flared like Freccia's as the beans rolled by. I imagine he could have booked me had he been in the mood, but the bell had just rung one and his own lunch awaited.

If Valeria's invasiveness gave me cause for complaint, my irreverence didn't help much either. A few weeks after discovering the missing grille in the gate, which *il fabbro* had removed so that Freccia could come and go, Valeria arrived home to surprise me plucking a tick from the dog's ear with her cosmetic tweezers. I was of course going to sterilise the tweezers after relieving Freccia of the parasite, but the scene was too much for Daniela's mother, who already found my love of dogs—or underdogs in Freccia's case—unusual. She was too shocked to speak, so I did my best to ease the tension by telling her to get in line and I'd do her next. When her jaw dropped even further I said I'd give her a discount if price was her concern. Daniela helped tremendously in such situations, laughing so contagiously that her mother could do little other than reluctantly follow suit.

Humour had always defused our bombs and disguised our differences, but in the context of the wedding, laughter was no longer a safety valve. At every opportunity Valeria grilled me on my religious beliefs. She once asked if I thought Man was perfect or a sinner, and my reply that he was a perfect sinner was not what she wanted to hear. The concept of having a private spirituality was not something Valeria could grasp. The only place you could find God, according to her, was in church. Fortunately, Daniela shared my view of religion, and plans for our wedding in the castle continued, even if Valeria and her God threatened a boycott.

Realising that Valeria was lonely nursing Franco all day, Daniela and I stopped by as often as we could. But as the wedding approached I found excuses not to go—the inquisition was driving me mad. I felt no need to ask Valeria why she went to church, so what gave her the right to ask why I didn't? Tensions rose and spirits dropped. Even Daniela and I started squabbling. Something had to be done and, as usual, it was Daniela who did it.

One evening, I was sitting alone at the beach house watching moonlight on the Mediterranean—that's not a film, by the way—when Daniela returned from her mother's. Her face was joyless, tired, and she could have carried home the shopping in the bags under her eyes.

'What a beautiful moon,' she said, squeezing into the armchair beside me.

'Want to get married on it?'

'No, I want to get married in the castle.'

'And your mother?'

'She'll be there. I've just been speaking to her. She'll be there.'

'What did you tell her?'

'I told her to show some faith in her daughter rather than God.'

Together, in perfect silence, reassuring when you're in love, disturbing when you're not, we watched the moon rise and the night fall.

For almost a week, Valeria kept her brittle promise to say nothing about our wedding. But when I called in one morning after observing a wedding in the castle to see what a civil service entailed, her mind was slow to remember that promise and her tongue quick to break it. I couldn't decide if the ceremony had been a farce or a fiasco, if only because it was both, the result of a lack of creativity and the best man forgetting the rings on the roof of his car. Marriage celebrants don't exist in Italy, so the mayor had married the couple and read laws rather than prayers. I was unenthused by what I had seen, but felt sure that with a little imagination our service could be special. Valeria wasn't of the same opinion, however, and let me know when I called in to pick up my scooter on my way home.

'Back so soon?' she asked rhetorically.

'Well, I wasn't invited to the reception and it was a short service.'

The service would have been even shorter without the ten-minute search for the rings.

'You see, Crris, here, only people with problems have a civil ceremony, which is probably why it was so quick.'

'Problems? What sort of problems?'

'People who are divorced, or pregnant perhaps.'

The bride had indeed been pregnant, something Don Filippo said was 'the greatest gift of the holy blessing God can give.' Only in certain circumstances it seemed.

'And what sort of *problems* are they?'

'Well, not *problems*, but if they're divorced then they can't get married in church.'

'Not unless they pay, you mean.'

A Sicilian friend of Daniela's had recently divorced and then wanted to remarry in church. The church would only give its consent in exchange for $40,000.

'The church is most accepting,' I attacked.

'The church has a strict morality,' defended Valeria.

'Which is hypocritical and for sale.'

We had got along better when we couldn't communicate.

The civil ceremony in the castle shed new light on Valeria's standpoint. She didn't so much object to our marrying out of church, she objected to the village assuming certain things about her 'children' that weren't true, like either I was divorced or Daniela was carrying more than a bunch of flowers. Valeria wanted to protect us from gossip, to conform to local custom and make a good impression—*fare la bella figura,* as the Italians call it.

When I told Daniela about the wedding in the castle, I said it had only lacked a sense of occasion because of the small number of guests, the mayor's monotone reading of the laws as though he was opening a new bridge, and a lack of music, flowers and other trimmings. It seemed an authentic 'shotgun' wedding: in fact the bride was so pregnant it appeared she might go into labour during the service. Maybe that's why they'd kept it quick. Daniela and I felt certain we could turn a civil ceremony into an event, but could we be bothered in a town that would find fault with it simply because it was different? So to keep our options open we decided to return to Soldignano and get the certificate after all. Naturally, Valeria saw this as a rethink and was delighted—we had finally seen the light.

Daniela justified the religious lessons we had missed through illness; the good thing about lying to a priest is that it's his job to forgive you. The course had been moved to Sunday evening, its last meeting coinciding with the Brazilian Formula One Grand Prix. Italian men follow *automobilismo* more religiously than religion, and only the brides turned up to collect their certificates. Don Filippo had left the groom's name blank on ours. 'Fill it in yourself,' he said to Daniela. 'Anything could happen between now and the end of June.' In addition to the certificate he gave each couple a Bible, the thirty-second edition of *Familiaris Consortio*—The Tasks of the Family—penned by the Pope, a pot plant which we called Don Filippo, and a silk apron with both our names on the pocket symbolising reciprocal service for life. When Daniela returned home with her hands full, around lap forty-seven if I remember correctly, I felt rotten for putting pistons before apostles. I should have gone with her to thank the priest for his generosity.

Don Filippo had put both names on Federica and Stefano's certificate as their wedding was only a week away and would surely go ahead as planned. No one had objected to their banns notice, and Stefano had certified that he had no rare diseases or African children. The couple were to wed in Don Filippo's church, and Valeria was hoping, or praying rather, that the occasion would convince Daniela and me that a traditional wedding was the wiser choice. And nothing could have been more traditional than Federica's wedding. Identical to the dozen Italian weddings Daniela has dragged me to, it was a long, dull, predictable afternoon, whose only sparks of originality were the excuses of guests for either not attending or leaving early.

The most exciting moment of Federica's wedding day was the accident I had on my way there. Having worked in the morning, Daniela had arranged to meet me at her mother's, where she could shower and fix her hair in a house with reliable hot water. That meant riding my Vespa up the hill to Valeria's, which I foolishly decided to do in my suit, my best suit, my only suit, the same suit I was planning to wear to my own wedding in two months' time. Helmetless and happy in delightful spring sunshine, rather than watch the road I was gazing at the sea when in the corner of my eye the road appeared to move. Turning my head I spied a metre-long black snake that had been sunbathing on the road until disturbed by my arrival.

To an Australian a black snake spells trouble. To a black snake so does a motorbike. We both took evasive action, me swerving left and the snake slithering right. This merely put us on a revised collision course, so I swerved abruptly in the other direction, losing control of my *motorino* and sliding along the asphalt. The snake fled the scene and my trousers were in tatters. Knees bleeding, I pulled into Valeria's driveway in search of sympathy and soapy water. After hearing my tale of woe, Valeria laughed and tossed me a towel. 'Those snakes are harmless,' she said. 'You should have ridden over it.' Before tensions over our wedding she would have washed my knees for me, like a second mother should.

Other than that, the day was uneventful. Federica's wedding went entirely to plan, a plan that had commenced over a year ago when she and Stefano decided to marry and work began on their house. Southern tradition stipulates that the new house be ready in time for the wedding. This is the parents' expense: his the house, hers the furniture. As though organising a wedding isn't stressful enough, Italians will actually include the construction of a house in their preparations. I once asked Davide, a friend from the tennis club, how his wedding plans were coming along. 'We should be okay,' he replied. 'They're installing the kitchen tomorrow and the fireplace next week.'

Davide's wedding was identical to Federica's. He too married his childhood sweetheart from the same village. He too had his house finished just in time. He too invited guests to view the house a week before the wedding, and to deliver their gifts at the same time as instructed on the invitation; and I thought bridal registers were tactless. He too watched an automatic priest perform a service the congregation knew by heart, the only novelty the couple's names. And he too treated friends and family to an eight-course meal which took almost as many hours to eat. It's a myth that Italians put on weight after their weddings. Italians put on weight *during* their weddings.

From 'here comes the bride' to 'here comes dessert', Federica's wedding lasted eight hours, and for six of those we were eating. We applauded the waiters as they emerged in a line from the kitchen to present each dish to the ballroom. The food kept coming despite the fact most guests had stopped eating hours ago. As Daniela sees it, Italian weddings are a culinary competition, a desperate attempt to outdo one's friends. But southern Italians are so busy trying to *fare la bella figura* that often they forget to have fun. There were no speeches, no laughter, no candid photos, no drunkenness. Only swollen stomachs and stretched smiles. And while there was a dance floor, by the end of the marathon meal everyone was too bloated to boogie. Cancel the images you have of Italian weddings being joyous galas of Mediterranean mayhem. I have yet to endure one where guests didn't spend most of the evening watching their watches. As far as I'm concerned, when Italians get married, 'the greatest gift of the holy blessing God can give' is not being invited.

The final inanity is the *bomboniere*—a gift given to guests perhaps to thank them for their staying power. Vast sums of money are spent on a banal memento, distributed as you leave and accompanied by a handful of sugar-coated almonds called *confetti*, so called because guests used to throw them at the couple but have since realised that rice causes fewer injuries. There is a *bomboniere* shop in almost every Italian town, thriving businesses catering for that perfect reminder of a forgettable day. So far I have picked up a turtle, an angel, a saucer, a thimble . . .

I am aware that Italian weddings are not designed to please Australian tastes, so why was Daniela complaining more than I was? Indeed most of the guests at Federica's wedding failed to see the fun in sitting at a table for six hours while waiters ferried as much food back to the kitchen as they then brought out again. Applause for each dish diminished as fast as our appetites. I invented an excuse to flee between course five and six, leaving Daniela to get a ride home with her mother. They had both wanted to come with me but were 'on duty', as Daniela put it.

My seat vacant, Zia Francesca spotted the perfect opportunity to put a word in Daniela's ear. Having travelled from her convent in Rome especially, the nun had brought a letter from the Pope blessing Federica's marriage and future progeny. Daniela and I would receive a similar letter, enticed her aunt, should we decide to marry in church. But if we didn't, no letter from the Pope, and no Zia Francesca.

'What?' asked Daniela. 'You wouldn't come?'

'They wouldn't give me the day off if I said it was to attend a civil ceremony.'

'And do you have to tell them what it's for?'

'*Sì.*'

'Can't you come as my aunt and not as a nun?'

'*No.*'

She was as black and white as her outfit.

As Valeria had hoped, Federica's big day helped Daniela and me choose the location of our own. As Valeria hadn't hoped, it would be Andrano's castle, saving Zia Francesca the train fare from Rome and the Pope another form letter. The venue for the reception would remain unchanged at La Tenuta Lucagiovanni—a sixteenth-century hunting lodge which guaranteed a four-course feed in less than ninety minutes. Preparations began for an unconventional wedding which Daniela and I, first and foremost, and then hopefully our guests, would enjoy.

Eight days to object

Daniela was ten when her father drew this sketch, her child's eye drawn to a picture whose beauty lies in its naiveté. As she grew up, time ruined her father but not the magic of his drawings, which Daniela treasured as memories of a man who no longer had a memory. She knew how happy it would have made Franco to announce her marriage to friends and family, and enabled him to do so by putting this picture on the cover of our invitation. It made me realise just how emotional an event the wedding would be for Daniela's family. Franco's absence was more conspicuous on special occasions, when years of sadness tinged a moment's celebration.

Designing the invitation was simple. Deciding who to send it to was not. Daniela's family and friends all received one of course, but I rather confused my friends by sending them an invitation together with a letter advising them not to come. Andrano is a remote and basic southern village where no English is spoken and road signs point only to similar unkempt outposts. I could hardly expect friends to be self-sufficient in a place where it took me a year to become so. I would have to attend to their every desire, and surely on such an occasion I was supposed to be attending to mine. My parents would already be a handful, and with half of Sicily blowing into town like the *Scirocco*, as well as friends from Milan, I had no choice but to encourage my Australian mates to stay put. Instead I invited them to a wedding party over Christmas, when Daniela and I would be in Australia for a delayed honeymoon.

The invitation was the first of many wedding preparations, some of which were routine, some of which were not. A few months ago I had flown to the Australian consulate in Milan to get documents for my driver's licence. Now it was back again to get documents for my wedding. Glancing at the 'No Impediment to Marriage' certificate in the lift upon leaving the consulate, my eyes stalled on the suspect line 'there is no law prohibiting an Australian citizen from marrying an Australian citizen'. Intending to marry an Italian citizen, when I reached the ground floor I sent the lift straight back to the third, where I showed the oversight to the document's author. 'Oh my God,' exclaimed the woman, who knew me well by now. 'This is the letter I've been giving people like yourself for years.' It was obviously such a formality I could have written it myself.

Back in Andrano, first on the 'to do' list was clothing. I needed a new suit after my brush with the black snake, and Daniela designed and made her dress with the help of a seamstress friend of her mother's. I was forbidden to see the dress but was allowed to see the shoes, joining Daniela on her search for a pair at the markets in Maglie. Daniela has a talent for looking expensively dressed in cheap clothes. On one occasion, in a doctor's waiting room in Sydney, a woman leant over her three-year-old *Woman's Day* to ask: 'Where did you get those shoes? They're gorgeous.' When Daniela replied 'Italy', the woman no doubt pictured the fashion avenues of Milan rather than the markets in Maglie, where a slovenly old man peddles discount footwear from a rusty van.

Daniela bought much of her wardrobe at the Maglie markets, which are famous for quality at low prices. There you can buy a pair of pants and have money left over to put in the pockets. Lower latitudes mean lower prices, and northerners notice the difference when they descend on the south during summer. One canny trader at the markets has coined his spiel around this difference. Like every Saturday, he was there the morning Daniela and I were hunting for shoes, standing among a miscellany of leather and laces, yelling: 'The women of Milan pulled their hair out when they saw these shoes at these prices!' On this occasion, unfortunately, he had nothing suitable, and I pulled out what was left of my own hair when we parted with a small fortune at a bridal wear shop for a pair of ivory high heels which Daniela wouldn't wear long enough to dirty the soles.

Swimming upstream in southern Italy gets the other fish talking. In synchronised schools they not only gossip about the nonconformist but feel duty-bound to inform it of the direction of the current. I could forgive family their invasiveness but accepting advice from strangers was hard to take. When Daniela and I went to look at wedding rings, what we wanted to buy mattered less to jewellers than what tradition dictated we buy. When I proposed to Daniela I gave her an engagement ring which she now wished to match with a wedding band. As the engagement ring was made of white gold, she was looking for a white gold wedding band.

'These are for weddings,' said a jeweller in Tricase, offering a selection of yellow gold rings. 'White gold is for the twenty-fifth wedding anniversary.'

'Could we see the white ones anyway?'

He shook the rings in their velvet tray.

'But these are the ones you need.'

I upset another jeweller by attempting to buy myself a yellow gold wedding band. 'What? The rings won't be the same colour? But they must be.' It was as if they'd be party to an illegitimate marriage by selling us different coloured rings, or perhaps *La Guardia di Finanza* could fine them for breach of tradition. And it's not only jewellers who are sticklers for custom. When Daniela went to the florist in Andrano to buy her mother some flowers for her birthday, she asked the shop assistant to arrange the *tulipani* in purple wrapping paper. 'Purple is for funerals,' said the shop-keeper. 'I can give you red or green.'

Eventually we found a young shop assistant in Maglie who realised the key to opening our wallets was keeping her mouth closed. To this day, however, few Italian friends aren't disturbed that Daniela's and my wedding rings are different colours, and even fewer hold their hyperactive tongues. The fact we are happily married seems irrelevant.

Surprisingly, Daniela's mother stayed quiet about the rings. Arthritic fingers defying decoration, her own wedding ring gathered dust on her dressing table. And on the orders of Mussolini, Valeria's parents and grandparents had been forced to hand over their wedding bands for the war effort. Who could blame her for thinking the rings irrelevant?

Organising the ceremony was next on the list. We had the assurance of the mayor that Andrano's castle was ours for the day and planned to hold the service in the interior courtyard. I had suggested doing it inside in case the drought broke during proceedings but Daniela had her heart set on the charming stone quadrangle. Just in case, we asked for the function room upstairs to be cleaned. We also asked the *vigile* to ensure the castle door would remain closed. Our fear was the mattress seller, whose ear-splitting spiel wasn't quite the background music we had in mind.

Andrano's mayor, Giuseppe Accogli, was tending his ill mother's bedside, so formalities would be conducted by the vice-mayor, Mario Accoto, a close friend of Daniela's family who put his hand up for the job. Daniela and I spent an afternoon with Mario translating vows into English for the benefit of my parents and ironing out creases in his clumsy pronunciation. Other than the vows and a poem my mother would read, the rest of the ceremony would be in Italian. My parents were outnumbered a hundred to two and we couldn't double the length of the ceremony for their ears only. Instead we organised written translations of other speeches and poems. Mario made a gallant attempt at translating his speech, which apart from calling the mayor the 'mere', was close enough.

To remember our Irish beginnings, Daniela thought some Celtic music might be appropriate and set about finding a harpist. A colleague of hers knew of a harpist in a nearby town and gave us her surname to look up in the phonebook. It might have been quicker to learn the harp. The phonebook had forty-one listings for Rizzo in a town of 2500 people, four of which lived on the same street. Sound like a lot? Well, of the 5000 *Andranesi*, 185 share the surname Accogli, including the mere mayor. At least we were looking for a big needle in a haystack.

A trip to the cemetery reveals the most common surnames in a southern village, which although posted on almost every grave are far from dying out. Andrano was founded by seven families who inter-married and themselves had large families. Sharing similar origins, many towns in the Salento have several highly diffused surnames, like Accogli, Accoto and Panico in Andrano, and Musarò, Turco and Longo in Tricase. Continued inter-marriage has reinforced these trends. Only immigration has diluted things slightly. I am fairly sure there is only one Harrison in Andrano. Look under A in the phonebook, however.

As if shared surnames don't cause enough confusion, southern Italians are in the habit of christening children after their town's spiritual protector, meaning villagers often share both first name *and* surname. Andrea is a popular Christian name in Andrano after the town's patron saint. However a saint needn't be a town's patron to have his name adopted. In Andrano's Chiesa di Sant'Andrea there is a statue of San Rocco standing between a dog and a boy with grazed knees; perhaps he too had come a cropper on his Vespa. According to religious legend, a wounded San Rocco was licked by a dog and miraculously healed. Under frequent invasion from land and sea, Andrano's turbulent history may have prompted San Rocco—protector of the wounded and lepers—to be revered by a population who wished their own wounds to be healed. Naming one's child after him was a superstitious means of achieving this. Once a year, Andrano pays homage to San Rocco. His statue is carried through the town and those named after him celebrate their *onomastico* or 'name day'. It's a long procession because, excuse the pun, every man and his dog is called Rocco in Andrano. I just wish they treated dogs with the respect they do saints.

I have three friends in Andrano named Rocco Panico, all of whom are cousins. To differentiate, they are known as Rocco *ingegnere*—Rocco the engineer, Rocco *geometra*—Rocco the surveyor, and Rocco *professore*—Rocco the teacher. All three came to our wedding, along with several other guests who shared the same names. I thought we would have to write tax file numbers on the seating plan. If that sounds absurd, local electoral lists show candidates' nicknames so that voters can tell them apart. And spare a thought for the postman in a town where houses have several addresses but their occupants the same names. No wonder the service is slow. They should just put the incoming mail bag in the piazza and let the locals sort through it.

After dozens of failed attempts at finding the harpist, which basically involved calling a stranger's house to ask if anyone on the premises played the harp, Daniela found an old woman who said she was sure a professor of music with the same surname as her lived at the end of the street. Perhaps it was his daughter who played the harp? 'I've never heard music coming from the house,' she told Daniela, 'but the harp is a very quiet instrument.'

The woman kindly offered to go and find out, calling back that evening with the news she had found our elusive harpist. Daniela was so grateful I thought she was going to invite her to the wedding. She took down the harpist's mobile number after learning that her family, surely one of few in Italy, let alone the Salento, didn't have the phone on at home. So there were forty-two Rizzos in one tiny town rather than the forty-one in the phonebook, and we would never have found the Rizzo we needed had we called them all. After such a tangled search, I hoped to God, or at least San Rocco, that she was a good harpist.

Preparations for the ceremony were almost complete. Only the paperwork remained. This was taken care of at the *municipio*, where Daniela and I signed a document declaring we were not related and our marriage would be legitimate. Andrano's town clerk, Paolo, a hobby farmer with much of the Salento under his fingernails, then posted an announcement of the wedding on the village notice board, after embellishing it with the required tax stamps of course. People had eight days to object.

During those eight days, I often wandered by the town hall to read a notice even I would have objected to a couple of years earlier, when Italy was that effervescent country I visited for cathedrals and Caravaggios, and I was in love with another woman—my ex-girlfriend. We had met at university and shared an interest in most things, including Italy, a country we visited together just days before parting company.

When she gave me my marching orders in a tiny French village, I had expected a lonely mixture of regret and self-annihilation to muddy the coming months. But then I went to Ireland, whose sense of humour soothed my wounds and trivi-alised my sadness. I found consolation in lively chat, empty glasses and full ashtrays. No one knew me, no one asked what was wrong, and sooner than I could have hoped the trauma of my break-up began to fade; though I may have just been too drunk to remember it.

Her own heart heavy with her father's recent illness, Daniela still managed to bring the Mediterranean sun to gloomy Dublin. Fate and separate taxis took us to the same pub the same night, where I filled her glass and she my wounded heart. Perhaps she was San Rocco's messenger, herself a healer of injuries. In that moment, however, as I asked her questions she needed a pocket dictionary to grasp, I had no idea who San Rocco was, just as I had no idea that we would one day marry in a town I had never heard of, but which I would soon call my second home.

Two years later, the announcement of our marriage outside Andrano's town hall was more than just a few lines of legal jargon. It marked the end of difficult years and hopefully the start of a fun future. Each time I read the notice I relived an episode of my move to Italy: the highs and lows of putting my life in a bag and changing language, country, culture, custom, even my name. Those highs and lows would no doubt continue with marriage. In fact Barzini's warning, which I had read on the flight to Italy, said that marriage would be our downfall and that Daniela might 'discredit me' and 'make me unhappy' as my wife. Why then would anyone take up the invitation on the notice board and object to that marriage going ahead? Anyone wishing us harm might be better off letting us wander, willingly, into a future full of risk.

Daniela's and my names looked mismatched on the marriage notice, hers full of vowels and mine crammed with consonants— they had finally spelt it correctly. Like Andrano and Sydney, we were worlds apart, and any bridge between the two might over-stretch and fatigue with time. Important questions lay ahead: like where we would settle down. Not which city but which country. Daniela had a stable job and a handsome pension awaiting her, but cashing it in would involve staying in Italy, which I couldn't imagine doing indefinitely. My love for Daniela seemed infinite. My love of her country did not.

Barzini may have been wrong to warn me off Daniela, but he was right when he tried to warn me off Italy. I had liked the place more when I visited for art and ice-cream. Now that I lived there, I could certainly do without many aspects of Italian life. I will never comprehend this way of life, just as I will never comprehend how the love of one Italian can atone for all her nation's faults. Why am I drawn to this hopeless country despite finding an array of reasons never to set foot here again? Could Italy's imperfections somehow make it perfect?

I asked myself if it was a mistake to marry a person from a country I adored one day and deplored the next. Maybe love wasn't the only prerequisite to marriage and logistics should be resolved first. I became anxious: my parents were packing their suitcases in Sydney and I was rethinking my marriage in Italy. My concern was like a clear sunrise turned cloudy. But were the clouds born of reason or nerves? 'Nerves,' decided Renato, who, by way of distraction, whisked me off to Tricase and thrashed me at tennis.

The eight days passed slowly, with nobody, other than my nerves from time to time, objecting to the marriage.

An exclusive villa on the outskirts of Maglie, La Tenuta Lucagiovanni was an expensive choice of venue for our reception. Valeria insisted Franco would have spared no expense on his daughter's nuptials, and as she was paying, well, it would have been rude to refuse. As the big day drew nearer, Daniela's mother appeared to have forgotten her objection to our non-church wedding, to the point of showing enthusiasm for the event. I think she was proud of our stubborn self-belief, for stubbornness to a Sicilian is an admirable trait.

After initial protests, Valeria had left Daniela and me to organise the ceremony, so I now left her and Daniela to organise the reception. As far as I was concerned it was their evening, as long as it could be Daniela's and my afternoon. La Tenuta Lucagiovanni, or Maglio as it's known locally, offered an array of table settings and floral arrangements which mother and daughter were free to select. In the weeks before the wedding they made numerous trips to the villa, deciding on everything from the height of the cake to the length of the candles.

Daniela returned from one of these trips to Maglio troubled. Having booked a pianist to play the grand piano in the dining hall, she had been warned to consider paying tax on the performance. Under Italian law, the pianist would be in breach of copyright unless we paid €100 to the Italian Society of Authors and Editors for the rights to the music we had chosen to accompany dinner. Someone at Maglio had convinced Daniela that *La Guardia di Finanza* had nothing better to do on a Friday evening than raid weddings demanding to see receipts for the background music and handing out fines if the tax hadn't been paid.

Confused about whether to pay or not, Daniela called the pianist, who said the tax was *legittima* but that the way around it, if the Receipt Police did turn up, was to say he was a guest who was simply playing a few sonatas out of the goodness of his heart. Obviously the tax had lost the pianist business—playing a CD during the meal would be cheaper—so he offered clients this escape route. But the problem, according to Daniela, who between taxes and traditions was becoming traumatised, was that if *La Guardia di Finanzia* stuck around at the reception, they would soon discover that our 'guest' was both an excellent pianist and an excellent friend, having volunteered to play non-stop for ninety minutes. And why did his coat have a tail?

The tax, like most in Italy, became the subject of much debate. Maglio said it was our choice whether we paid or not but they couldn't close their gates and deny access to officials. Raids had occurred in the past and ruined the evening for everyone. I voted not to pay, suggesting there wouldn't be a busker left in Italy were such a law enforced. And besides, no one got married on a Friday, so *La Guardia di Finanza* were far more likely to be playing cards in the squad room rather than out raiding weddings. If Maglio had said nothing our 'concert' would have gone ahead with the impunity of ignorance. Indeed why weren't we debating whether to pay tax on the harpist's performance in the castle? Because no one at the *municipio* had suggested doing so, and I hoped it stayed that way.

After days of deliberation, Daniela decided to pay, if only to stop the nightmares about men in grey suits storming her wedding like Hollywood cops. So one morning in June, with the last of the poppies drooping red by the roadside, we drove to an office in Maglie and paid what was essentially an insurance premium to keep our reception free from gatecrashers. We might just as well have driven to the police station and turned ourselves in for recording a film from the TV. I wonder which form the *carabiniere* in Loritano would use for that offence?

Tablecloths chosen and vows rehearsed, we began to relax and look forward to the day. My parents arrived and made themselves comfortable in the beach house. Dad had even brought his snorkel. That spirit of adventure was still keeping him young. They were enchanted by Andrano, particularly its piazza, and became fascinated by its ancient routines: the vegetable sellers' spiels, the ever-reliable bell. Dad had only been in town an hour before he figured out how many times a day it rang. I had done the same. It was wonderful to see them.

Valeria's house had undergone a Sicilian invasion and Daniela spent the eve of the wedding at her mother's being feted by extended family. I spent a quiet night watching the Australian Rules Football videos my father had brought for me, translating his speech into Italian, and chatting with my mother while she ironed Dad's Sydney Swans tie; I should have been flattered seeing he only wore it on special occasions.

All was in readiness and all appeared perfect—apart from the Swans tie. Most importantly, the weather looked superb. It hadn't rained for three months and a pink sunset promised calm.

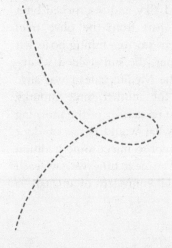

Wet bride, lucky bride

A deafening thunderbolt shook me awake, the precursor to a downpour which compensated for three months of aridity in one brief morning—the morning of my wedding. Unable to believe my ears, I dashed to the trembling French windows, where I found Daniela and my parents unable to believe their eyes, staring into the gloom that was usually a picture postcard.

I hugged the bride-to-be whose face resembled the weather. 'It's probably just a—BANG—morning storm, my love,' I said unconvincingly. 'It'll probably all be—RUMBLE—over in a few minutes.' My parents tried similar platitudes but it was impossible to comfort Daniela, who heard gossip rather than thunder. Town tongues would have a field day: a non-religious wedding on a Friday with different coloured rings; we had got what we deserved for snubbing proverb and priest.

Two hours later the deluge passed. Sky and sea turned blue, wind dropped, trees straightened—apart from the olive trees which appeared caught in a permanent storm—fishing boats left port, washing was hung from rooftops, the sun scalded white-washed houses and our stretch of the Mediterranean was alive again. Convinced it wouldn't rain for another three months, together with the florist we spent the remainder of the morning decorating the castle courtyard for what would be an outdoor wedding as planned. Then, in an attempt to inject some tradition into the day, I sent Daniela home. The next time we saw each other would be at the altar, or the civil equivalent of an altar—a desk with an ivory tablecloth.

Daniela spent the afternoon being smartened and snipped, while I went to La Botte, careful to avoid sunburn lest I look like a lobster in the photos. I was relieved we had finished the preparations in the morning, allowing me to swim rather than sweat in the hours before the wedding. So while my father snorkelled in sandals to guard against *riccio* spikes, I lazed on my towel and chatted with my mother, whose fair Soviet skin enjoyed the Northern Hemisphere's intact—for now at least—ozone layer. You still sizzle, only slower.

Our peaceful afternoon was shattered at precisely half-past four, ninety minutes before we were due at the castle, when my father, whose skin had shrivelled from too much time in the sea, asked: 'Is that likely to come this way, Chris?'

'Is what likely to come this way?'

He pointed to cloud behind the southern headland.

'That.'

'*Minchia!*' I exclaimed—Sicilian for 'cock', as multifunctional as 'fuck'.

'I thought you said it was always sunny in summer,' said Dad.

'Apart from this morning it hasn't rained for three months.'

'Law of averages says you're due then.'

Between his Swans tie and his law of averages I was starting to regret inviting him.

Before playing tennis, it's my habit to go up to Valeria's roof and look south towards Tricase to check the weather in that direction. Despite an absence of mountains, I have never seen such pockets of localised weather as those of the Salento; at times your right hand can be getting wet while your left is getting tanned. The exception is when the *Scirocco* brings a mass of cloud which blankets the Salento and looks ominous but rarely is. I hadn't seen Daniela's dress but was fairly sure it wasn't waterproof. So after my father's reminder of the laws of probability, I decided to drive up to Valeria's and take a look at the uninvited guest from her *terrazza*.

I met with protest at her front gate where a swarm of Sicilians assumed I'd come to see the bride. After explaining my visit, I was granted passage and accompanied onto the roof by the florist and Daniela's brother, both of whom were born in Andrano and should have known the local weather better than an Australian. With Valeria's bloomers hanging at our backs, the three of us sized up the cloud mass in the distance.

'What do you think?' I asked.

'*Scirocco*,' replied Francesco. '*Innocuo*.'

'*Scirocco*,' echoed the florist. 'Nothing to worry about.'

But had I a tennis appointment I wouldn't have been going anywhere. I'd seen the sky in this mood dozens of times.

'*Pioggia*,' I said assuredly. 'Rain.'

Fifteen minutes later rain was falling in Andrano and I was pulling out what was left of my hair. '*Non ti preoccupare, Crris*,' consoled the florist. 'We have a saying: *Sposa bagnata, sposa fortu-nata*'—Wet bride, lucky bride. One proverb warns not to marry on a Friday, another says bad weather is a blessing regardless of the day. Plenty of rhyme but not much reason to these Italian proverbs. Choose the one that suits you and have a nice day.

But the proverb that best suited me in that moment was an English one: *Many hands make light work*. As if someone had blown a whistle, Francesco, the florist, the harpist, the Sicilians, as well as two men from the *municipio*, scrambled in every direc-tion to move flowers, carpets, harp and microphones from the courtyard to the function room on the upper floor of the castle. Though we were now pressed for time, such a move had always been our contingency plan in the unlikely event of rain. We'd been assured by the *municipio* that the room would be clean. But take an Italian at his word and he'll take you to the cleaners.

And it was precisely the cleaners we needed next, for when we opened the door we found the function room in disarray, undergoing what appeared to be renovations. Spot-cloths and soft-drinks were scattered about the place, with chairs and tables stacked hurriedly in the corner. It was my fault—I should have checked the room when it rained that morning. But I had seen a wedding take place there just a few weeks before and it had been in immaculate shape. What the *minchia* had happened? Quite simply, neither we nor the *municipio* believed we would need the room. You get lulled into a false sense of security when you forget what a cloud looks like. Daniela had taught her English class the word 'cloud' in early April, and by late June was still waiting for a real-life example to float by the classroom window.

On my orders—a series of commands in which the word *minchia* featured heavily—the florist dismantled decorations in the courtyard while the rest of the working party, which now included the seamstress and hairdresser, who had finished smartening the bride, began smartening the room in which she was due to marry in forty minutes. A stooped old woman dressed in a black frock and slippers darted into the room and distributed brooms to bystanders. I'd never seen her before but she knew me, apparently. Or sort of knew me. 'Don't worry, Crristian,' she said in dialect. 'It'll soon look like a castle again.' To this day I have no idea who she was. She looked as if she lived in one of the cupboards under the stairs.

Lugging a 30-kilogram harp up two flights of stairs—I should have hired a violinist—I was tapped on the shoulder by Daniela's brother who informed me that the photographer had arrived and I was still in my swimmers. As though in a relay, Francesco relieved me of the bulky instrument and sent me home to dress, de-stress and collect my parents, who must have thought I'd fallen off Valeria's roof while checking the weather.

Foot to the floor, I was red-lining the Lancia when who should I encounter on the lonely stretch of road between Andrano and its port but the *carabinieri*, lollipop sticks ordering me to stop. Ignoring a man with a machine gun isn't a good idea, so I accepted their invitation and pulled off the road. I was speeding without a seat-belt but they either hadn't noticed or didn't care. It was a road-block rather than a speed trap, and they were more interested in looking for Albanian stowaways in my boot than in how fast I was going. With deliberate dishaste, my details were fed into a laptop computer. Fortunately it had no record of me, surprising given my summer outburst on the same stretch of road. I was home with ten minutes to spare, shaking with stress and still shouting obscenities my parents couldn't understand.

Strip, shower, shave and I was in my suit, knots in both my stomach and tie. Then back in the Lancia with my parents and the rings, taking a longer route via Marittima to avoid the *carabinieri*, who would probably have arrested the man in the suit on suspicion of stealing the car from the man in the swimmers.

Ten minutes late, light rain falling, we pulled into Piazza Castello to find guests eyeing the sky and tossing the word *Scirocco* about. Rudely perhaps, we raced upstairs to view what I had described to my parents as 'the castle broom cupboard'. In its place we found an elegantly decorated function room that appeared to have been spruced up weeks in advance. Tulips had replaced spot-cloths, the walls were hung with photos of yesteryear Andrano—if such a term is possible, I could see my reflection in the squeaky-clean floor, a red carpet divided neat rows of chairs and led to a table adorned with flowers at the top of the room. Behind the table stood three flags: the Italian, the European Union's and Andrano's coat of arms, by the window the harpist strummed a calm Celtic tune, and by the door stood my parents and my open-mouthed self, feeling as if a joke had been played on me. It was the sort of miracle you might ask for in church. Don't tell Valeria I said that.

My parents accused me of exaggerating the mess, but had they been standing in the same spot thirty minutes before, they would have witnessed a frantic bunch of locals racing like ants on a discarded sandwich, averting disaster by the barest of margins. It wouldn't have been a genuine Italian wedding without an element of drama, without the chance of everything falling apart. It was as if keeping the promise of cleaning the room in advance was more of an effort than the last-minute rescue. Italians only know how to win when there's everything to lose. By visualising disaster rather than hope, I had shown that despite residency, fluency, and my ability to balance a watermelon on a bicycle, I was still an outsider in Andrano. But in my view it had been an unnecessarily anxious afternoon. All it needed now was *La Guardia di Finanza* to arrive and start sniffing near the harpist. It's a stressful way to live.

Even when you know the bride is definitely coming because you can hear guests clapping her outside, the wait at the altar is a nervous one, particularly when you're made to wait as long as I was. Daniela had insisted that her father give her away, which meant shuffling at his pace from car to altar. Now I understood why she had wanted to hold the service in the courtyard: to save Franco the stairs. Watching father and daughter arrive, she leading him rather than he leading her, I realised what an appropriate choice of venue the castle had been. Franco had grown up among these ancient walls; learnt to play the violin in this very room. Had he been well he would have played a favourite sonata on his daughter's wedding day. Yet here he was, unable to manage the steps he had raced down as a boy, his head full of music, his life filled with promise. Inching down the aisle, shrunken inside his suit, the applause was for him as much as the bride. And though his stride was pained, his eyes were brighter than usual. He may have been a stranger to history, but something about him said he realised the present moment was special.

Guests squeezed into the room behind the bride and her sluggish chaperone, before Daniela guided Franco to Valeria, who would hold his arm for the rest of the evening, indeed for the rest of his life. I had only just regained my composure after the afternoon fiasco. Now it was stolen again by Daniela taking my hand and her place next to me. Had I been able to speak I would have whispered that she looked delightful, but my throat tightened as I wrestled back tears. It reminded me of the night we had met in that smoke-filled Irish pub, my eyes drawn to one vivid person amid a throng of blurred bystanders.

I have always told Daniela that her beauty is natural, an allure which make-up can only diminish. So I was glad to see that on our wedding day she had been minimalist with the mask, allowing liquorice eyes and sunshine skin to speak for themselves. Her hair was braided with flowers the ivory of her dress, which was summery, slender and speckled with pearls. Looking at her, breathing her in, cute and classy, stylish and sweet, I had never felt happier, but I had never felt weaker. Marrying Daniela was a mixed emotion, a celebration of my love for a woman who both completed and compromised me from the moment we met.

The unexpected price of moving to Italy was the feeling of alienation I felt from my former home and friends. The way of life I had known before Italy now felt foreign to me, but so too did the Italian way of life. So instead of feeling like a citizen of two countries, I felt like a nomad belonging to neither. A foreigner both at home and abroad, lost in a hybrid reality between Italy and Australia.

What's in a name? An identity. Chris the Sydney-sider and Crris the resident of Andrano were two intrinsically different people. Their names were pronounced differently, they spoke different languages with different accents, had different dress sense, a different sense of humour, ate different foods at different times, feared different things and enjoyed different pastimes. Chris the pilot and surfer, lover of the outdoors, deplored the smell of cigarette smoke, while Crris the café junkie and conversationalist sometimes smoked ten a day. Crris raised his voice to speak, something Chris's friends found irritating. And Chris disliked people who interrupted, something Crris found the key to survival. They were two separate people who probably wouldn't have gotten along. Indeed the only thing they had in common was their love of the same woman.

Rather than eliminate the distance between our two worlds, Daniela's and my love actually highlighted it. We were agreeing to share the same future even though we would always be different. Daniela and Chris could never be complete at the same time. In Australia, Daniella—pronounced very differently from Daniela—suffered the same schizophrenia Crris endured in Italy.

For the two of us to be together, one had to sacrifice their true identity. But love is worth it, which is why, despite the challenges that lay ahead, Daniela vowed to do what Barzini suggested to be beyond her: to love, honour and obey Chris and Crris, while I vowed to do likewise to Daniela and Daniella for as long as the four of us should live.

Shortly before seven, in the castle by Daniela's back garden, to the sound of the mattress seller doing his rounds and a Celtic melody, we were pronounced husband and wife by the vice-mayor of Andrano, who, in accordance with law and tradition, was wearing the tri-colour ribbon of the Italian Republic across the torso of his tailor-made suit. He looked splendid, like a well-wrapped wedding present.

The crowd clapped, our mothers wiped their eyes and my father whizzed around the room like a trapped fly taking more photos than the photographer. I was proud to call him my best man for the day, although Italians use the less flattering term *testimone,* meaning 'witness'—not like them to miss an opportunity to praise. He only stopped snapping to sign his name on the marriage certificate, a formality presided over by Paolo, the town clerk, who hadn't found time to clean his fingernails for the occasion. Everyone else had scrubbed up well though, especially the vice-mayor, whose signature on the certificate brought proceedings to a close. Now all I had to do was kiss 200 cheeks and I could go and get drunk.

Daniela and I were delighted with the ceremony, a mix of Italian law, Australian poetry and Irish music which, as one guest put it, displayed '*originalità, personalità e spiritualità.*' Through self-belief and stubbornness we had shown an equally stubborn village how to respect the beliefs of others, that the world is coloured rather than stained by such beliefs, and that accepting another's values is far more Christian than falling to your knees every time you see a stained-glass window. Even Daniela's mother would later speak of the 'unique spirituality' of our ceremony. She never actually apologised for the 'Italian Inquisition', but said enough for us to realise that she knew she should. For Daniela, her mother's blessing was better late than never.

After kissing our way through the crowd, we were showered with confetti and macramé boomerangs which Hiroshi, our Japanese friend from Milan, had painstakingly made. With the consent of the vice-mayor, Daniela and I then went up to the castle balcony to salute guests in the piazza below. What we had asked was exceptional. In two years I had stopped countless times to admire the balcony but was yet to see someone on it. The Baroque *balcone* is the sentimental symbol of Andrano. Sculpted from the castle's stone, its beauty is regal, lavish, ornate, and standing among its coronet and columns affords an excellent view of the town. The entire *centro storico* lies at your feet: Piazza Castello, La Chiesa di Sant'Andrea, and on the cobblestone laneway in the shadow of the bell tower, a mosaic of Andrano's coat of arms featuring *le sette spighe*—the seven ears of wheat— representing the agricultural origins of Andrano's seven founder families.

Centuries later, though from the balcony time has stopped, Andrano has 5000 residents, of which I am one, both officially and emotionally. Gazing across its uneven rooftops was a crowning moment. The rain had stopped, the cloud had lifted, and house-wives took to terraces to hang sheets in an hour's sunshine. Two years ago the laneways below were a maze. Now I could ride them blindfolded without hitting a pothole. And two years ago the woman who brought me to this curious village was a stranger. Now, her arm through mine, she was my wife.

'You look like Mussolini and his mistress!' shouted Concetta towards our stage. Concetta was Daniela's *testimone*, an appropriate choice of 'witness' as she had been travelling with Daniela in Ireland and held a special place in her heart. But the piazza was packed with special people that evening, who from the elevation of the balcony I could easily single out. Faces from my adventure who had displayed generosity, friendship, affection, and above all, the real Italy. Like Riccardo the police chief, with his key to the back door of every office in Lecce; proud Laura, who had forgiven me for feeding her prized gnocchi to a stray dog; Dr Nino, whose home-made *limoncello* made him more an anaesthetist than a doctor; silent Franco, stubborn Valeria and Francesco, who had mellowed greatly and turned from foe to friend; Antonio, Adele and little Asia, who hung precariously to her name; the now engaged Michele and Carla, whose parents had since forgiven them for lying about their trip to New York; and a brigade of Sicilian relatives from the hillside near Alcamo. Only Freccia was missing, rascal and four-legged friend, who died a few months before the wedding and was unable to play her part. To Valeria's horror, I had planned on the dog bringing the rings to the castle in a container attached to her collar. My father had loved the idea, the reason I knew he was the right person to stand in for my sorely missed mate.

Despite being told I resembled a Fascist, those moments on the castle balcony remain my most treasured memory of my wedding day and indeed my time in Andrano. Smiling and waving up towards us were family and friends from the Salento, Milano, Sicilia, Australia and Japan, all gathered in Andrano's piazza, cosmo-politan feet on small-town stone. In and around the crowd rode black widows on rusty bicycles returning from the cemetery, sunburnt farmers on jumpy tractors returning from the fields, and slick boys on Vespas going nowhere in particular as long as they made some noise. From my vantage point it looked wonderful, a typical Italian scene, the noisy comings and goings of people and machine. My life had changed dramatically but Andrano's remained the same. The *vigile* blew his whistle. The bell rang seven and three.

Leaving Andrano for the reception, car horns blaring and lights flashing, I stopped to salute Signor Api as our procession passed 'California'. Abandoning his bowser, my first friend in the village dashed to the car window with eager paces. '*Auguri!*' he exclaimed, leaning in to kiss my cheeks. 'Now can we see that *bambino*?'

After *aperitivi* and *antipasti* in an enchantingly lit garden, Maglio served a swift but sumptuous four-course meal in an unusual dining room. Consisting of three parallel halls separated by recurring open arches, the sixteenth-century structure was in fact Count Lucagiovanni's coach house and stables when he used the residence as a hunting lodge. In the central hall he parked his horse-drawn carriage, a picture of which hangs on the wall behind the grand piano, while in the other two he tethered his mounts. To the sound of soft—and legal—piano music we dined in the glorified garage, where elegantly dressed stable-hands catered to our every need.

I have been to a dozen Italian weddings and have yet to hear anyone other than a priest mark the occasion with a speech. So when Daniela fired up the microphone, even the staff gathered to listen to a novel idea. Daniela thanked all the right people for coming, I recounted some of the more embarrassing moments of my move to Italy, including requests for a paedophile and a kilometre of sausages, and my father stammered a tribute to his son and daughter-in-law in such cumbersome Italian that he earned more laughs than I did without even trying.

Cocktails and cake were served in the garden and the Count's liquor cabinet was raided. Maglio didn't provide beer at weddings, so I had made an advance request for a small supply. And 'small' was what I got; six bottles in fact, a puddle which Daniela's former English teacher from Lecce quickly mopped up. I was left drinking heavier artillery than I was used to, causing my powers of speech to dwindle as rapidly as the beer. But I was careful to hold on to staple phrases, '*grazie*' first and foremost.

The generosity of our guests deserved more than *grazie*. In Macedonia, apparently, guests pin money on the bride's dress. In southern Italy, when she's distracted, they slip it in her husband's pockets. By the end of the evening mine were bulging with little white envelopes containing over €6000, around $10,000 (not each unfortunately). The unwritten rule is that guests calculate the cost of their meals and give gifts of similar value. Ours had calculated well. From top-ups to toothpicks, Valeria had spent just over €6000 on the evening. But that was her gift to Daniela and me, so the cash in my trousers could stay. And I had wanted to get married elsewhere?

Only a few guests gave presents other than money, including Zia Francesca, who sent a two-foot-tall religious icon. I suggested setting a place for it at the dinner table but Daniela said that would offend.

Other than the boomerangs, Hiroshi had also crafted a life-size kangaroo which, at the tail end of the evening, I mounted and rode around the garden, making sure not to lose any envelopes from my pouch. Were the Count still alive he would probably have had me shot, stuffed and put on his mantelpiece. And when I hopped in Daniela's vicinity I got the impression she would do likewise. We had only been married ten minutes and already I was disgracing her. Barzini had suggested it would be the other way round.

As a rule, Italians refrain from overindulging—with alcohol at least—in the presence of others, for it has adverse effects on that prized goal—*la bella figura*. But I was far too busy enjoying myself to worry about impressing others. Hopping among hedgerows on a macramé kangaroo, it struck me that for all their famous flamboyance the Italians are remarkably formal folk with a code of conduct for every occasion; fish who swim spiritedly but rarely upstream, horses who buck but with blinkered eyes. Perhaps it stems from being part of an homogenous population whose history is ancient and which does things *en masse*, rather than the modern multi-culture to which I belong. *Bella figura* or not, I was staying on my kangaroo. I was, and always will be, Australian . . . I think.

After bewitching the beast in his headlights, Francesco drove Daniela and me to a hotel in Castro, where I flew further in the face of tradition by keeping my pants on to protect the treasure in my pockets. Now I understand why Italians don't get married on a Friday: because banks don't open until Monday. I checked the lock on the door several times. Where was San Denaro—the patron saint of money—when I needed him?

Satisfied that nobody had followed us, I finally gave my bride the attention she deserved. What a chaste woman Daniela's seamstress must be. She had sewn thirty-five buttons into the back of the wedding dress which even a sober man would have struggled to prise open before check-out. When I did finally disassemble her, I left on her exorbitantly priced high heels, so that I could get my kicks, and she her money's worth.

Passionate but gentle, and with one eye on the loot, our unconventional wedding day came to a conventional close; some rules should never be broken. Several months of stress were forgotten in a moment of total contentment. Even that nagging voice, so obsessed with where we would settle, fell silent for a while.

A dawn breeze caressed the curtain. A fishing boat puttered into port. A stray cat meowed in the street. Summer was returning to the Salento, the sun was gathering strength, and for three whimsical months, decisions about the future could wait.

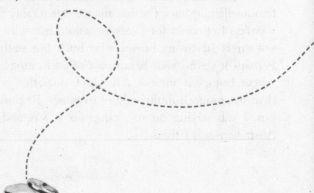

Author's note

Before writing about Italy, I had always believed there was no such thing as true non-fiction; writers must make their 'stories' as entertaining as possible, embellishing here and embroidering there. But over-gild the lily and that story might be deemed unbelievable, implausible, too absurd to be true.

Italy's Nobel Prize winning author, Luigi Pirandello, suggested no shrewd audience would believe the true story of Albert Heintz—protagonist in a love triangle who convinced himself, his wife and his lover that the best solution to their amorous impasse was for each of them to commit suicide. When his wife promptly did so, Albert and his mistress could no longer find a reason to discontinue their love affair, marrying shortly after the wife's funeral.

Pirandello, born rather aptly in the Sicilian town of Caos, claimed that any play or novel based on this story would be dismissed as unrealistic. 'This is because life,' said Pirandello, 'with all its brazen absurdities, small and large, has the invaluable privilege of being able to do without this ridiculous realism that art seems duty bound to adhere to. Any real event can be absurd; a work of art, if it is a work of art, cannot.'

While writing this memoir, I too had concerns about my experiences in Italy being deemed unrealistic, experiences which defied decoration and whose inherent humour and peculiarity were far more absurd than anything I could ever contrive. Like Federico Fellini's films, the most revealing Italian stories reflect rather than invent, holding an unpolished mirror up to the Italians whose best comedy is achieved when being serious.

And so here, unadorned, is the tale Italy told me during the years of my own love affair with an Italian, whose mother, I might add, was born a short distance from where Pirandello now rests. And I swear on his grave that despite some minor changes to disguise certain people and places, and to assist chronology, this is a true work of non-fiction which, while a blow to my ego perhaps, could never be considered a 'work of art'.

Acknowledgements

Without the love, support and professionalism of the following people, this book might be a manuscript gathering dust in a bottom drawer. Heartfelt thanks go to my selfless parents, for their encouragement, perceptive guidance, and for taking care of my German Shepherd while I was off chasing Italian skirt. To my wife, Daniela, for her brown-eyed patience, not only while I was locked away in the study but while I was taking my first clumsy steps in her country. To Richard Stokes, for laughter, friendship, and believing in the book enough to be its first advocate. To my agent, Isobel Dixon, whose skilled eye and expert efforts have literally made my literary dreams come true. It is a privilege to be assisted and represented by all the staff at Blake Friedmann. It has also been a privilege to work with the talented team at Murdoch Books: Juliet Rogers, Kay Scarlett, my ever-approachable editor, Colette Vella, and my copyeditor, Karen Ward, who made a daunting process fun. Thanks also to Sophie Hamley for showing faith in my writing and always putting the book first; to Giacomo Di Costanzo for his boundless enthusiasm; to Matthew Rich for his advice on my early efforts; to Grazia, Massimo and Rocco for their affection and acceptance; to Jaki Virtue for the lucky blue folder; to my brother for his literary courier service; to my sister for test-reading chapters; and to Graem Sims, who commissioned my first feature story and thus convinced me I could write. And *grazie*, above all, to the Italians, who showed me their eccentric lives and welcomed me to their whimsical world.

Bibliography

Barzini, Luigi, *The Italians*, Hamish Hamilton, London, 1964.

Bryson, Bill, *Neither Here Nor There*, Black Swan, London, 1998.

Cazzola, Franco, *L'Italia del Pizzo*, Einaudi, Turin, 1992.

Coluccia, Francesco, *Parleranno le Pietre: Testimonianze di Vita Andranese*, Gino Bleve Editore, Tricase, 1998.

Ginsborg, Paul, *A History of Contemporary Italy: Society and Politics 1943–1988*, Penguin Books, London, 1990.

Hersey, John, *A Bell for Adano*, Victor Gollancz Ltd, London, 1945.

Joyce, James, *Dubliners*, Penguin Classics, London, 2000.

Malatesta, Stefano, *Il Cane che Andava per Mare e Altri Eccentrici Siciliani*, Neri Pozza Editore, Vicenza, 2000.

Pantaleo, Giacomo, *Preistoria e Protostoria del Basso Salento*, Editrice Salentina, 1981.

Pirandello, Luigi, *The Late Mattia Pascal*, Dedalus European Classics, Huntingdon, 1987.

Richards, Charles, *The New Italians*, Penguin Books, London, 1995.

Robb, Peter, *Midnight in Sicily*, Duffy & Snellgrove, Sydney, 1996.

Severgnini, Beppe, *Inglesi*, Coronet, London, 1991.

Sigerist, Henry Ernest, *Breve Storia del Tarantismo*, Besa Editrice, Nardò, 1945.

Vidal, Gore, 'The City Today' from *Vidal in Venice*. In: Leccese Powers, Alice, *Italy in Mind*, Vintage Books, New York, 1997.

Several newspapers were consulted, including *Il Corriere della Sera, La Repubblica, Il Messaggero* and *The International Herald Tribune*. Material in this book was also informed by the Italian National Office of Statistics, ISTAT.